The Economic Development of Israel

PRAEGER SPECIAL STUDIES IN
INTERNATIONAL ECONOMICS AND DEVELOPMENT

The Economic
Development of Israel

Nadav Halevi
Ruth Klinov-Malul

Published in cooperation with
the Bank of Israel

by

FREDERICK A. PRAEGER, Publishers
New York · Washington · London

The purpose of the Praeger Special Studies is to make specialized research monographs in U.S. and international economics and politics available to the academic, business, and government communities. For further information, write to the Special Projects Division, Frederick A. Praeger, Publishers, 111 Fourth Avenue, New York, N.Y. 10003.

FREDERICK A. PRAEGER, PUBLISHERS
111 Fourth Avenue, New York, N.Y. 10003, U.S.A.
77-79 Charlotte Street, London W.1, England

Published in the United States of America in 1968
by Frederick A. Praeger, Inc., Publishers

Library of Congress Catalog Card Number: 68-17557

Printed in Israel at the Jerusalem Post Press, Jerusalem

This book is one of a series of studies carried out under the guidance of the Advisory Council for the Israel Economic and Sociological Research Project, set up in close cooperation with the List Institute, Basel.

The authors and publishers express their appreciation to Professor Edgar Salin of the University of Basel, who initiated the project; to the List Institute and its director, Professor H. W. Zimmermann; and to the Israel Advisory Council, for the guidance, encouragement, and financial aid which made this study possible.

PREFACE

This book is one of the studies carried out between 1962 and 1965 as part of the List Institute Israel Project. While the other studies in the series dealt with particular aspects of Israel's economy, the present book is a general survey of the development of the economy. The data originally covered the period 1949–63, but because additional information became available before the study was completed, the figures relating to the magnitudes of economic growth have been updated through 1965. However, some of the discussion of policy, though referring to later developments, does not present any data for the years after 1963. Some recent developments which took place while this book was in the last stages of production—such as the Six Day War and the ensuing political uncertainty—suggest that some of the major economic problems of the future may be very different from those of the period dealt with in this book.

Since both authors worked together over five years in developing a course on the economy of Israel for the Hebrew University, much of their individual knowledge in the subject has become joint property. However, it was convenient to share out the various chapters according to each author's comparative advantage. Ruth Klinov-Malul bears the principal responsibility for Chapters 4, 5, 7, and 11, and Nadav Halevi for Chapters 2, 6, 8, 9, and 10. All chapters have had to pass the scrutiny of the co-author, and some, such as Chapters 1 and 3, have passed back and forth so often that neither author can be singled out as mainly responsible.

The list of people and institutions who helped in one way or another is long. We wish first to thank those who contributed to the entire project: Professor E. Salin of the List Institute, the Governor of the Bank of Israel, Mr D. Horowitz, and Dr Y. Foerder of the Bank Leumi Le-Israel, who initiated the project; Dr Y. Bach, who acted as honorary executive secretary, and Dr F. Ginor and Dov Genachowski of the Bank of Israel, who carried much of the administrative burden.

Being a general survey, this book relies heavily on the work of others, and appropriate references are made in the text. We must, however, acknowledge our debt to colleagues who supplied us with data and explanations based on their current research; they include H. Ben-Shahar, A. L. Gaathon, Z. Lubetzki, the late A. Morag, G. Ofer, and M. Sarnat. The Balance of Payments Section and the National Accounts Department of the Central Bureau of Statistics and the Research Department of the State Revenue Administration were extremely helpful in supplying the results of current research.

We were fortunate to receive comments on earlier drafts from many scholars. It is a pleasure to record our debt to Y. Bach, R. A. Easterlin, A. L. Gaathon, F. Ginor, E. Kleiman, M. Michaely, the late A. Morag, H. Pack, D. Patinkin, H. Rosovsky, and Z. Sussman. We are particularly indebted to Simon Kuznets whose penetrating comments on the entire manuscript were extremely helpful and stimulating. None of these scholars is, of course, responsible for our inability to make the fullest use of their suggestions.

We also wish to thank those who carried much of the technical burden: E. Pazner and Z. Ginsburg, who gave research assistance on the material for Chapter 9; Ofra Zack, who typed the early drafts; Margret Eisenstaedt, our editorial assistant; Moshe Felber, who saw the study through the press; and Susanne Freund, who, as editor, was responsible for transforming a raw manuscript into a book.

The study was made possible by a grant from the Advisory Council for the Israel Economic and Sociological Research Project (in cooperation with the List Institute, Basel), to which we extend our thanks.

Finally, we are grateful to the Bank of Israel, which undertook the publication of the study.

N. H.
R. K. M.

Jerusalem
October 1967

CONTENTS

ix

LIST OF TABLES

ABBREVIATIONS AND SYMBOLS

AID	Agency for International Development
Abstract	Statistical Abstract of Israel
Bulletin	Statistical Bulletin of Israel
CBS	Central Bureau of Statistics
c.i.f.	Cost, insurance, freight
COL	Cost of living
DLF	Development Loan Fund
DM	Deutschmark
f.o.b.	Free on board
GDP	Gross domestic product
GNP	Gross national product
ILO	International Labour Office
LP	Palestine pound
n.e.s.	Not elsewhere specified
NNP	Net national product
OECD	Organisation for Economic Co-operation and Development
USOM	United States Operations Mission

–	zero
0	less than half last digit shown
..	not available

Year notation: Unless otherwise specified, the form 1961/62 refers to the fiscal year from April to March; the form 1961–62 indicates two calendar years.

PART I

INTRODUCTION

CHAPTER 1

INTRODUCTION

A survey of a country's development may often contain so many details that the main outline is obscured. It is our aim in this introductory chapter to give the reader such an outline, first in terms of the characteristics of the whole period covered (1948–65), and then in terms of the main developments by sub-periods.

The three salient features of the economy since the establishment of the State of Israel in 1948 have been free immigration, resulting in a very high rate of population growth; a large capital import; and a rapid growth of total and per capita product. The economy of the Jewish community under the British mandate (1917–48) developed along broadly similar lines, but both the orders of magnitude and the way in which problems were tackled were different.

Free immigration was a political aim of the Jewish community during the mandate, and although this aim was not achieved, the ratio of immigration to the existing Jewish population was very high, causing a population increase unparalleled in the twentieth century. Free immigration of Jews had been one of the main issues of the campaign for independence and was legally guaranteed by Israel, opening the country to an influx of immigrants until 1951; ever since there has been a continuous (though reduced) stream of immigration. As a result, the population has grown much faster than in other countries.

The main economic challenge under these circumstances has been to maintain, or even raise, per capita income, i.e., to provide the population with increasing amounts of capital and with the education and skills necessary to exploit it. The difference between the mandatory and the State period in this respect seems to be in the source of education and of capital accumulation. During the mandate, a large part of both was provided by the immigrants themselves: most capital (at any rate since the early 1930's) was supplied through transfers made by

3

immigrants, while a comparatively high level of education had been obtained by the immigrants in their countries of origin. In contrast, most immigrants who arrived after 1948 lacked financial means and had, by and large, a much lower level of education and skill than the resident population.

The accumulation of tangible capital after 1948 could therefore be carried out either by very high domestic saving, or by importing capital by means other than immigrant transfers. The second method was chosen, and the government and public institutions raised loans and grants abroad. (There had been such fund-raising under the mandate too, but it accounted for a much smaller proportion of total capital import.) Consequently, the public sector gained control over a very large part of investment resources, and hence, over economic activity in general.

This is one of the reasons for the far-reaching intervention of the public sector in economic activity. Added to this is the socialistic tradition built up during the mandate. Mapai, the leading party in the government of Israel since 1948, is a moderate socialist party; the Histadrut, the roof organization of trade unions, is one of the most powerful public institutions in the country. The result is a mixed economy in which the public sector and Histadrut have undertaken, partly by necessity and party on ideological grounds, extensive functions in the economy. In recent years private capital imports in the form of private investment and personal restitutions from Germany constitute a larger share of total capital import. The degree of intervention and its forms are therefore in flux.

Another corollary of capital imports is the very large deficit in the current account of the balance of payments. Such a deficit influences the allocation of resources and the structure of product. Two of its principal effects are the high rate of investment and the large share of services in Gross National Product. A third, more obvious, effect is the growth of external debt and the resulting need to divert an increasing part of resources to exports.

Let us return to changes in the population. The very fact that it grew not only induced import of capital, but also brought about far-reaching social and economic changes. As mentioned, immigrants who arrived after 1948 had a much lower level of education and skills than the resident population. The initial impact of this immigration was a widening of income and wealth inequality and simultaneously of social inequality. The integration of immigrants therefore became a major problem. Economically, this meant large-scale investments, not only in housing and employment facilities, but also in health, education and vocational training. Far from having been solved, the problem of integration is perhaps the main challenge facing Israel in the future.

The third of the features noted above is the very rapid increase in total and per capita product. In spite of the changes in the composition of the population and the labor force, Israel succeeded in raising per capita product by an annual average of about 5 per cent. Although a considerable part of this growth resulted from the high rate of investment, improvement in efficiency was an important contributing factor. The increase in resources and incomes and the concomitant reduction in unemployment through 1964 are, in our view, the main achievements of the economy. The maintenance of high levels of growth and employment, while reducing the dependence on capital inflow, remains a major challenge.

This book is an attempt to trace the developments outlined in a more systematic manner. Part I is introductory and includes a summary of the main developments during the mandate and a description of the institutional framework of the economy. In Part II, changes in the population and the labor force are described in Chapters 4 and 5; Chapter 6 surveys the growth, structure, and distribution of national product; Chapter 7 deals with capital and productivity; and Chapter 8 discusses the balance of payments and particularly the capital inflow. Part III discusses three aspects of the economic policy of the public sector and the Histadrut: fiscal policy, foreign exchange policy, and monetary and wage policy. Since the chapters deal with specific subjects rather than with developments by periods, a short summary of the sub-periods is presented here.

1948–51: The Austerity Period

The dominant characteristic of the period is mass immigration, which doubled the population. Once armistice agreements had been signed, full attention could be turned to economic problems, and these were considerable. The major tasks were supplying food, clothing, and shelter to the stream of new immigrants, finding employment for both immigrants and demobilized soldiers, and organizing the economic system, including setting up a civil service and independent foreign exchange, monetary, and fiscal systems. Most of the immigrants came without financial means. Thus, the burden of dealing with immigrant absorption fell upon the public sector. Two main policy measures characterize the period. The first was the austerity program, which consisted of stringent price control and rationing of food and other basic necessities, raw materials, and foreign exchange. This was designed mainly to ensure minimum standards of consumption for the entire population. The second was extensive public investment activities, financed primarily by inflationary means. Not only was the issue of currency made an instrument of fiscal policy, but there was no effective monetary policy to curb the expansion of loans to the public.

Two major fields of direct public activity were agricultural settlement and housing. Agricultural settlement was for several reasons viewed as an ideal way of absorbing immigrants: (a) there was a sudden abundance of cultivable land previously cultivated by Arabs who fled from Israel during the war; (b) expansion of agricultural production was an immediate and obvious necessity; (c) agricultural settlement served the purpose of dispersing the population in a way which created strong ties between the settlers and their land; (d) ideologically as well as economically, it was felt desirable that the proportion of agricultural population should rise.[1]

Housing had to meet another immediate need. In fact, all kinds of temporary shelter had to be provided (in addition to some 50,000 abandoned dwellings of various qualities). Little consideration could be given at that time to the utilization of housing for the dispersal of the population. Thus, most non-agricultural immigrant housing was in the vicinity of existing cities.

The basic objects of economic policy were to a large extent achieved: for most of this period minimum consumption standards were provided for everyone, no one was without some kind of shelter, at no other time was such a relatively large share of resources devoted to investment, and output increased rapidly while unemployment declined. The number of agricultural settlements doubled (though some, established in strategic locations such as the approaches to Jerusalem, did not achieve economic stability), and output of food increased very rapidly.

Several major problems remained unsolved: unemployment was still very high, about one fifth of the population lived in inadequate temporary housing, and foreign exchange reserves were very low. These undoubtedly reflect the sheer magnitude of the problems faced. But in addition, several other problems arose from the policy system itself. Planning and administration were of poor quality and could not

---

[1] One of the terms of reference given to Gaathon for the preparation of his Four Year Development Plan was that the share of the population in agriculture should rise to 24 per cent, a figure never actually approached. See L. Gruenbaum (Gaathon), *Four Year Development Plan of Israel: 1950–1953* (Tel Aviv: Prime Minister's Office, Department of Economic Research, 1950).

adequately substitute for the price system as allocators of resources. The public held large real balances created by the government's inflationary financing; by 1951, the failure to drain these off had combined with general disillusionment with the system to make the black market more of a rule than the exception it had been in 1949.

To sum up: This period combined the most severe problems with the greatest amount of government intervention in the economy. We do not feel that such unusual demands on the economy could have been met without resort to extensive controls, yet even massive intervention could not adequately cope with the tremendous problem posed by mass immigration. Many mistakes were certainly made, but not all of them could have been avoided given the state of administrative organization at that time and the magnitude of the problems involved. The resource misallocation created and the complete collapse of the system towards the end of the period have had a by-product, as Patinkin has pointed out: "No subsequent government has seriously considered returning to comprehensive price controls and rationing as a primary means of dealing with inflationary pressures."[2] It is, however, also true that no comparable problems have arisen since.

1952–53: THE NEW ECONOMIC POLICY

As 1951 drew to a close, two sets of problems remained. The first consisted of those unsolved in the earlier period: severe unemployment; a large part of the population living in temporary housing; and foreign exchange shortage, despite success in developing new sources of aid such as U.S. grants and State of Israel Bonds. The second type of problem arose from the economic policy of the preceding period: strong inflationary pressures and a highly distorted price structure.

Two major changes in policy were made: the first is what is known as the New Economic Policy—cessation of government inflationary finance, attempts to curb private credit, and devaluation. Some price controls were relinquished and others were set at much higher rates with a consequent increase in the domestic price level that decreased the value of the money supply and altered the ratio of domstic to foreign prices. The second policy change, frequently overlooked, was no less important: public policy to increase immigration was abandoned (although immigration remained, in the legal sense, free). It was acknowledged that immigration could not be exogenous to domestic policy. It

---

[2] Don Patinkin, *The Israel Economy: The First Decade* (Jerusalem: Falk Project, 1960), p. 111.

was decided that the economy must absorb those immigrants who had already arrived before large-scale immigration could be resumed.

The New Economic Policy was successful in slowing down the expansion of the money supply and in reducing real balances by raising domestic prices. However domestic price levels rose relatively to foreign prices, making further devaluation necessary. The reduced real effective demand made itself felt in a decline in the rate of growth (and even the level) of product per capita and in greater unemployment, primarily the result of a slump in housing and investment activity. The deficit on current balance-of-payments account was reduced, chiefly because imports fell off. The dilemma of how to reduce import surplus without stifling growth was not resolved.

1954–59: The Period of Growth

Although this period was not homogeneous, several major objects were retained throughout: to reduce unemployment and to increase and then maintain a high rate of growth of output and income per capita.

The policy measures taken to achieve these aims were varied. Public budgets were expanded and development loans were given on very favorable terms. Monetary policy was eased, compared with the preceding period. However, the establishment of the Bank of Israel in 1954 and the ensuing separation of monetary from fiscal administration led to continuous efforts to curb inflation while encouraging growth.

In 1954 and 1955 GNP and GNP per capita grew rapidly and unemployment declined. The balance of payments situation improved, despite some increase in the deficit in 1955: unilateral and capital receipts—the Jewish Agency consolidation loan, reparations and restitutions, and bond sales—all grew and facilitated building up foreign exchange reserves and reducing short-term debts.

It is difficult to ascertain how much of the increase in output in 1954–55 was due to an improved structure of production resulting from greater reliance on the market mechanism, how much of it was due to the easing of anti-inflationary policy, and how much resulted from the realization of the investments made in 1949–51. Of great importance was the increase in public investment in 1954 and the resumption of private investment in 1955.

The Sinai Campaign makes 1956 an exceptional year: defense expenditures were very high and the use of deficit financing created demand inflation and greatly increased the balance of payments deficit. Immigration picked up and rose to 70,000 in 1957, higher than in any other year since 1951.

The 1957–59 period was marked by fairly steady growth in product and product per capita; unemployment had declined to less than 6 per cent by the end of the period. The balance of payments deficit was fairly steady. Foreign exchange balances were reduced in 1957, and started to improve thereafter as the capital inflow grew. Annual price increases became moderate.

With inflation apparently under control, unemployment falling, and the housing situation much improved, attention was diverted to other objects. Although investment in agriculture continued, it was realized that the branch could not be expanded much further and that manufacturing must play a more important role in providing employment and output and in improving the balance of payments. Direct controls were virtually abolished, and subsidies, budgetary loans, and various protective devices were used to stimulate industry. Of these, the most important was quota restrictions on imports competing with local manufactures. The first industrial development plan or forecast was drawn up. More attention was devoted to profitability considerations in projects submitted to the government.

During this period, dispersal of the population became an explicit aim. Public housing and industrial policy were used for this purpose; new development towns were founded and received priority in the allocation of public funds. Industries were established in the development areas primarily to provide employment, thus often ignoring other economic criteria. However, employment opportunities lagged in the development towns and manufacturing did not succeed in preventing this. Not only was unemployment generally higher there than elsewhere, but the proportion of manufacturing employment was lower than in the established urban areas.

1960–64: FULL EMPLOYMENT AND THE SECOND NEW ECONOMIC POLICY

The period as a whole was one of prosperity and unemployment virtually disappeared, but two other problems gained prominence. The first was the increase in the import surplus. Although capital inflow—in particular, private investments and restitutions transfers—exceeded the current account deficit sufficiently to build up substantial foreign exchange reserves, it was realized that the growth in import surplus should be curbed. Second, a complex system of effective exchange rates and protective practices complicated any attempt at a realistic economic appraisal of projects and led to misallocation of resources.

In February, 1962, a second New Economic Policy was announced, consisting primarily of a devaluation of the Israel pound to IL 3.00/$ 1.

This was designed to eliminate multiple rates and to improve the balance of payments. Hidden subsidies for some exports and widespread tariffs on imports prevented the new rate from being effective. There was some shift from administrative to fiscal protection of domestic manufactures; agriculture continued to enjoy administrative protection. A devaluation at a time of full employment could improve the balance of payments only if domestic "absorption" was decreased, i.e., by reducing either consumption or investment in order to divert a larger share of resources to reducing the import surplus. This necessitates a vigorous anti-inflationary fiscal and monetary policy, but neither was forthcoming. Indirect price controls were used to prevent domestic prices from rising. These controls were successful, for almost two years, in preventing the aggregate price level from rising as much as it otherwise would have done as a result of the great increase in the supply of money, at least in agriculture and manufacturing. But little official attention was given to the fact that the object of price stability, initially part of the more general object of improving the balance of payments, had little meaning when it stood alone, unaccompanied by an absorption policy. In housing and land, whose prices were uncontrolled, the full impact of inflationary pressure was reflected in a considerable amount of speculation. The rise in real balances combined with the liberalization of import policy to increase the balance-of-payments deficit to over $ 500 million in 1964. Industrial exports grew more slowly. Thus, the New Economic Policy failed to attain its principal aims.

1965: A TURNING POINT

Two developments may mark 1965 as a turning point. First, immigration was at an ebb; this entailed a reduction in public investment, especially in residential building. Second, during 1965 monetary and wage policy underwent a transformation. The Bank of Israel succeeded in curbing the expansion of money and credit supply, thus arresting demand inflation. On the other hand, the public sector did not withstand pressure and raised wages and salaries of employees by about 30 per cent. The combined result was the onset of cost inflation, a slower rate of GNP growth, and rising unemployment. Another result of the recession was that the import surplus decreased.

Recent data indicate an intensification of the recession: a market decline in the growth rate of product and an absolute decline in investment, a sharp increase in unemployment, and a further reduction in the import surplus. It is the government's view that such a recession is necessary in order to improve the balance of payments situation, but whether or no the improvement will outlast the recession remains to be seen.

Some Concluding Remarks

The economy of Israel has been marked by several notable achievements in its short history. The mass immigration of the early years and the following smaller inflow of immigrants have been more or less integrated into the country's economic life. National product has expanded at a substantial rate, and income per capita—the most widely used measure of economic growth—has risen rapidly. Much of this growth has been due to a high rate of capital formation, made possible by massive capital inflow, but part of it is explained by increased productivity.

Yet several problems have emerged which may continue to trouble the economy for at least the next decade. One of these is the balance of payments deficit, which substantially contributed to Israel's growth in the past. Some time within the next few years, the capital inflow will decrease substantially. By definition, the balance of payments will balance, but will it be at a high level of foreign trade, fully utilizing the advantages of international specialization, or will it be at a high level of autarky? Recent events suggest that the transformation of the economy made necessary by a lower level of capital inflow may be a difficult one involving severe dislocations.

No less crucial a problem lies in the way that past immigration has been absorbed. The growth in income per capita has been accompanied by a trend of widening income differentials. Economic factors, such as the differences in the level of education, provide a partial explanation of why the veteran population increased its lead over the new immigrants, particularly those from Africa and Asia. But the creation of a marked economic cleavage between the two groups—contrary to the historical ideological aspirations of the Zionist movement—may well be the major issue of the next decade. The dislocations which are apt to arise from attempts to cut the balance of payments deficit could intensify this problem. The slowing down of growth in 1965 and 1966 and the 1966 increase in unemployment suggest that some of the economic absorption of immigration may have been illusory.

Lastly, this book deals extensively with the subject of the government's role in Israel's economic development. The degree and modes of intervention are both in flux. The role of the government in the past has been determined more by economic factors, such as the size and composition of immigration and the flow of foreign capital, than by ideology. Both these factors may change in the future: immigration may dwindle, and import of capital may be reduced, with a larger part of it being received directly by individuals. Consequently, direct intervention by the public sector may become less important. Perhaps during the coming decade a more explicit formulation of the government's role in the economy will evolve, as regards both spheres of activity and methods of intervention.

The State of Israel came into being on May 15, 1948. On that day,
the country already had a sizable Jewish population and a fairly well-
developed economy. The political situation presented new opportunities
for economic growth, and it is with this that we are primarily concerned.
But we must first examine the economic development of the Jewish
sector in Palestine before the establishment of the State. This is important
for two reasons: first, the subsequent development rested on the economic
base existing in 1948, and to a great extent continued the trends of the
earlier period; second, post-1948 economic policy was a product of
economic thought and opinion shaped by the experience of the earlier
period.

The Jewish effort to rebuild Palestine as a national home in modern
times started, of course, before British replaced Ottoman rule in
Palestine following World War I. Any comprehensive survey of the
ideological, political, social, and economic development of Palestine
should really cover the period from 1882 to 1918. But although important
economic experience was gained and various institutions developed during
this earlier period, the study of actual economic growth can begin in
1920.

In examining the mandatory period our limited purpose is to
describe the background of the economic structure inherited by the
State of Israel in 1948. Consequently, we make no attempt to survey
the pre-State economy in detail.[1]

---

[1] The economy of Palestine has been surveyed in several books. Well-known
works in Hebrew are: A. Bonné, *Palestine, the Country and the Economy*
(Tel Aviv: Dvir, 1936); D. Horowitz, *The Economy of Palestine and Its
Development* (rev. ed.; Tel Aviv: Mosad Bialik, 1948); D. Horowitz, *The
Economy of Israel* (Tel Aviv: Massada, 1954), part I. The best known works
in English are: S. B. Himadeh (ed.), *Economic Organization of Palestine*
(Social Science Series No. 11; Beirut: American University of Beirut, 1938);

Jewish aspirations to return to Palestine and rebuild a Jewish homeland were greatly encouraged by the Balfour Declaration of 1917 and
the British occupation of Palestine, but the political situation was never
free of controversy.[2] The Jews considered the Mandate for Palestine
to be a clear commitment to the idea of developing a Jewish national
home there.[3] The Arabs never ceased to regard Palestine as an Arab
country and the development of a Jewish national home as a violation
of their rights and of promises made them. Their hostility grew with the
Jewish population in Palestine and with the success of neighboring Arab
countries in achieving independence. This hostility was directed against
the Jews, but even more against the Government of Palestine. Arab
antagonism resulted in violence and bloodshed on several occasions,
most extensively in 1929 and in the armed conflicts of 1936–39.

The British were caught in the middle: every act and statement
which facilitated Jewish immigration and the economic development
of the Jewish sector aroused antagonism in the Arab sector; every con-
cession to Arab demands was viewed by the Jews as a betrayal of the
major commitment under the mandate. A Royal Commission concluded
in 1937 that the Mandate was inherently unworkable: clauses calling
for the building of a Jewish homeland conflicted with those guaranteeing
that nothing should be done to prejudice the position of the Arab population. The Commission suggested that partitioning the country was
the only possible solution;[4] however, it was not accepted at the time.
In 1939, the Palestine government clamped tight restrictions on Jewish
immigration, and this seriously impaired its relations with the Jewish
community.

After World War II ended, the continuance of the government's
restrictive immigration policy led to open Jewish hostility and to armed
conflict. The British government, unable to solve the problem, presented

---

David Horowitz and Rita Hinden, *Economic Survey of Palestine* (Tel Aviv:
Jewish Agency, 1938); the most comprehensive work is Robert R. Nathan,
Oscar Gass, and Daniel Creamer, *Palestine: Problem and Promise* (Washington:
Public Affairs Press, 1946).

2 The reader interested in an objective and comprehensive survey of political
developments during the mandate is referred to J. Hurewitz, *The Struggle
for Palestine* (New York: Norton, 1950).

3 The Mandate came into force on September 29, 1923, but its main provisions
were actually applied from the summer of 1920 when a civil administration was
established in Palestine.

4 *Report of the Palestine Royal Commission,* Cmd. 5479, 1937. This report
will be referred to as the *Peel Report.*

it to the United Nations, which, on November 29, 1947, voted for the partition of Palestine and the setting up of separate Jewish and Arab states. Despite the invasion of Palestine by the armies of the neighboring Arab States in an attempt to forestall this solution, the State of Israel successfully survived the war.

It is against this background that we shall survey the economic development of Jewish Palestine.

ECONOMIC GROWTH

Population

The Jewish population of Palestine started to grow rapidly in 1882, from 24,000 in that year to about 85,000 in 1914, declining, however, to some 56,000 during World War I—roughly the level at the turn of the century.[5]

TABLE 1.   *Population: Selected Years, 1919–48*[a]

| | Thousands | | | Per cent | | |
	Total	Jews	Non-Jews	Total	Jews	Non-Jews
1919 (March)	648	65	583	100.0	10.0	90.0
1922 (October)	752	84	668	100.0	11.2	88.8
1931 (November)	1,033	174	859	100.0	16.9	83.1
1939 (December)	1,506	450	1,056	100.0	29.9	70.1
1947 (December)[b]	1,899	630	1,269	100.0	33.2	66.8
1948 (May)	..	650	..			

[a] Census results for 1922 and 1931; the figures for other years are estimates.
[b] Excluding Bedouins, estimated at 67,000 in December, 1944.
SOURCES: 1919—*Report of the Palestine Royal Commission,* Cmd. 5479, 1937 (*Peel Report*), p. 156.
Other years—Jews: *Abstract 1966,* No. 17, p. 22; the 1939 figure is from M. Sicron and B. Gil, *Jewish Population by Sex, Age and Country of Birth, 1931–1954* (Special Series No. 37; Jerusalem: CBS, 1955), p. 3, Table 1.
Non-Jews: Government of Palestine, *A Survey of Palestine* (Government Printer, 1946), Vol. I, p. 141, Table 1; the 1947 figure is from Avner Hovne, *The Labor Force in Israel* (Jerusalem: Falk Project, 1961), p. 29, Table 8.

Table 1 shows that the non-Jewish population of Palestine increased more than the Jewish population in absolute terms, but that the Jewish population grew far more rapidly: while the number of non-Jews

[5] *Abstract 1966,* No. 17, p. 22.

doubled, the number of Jews rose tenfold, from one tenth of total population at the start of the mandatory period to one third at its close.

Arab population growth was fairly steady, being due mostly to natural increase. The rate of natural increase of Moslems accelerated and reached about 28 per thousand in 1941. This high rate was the result of a high birth rate, about 50 per thousand, and a death rate that had declined to about 20 per thousand.[6]

The Jewish rate of natural increase was about 20 per thousand,[7] which, though high by international standards, was much lower than that of Arabs. The main source of population growth among Jews was immigration, which accounted for about 72 per cent of the total growth in Jewish population in 1919–48,[8] a figure that underestimates the importance of immigration since immigrants were responsible for most of the natural increase. Because immigration fluctuated considerably, the annual rate of increase of the Jewish population ranged from 0.2 per cent in 1927 and 0.3 in 1946 to 27 per cent in 1934.[9]

About 487,000 Jews immigrated to Palestine from 1919 to May, 1948. During the same period, there were 60,000 emigrants, so that net immigration was about 427,000.[10] Immigration to Palestine is usually divided into waves (aliya in Hebrew), and Table 2 summarizes gross immigration in this way.

The quality of the immigrants and the Jewish population
Much has been written about the quality of the Jewish immigrants who came to Palestine. Some aspects of quality are measurable, at least conceptually: age structure, life expectancy, literacy, and education levels. But there are other, unmeasurable, qualities which are no less important; among these are idealism, optimism, dedication, and readiness for self-sacrifice, all at various times decisive. Moreover, all or even most of the immigrants need not have these qualities; even during the second and third aliya, probably only a minority were imbued with the high

---

[6] Figures on Moslem natural increase are taken from Z. Abramovitz and I. Guelfat, *The Arab Economy* (Tel Aviv: Hakibbutz Hameuchad, 1944; Hebrew), p. 7.

[7] *Abstract 1966*, No. 17, p. 56.

[8] Moshe Sicron, *Immigration to Israel: 1948–1953* (Jerusalem: Falk Project and CBS, 1957), Statistical Supplement, p. 3, Table A3.

[9] Computed from data in *Abstract 1949/50*, p. 18; Sicron, *op. cit.*; and the *Peel Report*.

[10] Sicron, *op. cit.*, Statistical Supplement, p. 3, Table A2.

idealism attributed to the *aliya* as a whole. But it was this minority, many of whom had gone through special training in Zionist centers abroad, who set the tone for economic, social, and political developments in Palestine.

TABLE 2.   *Waves of Immigration: 1882–1948*

	(thousands)
First Aliya (1882–1903)	20–30
Second Aliya (1904–1914)	35–40
Third Aliya (1919–1923)	35
Fourth Aliya (1924–1931)	82
Fifth Aliya (1932–1938)	217
World War II (1939–1945)	92
Post World War II (1946–May, 1948)	61

SOURCE: Moshe Sicron, *Immigration to Israel: 1948–1953* (Jerusalem: Falk Project and CBS, 1957), p. 21, Table 1.

Turning to such more measurable properties as are important for a productive labor force, we find that the immigrants (and hence the population) were on the whole of high quality.

Age distribution: Registered immigrants were young: less than 16 per cent of those arriving during 1929–48 were over 44, and close to half were between 15 and 29.[11] The population was thus concentrated in the age groups most suited for participation in the labor force. Throughout 1931–47, at least half the Jewish population was in the 15–44 age group (Table 3).

Formal education: In 1931, 93.4 per cent of Jewish males aged 7 and over were literate, as were 78.7 per cent of Jewish women;[12] all indications are that till 1948 these high levels of literacy were at least maintained. Using the data of a study of educational standards in Israel in 1954, Easterlin has estimated the per cent of the Jewish population in 1948, aged 24 and over, who had completed secondary and higher education. He found that the educational level of this population was among the highest in the world, as measured by completion of both

[11] *Ibid.*, Statistical Supplement, p. 11, Table A17.
[12] E. Mills, *Census of Palestine* (Government of Palestine, 1933), Vol. I: Report, p. 215, Subsidiary Table No. I.

secondary and higher education. Almost 10 per cent of men had completed higher education, a higher rate than in the United States in 1950, and more than twice as high as in any other country for which Easterlin found data.[13]

TABLE 3.   *Age Structure of Jewish Population of Palestine: End of Selected Years*

(per cent)

	1931	1939	1942	1947
0–14	32.7	27.5	27.2	29.5
15–29	31.9	26.8	24.5	24.5
30–44	19.7	28.4	30.0	26.9
45–64	11.5	12.9	13.6	15.0
65+	4.2	4.4	4.7	4.1
Total	100.0	100.0	100.0	100.0

SOURCE: Sicron and Gil, *op. cit.,* Tables 1 and 2.

Health: The general level of health is indicated by life expectancy estimates: the life expectancy of Palestine Jews rose by about 10 years from 1926–27 to 1942–44, when it attained the high level of 64.1 years for men and 65.9 years for women.[14]

Occupation: The occupational distribution of the Jews in Palestine will be discussed below; what is important here is that many of the immigrants had some previous skill. Of all immigrant earners arriving during 1919–47, 15 per cent had experience or training in agriculture, 36 per cent in crafts and industry, and 12 per cent were in the professions (not including 4 per cent in clerical occupations). Most significant, only 13 per cent were unskilled laborers.[15]

Capital inflow and investment in the Jewish sector

There are unfortunately no data on total capital formation during the mandatory period. However, estimates of Palestine's balance of payments show that the country was a net importer of capital, much of which

[13] Richard A. Easterlin, "Israel's Development: Past Accomplishments and Future Problems," *Quarterly Journal of Economics,* LXXV (February 1961), 71.

[14] Department of Statistics, *Statistical Abstract of Palestine 1944–45* (Jerusalem: 1946), p. 27, Table 18.

[15] Sicron, *op. cit.,* Statistical Supplement, p. 17, Table A26.

financed capital formation. In most years, and over the period as a whole, Palestine had a balance of payments deficit. The statistics available are insufficient for a comprehensive estimate of the balance of payments—statistics on services transactions are particularly meager—but it is generally accepted that the missing items would not significantly affect the size of the deficit.

TABLE 4.   *The Balance of Payments of Palestine: 1922–47*

(LP millions)

	1922–39		1940–47		1922–47	
	Credit	Debit	Credit	Debit	Credit	Debit
A. Current account						
Merchandise trade	52	171	129	313	181	484
Transactions with armed						
forces in Palestine	8	–	180	–	188	–
Total	60	171	309	313	369	484
B. Unilateral transfers (net)						
Immigrant transfers	75	–	35	–	110	–
Transfers by Jewish						
public institutions	25	–	40	–	65	–
Transfers by non-Jewish						
public institutions	6	–	4	–	10	–
Transfers by government	3	–	7	–	10	–
Total	109	–	86	–	195	–
C. Capital account (net)						
Private investments	26	–	–	10	16	–
Government investments	–	2	–	9	–	11
Balance abroad and in-						
vestments of banking						
system	–	6	–	48	–	54
Balance abroad and in-						
vestments of Palestine						
Currency Board	–	9	–	35	–	44
Total	26	17	–	102	16	109
Total A through C	195	188	395	415	580	593
D. Errors and omissions	–	7	20	–	13	–

SOURCE: Michael Michaely, *Foreign Trade and Capital Imports in Israel* (Tel Aviv: Am Oved, 1963; Hebrew), p. 2, Table 1.

Table 4 presents estimates of the balance of payments for 1922–47, divided into two markedly different sub-periods. In each of the years 1922–39 there was a deficit, i.e., imports of goods and services exceeded exports of goods and services. For the period as a whole, the difference was over LP 110 million. This import surplus was made possible by the foreign capital available, mostly in the form of unilateral transfers.

During 1940–47, the large expenditures for supplying the armed forces almost balanced the merchandise trade deficit, and the current account deficit was only LP 4 million. At the same time, capital transfers from abroad continued, more rapidly than in 1922–39, so that sterling balances were accumulated which were technically capital exports.

The main source of capital inflow was transfers by immigrants, which almost matched the deficit in the balance of payments of the whole period. However, two thirds of immigrant transfers were made during 1922–39, when they covered only two thirds of the deficit.

There were also substantial unilateral transfers by Jewish institutions, the most important of which were the financial instruments of the Jewish Agency. These alone transferred some LP 12 million during the interwar years, about two thirds of all transfers by national institutions made in this period.[16]

Private investment was relatively slight [17] and occurred only in the interwar period; during the war there was a net outflow in this item. Yet, considering that compared with other underdeveloped countries Palestine had little to offer the foreign investor, the figures are surprisingly high and reflect the fact that Zionism played an important part in private investment too.

Table 4 does not distinguish between the Jewish and non-Jewish sectors. But it is clear that most of the capital inflow was Jewish, and it rose and fell with immigration primarily because immigrant transfers was the largest single item.

From the end of World War I and until 1927, Egyptian currency was legal tender in Palestine. At the end of 1927, a Palestinian currency was introduced: it was a 100 per cent coverage system, with Palestine pounds being issued and redeemed for sterling at a one-to-one ratio by the Palestine Currency Board.[18] Thus, all local currency was backed by

---

16 The figures are from A. Ulitzur, *National Capital and the Building of Palestine* (Jerusalem: Palestine Foundation Fund, 1939; Hebrew), pp. 240, 271.

17 The figures are somewhat understated since immigrant transfers included sums belonging to Jews who did not immigrate at the time.

18 An interesting description of the Palestine currency system is contained in

foreign exchange held abroad and generally invested in British securities. One result of this system was freedom from the modern affliction of foreign exchange shortage, for in effect the Palestine currency was itself foreign exchange. The obverse of this was that the money supply was linked to the balance of payments. The constant supply of foreign capital made it possible for Palestine to be a net importer without the necessity of reducing domestic currency in circulation. The capital inflow affected the supply of money when it was not matched by the import surplus.[19] Thus, the capital inflow affected economic activity in two ways, in accordance with the classical gold exchange standard mechanism: (a) when the inflow in effect consisted of transfers in kind, additional real resources were provided directly; (b) when the supply of money was increased, the result was expanded economic activity and employment, as well as price changes and the consequent changes in foreign trade, until the process was stopped or reversed.[20]

Up to World War II, the volume of imports was largely determined by the availability of Jewish capital inflow, since exports were hardly sufficient to pay for the import requirements of the expanding economy. Years of large capital inflow were also years of large imports and large import surpluses. But even in years of relatively small capital inflow, the ratio of imports to national income was unusually high: 42 per cent in 1936 and 48 per cent in 1939.[21]

Between the wars, Palestine had negative savings, that is, capital inflow exceeded total net domestic investment: as well as providing for all new investment, capital inflow also contributed to consumption.

Gaathon's 1936 data show a high ratio—44 per cent—of investment to national income in the Jewish sector. The Jewish Agency prepared estimates of Jewish investment in 1932–39, and the series is presented in Table 5.[22]

Robert David Ottensooser, *The Palestine Pound and the Israel Pound* (Geneva: Librarie E. Droz, 1955).

[19] The connection between capital inflow and money supply was not fully automatic because of changes in holdings of foreign exchange balances.

[20] An interesting and exhaustive examination of the adjustment mechanism of Palestine's balance of payments has been made by Asher Halperin, "Palestine's Balance of Payments 1932–1946" (unpublished doctoral thesis, Princeton University, 1954). A briefer discussion can be found in M. Michaely, *Foreign Trade and Capital Imports in Israel* (Tel Aviv: Am Oved, 1963; Hebrew), Chapter 1.

[21] Michaely, *op. cit.*, pp. 7–8, Tables 2 and 3.

[22] There are several versions of the Agency estimates in the literature. We use

TABLE 5.   *Jewish Investment and Capital Inflow: 1932–39*

(LP thousands)

	Investment						Capital inflow
	Land	Citrus and mixed farming	Construction and public works	Industry and crafts	Other	Total	
1932	150	1,400	1,000	1,100	200	3,850	4,570
1933	850	2,150	2,750	500	300	6,550	7,680
1934	1,650	1,750	4,000	1,300	700	9,400	11,090
1935	1,700	1,000	5,750	1,600	650	10,700	10,840
1936	150	1,000	4,000	1,100	550	6,800	7,080
1937	400	1,000	3,000	1,000	600	6,000	5,540
1938	170	800	2,100	900	730	4,700	6,390
1939	380	900	2,000	900	620	4,800	6,870
Total 1932–39	5,450	10,000	24,600	8,400	4,350	52,800	60,060
Per cent	10.3	19.0	46.6	15.9	8.2	100.0	

SOURCES: Investment, rounded to nearest 10,000, is taken from D. Horowitz, *The Economy of Palestine and Its Development* (rev. ed.; Tel Aviv: Mosad Bialik, 1948; Hebrew), pp. 19 and 24.
Capital inflow—Jewish Agency, *Statistical Handbook of Jewish Palestine 1947* (Jerusalem: 1947), p. 375.
Jewish year figures were prorated by quarters to approximate calendar years.

Comparing investment with immigration figures shows that Jewish investment and immigration were highly correlated; the correspondence is particularly marked in construction, which amounted to almost half of all Jewish investment during 1932–39.

---

those appearing in D. Horowitz, *The Palestine Economy and Its Development, op. cit.,* pp. 19, 24. The 1936 figure is from L. Gruenbaum (Gaathon), *National Income and Outlay in Palestine 1936* (Jerusalem: Jewish Agency, 1941), p. 57, Table 29.
The differences between Gaathon's and the Agency's figures are primarily due to the inclusion of durable consumer goods in the Gaathon figures.

National income

There are no firm estimates of Palestine's national income before 1936.[23] All available data indicate that before the first world war the economy of Palestine was poor and primitive. The general picture that emerges is of an underdeveloped and underpopulated economy with very low standards of living, 80 per cent of whose income originated in primitive agriculture. The small Jewish community, most of them petty traders, artisans, and people living on charity, were not much better off than the Arab population.[24]

By 1936 the situation had changed considerably, particularly in the Jewish sector. International comparisons and per capita income rankings made for 1938 and 1939 (when the Palestine figures were somewhat lower than in 1936) ranked Palestine well above the primitive countries of the world, but below the most developed, somewhere in the lower ranges of the upper middle class.[25] Thus, the period betwen 1919 and 1936, for which data were not available, was probably one of considerable growth in aggregate and per capita national income.

The Jewish economy did not, however, grow steadily during the period. Development began with the enthusiastic Zionist immigration that followed the Balfour Declaration. For the first few years it was difficult to find jobs for these immigrants, many of whom turned to temporary employment in public works, and ended up in non-agricultural activities because insufficient means were available to settle them on the land. A sudden surge in immigration in 1924 and 1925 was followed by a severe depression, and many Jews emigrated. Ruppin

---

[23] The first detailed estimates were prepared by A. L. Gaathon for 1936 [Gruenbaum (Gaathon), *op. cit.*].

[24] The estimate of income originating in agriculture is taken from M. Novomeysky ["The Industries of Palestine," *Bulletin 4/5 of the Palestine Economic Society* (May 1925)], who cites earlier works by Ruppin and Wilbuschewitsch. Similar estimates appear in Government of Palestine, *Report of the Wages Committee* (1943), p. 4.

The situation of the Jews in 1907 is described by Arthur Ruppin, *Three Decades of Palestine* (Jerusalem: Schocken, 1936), pp. 1–14. This is a magnificent collection of speeches and essays by a central figure in the development of Palestine.

[25] The international comparisons mentioned are in W. S. and E. S. Woytinsky, *World Population and Production* (New York: Twentieth Century Fund, 1953), p. 392; and in S. Kuznets, "International Income Levels," *Economic Changes* (New York: Norton, 1953), p. 220.

blamed the depression on the fact that financial means were inadequate for the absorption of the middle-class Polish immigration of 1925.[26] By late 1928 the economy had begun to pick up again and conditions improved gradually, except for a temporary setback caused by political conflict and Arab terrorism in 1929. Although economic growth was slower during the depression, it did not stop. Land purchase and settlement continued, and agricultural and industrial production rose. According to Jewish Agency figures which, though not entirely reliable, probably reflect the trend, production per capita and consumption per capita (in constant prices) rose by well over 50 per cent between 1922 and 1928–30.[27] However, much of this increase occurred before the mid-decade depression. Other figures, based on even more questionable data, suggest that the standard of living did not rise at all between 1926 and 1931.[28]

The 1932–35 period was one of boom in Palestine. Immigration (mainly from Poland and Germany) reached previously unparalleled figures; capital inflow was at a peak; investment, production, and exports increased rapidly and unemployment virtually disappeared.[29]

For the post-1935 period there are several estimates of national income.[30] Despite considerable problems of comparison, not least of which is the tremendous rise in prices, the estimates point up the following developments: (a) In 1939 aggregate and per capita national income for both Jews and Arabs were lower than in 1936. (b) By 1945, substantial gains had been made in real aggregate and per capita income in both sectors, not only in comparison with the depressed year 1939,

---

[26] Ruppin, *op. cit.*, p. 173.

[27] Jewish Agency, *The Jewish Case Before the Anglo-American Committee of Inquiry on Palestine* (Jerusalem: 1947), p. 181 (statement by Mr Horowitz).

[28] A. Nizan, *The Standard of Living in Palestine (Israel) During the Last 20 Years* (Special Series No. 7A; Jerusalem: CBS, 1952; Hebrew), p. 34.

[29] D. Horowitz presents a detailed discussion of the prosperity of 1932–35 and the depression of 1936–39 in *The Economy of Palestine and Its Development, op. cit.,* Chapter 1. However, the reliance of the analysis of the boom and depression on an overproduction theory of the business cycle is open to argument.

[30] Gruenbaum (Gaathon), *op. cit.;* G. E. Wood, *Survey of National Income of Palestine* (Jerusalem: Government Printer, 1943); P. J. Loftus, *National Income of Palestine 1944* (Jerusalem: Government Printer, 1946); P. J. Loftus, *National Income of Palestine 1945* (Jerusalem: Government Printer, 1948); A. L. Gaathon, "National Income," *Encyclopaedia Hebraica*, Vol. VI (1957; Hebrew), pp. 729–30; here Gaathon uses the estimates listed above and includes his own rough estimates for 1947.

TABLE 6. Income, Employment, and the Product-Worker Ratio, by Industry: Selected Years

(per cent)

| | 1931 Jewish employment | 1936 Employment | | 1936 Product | | 1945 (Jews) | | 1947 Jewish employment | Product-worker ratio[a] | | |
| | | Jews | Non-Jews | Jews | Non-Jews | Employment | Product | | 1936 Non-Jews $(5) \div (3)$ | 1936 Jews $(4) \div (2)$ | 1945 Jews $(7) \div (6)$ |
	(1)	(2)	(3)	(4)	(5)	(6)	(7)	(8)	(9)	(10)	(11)
Agriculture	22.1	21.4	62.1	11.0	26.7	13.7	10.9	12.6	0.43	0.52	0.79
Industry	23.8	20.1	8.4	25.9	13.6	31.8	41.3	26.5	1.62	1.29	1.30
Construction	8.7	9.4	3.1	10.6	2.2	5.0	4.9	8.7	0.70	1.13	0.97
Transport	5.5	5.3	} 12.2	7.6	} 23.6	5.2	6.9	} 6.3	} b	1.41	1.34
Commerce	14.1	15.7		29.2		15.0	19.0	19.4		1.86	1.27
Public services	15.2	18.1	} 14.2	10.4	} 33.9	21.3	11.4	} 18.6	} b	0.56	0.58
Personal services	10.6	10.0		5.3		8.0	5.6	7.9			
Total	100.0	100.0	100.0	100.0	100.0	100.0	100.0	100.0	1.00	1.00	1.00

[a] Ratio to total (=1.00). Calculated from less rounded figures underlying columns (2), (3), and (6).

[b] Not meaningful, since no adjustment has been made for industrial classification differences between employment and product; in particular, the product of ownership of dwellings has not been excluded.

SOURCE: Non-Jews—Robert R. Nathan, Oscar Gass, and Daniel Creamer, *Palestine: Problem and Promise* (Washington: Public Affairs Press, 1946), p. 150.

Jews—Gur Ofer, *The Service Industries in a Developing Economy: Israel As a Case Study* (Jerusalem and New York: Frederick A. Praeger with the Bank of Israel, 1967): Table 4.6 (1931 and 1947); product-worker ratio from Table 4.10, and employment and product from underlying worksheets giving data adjusted for classification differences (1936 and 1945).

but also in comparison with 1936. (c) Between 1936 and 1945 per capita real income grew faster in the Arab sector than in the Jewish sector. (d) Although no reliable estimates are available for 1947, Gaathon's figures suggest that real aggregate and per capita income continued to increase rapidly in both sectors after the war.

Table 6 presents national income, earners, and income per earner by industry in 1936 for the Jewish and Arab sectors separately.

In terms of origin of national income, Palestine was no longer a predominantly agricultural country by 1936; this is true of both sectors. The relative contribution of agriculture to national income was almost three times as high in the Arab as in the Jewish sector. The difference was made up by manufacturing and construction; there was little difference between the two sectors in the total figure for the other branches.

In terms of employment there were major differences between the sectors. Each non-agricultural branch accounted for a greater share of employment in the Jewish than in the non-Jewish sector; in agriculture the situation is reversed, for over 60 per cent of the Arab labor force was still engaged in agriculture.[31]

Income per earner [32] in agriculture was below average in both sectors. In the other branches, inter-industry differences were much wider in the Arab than in the Jewish sector.

Finally, the combination of relatively heavy employment in agriculture in the Arab sector with a low product-worker ratio, explains much of the difference between the two sectors in per capita income.

Let us turn now to structural changes in the Jewish sector between 1936 and 1945. Table 6 also shows Jewish sector data for 1931 and 1947. The most significant change in the industrial origin of national income is the rise in the share of manufacturing from 26 per cent in 1936 to 41 per cent in 1945, mainly at the expense of construction, trade, and finance. Since the corresponding figures for the non-Jewish sector show that the share of manufacturing fell from 13.6 per cent to about 10.8 per cent, it is clear that this happened only in the Jewish sector.[33] Also of interest is the increase in the share of agriculture despite an

---

[31] The Arab employment estimates, being essentially projections of 1931 census data, are not very reliable. Furthermore, agricultural employment is the weakest part of the estimates.

[32] Shown as a ratio to the average (=1). We shall refer to this as the product-worker ratio.

[33] These figures are based on Table 6 for 1936, and on P. J. Loftus, *National Income of Palestine 1945, op. cit.*, p. 18.

absolute and relative decline in citrus production and exports. This was primarily due to the demand for food of the armed forces.

The tremendous increase in manufacturing activity was the result of two factors. First, the great wartime demand, much of it resulting from the activity of the Middle East Supply Centre; second, Palestinian industry had virtually total protection, a result of geographical isolation. Under these hothouse conditions, many enterprises flourished that might not have done so in more normal conditions. A Survey of Palestine (1946) tried to classify manufacturing branches according to their vulnerability to competition in peace time. Although such a classification is largely arbitrary, some rough indication of the effect of protection may be gained by comparing industrial net output in 1942 and 1939. The comparison shows the ratio of 1942 to 1939 net nominal output to be 4.15 in the "non-vulnerable" class, 4.69 in the "slightly vulnerable" class, 5.06 in the "more vulnerable" class, and 5.45 in the "highly vulnerable" class: there appears to have been more expansion in the branches most dependent on protection. However, when some allowance is made for statistical discrepancies in coverage in the two years, the range narrows from 4.72 in the "non-vulnerable" to 5.40 in the "highly vulnerable" class.[34]

Even allowing for possible undesirable investment due to overprotection, there is no doubt that the war-induced expansion marked the emergence of real manufacturing as opposed to crafts.

While employment in manufacturing rose, relative employment in agriculture and construction in 1945 was much lower than in 1936 and 1931 (Table 6). By 1947, employment had risen in construction but not in agriculture, and the share of manufacturing remained high at least to the end of the mandate, though it fell somewhat below the wartime peak. Of particular interest is the fact that the unusually high proportion of earners in services, often noted in studies on Israel, was typical of the mandatory period as a whole.[35]

The difference between income and employment is brought out in columns (10) and (11) of Table 6, which show a rise in the agricultural

[34] The classification is given in Government of Palestine, A Survey of Palestine (Government Printer, 1946), Vol. III, pp. 1265–71. Figures in the text are calculated from Department of Statistics, Special Bulletin 20 (Government of Palestine, n.d.).

[35] A comprehensive discussion of the overconcentration in services during the mandate is contained in Gur Ofer, The Service Industries in a Developing Economy: Israel As a Case Study (Jerusalem and New York: Frederick A. Praeger with the Bank of Israel, 1967).

product-worker ratio and a decline in that of commerce. It is particularly interesting to compare agriculture with manufacturing. Agricultural income per earner was only 40 per cent of that of manufacturing in 1936, but it had risen to 61 per cent by 1945.[36]

This rise in agricultural per-earner income (relative to manufacturing) may reflect changes in physical output per worker, or it may be the result of differential price movements. We were able to make several rough computations to eliminate price influence and can draw the following conclusions:[37]

Agricultural product rose less than total national product in real terms, when separate price indexes are used to deflate agricultural and other product. Thus, the increase in the share of national product originating in agriculture, shown in Table 6, is due wholly to the rise in agricultural relative prices.

The number of workers in agriculture declined slightly, whereas the number in manufacturing rose considerably. Deflating output per worker by the separate indexes used above shows that output per worker in agriculture rose less than output per worker in manufacturing.

It is somewhat misleading to talk of agriculture as one branch, because during this period there were opposite developments in the two main sub-branches, citriculture and mixed farming. Exports of citrus

[36] Kuznets, making such a comparison between 1936 and 1954, arrives at a similar change and considers it of some significance. If so, it is important to observe that much of this change does not reflect the transition from the mandate to the independent State of Israel, but actually took place before 1948, probably as a result of World War I. [S. Kuznets, "The Economic Structure and Life of the Jews," in *The Jews*, ed. Louis Finkelstein (3rd ed.; New York: Harper and Brothers, 1960), Vol. II.]

[37] Our procedure was as follows: agricultural product was deflated by using Dr Ludwig Samuel's index of agricultural prices for 1938/39, as quoted in Nathan, Gass, and Creamer, *op. cit.*, p. 213 (price changes between 1936 and 1939 are ignored). Manufacturing and other product were—for want of a more appropriate index—deflated by the cost-of-living index, which is biased downward, so that the rise in real non-agricultural output is exaggerated. To compensate for this, an alternative deflation was made with the cost-of-living index adjusted upwards by 15 per cent in 1945. This is a maximum allowance for the bias. The "Report on the Cost-of-Living Index" submitted to the War Economy Advisory Council estimated that the index understated the cost of living by 15 per cent at the end of 1943. Even if this applied in 1943, the index was much closer to the truth in 1945. Conclusions in the text are those valid within the range of results obtained by using the alternative deflators.

declined steeply during the war: in 1936 citrus accounted for almost half the Jewish sector's agricultural income, and its share had declined to less than 10 per cent by 1945.[38] Excluding citrus, Jewish real farm output rose by about two thirds between 1939 and 1945.[39] Thus, the apparent relative lag in real farm output was due solely to the decline in citrus; other farm output rose about as fast as the rest of the economy. Moreover, the fall in farm employment was a direct result of the decline in citrus, since non-citrus employment rose.[40]

ECONOMIC POLICY

National economic policy lies primarily in the domain of government. But any consideration of economic policy in Palestine must distinguish between the policies of the mandatory government and those of the Jewish national institutions; the latter require some elaboration.

A fundamental aspect of the development of Jewish Palestine is that it was of external origin and control: Zionism was a movement of world Jewry. In time, the Jewish community in Palestine became of greater consequence in directing its own affairs and affecting Zionist policy, but throughout the mandatory period, Jewish institutions representing much more than just the local community were paramount in organizing and directing the stream of men and money to Palestine.

Article 4 of the Mandate for Palestine specified that:

An appropriate Jewish Agency shall be recognized as a public body for the purpose of advising and cooperating with the Administration of Palestine in such economic, social and other matters as may affect the establishment of the Jewish national home and the interests of the Jewish population in Palestine, and, subject always to the control of the Administration, to assist and take part in the development of the country.

The World Zionist Organization served as the recognized public body

---

[38] The computation is based on 1945 citrus output figures given in Jewish Agency, *Statistical Handbook of Jewish Palestine 1947* (Jerusalem: 1947), and on total agricultural output in P. J. Loftus, *National Income of Palestine 1945, op. cit.,* p. 18; 1936 figures are based on L. Gruenbaum (Gaathon), *Outlines of a Development Plan for Jewish Palestine* (Jerusalem: Jewish Agency, 1946), Appendix Table 3.

[39] Nathan, Gass, and Creamer, *op. cit.,* p. 215.

[40] Estimated from Jewish Agency, *Statistical Handbook, op. cit.,* p. 67, and Jewish Agency, *Statistical Bulletin 1946,* p. 18. The methods of estimating farm employment are discussed in Gruenbaum (Gaathon), *Outlines, op. cit.,* p. 24.

until 1929, when the Jewish Agency for Palestine was organized to include non-Zionist representatives. The Agency was the chief Jewish national institution and dealt with political, social, and economic matters. Its main financial instruments were the Palestine Restoration Fund (1917–21) and, after 1921, the Palestine Foundation Fund.

A second institution, closely connected with the Jewish Agency, was the Jewish National Fund, which, since its founding at the World Zionist Congress of 1901, had been devoted to purchasing land in Palestine, thus converting it to "national land."

Besides a host of philanthrophic bodies, several public institutions supplemented the activities of the Jewish Agency. One of the more important of these was Hadassah, the Women's Zionist Organization of America, which specialized in medicine, public health, and social work.

The national and allied public institutions were the main instruments through which the energies, resources, and aspirations of world Jewry were directed towards the building in Palestine of a Jewish national home. These institutions, and first among them the Jewish Agency, represented Jewish economic policy in Palestine.

Approaches to economic policy

Economic policy in Palestine was subordinated to political objectives. This was true of British, Jewish, and Arab institutions. The Jews were interested in establishing as rapidly as possible a large Jewish community in Palestine, and Jewish economic policy had to serve this primary aim.[41] It is unfair to say, as many Jewish authorities have said, that the mandatory government did its best to hamper the development of Jewish Palestine: certainly the tremendous growth of the Jewish sector contradicts such a view, unless one also accuses the British administration of complete incompetence! But there is ample evidence that, as it became clear that Great Britain had gotten into a political dilemma in Palestine, British policy towards the Jewish sector became increasingly restrictive.

British and Jewish thinking also differed as to the economic role of government. The government's attitude was quite clear: its main task was to form and maintain a framework for private or institutional initiative. To this end law and order was to be maintained and some social services provided. However, except for public works such as the

---

[41] Ruppin, in an address to the 13th Zionist Congress in 1933, expressed his regret that the Zionist Movement was mainly interested in politics and that "... interest in economic questions still takes second place." (*Op. cit.,* p. 107.)

communication and transport network, and with other minor exceptions, the government did not consider direct participation in economic development or the maintenance of economic stability to be among its legitimate functions. In any event, the official position was that "sound financial management" would limit the government's role.

This attitude has been severely and, on the whole, justly criticized;[42] yet one must distinguish between the criticism of the Palestine government as overly conservative and lacking in initiative, and similar criticism which regarded this attitude as a reflection of British policy in general, and not one peculiar to the Palestine government. Surely the thinking underlying the economic policy in the United Kingdom itself during the depressed years 1924–31, when the gold standard was maintained at an unrealistic exchange rate regardless of consequences, cannot be accused of being too conservative in Palestine alone. Furthermore, although modern economic thinking may legitimately condemn the economic policies of the past, it is not permissible to extend such criticism to the intentions of policy-makers at work within the climate of their time. Even so, some of the examples discussed below show that the Palestine government was criticized by British commissions as well. Moreover, starting in 1931, there was a drastic reversal of policy in England as regards government activities to stimulate the economy; but this revolution did not extend to Palestine or to British colonies in general. The Palestine government and the British Treasury (which exercised the ultimate control over fiscal matters in British dependencies at the time) remained conservative in the extreme. Thus, there is some justification for criticizing the divergence in economic thinking at home and in Palestine, at least during the 1930's.

Jewish criticism was on several levels. The Palestine government was taken to task for not showing greater initiative in the economic development of the country. But by and large, the Jewish institutions were ready to accept most of the responsibility for the development of Jewish Palestine, and consequently, most criticism of the government concerned what was felt to be interference with Jewish development activities.

These general attitudes may become clearer from a consideration of several areas of policy.

Immigration policy

The Jewish Agency's main tasks were to encourage and finance Jewish immigration and to provide facilities for its absorption in Palestine.

---

[42] Cf. Nathan, Gass, and Creamer, *op. cit.*, p. 338.

Yet despite Zionist efforts, only a small part of the large stream of Eastern and Central European Jewish emigrants came to Palestine until restrictions on immigration to other countries, particularly the United States in the 1920's, limited opportunities of settlement elsewhere. Thus, during 1920–23, only 10 per cent of world Jewish migration came to Palestine, 21 per cent during 1924–31, 53 per cent during 1932–38, and somewhat less thereafter until 1948.[43]

Two other factors affected the decision of Jews to come to Palestine. One was economic conditions in Palestine. The depression after 1925 not only reduced immigration, but there was even net emigration, while the boom of the early 1930's encouraged immigration. The second and for many years dominant factor was British immigration policy.

The mandatory government almost from the first based its official immigration policy on the economic absorptive capacity of Palestine. This position, first expressed clearly in the Churchill White Paper of 1922,[44] was often reiterated.[45]

In accordance with this principle, several economic categories were established for potential immigrants and permits were issued for each category.[46] Broadly, the classification differentiated between capitalists (i.e., those who had sufficient resources for their own absorption), members of liberal professions who were required to have more modest sums (this category was virtually abolished after 1935), persons with prospective employment (who received permits according to a labor schedule), and dependents. Upon request from the Jewish Agency, the labor schedule was determined every six months by the government, whereupon the Jewish Agency, as a sort of blanket employer, was permitted to allocate the permits among prospective immigrants. Thus, in practice, absorptive capacity was not a measure of the economic potential of Palestine but rather of how many job opportunities would be available in the coming six-month period.

Although the Zionist Executive was frequently unhappy with official

---

[43] Sicron, *op. cit.*, p. 24, Table 2.
[44] *British Policy in Palestine,* Cmd. 1700, pp. 17–21, reprinted in Jewish Agency, *Book of Documents Submitted to the General Assembly of the United Nations 1917–1947* (New York: 1947).
[45] See, e.g., the policy letter of February 13, 1931, from the Prime Minister to Dr Weizmann, reprinted in *ibid.*
[46] A detailed discussion of these categories may be found in Government of Palestine, *A Survey of Palestine,* Vol. I, 1946, Chapter VII, and a more complete analysis in D. Gurevich, A. Gertz, and R. Bachi, *The Jewish Population of Palestine* (Jerusalem: Jewish Agency, 1944; Hebrew), pp. 21–24.

immigration policy during the 1920's, it was only in the 1930's that dissatisfaction became acute. In only four six-month periods during the 1930's did the mandatory government approve as much as 50 per cent of the Jewish Agency's labor schedule.[47] The Jewish Agency complained that the mandatory government tended to apply political rather than purely economic criteria both in interpreting absorptive capacity and in the day-to-day implementation of policy. Jewish sources maintained this opinion despite the fact that it was rejected by the Palestine Royal Commission of 1937, which concluded that the Administration had based its immigration policy solely on economic criteria, taking no account of political, psychological, or social considerations.[48]

Quite apart from the routine application of immigration policy, there was a theoretical argument over the ultimate absorptive capacity of Palestine. The mandatory government's attitude seems to have been that this was mainly a question of how much land could be made available for Jewish settlement without lowering the standard of the Arabs. This resulted from making rather rigid assumptions about the amount of land per settler and from taking a skeptical view of the possibilities of absorption in industry. Generally, the absorptive capacity of Palestine was thought to be practically exhausted. Dr Weizmann quotes Sidney Webb as saying in 1929: "There is no room to swing a cat in Palestine."[49] The Shaw Report of 1930 warned of excess immigration and the Simpson Report of 1930 concluded that there was no margin of land available for agricultural settlement of new immigrants.[50]

The Jewish Agency attacked these specific conclusions. In several memoranda it sought to make the following points:[51] (a) the mandatory government's estimates of cultivable land were much too low;[52] (b)

---

[47] See Gurevich, Gertz, and Bachi, *op. cit.*, p. 30, the table showing requests and approvals of labor schedules between April, 1924, and March, 1939.

[48] See, e.g., Jewish Agency, *Memorandum Submitted to the Palestine Royal Commission* (London: 1935), Chapters X and XVI, and *Peel Report*, pp. 293–97 and 299.

[49] Jewish Agency, *The Jewish Case before the Anglo-American Committee of Inquiry on Palestine* (Jerusalem: 1947), p. 19.

[50] Sir John Hope Simpson, *Palestine: Report on Immigration, Land Settlement and Development*, Cmd. 3686, HMSO, 1930; *Shaw Report*, Cmd. 3530, 1930.

[51] The Jewish arguments may be found in several Jewish Agency publications: *Memorandum Submitted to the Palestine Royal Commission*, *The Jewish Case*, and *The Jewish Plan for Palestine* (Jerusalem: 1947).

[52] A classic among the many attacks on the cultivable area estimates is Ruppin, *op. cit.*, pp. 205–28.

Jewish purchases of land from Arabs did not lead to any significant displacement of Arab farmers; (c) the absorptive capacity of land should be estimated on the basis of modern agricultural techniques, not on average yields of *fellah* farms; [53] (d) there were absorption opportunities outside of agriculture.

More generally, the Jewish case was based on two main lines of argument. First, that economic absorption was not a fixed quantity, but an expanding concept, a function of the economic development of the country. Second, that Jewish immigration, far from filling a vessel of limited volume, was itself the main factor raising economic absorptive capacity. The soundness of this approach was accepted by the Palestine Royal Commission in 1937, which concluded that "... so far from reducing economic absorptive capacity, immigration increased it." [54]

However, the result of this change in view was not a call for more immigration, but a switch to political criteria. The Royal Commission recommended abandonment of the principle of economic absorptive capacity and its replacement by a political criterion which would limit Jewish population to one third of the total population, after allowing 75,000 immigrants to enter over a five-year period so as to allow the Jewish population to reach this level. This policy was in effect adopted in 1938 and officially declared in the White Paper of 1939 (Cmd. 6019). As mentioned, the restrictions on immigration during and especially after World War II were the main cause of the Jewish community's antagonism to the mandatory government and of the eventual bitter end of the mandate.

Land and settlement policy

Land purchase and agricultural settlement were the pillars of Zionist policy. About 40 per cent of all expenditures of the national institutions in 1917–39 were for these purposes.[55] A number of connected factors explain why the Jewish institutions considered these activities so important: (a) agricultural settlement in general and land purchase in particular were politically important in establishing the "Jewishness" of Palestine; (b) land purchase by the Jewish National Fund was considered necessary in order to "nationalize" the land and remove it from

---

[53] Sir John Hope Simpson, *op. cit.*, had called for agricultural development which would increase absorptive capacity in the future, but this part of his report was carefully ignored by the mandatory government; see *Peel Report*, p. 73.

[54] *Peel Report*, p. 62.

[55] Ulitzur, *op. cit.*, p. 273 (adjusted by figures from his earlier chapters).

speculative dealings; (c) there was an ideological goal of "back to the land" to reverse the diaspora structure of Jewish economic life; (d) it was felt that the proper economic sequence of development should start with agriculture; (e) it was assumed that private initiative and capital could be attracted to industry but that only public capital could provide a sound agricultural base (except for citriculture).

The last point reflects what was perhaps the basic attitude of the Jewish national institutions: Palestine was not very inviting economically; it was therefore the function of the institutions, as representatives of world Jewry, to create the economic environment for the absorption of immigration—a recognition that much of the investment in land purchase and agricultural settlement would be social, as opposed to private cost.

The government's attitude to the purchase of land was attuned to the absorptive capacity argument. It was feared that the purchase of land by Jews from Arabs would displace Arab farmers and lower their standard of living. The British were particularly incensed by the clause in Jewish National Fund land leases forbidding the employment of Arab labor. This attitude persisted despite the fact that the Jewish Agency was generally able to prove that complaints about the displacement of Arab farmers were greatly exaggerated, and that the standard of living of Arabs, including farmers, had risen considerably. Consequently, purchase of land by Jews was often hampered by administrative and legal complications. In February, 1940, land purchase from Arabs was legally forbidden in all but a very small area of Palestine.

The Jewish concept of agricultural settlement as national overhead investment was foreign to the point of view of many of the mandatory government economists. How opposed the two attitudes were can be seen from the following quotation from Sir John Hope Simpson (who himself called for a greater accent on economic development):

It is undesirable, from the point of view of ordinary morality, that colonists should be allowed to benefit by the large expenditure which has been made for their settlement and yet to escape the payment of the amounts spent upon them. Nothing could be worse than that the Jewish immigrants should feel that they have the right to be established in Palestine at the expense of others.[56]

Monetary and fiscal policy

The monetary system itself was such as to preclude an active monetary or foreign exchange policy on the part of the central authority; the

[56] Simpson, *op. cit.*, p. 50.

Government of Palestine did not concern itself with monetary policy, there was no central bank, and the Palestine Currency Board played a technical role of response, not initiation. There was no room for exchange rate policy, and though this eliminated the possibility of foreign exchange shortage, it also greatly restricted compensatory monetary policy. Undoubtedly, a more flexible monetary system would have moderated the boom of 1932–35, and, more important, the recession of 1936–39. Furthermore, the absence of a central bank forced even the largest Jewish banks to keep very high reserve ratios. The defects of this system from the point of view of Palestine have been pointed out, but there is no reason to believe that there was any concerted opposition to the system as such on the part of the Jewish authorities. For example, as late as 1946, Eliezer Hoofien, one of Palestine's most influential bankers, expressed his belief that the foreign exchange system was beneficial from the point of view of capital inflow, and was therefore more important than having a central bank and independent monetary policy.[57]

The Government of Palestine had an extremely conservative fiscal policy. Even the Palestine Royal Commission found that "the effect of Treasury control has been to secure in a young country with a multitude of financial and economic problems a conservative and sometimes a restrictive policy." [58] This conservatism made itself felt in two ways: the size of the government budget and its composition.

The domestic receipts of the government were equal to about 13 per cent of the net national product of Palestine in the years 1936, 1943, and 1945, and expenditures were not much different.[59] The major sources of income were indirect taxes, primarily on imports; in fact, no income tax was imposed until 1940. Although the tax structure has often been criticized, one scholar finds much to justify it in the situation of a foreign government confronted by two antagonistic sectors.[60]

The almost complete reliance on taxation and the insignificant use made of loan financing for regular government activities were perhaps more to be deprecated. A frequent complaint against the Palestine Currency Board was that it invested Palestinian funds in foreign securities. It has been pointed out that it would have been more to the point to

---

[57] Jewish Agency, *The Jewish Case, op. cit.*, p. 237. We are indebted to Dr Gaathon for clarifying Hoofien's views. A contrary opinion is expressed in Nathan, Gass, and Creamer, *op. cit.*

[58] *Peel Report*, p. 206.

[59] Amotz Morag, *Public Finance in Israel: Problems and Development* (Jerusalem: The Magnes Press, 1967; Hebrew), p. 1.

[60] *Ibid.*, pp. 2–3.

blame the government for not issuing obligations in which the Palestine Currency Board could invest.[61]

The customs tariff was often criticized by the Jews for not giving proper protection to industry and for bearing too heavily on raw materials, and by the Arabs for giving too much protection to Jewish industry. The government's policy, gradually developed after 1925, was to free most raw materials and machinery from duties, to give moderate protection (from 1927) to some local industry, and to give greater protection to grain cultivation.[62] The Jews also objected strenuously to the strict adherence to Article 18 of the Mandate which by ensuring equal tariff treatment to all members of the League of Nations, prevented the use of reciprocal commercial arrangements for Palestine to improve trade at a time when they were in widespread use. Both Michaely and Morag, in their previously cited studies, have concluded that the actual damage resulting from this clause, though not subject to measurement, has probably been greatly exaggerated.

Jewish, Arab, and even British commissions criticized the inadequacy of expenditures on economic development and social services, particularly the very small sums spent on health and education.[63] Even during the prosperous years 1932–35, when budget surpluses were accumulating, the government did not see fit to expand expenditures substantially.[64]

The main Jewish complaint was that the Jewish sector paid a much larger share of government revenue than it received of government expenditures. This point reveals a fundamental difference in the attitudes of the Jewish institutions and the government as regards the relationship between the Jewish and the Arab sectors. The government tried to consider Palestine as one economy. In keeping with this, it was in the best tradition of progressive fiscal policy (which the Jews, even more than the British, accepted)[65] that the richer Jewish community should give more and the poorer Arab community should receive more. The

---

[61] Nathan, Gass, and Creamer, *op. cit.,* p. 300.

[62] The development of tariff protection is reviewed in Government of Palestine, *A Survey of Palestine,* Vol. III, pp. 1252–62. The Arab view is presented in M. F. Abcarius, *Palestine Through the Fog of Propaganda* (London: Hutchinson, n.d.), Chapter VIII.

[63] Cf. Nathan, Gass, and Creamer, *op. cit.; Simpson Report; Peel Report;* and Abcarius, *op. cit.*

[64] Morag considers this a good example of the government's very restricted view of its legitimate functions (*op. cit.,* p. 5).

[65] Morag points out that British official fiscal policy never claimed to be progressive, but rather proportional (*ibid.,* p. 10).

Jews, on the other hand, were primarily concerned with the development of Palestine as an economy able to absorb more Jews. They therefore saw no contradiction in criticizing the government for not doing enough to develop the Arab economy and at the same time demanding that Jewish taxes should pay for proportional services to the Jewish sector. This difference in viewpoint is apparent in land and labor policy as well. The two communities were really two separate economies. In addition to land, Jews bought some agricultural goods from Arabs and sold them some industrial goods, and many Arabs worked in Jewish agriculture and building. But it has been estimated that in 1936 total intersectoral trade in final and intermediate goods and services came to only about 7 per cent of Palestine's national income.[66]

The Jewish institutions provided for most of the Jewish sector's needs. In 1936–39 the Jewish institutions spent almost twice as much on health as did the government.[67] The institutions spent heavily for economic development as well as for the social services of the Jewish community, mainly health and education. Relying primarily on financing from abroad, the financial resources of the Jewish institutions together were smaller than those of the government, which relied almost exclusively on local taxation, the major share coming from the richer Jewish sector. During 1917–39 the national institutions alone spent a total of over LP 20 million, of which about 32 per cent went to social services, about 8 per cent to industry, trade, and urban settlement, and, as mentioned above, some 40 per cent to land purchase and agricultural settlement.[68]

It has been estimated for 1920–45 that Jewish institutions raised about LP 40 million, the National Council (*Vaad Leumi*) and the local authorities LP 20 million (about half of it by taxation), while sick fund receipts and the sale of education services brought in another LP 20 million. Despite having to provide a major share of the LP 100 million government revenue, the Jewish sector was able to raise some LP 80 million for its own public service activities.[69]

[66] Computed from Gruenbaum (Gaathon), *National Income and Outlay in Palestine, 1936, op. cit.*, pp. 19, 21. Since 1936 was a year of open hostility, this may be less than in peaceful years. A discussion of the relations between the sectors is presented in Yoram Ben-Porath, *The Arab Labor Force in Israel* (Jerusalem: Falk Institute, 1966).

[67] Computed from Nathan, Gass and Creamer, *op. cit.*, p. 349 .

[68] Ulitzur, *op. cit.*

[69] Ofer, *op. cit.*, p. 119.

Conclusion

Unlike the Government of Palestine, the Jewish national institutions adopted an attitude towards public responsibility for economic development that was foreign to most of the non-Communist world until the 1950's. Whereas the mandatory government did maintain (though not always successfully) the legal framework that was a prerequisite for the development of Palestine, it is to the Jewish national institutions, and of course the human material which came to Palestine, that most of the credit for the development of Jewish Palestine must be given. This development would have been much greater had the government shared the attitude of the Jewish institutions both to aims in Palestine and to the role of government in achieving these aims. Since the Jewish institutions were public in only a narrow sense and did not have most of the basic powers of government, their role, though vital, was limited. With the advent of the State of Israel, the stage was set for a meeting of two strands of policy for economic development: the acceptance of economic development as a primary goal of government economic policy in all its forms and the continuation of the national institutions' activities in channeling the contributions of world Jewry towards the development of Israel.

It is the purpose of this chapter to survey briefly the main institutions which comprise the non-private sector of the economy—the government, the national institutions, and the Histadrut (the General Federation of Labor)—and the extent and modes of their economic activity. Although it is difficult to assess accurately their weight in the economy, it is certainly considerable compared with most Western countries.

The importance of the non-private sector (i.e., the sector comprising the three institutions mentioned) in economic activity has its roots in the mandatory period. It was not to be expected that immigration of Jews to Palestine, which was the central aim of the Zionist movement, would be motivated by economic profitability. Hence, irrespective of socio-economic ideology, there was a consensus that immigration should be subsidized by world Jewry and organized by a "public" sector.

The same line of thought prevailed as regards the allocation of resources in Palestine: some economic activities had political priority but were not profitable enough to attract private enterprise. A relevant example is the purchase of land from Arabs. Since land was a prerequisite of political independence, economic considerations played a secondary part in determining requirements. The same goes for agricultural settlements: their establishment was often undertaken out of political considerations. These three activities—immigration, land-purchase, and agricultural settlement—were largely financed by the financial instruments of the national institutions. More important, the idea that individuals have an order of priorities which differs from that of the community served as a justification for public intervention in many fields during the State period.

Another aspect of a trend of thought shared by the majority of the Zionist movement is that the Jewish community (and later the population of Israel) was never expected to adjust its standard of living to local production conditions. During the mandatory period Jews sought to maintain a higher standard of living than Arabs; this was accomplished in several ways: through the higher quality of the Jewish labor force; through the import of capital which made it possible to raise capital per worker to a level higher than in the Arab sector; and by combating Arab competition in the commodity and labor markets. The same idea of maintaining a standard of living above that guaranteed by the Gross National Product persists today, and it still means importing capital.

Last, but not least, is the socialist tradition of the labor movement. Until the 1930's most of the immigrants came from Eastern Europe, and were strongly influenced by socialist movements there. Palestinian conditions of labor organization differed in two ways from those in Europe. First, there was no solid base of established population, so that there was neither a "working" nor a "capitalist" class; the new socio-economic pattern did not, therefore, clash with any pre-existing regime. Second, capital was, as stated, largely concentrated in the hand of national institutions and allocated at their discretion. Both factors made it possible for the labor movement to mobilize capital and to enter production by setting up its own enterprises, cooperatives, and social services. To this day, labor is dominant in agriculture, which did not (except in citriculture) attract private entrepreneurs.

Much of the power of the labor movement was derived from the degree of centralism under the Histadrut. Since there was no established labor force, and since immigrant workers had many common interests, there was far less conflict between trade unions than in other countries. On the production and services side, considerations of scale favored a roof organization. The relative homogeneity of political views—Zionism on the one hand, and socialism on the other—facilitated centralization and made the Histadrut a political power.

With the establishment of the State other factors also came into play in strengthening the role of the non-private sector. There was the concentration of capital imports in the hands of the public sector, while the continuous inflation, combined with foreign-exchange control, entailed a complicated mechanism of interference with free-market prices.

We shall now outline the scale and modes of activity of the public sector and the Histadrut.

THE GOVERNMENT

Since 1948, the government has been led by the same moderate labor party, Mapai; but since Mapai has not succeeded in gaining an absolute majority at any election, coalition governments have been the rule.

Mapai dominance has meant the acceptance of decisive government influence in economic affairs, particularly in development, whereas the necessity of working in coalition has created a tendency to avoid extreme positions.

The legal framework within which the government works is still in flux: it is a combination of Ottoman, British, and Israeli legislation, and there is as yet no unified system of law.[1]

One way of trying to gauge the importance of government is through estimates of public consumption and investment. Such an approach, of course, underestimates the government's real power, since it fails to take into account its influence through policy—fiscal, monetary, foreign exchange, and the like.

Direct activity:[2] In 1959, about 55 per cent of total investment was financed by the public sector.[3] Most of it was direct investment, the public sector acquiring ownership of the capital; the rest was through loans. The public sector share in investment is higher in Israel than in any other non-Communist country for which data are available. Many public sector enterprises are owned jointly by the government and national institutions, the Histadrut, and private enterpreneurs.[4] Some investments are only initially owned by the public sector; an example is dwellings, which are eventually transferred to the tenants. The government thus uses its resources to gain complete ownership, to enter into partnership with private capital, to make loans, and sometimes to give grants. This raises the question of what fields the government should enter and of what criteria should apply to the choice between alternative methods of investment finance. As will be seen later (Chapter 9), there is no consistent and well-defined policy, and a common criticism is that arbitrary investment decisions have led to too many mistakes.

Israel also ranks high in public consumption, which comes to between 15 and 20 per cent of domestic resource-use. This is similar to the level

---

[1] We shall not discuss this subject, which, in its economic aspects, is comprehensively dealt with in Meir Heth, *The Legal Framework of Economic Activity in Israel* (Jerusalem and New York: Frederick A. Praeger with the Bank of Israel, 1967).

[2] This section is based on Haim Barkai, "The Public, Histadrut, and Private Sectors in the Israeli Economy," *Sixth Report 1961–1963* (Jerusalem: Falk Project, 1964), Chapters 5 and 6.

[3] I.e., central government, local authorities, and national institutions (see below, p. 43).

[4] A public enterprise is defined as one in which at least 50 per cent of the shares are owned by the government and national institutions.

found in developed non-Communist countries such as the United States, Britain, and Sweden.

Indirect activity: This includes policy implementation, which cannot be measured directly; even so, it is clear that the influence of indirect government activity is very great indeed. Some of the more important effects will be discussed in later chapters on policy; here we shall stress only one factor. Policy measures can be specific, discriminating between, say, enterprises or commodities, or they can be general, acting at a macro-economic level. Because of the government's extensive direct operations, and because the whole economy is quite small, specific discriminatory measures have been widely used. To give only two examples: foreign exchange policy is marked by the existence of dozens of effective exchange rates; also, the terms of financing private investment vary widely. Thus, the prevailing type of policy lies somewhere between the use of macro-economic variables to guide the economy, and planning on the micro-economic level. Although there have been several attempts to draw up comprehensive plans,[5] no administrative steps have ever been taken to implement them.

It would be interesting to know whether direct and indirect government activity has increased or decreased during the period. No systematic attempt has been made to answer this question. Direct activity, measured by the share of GDP originating in the public sector, has been roughly constant since 1953.[6] There are no figures for 1948–52, but it is reasonable to assume that the public sector share of GDP was considerably higher then. The same appears to be true of indirect activity, though no proof of this is readily available. Up to 1952, price controls, for example, were much stricter than they have been at any time since; but no clear trend can be discerned without further research.

THE NATIONAL INSTITUTIONS

The national institutions are the Jewish Agency, the Foundation Fund (the financial arm of the Agency), the Jewish National Fund, and the Zionist Organization. They are usually added to central and local government to complete the public sector. The rationale for considering the national institutions as part of general government is that they were set up in order to undertake many government functions. The mandatory

---

[5] See A. L. Gaathon, "Economic Planning in Israel, Its History and Problems," *Israel Economy: Theory and Practice,* ed. Joseph Ronen (Tel Aviv: Dvir, n.d.; Hebrew), pp. 179–202.

[6] Barkai, *op. cit.,* p. 26, Table 1.

government recognized the Zionist Organization, and later the Jewish Agency, as the principal (though not the only) representative of Jewish interests in Palestine.[7] After 1948, when a government was formed, it was natural for its ministries to replace Jewish Agency departments (and for Agency department heads to become ministers—for example, the head of the Agency's political department became foreign minister). But although some departments were abolished and others curtailed, not all activities were shifted to the government. In particular, the institutions retained some important economic functions.

There were two reasons for this. First, the rebuilding of Palestine had always been considered the task of the Jewish people everywhere, and not only of those in Palestine. Although the creation of the State of Israel brought about some automatic changes,[8] it did not alter the primary task of developing the country. World Jewry had functions to perform and therefore also the right to be represented in the organizations executing these functions. Besides, world Jewry has been a major financial source. Donors are interested in having some control over their donations, and institutional arrangements in the donor countries make it administratively, financially, and perhaps legally, preferable to raise money for philanthropic institutions rather than for a foreign government; the framework of the national institutions was therefore retained.

The main economic tasks of the Jewish Agency have been connected with immigration. During the period of mass immigration, the financial resources of the Agency proved inadequate, and the government had to join in. The Agency still remains responsible for bringing immigrants to Israel, and for the provision of their immediate needs. Their permanent absorption is a joint undertaking, with the Agency prominent in housing and agricultural settlement.

However, the Agency's activities are by no means restricted to immigration and agriculture. Jewish Agency departments and firms (wholly or partly owned) are active in virtually every branch of economic activity, including the country's largest bank and the national shipping line.

The institution whose position was ostensibly most undercut by the

---

[7] The functions of the national institutions during the mandatory period are discussed in Chapter 2.

[8] For example, the political role of the World Zionist Organization had to be defined anew; in fact, this redefinition has become a continuous process. The status and functions of the Jewish Agency, as recognized by the Government of Israel, were spelled out in a special law in 1952.

creation of the State was the Jewish National Fund. For almost half a century its primary function had been to purchase land, thus creating national land to be used for settlement. After the mass exodus of Arabs in 1948 the government became the custodian of most of the country's land. In 1960, an agreement was signed whereby the administration of all publicly owned land was entrusted to a new joint government–Jewish National Fund organization, the Israel Lands Administration. The Jewish National Fund became responsible for all land amelioration and afforestation on publicly owned land.

THE HISTADRUT

An important part of the Zionist Movement has been Labor Zionism, an intermingling of Zionism and socialism. The basic idea of this movement has been to develop a national home along socialist lines, in the sense of creating a new society, not necessarily defined in the same way by the various labor parties. Groups affiliated to these parties were formed, consisting of pioneers seeking not only to make a living in Palestine, but to do so through their own manual labor. The competition of Arab labor and the difficulties of adjusting to a new way of life led to various experiments in cooperative endeavor ranging from mutual aid provided by the labor parties or unions, to the first collective and cooperative settlements. In 1920, the Histadrut was organized and adopted a tradition which saw the tasks of organized labor as the development of the economy so as to provide new jobs for Jewish workers, and at the same time providing mutual aid and trade union protection.

Consequently, the Histadrut is a multi-purpose organization. It is primarily a giant labor union, representing the majority of workers in the country. As such, it performs the usual trade union functions, the most important of which is to negotiate terms of employment. Thus, perhaps the major direct influence of the Histadrut in recent years is on wage policy, to be discussed in Chapter 11. The Histadrut provides its members with numerous social services, far beyond what is usually provided by trade unions. The most important of these is medical care: 72 per cent of the population received the benefits of the Histadrut's sick fund in 1965.[9]

But where the Histadrut departs most radically from usual trade union practice is in its entrepreneurial activities; these are numerous, complex, and important in almost every branch of the economy. There

[9] *Abstract 1966,* No. 17, pp. 141–44, Tables E/20–E/23. The Histadrut sick fund covers 87 per cent of the *insured* population.

are four main types of Histadrut enterprise: collective settlements (kibbutzim), cooperative settlements (moshavim), producer cooperatives, and corporations owned by Hevrat Ovdim, the Histadrut holding company.

The kibbutzim are chiefly agricultural settlements based on communal production and consumption. But they have been turning more and more to industry: it has been estimated that in 1959, their net product from manufacturing was about the same as from agriculture.[10]

The moshavim are smallholders settlements, with cooperative marketing and purchasing, and with strongly held principles of mutual aid and "self labor"—abstention from employing hired labor.

Producer cooperatives range from small workshops to large utilities such as the bus cooperatives which dominate urban and inter-urban passenger transport. They too are based, at least in theory, on the principle of "self labor."

Hevrat Ovdim is the corporate form of the Histadrut: each member of the Histadrut automatically has a "share" in Hevrat Ovdim, and the same people constitute the governing bodies of both organizations.[11] Companies owned by Hevrat Ovdim are active in manufacturing, mining, construction, commerce, transport, and other services. Some firms are wholly owned by Hevrat Ovdim or its enterprises, and some are joint ventures with public or private interests.

The four parts of the sector are not equally subject to central Histadrut control, and there is also a wide range of motives among the various enterprises. Nevertheless, there are grounds for separating the Histadrut from the private sector: in undertaking an activity, Histadrut enterprises retain the idea that they are supposed to serve a national or class interest. The Histadrut sector therefore holds a position somewhere between the public and private sectors.

The extent of Histadrut influence on economic activity is hard to assess. Wage policy is discussed in a later chapter, but politically the Histadrut also has real indirect influence. Political control of the Histadrut is through the same labor parties active in national politics. In fact, the same people are frequently active in both government and Histadrut. At the very least, all members of labor parties are also Histadrut members. Professor Lerner once said, only half in jest: "The workers have a Histadrut, and the Histadrut has a government." The situation is much more complicated than that, with the lines of control not

---

[10] Barkai, *op. cit.*, p. 46, Table 7.
[11] *Ibid.*, Appendix A.

necessarily running in only one direction. Certainly in recent years they have run more in the opposite direction. The relationship between the Histadrut and the government, and the difficulties inherent in the all-embracing nature of the Histadrut are fascinating subjects but cannot be dealt with here.[12]

[12] For a discussion of some of these difficulties, see Nadav Halevi, "The Israeli Labor Movement," *The Annals of the American Academy of Political and Social Science*, CCCX (March 1957), 172–81. One problem, the relationship between management and labor in Histadrut enterprises, is the subject of a List Institute study by Theo Pirker, *Die Histadrut* (Basel and Tübingen: Kyklos-Verlag and J.C.B. Mohr, 1965).

PART II

MAGNITUDES OF GROWTH

4 POPULATION

A rapid population growth, in which immigration played a considerable part, was typical of both the mandatory and State periods. The population of Palestine grew by 3.8 per cent annually from 1919 to 1947, while the Jewish population grew by 8.3 per cent annually (Table 1). By comparison, in 1948–65 the annual growth rate of the total population was 6.3 per cent. In all, population rose from 915,000 at the end of 1948, to 2.6 million at the end of 1965. These figures must, however, be qualified: the benchmark is 1948, after a large part of the Arab population had emigrated. In 1947, i.e., before the establishment of Israel and the Arab emigration, the total population of what subsequently became Israeli territory was 1.4 million.[1] On this basis, the annual rate of growth is 3.5 per cent, very close to the mandatory rate.

It is difficult to decide which is the better benchmark; each is valid in some cases and inappropriate in others. The 1948 base stresses political aspects, whereas the 1947 base indicates that any view of population growth must take account of the cultivated land, buildings, and equipment abandoned by the Arabs who left.

In any event, the choice of benchmark is moot until 1951 and the first three or four years of the State period should be discussed separately. Starting at 1948, these years saw very rapid growth (20 per cent annually) not subsequently equaled or even approached. Looked at from the 1947 benchmark, 1948–51 is the period in which population returned to its former level, so that we may speak of an expanding population only from 1951 on.

[1] Jewish population was 630,000 (Table 1). Avner Hovne, *The Labor Force in Israel* (Jerusalem: Falk Project, 1961), p. 29, Table 8, estimates the non-Jewish population of "pre-Israel" (i.e., the territory within the borders set by the 1949 Armistice agreements) at 763,000. Deducting the 156,000 non-Jewish population of November, 1948 (Table 7), gives an estimate of around 610,000 Arab refugees. This is low compared with the U.N. estimates.

Whichever base-year we use, the annual rate of growth is much higher than the 0.5 to 1.5 per cent found in developed countries.[2]

TABLE 7.   The Population: 1948–65[a]

(thousands)

	Total	Jews	Non-Jews	Total: per cent increase over preceding year
1948	914.7	758.7	(156.0)[b]	..
1949	1,173.9	1,013.9	160.0	28.3
1950	1,370.1	1,203.0	167.1	16.7
1951	1,577.8	1,404.4	173.4	15.2
1952	1,629.5	1,450.2	179.3	3.3
1953	1,669.4	1,483.6	185.8	2.4
1954	1,717.8	1,526.0	191.8	2.9
1955	1,789.1	1,590.5	198.6	4.2
1956	1,872.4	1,667.5	204.9	4.7
1957	1,976.0	1,762.8	213.2	5.5
1958	2,031.7	1,810.2	221.5	2.8
1959	2,088.7	1,858.8	229.9	2.8
1960	2,150.4	1,911.3	239.1	3.0
1960[c]	2,154.1	1,910.8	243.3	..
1961	2,234.2	1,981.7	252.5	3.7
1962	2,331.8	2,068.9	262.9	4.4
1963	2,430.1	2,155.6	274.5	4.2
1964	2,525.6	2,239.2	286.4	3.9
1965	2,598.4	2,299.1	299.3	2.9

[a] End of year figures.
[b] Estimate for 8.XI.1948 of population within borders of Israel as set by the 1949 Armistice Agreements. Jewish population at this date was 716,000.
[c] New series (permanent population) based on the Census of 22.V.1961. The old series (present population) is based on the Registration of Population of 8.XI.1948.
SOURCES: *Abstract 1966*, No. 17, p. 20, Table B/1; permanent population in 1960 from *Abstract 1964*, No. 15, p. 12, Table B/1.

When the State was established, the immigration restrictions imposed by the mandatory government were abolished by the Declaration of Independence and the Law of Return (1950) which provides, with minor reservations, for the right of every Jew to immigrate and become an Israeli citizen.[3] In addition, positive measures were taken to encourage

[2] U.N., *Demographic Yearbook 1962* (New York: 1963), Tables 14 and 18.
[3] *Laws of the State of Israel*, Authorized Translation (Jerusalem: Government

immigration. As a result, the population nearly doubled in 1948–51. Thereafter, immigration decreased, but still accounted for 42 per cent of total and 47 per cent of Jewish population growth. The average for the whole 1949–65 period is 64 per cent for Jews, which is comparable to the 72 per cent for Jewish population increase during 1919–48.[4]

The rate of population growth (Jews and non-Jews combined) is similar to that of the mandatory period. Also, the share of immigration in the Jewish population increase is similar in the two periods. But the similarity ends here since the population has acquired a new structure. This chapter is confined to 1948–65.[5] The main structural changes, discussed in this and the next chapter, were the initial decline in the level of education due to immigrants having fewer years of schooling and the increase in the proportion of children in the population due to the immigrants' high fertility rate.

IMMIGRATION

During the mandatory period, and especially after 1930, immigration was to a large extent determined by quotas. After 1948, when immigration not only became legally free, but when steps were taken to increase it, social and economic determinants came to the fore.

The first influx of immigrants was from Eastern Europe (mainly from Bulgaria, Poland, Hungary, and Romania), and from Arab countries (mainly Yemen and Iraq) involved in the War of Independence (1948–49); this immigration included displaced persons from concentration camps. These groups undoubtedly immigrated because of political and social conditions in these countries, and because of the persecution during World War II. Special bodies were established by the Jewish Agency to organize the mass immigration. Sometimes, in both Europe and the Middle East, agreements were made with the governments concerned, and entire communities immigrated as a result. Because of the difficult situation of Jews in these countries and because it was not at all certain that their governments would continue to let them emigrate, this operation was called "rescue" immigration.

Printer), Vol. 4, p. 114. The reservations are: immigration is subject to the discretion of the Minister of the Interior if a prospective immigrant is liable to endanger public health or security; also if he is suspected of crimes against the Jewish people.

4 Figures in this paragraph are from Chapter 2, p. 16, from Tables 7 and 8, and from the sources to these tables.

5 For the mandatory period, see Chapter 2.

TABLE 8. *Jewish Immigration,*[a] *by Continent of Birth: 1948–65*

	Gross immigration			Emigration	Net immigration	
	Total	Asia-Africa	Europe-America		(1)–(4)	(5) as per cent of population increase
	(thousands) (1)	(per cent) (2)	(3)	(thousands) (4)	(thousands) (5)	(6)
1948[b]	101.8	14.4	85.6	1.0	100.8	..
1949	239.6	47.3	52.7	7.2	232.4	91.1
1950	170.2	49.6	50.4	9.5	160.8	85.0
1951	175.1	71.1	28.9	10.1	165.0	81.9
1952	24.4	71.6	28.4	13.0	11.4	24.9
1953	11.3	75.1	24.9	12.5	−1.2	−3.6
1954	18.4	88.7	11.3	7.0	11.4	26.9
1955	37.5	92.9	7.1	6.0	31.5	48.8
1956	56.2	86.7	13.3	11.0	45.2	58.7
1957	71.2	42.5	57.5	11.0	60.2	63.2
1958	27.1	44.3	55.7	11.5	15.6	32.9
1959	23.9	33.2	66.8	9.5	14.4	29.6
1960	24.5	29.0	71.0	8.5	16.0	30.5
1961	47.6	47.3	52.7	7.0	40.6	57.3
1962	61.3	78.5	21.5	7.5	53.8	61.7
1963	64.4	69.3	30.7	11.1	53.3	61.5
1964	54.7	..	..	8.4	46.3	55.4
1965	30.7	..	..	7.8	22.9	38.2
1948–65	**1,240.0**	55.4[c]	44.6[c]	**159.6**	**1,080.4**	63.6[d]

[a] Column (1) includes tourists settling (22,400 during 1948–65). The continent-of-origin breakdown excludes tourists settling and "origin not known" (19,400 during 1948–63, 18,800 of them in 1948–51). Discrepancies in the total of the absolute figures are due to rounding.
[b] From May 15.
[c] 1948–63.
[d] 1949–65.

SOURCES: *Abstract 1966,* No. 17, as follows: Column (1) from p. 91, Table D/3. Columns (2) and (3) from p. 92, Table D/4. Column (4) from p. 103, Table D/14; for 1961–65 this table gives only total emigration, and the figure for Jews was obtained by deducting net emigration of non-Jews from p. 21, Table B/2.
Column (6)—the annual increase in Jewish population was calculated from Table 7.

After 1951 rescue immigration became less important. One exception was the immigration from Hungary and Egypt in 1956 and 1957 which followed the Hungarian uprising and the Sinai Campaign. Some of the North African immigration can also be considered a rescue operation, since Jews often suffered along with the Europeans from anti-French campaigns there.

Otherwise, immigration became more and more a matter of individual choice, rather than being an immediate necessity for entire communities, and was thus more affected by current conditions in Israel and by the cost of immigration in its broadest sense.

Relevant economic factors included, first of all, financial participation of the Jewish Agency and the government in the cost of immigration. In 1948–51, the Agency financed the transportation of practically all immigrants and set up transit camps which provided food, medical care, and other essentials for the first few months after immigration. In November, 1951, when internal economic pressures were mounting and rescue immigration ceased, a joint Agency–government body decided to reduce the Agency's participation in immigration costs, limiting it to young or skilled immigrants.[6] This decision sharply reduced immigration, especially from Iran and Morocco, the main sources at the time. Since then, public financing of immigration costs has remained a matter of discretion, although it was granted more freely after 1954.

Before discussing the prospects of future immigration, we should remark that the migration of the 1950's brought about a notable change in the geographical distribution of world Jewry. In 1947/48 there were about 11.3 million Jews, roughly half of them (5.8 million) in America (mainly in the United States) and a quarter (2.8 million) in the Soviet bloc; the remainder were in the rest of Europe (about 1 million), in Africa (0.7 million), and in Asia—other than Israel—(0.4 million). About 6 per cent of all Jews (0.6 million) lived in Israel. Since then, the map of world Jewry has changed: by 1961, around 15 per cent of Jews were in Israel; the share of the non-U.S.S.R. Soviet bloc had declined from 7 per cent to 3 per cent and that of the Islamic countries from 8 per cent to 4 per cent. The shares of Western Europe, America, and the U.S.S.R. did not change: there was natural increase, of course,

---

[6] The conditions for financing "non-rescue" immigration were: 80 per cent of immigrants must be between the ages of 15 and 35, or skilled workers, or owners of at least $ 10,000 worth of capital; unskilled workers were required to agree in writing to work at assigned jobs for two years after immigration. [Jewish Agency, *Immigration Papers,* No. 20 (November 1952), p. 3 (Hebrew).]

TABLE 9. *World Jewish Population: 1947–48 and 1961*

| | *(thousands)* | |
	1947–48	*1961*
Total	**11,330**	**12,866**
Israel	*650*	*1,937*
Asia (other than Israel)	*430*	*182*
Turkey	80	50
Iraq	120	6
Iran	90	80
Yemen and Aden	50	4
Others	90	42
Africa	*730*	*500*
Tunisia, Morocco, and Algeria	470	360
Egypt	75	7
Union of South Africa	100	110
Others	85	23
Europe—Soviet Bloc	*2,761*	*2,709*
U.S.S.R.	2,000	2,345
Romania	380	200
Hungary	170	100
Poland	100	32
Others (including Yugoslavia)	111	32
Other Europe	*959*	*1,021*
United Kingdom	350	451
France	235	375
Others	374	195
America and Oceania	*5,800*	*6,517*
U.S.A.	5,000	5,500
Canada	180	275
Brazil	110	125
Argentina	350	400
Others	160	217

SOURCES: 1947–48—Moshe Sicron, *Immigration to Israel: 1948–1953* (Jerusalem: Falk Project and CBS, 1957), Statistical Supplement, p. 30, Table A42. 1961—*American Jewish Year Book 1961.*

but little migratory movement between them and the rest of the world (Table 9).

Eastern Europe (other than Russia) and the Islamic countries were the principal countries of Jewish emigration. In 1961 they still had 900,000 Jewish inhabitants—60 per cent in Islamic countries and 40 per cent in Eastern Europe. But only a few of these Jews are likely to immigrate to Israel. Any future immigration will therefore have to come from America and Western Europe.

Here the cost of immigration is much higher owing to the higher standard of living to be forgone. Although economic conditions in Israel have improved vastly since 1948, they now have to compete with conditions in more developed countries. Also, since immigration has become more a matter of personal choice and less one of political asylum, social, cultural, and economic conditions in Israel have an increasing influence on the volume of immigration. Under present conditions, there is little immigration-by-choice, and it is probable that in the near future total immigration (and with it, population growth) will slow down.

We have not discussed the prospects of immigration from the U.S.S.R. Should any occur, it would probably open an entirely new phase in the economic development of the country.

NATURAL INCREASE

Natural increase is higher in Israel than in most developed countries, averaging about 1.9 per cent between 1961 and 1965, and more than 2 per cent in the 1950's (Table 10) compared with 0.5 to 1.5 per cent in Western Europe and America. Even if immigration dwindles, the population may thus grow fairly rapidly through natural increase alone.

However, the rate of population growth has been declining steadily, a process which can be better understood by distinguishing between Jews and non-Jews.

Table 10 shows that the birth rate of Jews has declined since 1951–55, while the death rate has been fairly stable: as a result, natural increase dropped from 2.4 per cent in 1951–55 to 1.6 per cent in 1961–65. By contrast, the natural increase of non-Jews rose from 3.7 per cent in 1951–55 to 4.3 per cent in 1961–65, the combined result of a declining death rate and rising birth rate. The drop in the rate of natural increase of the total population therefore reflects the drop in the Jewish birth rate. Two processes may underlie this decline: the tendency of Jewish women of child-bearing age to have fewer children and the decline in the percentage of women of child-bearing age in the Jewish population.

The tendency of women to have children is often measured by "total fertility,"[7] which shows a decline from 4.0 in 1951 to 3.3–3.5 in 1958–64.

TABLE 10.   *Births, Deaths, and Natural Increase: 1951–65*

(crude rates per thousand mean population)

	1951–55	*1956–60*	*1961–65*
Live births			
Total	31.5	27.3	25.2
Jews	29.8	25.0	22.3
Non-Jews	46.3	47.9	50.2
Deaths			
Total	6.7	6.1	6.1
Jews	6.3	5.9	6.1
Non-Jews	9.7	8.2	6.6
Natural increase			
Total	24.8	21.2	19.1
Jews	23.5	19.1	16.2
Non-Jews	36.7	39.7	43.5

SOURCE: *Abstract 1966,* No. 17, pp. 55–57, Tables C/1–C/3.

From these figures only one might conclude that the size of families is declining, but this would be wrong. The measure is subject to an upward bias which increases with immigration. One adjustment for the bias shows that fertility stood at a steady 3.5 children throughout the period, while a second adjustment even showed an upward trend.[8]

---

[7] The number of live births of a woman throughout her life, calculated from the age-specific fertility rates of a given year. See *Abstract 1966,* No. 17, p. xxxvi, and p. 73, Table C/21 for the data.

[8] The accepted measure of fertility used in the official statistics is $F = \sum_i \sum_a \frac{B_i(a)}{P_a}$ where B is the number of births; i is the birth order (i.e., first, second, third, etc.); a is age; and P_a is the population of women at age a. The measure is inadequate in Israel because of large-scale immigration: under these conditions, $\sum_a \frac{B_1(a)}{P_a}$ may be greater than unity, which is absurd; also, the magnitude $\sum_a \frac{B_i(a)}{P_a}$ may not decline when i increases. Two corrections have been

That family size has been stable is confirmed by the consumer expenditure surveys, which show that the average family had 3.9 members throughout the 1950's.[9]

This stable total fertility in the Jewish population results from opposing trends. Families with a high fertility rate immigrated from Asia-Africa; there is also some tendency for family size to rise among those of European origin. On the other hand, Asia-Africa immigrants tend to reduce family size after living in the country for several years.

The decline in birth rates must therefore be ascribed to the decline in the proportion of women of child bearing age (20–44) in the Jewish population, from 40 per cent in 1951 to 31 per cent in 1965 (Table 12).[10] Among non-Jews, the share of the age group rose slightly in the period, and this is reflected in the birth rates.[11]

Estimates of future natural increase thus depend very much on projections of the age structure of the Jewish population. The official population projection to 1969 assumed that the share of the 15–44 age group would grow,[12] with a consequent rise in the crude birth rate. However, the projected aging of the population will also raise the death rate. This seems to indicate that natural increase will stabilize at around 1.9 per cent.

Combining the results of our findings on immigration and natural increase, we may conclude that in the near future population will grow more slowly than in the past, but still faster than in many other countries.

JEWS AND NON-JEWS

In 1947, non-Jews were 67 per cent of the population in all Palestine and 55 per cent in the area that subsequently became Israel.[13] By the end of 1949 the proportion had fallen to 14 per cent, owing to the

---

suggested by R. K. Gabriel, *Marriage and Births in Israel* (Jerusalem: The Hebrew University, 1960; Hebrew mimeograph), Chapter 5. Both produce figures which show no decline in fertility since 1948.

[9] CBS, *Family Expenditure Surveys, 1950/51—1956/57—1959/60* (Special Series No. 148; Jerusalem: 1963) pp. 8, 52, 170.

[10] Table 12 shows figures for both sexes together, but the figures for women only are virtually the same.

[11] The fertility rates of non-Jews, available only from 1958, show an uneven tendency to rise.

[12] CBS, *Projections of the Population of Israel up to 1969* (Special Series No. 179; Jerusalem: 1965).

[13] Hovne, *op. cit.*, pp. 13, 29.

mass exodus during the War of Independence; by 1951, the proportion had dropped to 11 per cent, at which level it has remained during the rest of the period covered (Table 7). This means that the natural increase of non-Jews equaled Jewish natural increase and immigration combined. It also means that if the Jewish population is going to grow more slowly in the future, the proportion of non-Jews will increase.

The two population groups differ both socially and economically. In 1961, only 15 per cent of Jews lived in villages, the figure for non-Jews being 74 per cent.[14] Most non-Jewish villages are concentrated in Galilee and in the hilly region east of the central coastal plain (the so-called Little Triangle), so that most non-Jews live in their own rather isolated communities. This state of affairs has been aggravated by legal restrictions (abolished only recently) on the freedom of movement of non-Jews. The labor force, however, is much more mobile than the whole population, so that many non-Jews work quite far from where they live. The standard of education of non-Jews is much lower than that of Jews. The social and economic integration of non-Jews therefore involves problems different from those confronting Jewish immigrants and justifies a separate discussion, not attempted here, of non-Jewish communities.[15]

CONTINENT OF ORIGIN OF JEWS

The Jewish population is often classified by three groups of origin: Europe-America, Asia-Africa, and Israel-born. Immigration has raised the share of the Asia-Africa group in Jewish population. Table 11 (panel A) shows that the Europe-America group declined from 55 per cent in 1948 to 31 per cent in 1965, while the Asia-Africa group rose from 10 to 28 per cent. An additional breakdown of the Israel-born by father's continent of birth is available from 1961; if this is taken into account, around 45 per cent of the population belong to the Asia-Africa group (see panel B of Table 11).

The classification by continent of origin has wide application: educational level, income, and labor force participation are all higher in the Europe-America group. Moreover, since Europe-America families are smaller, their standard of living as measured by per capita expenditure or income is relatively even higher than suggested by aggregate figures.

[14] According to the 1961 census of population (*Abstract 1962*, No. 13, p. 39, Table 7). Subsequent data show little change.

[15] Such a discussion may be found in Yoram Ben-Porath, *The Arab Labor Force in Israel* (Jerusalem: Falk Institute, 1966).

TABLE 11.   *Jewish Population, by Continent of Origin:*
            Selected Years, 1948–65[a]

(per cent)

	Total	Europe-America	Asia-Africa	Israel
A. By continent of birth				
1948[b]	100.0	54.8	9.8	35.4
1951	100.0	46.9	27.6	25.5
1954	100.0	41.7	26.9	31.4
1957	100.0	37.1	29.0	33.9
1960	100.0	35.0	27.6	37.4
1963	100.0	32.2	29.0	38.8
1965	100.0	31.3	28.3	40.4
B. By continent of origin[c]				
May 5, 1961	100.0	52.8	41.8	5.4
1961	100.0	51.6	42.8	5.6
1962	100.0	50.1	44.2	5.7
1963	100.0	48.8	45.4	5.8
1965	100.0	47.6	46.2	6.2

[a] December 31 unless otherwise specified.
[b] November 11.
[c] Continent of birth of foreign-born and father's continent of birth for Israel-born (38 per cent of total at the census date).
SOURCE: A. *Abstract 1966*, No. 17, p. 45, Table B/16.
          B. *Ibid.*, p. 40, Table B/15 and *Abstract 1964*, No. 15, p. 37, Table B/17.

AGE STRUCTURE

We distinguish five age groups in the population: childhood (0–14 years), adolescence (15–19), early working age and fertility age (20–44), late working age (45–64), and old age (65+). In making use of this grouping we have borne in mind (a) the labor market: 20–64 is the principal working-age group; the subdivision into early and late working age is particularly important since immigrants aged over 45 find it difficult to get work; (b) the country's expenditure on education; and (c) the volume of pension and welfare payments, for which the 65+ group is the relevant one.

The percentage of children aged 0–14 is higher in Israel than in most European and developed American countries and similar to that in

Asia and underdeveloped American countries.[16] It rose steadily from 1948 to 1960, among both Jews and non-Jews, but then began to decline.

TABLE 12.   *Age Structure, by Population Group: Selected Years, 1948–65*[a]

(per cent)

	Total	0–14	15–19	20–44	45–64	65+
Jews						
1948	100.0	28.6	8.4	44.0	15.1	3.9
1951	100.0	30.9	8.4	39.7	16.9	4.1
1955	100.0	33.5	7.6	35.9	15.8	7.2
1961	100.0	34.8	7.9	32.0	20.0	5.3
1963	100.0	33.6	10.0	31.4	19.2	5.8
1965	100.0	32.4	10.7	31.0	19.6	6.3
Non-Jews						
1955	100.0	45.7	10.5	27.5	10.8	5.5
1961	100.0	46.6	10.6	28.5	10.1	4.2
1963	100.0	48.6	9.7	28.3	9.2	4.2
1965	100.0	50.0	8.8	28.3	8.7	4.2
Total						
1955	100.0	34.8	7.9	35.0	17.5	4.8
1961	100.0	36.1	8.2	31.6	18.9	5.2
1963	100.0	35.2	9.9	31.1	18.3	5.5
1965	100.0	34.4	10.5	30.8	18.3	6.0

[a] December 31 except for 1948 (November 8) and 1961 (May 22).
SOURCE: *Abstracts,* as follows: *1962,* No. 13, p. 45, Table 11; *1963,* No. 14, pp. 39, 41, Tables 15 and 17; *1964,* No. 15, pp. 29–31, Tables B/12–B/14; *1966,* No. 17, p. 37, Table B/12.

The share of the working-age group (20–64) is smaller than in developed countries and has declined throughout the period, so that its net effect (i.e., with participation rates held constant) would have been to reduce the ratio of earners to dependents. Within the 20–64

[16] U.N., *Demographic Yearbook 1956* (New York: 1957), pp. 164–78, Table 4. See also Gur Ofer, *The Service Industries in a Developing Economy: Israel As a Case Study* (Jerusalem and New York: Frederick A. Praeger with the Bank of Israel, 1967), p. 154, Appendix C, for data on the 15–19 age group in various countries.

group, the share of the older group rose, while that of the 20–44 group fell steeply. The share of the 65+ group has been growing slowly, but is still below that found in developed countries.

To sum up: The structure of the population is similar to that of less-developed countries, with a high proportion of children, and a low proportion of working-age and old people. The main consequence is a comparatively low proportion of labor force in the population. But, while such an age structure is typical of less-developed countries, where it reflects a combination of high birth rates with high death rates, in Israel both birth and death rates are lower. Death rates are especially low, and the life expectancy of Jews is as high as 70 years for men and 73 for women.[17] If immigration (especially from Asia-Africa) declines, it is probable that the percentage of children will decline while the percentage of older people rises, so that the age distribution will become more similar to that of developed countries.[18]

POPULATION: 1964–65

The population, which grew by 4.2 per cent in 1963, grew by 3.9 per cent in 1964 and 2.9 per cent in 1965—a typical percentage for low-immigration periods; immigration in fact contributed less than half of the increase (Tables 7 and 8).

In 1964 and 1965 the natural increase of Jews rose for the first time in many years; the natural increase of non-Jews continued to rise.[19]

The age structure followed the pattern set in recent years of a decline in the proportion of children, a rise in that of pension-age population, and, within the working-age group, a decline in the younger (20–44) and a rise in the older (45–64) groups (Table 12).

The relatively low immigration of the last two years is reflected in the rising percentage of Israel-born. The ethnic structure of the population has followed recent trends: the proportion of Asia-Africa continued to rise, and reached 46 per cent in 1965 (panel B of Table 11). The proportion of non-Jews has remained at about 11 per cent.

---

[17] *Abstract 1966,* No. 17, p. 83, Table C/31. There are no figures for non-Jews.
[18] See CBS, *Projections of the Population of Israel up to 1969, op. cit.,* p. 16, Table 14.
[19] *Abstract 1966,* No. 17, pp. 56–57, Tables C/2 and C/3.

The various aspects of population growth discussed earlier are relevant also to the labor force. The chief relevant fact is the rapid growth of population, since labor force grew at roughly the same rate. The first important issue is, therefore, that of supplying employment to the additional manpower.

The characteristics of immigration described in Chapter 4 must be taken into account. The standard of education of immigrants was below that of the veteran population, and special measures were therefore needed in order to integrate them into the rapidly developing economy. The same is true of the level and type of skills of immigrants; these are discussed in the second part of this chapter. The last part of the chapter deals with changes in the age structure of the population, which tended to lower the ratio of earners to dependents.

LABOR FORCE, EMPLOYMENT, AND UNEMPLOYMENT

Employment and unemployment

Since 1950, the labor force has been a fairly stable 36 per cent of total population;[1] in absolute terms, it grew from 450,000 in 1950 to 910,000 in 1965 (Table 13). The first question is how far the economy succeeded in providing jobs for a labor force that doubled in 15 years.

Before answering this question, we must qualify the concepts of labor force and unemployment. In the early years of the State, immigrants spent their first few months in the country in transit camps. They were there entitled to free camp services (board and lodging) only if they did not work, and thus had no inducement to look for jobs, although they would probably have done so in normal circumstances. This type of unemployment had virtually disappeared by 1953, when evacuation

---

[1] In 1949 the ratio was 32.4 per cent; it then rose to 35.5 per cent in 1950, as a result of demobilization (see Table 13).

to *maabarot*[2] was complete. In Table 14 we present two unemployment estimates, the second of which takes this fringe group into account.

TABLE 13.   *Labor Force Participation: 1949-65*

	Civilian labor force[a] (thousands)	Participation rate[b] (per cent)	
		Total	Jews
A. Old series			
1949	342.9	32.4	34.4
1950	450.1	35.5	37.4
1951	545.0	36.5	38.2
1952	584.0	36.4	38.0
1953	598.6	36.3	37.9
1954	608.0	36.0	37.6
1955	619.3	35.4	36.9
1956	646.1	35.3	36.8
B. New series			
1957	689.8	35.7	37.4
1958	698.3	34.9	36.4
1959	714.5	34.6	36.0
1960	735.8	34.8	36.1
1961	774.5	35.4	36.7
1962	818.4	35.8	36.8
1963	839.5	35.3	36.6
1964	883.6	35.7	37.1
1965	912.4	35.6	37.1

[a] Panel A figures estimated by applying to the population the age–sex–country-of-origin specific rates found in the 1958 Labor Force Survey. Panel B figures are from the LFS results in each year.
[b] Participation in total mean population.
SOURCES: Population—*Abstract 1966*, No. 17, p. 20.
Labor Force—1949–56: Avner Hovne, *The Labor Force in Israel* (Jerusalem: Falk Project, 1961), pp. 12–13, Summary Table.
1957–61: CBS, *Labour Force Surveys 1955–1961* (Special Series No. 162; Jerusalem: 1964), pp. 2, 4.
1962: *Abstract 1963*, No. 14, pp. 486, 488.
1963–65: *Abstract 1966*, No. 17, pp. 290, 292.

In 1949, a year after the establishment of the State, unemployment was very high: 14 per cent when immigrant camps are included, and about 10 per cent when they are not. In the next two years, unemployment declined despite mass immigration. This was achieved through

[2] Hastily erected shanty towns, some of which later developed into new towns.

government employment in construction and public works, to a considerable extent financed by printing money. The consequent inflationary pressure led to a policy reappraisal in 1952; the New Economic Policy of 1952–53 meant, among other things, the virtual cessation of government deficit financing, and as a result unemployment rose to a peak of 11 per cent in 1953. Since then it has declined steadily, and was only 3.6 per cent in 1965. In addition, some of the age-specific labor force participation rates rose, notably of elderly men (see Table 27), and this can be viewed as a reduction in disguised unemployment.

TABLE 14.   *Employment and Unemployment: 1949–65*

(thousands)

	Civilian labor force	Potential labor force in immigrant camps	Unemployment	Unemployment as per cent of labor force[a]	
				A	B
	(1)	(2)	(3)	(4)	(5)
A. *Old series*					
1949	343	17	33	9.5	13.9
1950	450	22	31	6.9	11.2
1951	545	12	33	6.1	8.1
1952	584	6	42	7.2	8.1
1953	599	2	67	11.3	11.5
1954	608	2	54	8.9	9.2
1955	619	–	46	7.4	
1956	646	–	51	7.8	
B. *New series*					
1957[b]	690	–	48	6.9	
1958	698	–	40	5.7	
1959	714	–	39	5.5	
1960	736	–	34	4.6	
1961	774	–	28	3.6	
1962	818	–	30	3.7	
1963	840	–	30	3.6	
1964	884	–	30	3.3	
1965	912	–	33	3.6	

[a] Variant A [column (3) ÷ column (1)] excludes the labor force potential of immigrant camps included in Variant B [columns (3) + (2) ÷ columns (1) + (2)]. Variant A was calculated from less rounded figures given in the sources.
[b] Average of two surveys, conducted in June and November.
SOURCES: Labor force and unemployment—see sources to Table 13.
    Immigrant camp potential—Hovne, *op. cit.,* p. 82, Appendix Table B.

An international comparison shows that in recent years Israel's un-employment was the same as or lower than in several developed coun-tries. Comparable figures for 1961 (when unemployment was 3.6 per cent of labor force in Israel) were (in per cent): U.S.A.—7.2; Canada—6.7; Finland—1.2; Italy—3.4; Egypt—4.7. These figures are derived from labor force surveys; typical rates in countries where unemployment is measured in other ways (such as labor exchange or trade union registration) were (in per cent): Belgium—6.0; Ireland—5.7; Den-mark—3.9; Austria—2.7; and West Germany—0.8.[3]

Since Israel's labor force has grown more than two and a half times since 1949, the low unemployment rate is an economic achievement of prime importance. How is it to be explained?

In the long run, the employment of labor is connected with economic development as a whole, i.e., with the growth of factors other than labor, such as reproducible capital and cultivable land. By itself, however, the growth of these factors does not ensure the immediate employment of additional manpower, and the government and public institutions have therefore followed a deliberate full-employment policy. Some of the measures used are in the monetary, fiscal, and wage-policy spheres, and will be discussed in later chapters. Here we confine ourselves to those with a direct bearing on the labor market.

Employment policy

Employment policy concentrated principally on three areas. First, State-controlled labor-exchanges were organized and conditions laid down for filling vacancies; second, the government and other public bodies allocated funds for direct expenditure on unemployment relief works; third, subsidies to enterprises were conditional on the employment of specified numbers of workers. Formally at least, the government did not intervene in wage determination (except in so far as it negotiated, as an employer, with its own employees); wages were fixed by direct bargaining between employers and employees.

Labor exchanges: The general labor exchanges are the principal channel for finding work. They were set up during the 1930's slump by the Histadrut and the employers associations, and all employers signing a Histadrut-approved collective agreement undertook to hire labor only through labor exchanges.

In allocating jobs, the exchanges were guided by a system of priorities which took account of trade qualifications, socio-economic conditions,

---

[3] ILO, *Yearbook of Labour Statistics 1962* (Geneva: 1962).

and Zionist background. The trade qualifications involved a distinction between the various categories of skilled workers and unskilled laborers, while the other two criteria were applied within each trade. Since more than 80 per cent of those registered were unskilled laborers, the skill criterion had little significance during periods of immigration pressure, and particularly in the years of mass immigration. Socio-economic conditions taken into account were duration of unemployment and size of family. The national background criterion meant length of residence in the country and service in the army and in Hagana (the Jewish sector's underground defense organization during the mandate).

The Employment Service Law, 1959, which nationalized the labor exchanges and placed them under the supervision of the Ministry of Labor, on the whole perpetuated these principles. Employers were obliged to hire workers through the exchanges; the only exception to this is professional and managerial staff, who may be engaged without recourse to a labor exchange.

The creation of a virtual monopoly in supplying manpower to firms made it much easier to apply socio-economic criteria in giving priority to those who needed it most. As full employment conditions developed, the function of the labor exchange in fitting the worker to the vacancy became increasingly important. But the social criteria for work priority had become so firmly rooted that this function could not be effectively carried out. Permanent absorption into the labor force may have suffered from the application of the existing priority system.

Direct government expenditure: It is difficult to segregate government outlays intended mainly for unemployment relief from those intended for other purposes, where a reduction in unemployment is incidental. It is the practice of government agencies to record as "relief works" any employment provided directly by the Employment Division of the Ministry of Labor through its current operations budget, as well as employment provided by other employers but subsidized from this budget.

Available estimates for the early 1950's[4] suggest that, using the definition given above, the proportion of employed labor force in relief works was quite small—about 1.5 per cent. Since the late 1950's the total number of work days provided seems to have been greater,[5] but most

---

[4] Ministry of Labour, *Monthly Review of Labour and National Insurance,* VII (July–August 1955; Hebrew), 40.

[5] *Abstract 1959/60,* No. 11, p. 322, Table 18; *Abstract 1962,* No. 13, p. 418, Table 23; and *Abstract 1966,* No. 17, p. 327, Table K/26.

of them are for the old and handicapped on the margin of the labor force. One of the main effects of relief works is, therefore, to raise the participation rate of older people; their contribution to reducing open unemployment is less important.

Subsidies for raising employment: The government has also deliberately influenced the volume of employment by granting various privileges to firms that guarantee to engage a specified number of workers. Here, large firms were preferred to small ones, and labor-intensive to capital-intensive ones.

The commonest benefits were credit on terms easier than those of the private market, and protection against competition, local or foreign. These measures created a large gap between the system of costs facing the individual manufacturer and the system of real costs facing the economy; "employment-raising" firms that were profitable to their owners but not to the economy were often encouraged in this way. Direct subsidization of wages was seldom employed, just as the government took no steps to influence the wage level directly.[6] As unemployment declined, so did the importance of employment as a criterion for allocating capital from government budgets.

The composition of unemployment

Although the general level of unemployment was low in recent years, it was still quite high among some sections of the population. We shall begin by presenting the findings on the duration of unemployment.

The labor force surveys provide only sporadic data on this subject, so that labor-exchange data must be used. Here, too, there are no direct monthly figures on the persistence of unemployment, but it is possible to calculate the average number of months of registration during each year, per person registered.[7]

Combining the intra-month with the inter-month information, we

---

[6] There is, however, limited support for industrial wages in development areas.

[7] The calculation is as follows: the average monthly number of persons registered is divided by the total number of persons registered during the year, and multiplied by 12. The rationale of the procedure is: if the same persons register each month throughout the year, the annual number of registrants equals the monthly number of registrants. The quotient is unity, and multiplied by 12, it means that each person registered during 12 months. Conversely, if new people register each month, the quotient is 1/12, and the result is 1, which means that after one month registrants find a job that lasts for at least the current year. [*Abstract 1965,* No. 15, pp. 284–85, 288; Employment Service, *The Employment Service in Figures,* Vol. I (IX), 1960 (Hebrew).]

get the following picture: during 1949, a year of high unemployment (Table 14), median unemployment within the month was 7 days, and it took 2.4 months to find permanent work. The time needed was in fact even longer, since at that period new immigrants spent an average of around three months in transit camps before applying to a labor exchange.

As unemployment declined in 1950–51, the number of unemployment days within the month also declined, but not the number of months during which a person was registered. This supports the hypothesis (see pp. 65–66 above) that at this time it was the temporary jobs offered by the government that were responsible for a significant part of the reduction in unemployment. During the period of peak unemployment (1952–53) both unemployment days within the month and the number of months of registration went up, so that in 1953 it took about 4.5 months to find permanent work. Since then there has been a fairly systematic decline in all indicators of unemployment. By 1963, the average number of months of registration had fallen to less than 2, and the median within-month number of days to 4.

TABLE 15.   *The Duration of Unemployment: 1952–56*

(per cent)

Year of first registration (x)	Persons returning to the labor exchange in the year x+i, as per cent of persons first registered in the year x			
	x+1	*x+2*	*x+3*	*x+4*
1952	..	..	17.7	13.6
1953	..	22.3	15.8	13.2
1954	39.3	22.6	17.1	..
1955	48.9	34.3	..	..
1956	56.4	..	..	..

SOURCE: Workers' General Labor Exchange Center, *The Labor Exchanges in Figures* (Hebrew): Table 5 in Vol. III, Table 6 in Vol. IV, and Table 7 in each of Vols. V–VIII.

Another point of interest is how many of the new registrants of any year registered again in the next year, the year after, and so on. A partial answer to this question is presented in Table 15, which shows that between 40 and 55 per cent of applicants returned to the labor exchange in the year after first registration; between 20 and 35 per cent returned two years after they first registered, including some who did not apply in the intervening year, and between 13 and 17 per cent returned after more than two years.[8]

As stated, these data refer only to persons applying to labor exchanges. Unemployed who looked for work in other ways and new immigrants in transit camps are excluded. Of those who do not usually apply to labor exchanges the two most important groups are non-Jews and residents of new moshavim (cooperative villages); as these two groups were especially hard hit by unemployment, the data of Table 15 are biased downward.

The pattern of unemployment shows high rates for new Asia-Africa immigrants and non-Jews, while the vulnerable age-groups are 14–17 and 55–64. To what extent did these groups benefit from the general reduction in unemployment? In 1955–56, when average unemployment was 7.6 per cent, the 55–64 age group had a rate of 8.7 per cent; by 1961–63, their rate was just over 2 per cent, compared with average employment of 3.6 per cent, and this represents a considerable relative improvement. Unemployment of non-Jews also declined somewhat faster than the average, but here the trend was uneven and less marked.[9] The relative position of new Asia-Africa immigrants did not change much: in 1955–57, their unemployment rate of 12.6 per cent was 1.7 times the average, and in 1961–63 it was still 1.6 times the average (at 5.7 per cent). The most vulnerable group was youths aged 14–17: in the six years during which average unemployment declined from 7.5 to 3.5 per cent, the rate for this group only declined from 17 to 14 per cent; their share in total unemployment has doubled, to reach over 25 per cent in 1961–63.[10]

---

[8] The data from which the table was compiled enable us to compute what percentage of first registrants in the year x returned to the labor exchange in the years x+1, x+2, etc. Those returning cannot, however, be identified: there is no way of knowing whether 1956 registrants, for example, whose first year of registration is given as 1954, also returned to the exchange in 1955.

[9] Cf. Yoram Ben-Porath, The Arab Labor Force in Israel (Jerusalem: Falk Institute, 1966), p. 80, Table 5–6.

[10] This paragraph is based on Table 14, and on data from CBS, Labour Force Surveys 1955–1961 (Special Series No. 162; Jerusalem: 1964), pp. 8, 25; CBS, Labour Force Surveys 1962 (Special Series No. 152; Jerusalem: 1964), p. 38; and CBS, Labour Force Surveys 1963 (Special Series No. 176; Jerusalem: 1965), pp. 6, 11.

EDUCATIONAL LEVEL AND OCCUPATIONAL AND INDUSTRIAL STRUCTURE

Educational level

The earliest information available on this subject is data derived from the June, 1954, Labor Force Survey.[11] These data refer to the Jewish population aged 15 and over, and distinguish between those in the country before 1948 (veterans) and new immigrants. The figures for veterans give a rough idea of the educational standard of the Jewish population as it was in 1948.[12] The most remarkable feature is the very high proportion of people—about one third—who completed secondary and higher education. Such a high level would be impressive even in Western Europe and the United States, whose economies are far more advanced than Israel's. It came about because education was imported by the European immigrants who were the main addition to the adult population during the mandatory period. Thus, 55 per cent of the veterans from Western and Central Europe and 35 per cent of those from Eastern Europe had received secondary and higher education.[13]

While Israel enjoyed a high proportion of educated citizens, its economic level, whether in terms of per capita product or capital per employed person, was, by international standards, much lower. This had a number of consequences. First, whether the educational standard would rise depended mainly on the composition of immigrants, since it was difficult to allocate a sufficient share of the country's limited resources to maintaining the standard set by European Jewry. Second, the comparatively low level of technology meant that there were not enough jobs requiring qualified people, so that many had to do work that, vital though it was at the time, did not make use of their qualifications. This qualified manpower later contributed to the country's rapid economic growth. A third result of the gap between

---

[11] O. Schmelz, *Standard of Education of the Population, June 1954* (Special Series No. 66; Jerusalem: CBS, 1958), cited in Ruth Klinov-Malul, *The Profitability of Investment in Education in Israel* (Jerusalem: Falk Institute, 1966), p. 8, Table 2–1.

[12] Sampling errors apparently caused a downward bias in the education standard. Moreover, the sample was taken in 1954, and the veteran group therefore includes persons who became 15 years old in the intervening six years, and excludes veterans who died or emigrated.

[13] Richard A. Easterlin, "Israel's Development: Past Accomplishments and Future Problems," *Quarterly Journal of Economics,* LXXV (February 1961), 63–86.

the educational and technological levels was greater equality of incomes than is found in Europe and the United States.[14]

By 1954, the average educational level had declined considerably: the proportion with secondary and higher education dropped from 34 per cent of male veterans to 25 per cent of all Jewish men, while at the other end of the scale the proportion of men with less than 5 years of primary schooling rose from 22 per cent to 33 per cent.[15] This was mainly due to the composition of the immigrants of the early 1950's. In 1951 free compulsory education was provided for the 5–13 age group (i.e., until the fourteenth birthday), but some years passed before it had any effect on the over-15 population. At the time, the educational system could not cope with the decline in the educational standard.

TABLE 16. *The Occupational Structure of Veterans: 1948 and 1954*

		(per cent)
	1948[a]	*1954*
Liberal and technical professions	11	14
Managerial and clerical	14	21
Sales and trade	9	11
Agricultural	14	10
Industry, crafts, and construction	38	32
Services and transport	14	12
Total	100	100

[a] All persons employed on 8.XI.1948.
SOURCES: *Abstract 1950/51*, No. 2, p. 20, Table 7; and CBS, *Labour Force Survey June 1954* (Special Series No. 56; Jerusalem: 1957), p. 44.

In the meantime, the economy developed at great speed. Real gross national product per capita rose by 41 per cent from 1950 to 1955 (Table 29). Real capital per employed person increased by 10.2 per cent annually from 1950 to 1955, and by 6.9 per cent from 1955 to 1960.[16]

[14] Giora Hanoch, "Income Differentials in Israel," *Fifth Report 1959 and 1960* (Jerusalem: Falk Project, 1961). See also Chapter 6, p. 119.

[15] Klinov-Malul, *loc. cit.* This comparison (from data of the 1954 labor force survey) is between 1948 and 1954, but there is evidence that most of the decline in the standard of education had already taken place by 1951 or 1952 [Joseph Baruh, "Changes in the Quality of Labor Input in Israel, 1950–61," *Bank of Israel Bulletin*, No. 25 (April 1966), 32–43].

[16] See Chapter 7, Table 45.

The demand for educated manpower rose steadily and was filled partly by the hitherto "wasted" qualified people.

The immediate result was the widening of income differentials due to skill and education. A second result was that veterans shifted from agriculture, industry, services, and transportation into liberal professions and technical, managerial, and clerical occupations (Table 16).

TABLE 17.   *Median Number of Years of Education of Foreign-Born Males, by Age and Length of Residence: 1961*

Age-group	Year of immigration				
	Up to 1947	1948–51	1952–54	1955–57	1958–61
14–29	9.6	8.4	7.8	8.1	8.9
30–44	8.9	7.8	7.1	7.3	8.2
45–64	10.2	7.2	6.1	7.1	7.7
65+	9.1	6.2	6.6	6.1	6.7
Total 14+	9.9	7.7	7.3	7.6	8.2

SOURCES: CBS, *Languages, Literacy and Educational Attainment—Part I* (Census Publication No. 15; Jerusalem: 1963), p. 79, Table 31.

Once mass immigration was over, and until 1961 (the year of the population census) the educational level remained more-or-less the same. The later immigration had a somewhat higher standard, with 8.2 median years of schooling for the 1958–61 immigrants, compared with 7.7 and 7.3 for the 1948–51 and 1952–54 immigrants, respectively (Table 17).[17] The educational gap between the resident population and new immigrants therefore narrowed. The scope of the country's educational system was also growing. School attendance at age 14–17 rose from 43 per cent in 1952 to 57 per cent in 1964; the percentage of the 20–24 age group attending institutes of higher learning rose from 3.0 to 10.8 in the same period.[18] Since immigration played a smaller part in the growth of the adult population than at the beginning of the decade,

[17] The data are from the 1961 population census and are therefore affected by the local educational system for the period between immigration and the census year.

[18] Attendance at 14–17 from *Abstract 1962,* No. 13, p. 486, Table 9; and *Abstract 1965,* No. 16, p. 584, Table T/14. Attendance at 20–24 calculated from *Abstract 1963,* No. 14, p. 38, Table 15; *Abstract 1965,* No. 16, p. 40, Table B/15; and *Abstract 1966,* No. 17, p. 605, Table T/25.

the local educational system became more important in determining educational level.

Demand for skilled and educated manpower continued to grow, and since there was no significant rise in the average level of education, some of this demand was absorbed by increasing income differentials. In recent years increasing income inequality has become a major issue, chiefly because income and educational differences tend to correspond to country-of-origin differences: it is the immigrants from Asia-Africa who are largely concentrated at the lower end of the scale.[19] The country's educational system thus has the twofold task of raising the average level of education and reducing the inequality of its distribution. As stated, there has been no marked rise in the average level, but some reduction in inequality is reflected in figures on post-primary schooling for three recent years: the attendance rate at 14–17 of children of Asia-Africa parents rose faster than that of children of Europe-America parents. Nevertheless, there was still a wide gap in 1965/66: the rate for the children of Europe-America parents was 71 per cent, compared with 41 per cent for children of Asia-Africa parents.[20]

Occupational structure

As with formal education, technical and occupational skills arrived from abroad "ready made." Since most of the labor force growth was derived from immigration, the main problem confronting the economy was to allocate immigrants to essential jobs while making use of their skills and to reallocate the veteran labor force.

Table 18 shows that almost half the Jewish employed persons in Israel in 1954, and two thirds of those who immigrated between 1948 and 1954, had had previous occupations abroad. What did they actually bring to the country?

Kuznets has described the characteristic features of the industrial and occupational structure of diaspora Jews,[21] a structure that was conditioned by the minority status and migration of Jews throughout the world. Migration often meant lack of tangible capital and of skills suited to the new host country, while as a minority Jews suffered from varying degrees of socio-political discrimination.

---

[19] See Chapter 6, pp. 119–21.

[20] *Abstract 1966*, No. 17, p. 598, Table T/16.

[21] S. Kuznets, "Economic Structure and Life of the Jews," *The Jews*, ed. Louis Finkelstein (3rd ed.; New York: Harper and Brothers, 1960), Vol. II.

These factors often restrained Jews from engaging in agriculture even where no formal barrier existed, since agriculture requires the accumulation of tangible capital and specialized knowledge. Moreover, competition between producers is often stiffer than in other sectors, since agriculture is a declining industry in many countries.

TABLE 18. *Jewish Employed Persons Previously Employed Abroad: 1954*

	Thousands	Per cent
Total Jewish employed persons	**474.4**	**100.0**
Gainfully employed abroad	211.0	44.5
Not gainfully employed abroad[a]	263.4	55.5
Veterans[b]	*193.5*	*100.0*
Gainfully employed abroad	68.6	35.5
Not gainfully employed abroad	124.9	64.5
New immigrants[c]	*224.3*	*100.0*
Gainfully employed abroad	142.4	63.5
Not gainfully employed abroad	81.9	36.5
Israel-born	*56.6*	

[a] Includes Israel-born.
[b] Immigrated before 1948.
[c] Immigrated 1948–54.
SOURCE: CBS, *Labour Force Survey June 1954, op. cit.,* pp. 46, 48.

Two other branches in which Jews were rarely employed were transport and public services, both of which were often State monopolies closed to Jews.

Their exclusion from agriculture, transport, and public services led Jews to concentrate in trade (particularly retail) and small crafts. In both, relatively little capital is required, and the specialized knowledge acquired is easily transferred from one country to another. These occupations are also comparatively independent of the majority population and, in particular, of political institutions. Another sphere in which Jews were prominent was the liberal and technical professions. Here also the favored professions were those least dependent on public authorities, such as medicine, law, and religion.

The occupational pattern of diaspora Jewry can also be seen among immigrants to Israel. Very few were engaged in agriculture, transport, and personal services, while there was a high proportion in industry, crafts, and trade, as well as in liberal and technical professions (Table 19).

TABLE 19.   *Immigrants,*[a] *by Occupation*
              Abroad: 1949[b]*–61*

	(per cent)
Liberal professions	8.8
Clerical, administrative	12.3
Commercial	15.0
Transport	3.8
Agriculture	4.8
Industry, crafts, construction	45.4
Personal services	2.7
Others[c]	7.2
Total	**100.0**

[a] Male earners.
[b] From 1.IX.1948.
[c] Mostly unskilled.
SOURCES: Moshe Sicron, *Immigration to Israel: 1948–1953* (Jerusalem: Falk Project and CBS, 1957), Statistical Supplement, p. 70, Table A90.
Abstract 1964, No. 15, p. 84, Table D/8.

The move to Israel greatly changed the occupational structure of the immigrants. In 1954 it was found that 60 per cent of all immigrants who had been employed abroad had changed their occupation between 1948 and 1954 (Table 20). The calculation was made for only ten broad occupational groups. It was mostly trade and service workers who changed their occupation, but clerks, artisans, and industrial workers were also mobile.

The direction of change was mainly into the unskilled class. Of those changing occupation, almost 50 per cent of immigrants previously engaged in trade, manufacturing and crafts, or services became unskilled laborers, as did over one third of those who had been clerks; altogether, 31 per cent of those changing occupations became non-agricultural unskilled laborers. The second marked shift was to agriculture: 29 per cent of persons changing occupation went into agriculture, over a third of them as unskilled laborers. A third shift was to manufacturing, crafts, and construction, 10 to 20 per cent of immigrants

TABLE 20. New Immigrants,[a] by Occupation Abroad and in Israel: 1954

(per cent)

Occupation abroad	Per cent of total[b] who changed occupation in Israel	Occupation in Israel							
		All those changing occupation	Clerks	Sales workers	Agriculture	Industrial, crafts, and building	Services	Unskilled laborers	Others[e]
Liberal professions	35.9	100.0	29.5	15.3	7.3	11.1	7.8	23.4	5.6
Clerks	54.5	100.0	–	12.5	8.8	19.6	14.9	35.5	8.7
Sales workers	77.3	100.0	8.0	–	19.0	16.6	8.8	42.2	5.4
Industrial, crafts, and building workers	51.9	100.0	3.5	8.7	21.4	–	9.6	52.4	4.4
Services	55.4	100.0	2.9	13.2	17.9	11.7	–	52.7	1.6
Unskilled laborers	38.1	100.0	1.1	18.6	16.3	36.5	16.8	–	10.7
Total	59.0[d]								

[a] Immigrated 1948–54.
[b] Total is the 142,400 new immigrants gainfully employed abroad (see Table 18).
[c] Includes professional, technical, and related workers; managerial workers; drivers and other transport workers.
[d] Includes earners in occupations abroad not shown in the detail (agricultural workers and the occupations listed in note c).

SOURCE: CBS, Labour Force Survey June 1954, op. cit., Table 25.

who had been white-collar workers abroad going into these industries.[22] This was partly the result of public planning, particularly in agriculture and construction. It was also partly due to language difficulties and to the fact that technical knowledge acquired abroad was not in demand in Israel.

TABLE 21.   *Jewish Employed Persons, by Occupation,*[a] *Length of Residence, and Continent of Birth: 1961*

(per cent)

	Total	Israel-born	Europe-America: Immigrated			Asia-Africa: Immigrated		
			Before 1948	1948–1954	1955 and later	Before 1948	1948–1954	1955 and later
Professional, technical	13.3	21.3	16.8	12.3	16.8	6.5	5.9	4.9
Administrative, clerical	19.3	23.5	29.0	18.3	13.4	15.7	9.9	7.6
Traders	8.7	4.5	10.8	12.4	6.3	12.9	6.1	4.4
Farmers	12.1	12.9	8.1	8.1	11.0	8.5	17.7	28.1
Transport	4.8	7.3	5.0	5.0	1.6	6.1	3.9	2.1
Construction	7.2	3.6	4.7	6.9	5.1	9.3	12.3	12.1
Industrial	23.1	19.0	17.2	24.8	30.8	24.2	28.8	26.2
Services	11.6	7.8	8.4	12.3	14.9	16.7	15.4	14.5
Total[b]	100.0	100.0	100.0	100.0	100.0	100.0	100.0	100.0

[a] The occupational description is here given in abridged form. The full description may be found in the source.
[b] Figures may not add to 100 owing to rounding.
SOURCE: CBS, *Labour Force—Part I* (Census Publication No. 9; Jerusalem: 1963), pp. 234–35, Table 56.

Table 21 shows the occupation of immigrants in 1961, by period of immigration; from these data it is possible to gauge the extent to which the change was permanent. Table 22 supplements it by comparing the occupational structure of the 1948–54 immigrants in 1954 and 1961. Both tables show that the share of professional, administrative, clerical, and transport workers rises with length of residence. The last two occupations were not at all typical of Jews in their countries of origin, but, together with the liberal professions, were typical of the Israel-born. Thus, as immigrants stay longer in Israel they do not

[22] Figures in this paragraph are from Table 20 and from its source.

return to their previous occupation but tend to adapt to demand conditions in Israel. Another occupation whose share in employment rises with length of residence is trade. However, unlike the white-collar occupations, the percentage engaged in trade is much lower for the Israel-born than for veteran immigrants, whose pattern perhaps reflects the occupation abroad. The per cent engaged in agriculture declines with length of residence, and is somewhat lower for immigrants than for the Israel-born. This pattern may also be a reflection of the pre-immigration occupational structure.

TABLE 22.   *New Immigrant Employed Persons,*[a] *by Occupation*[b] *in Israel: 1954 and 1961*

(per cent)

	1954	1961
Professional, technical	6.5	9.3
Administrative, clerical	10.5	14.3
Traders	9.6	9.4
Farmers	17.8	12.6
Transport	2.7	4.5
Industrial and construction	42.2[c]	36.2
Services	10.7	13.7
Total	**100.0**	**100.0**

[a] Employed persons who immigrated in 1948–54; for 1954, the data include those who immigrated up to the Survey date (June).
[b] See note a in Table 21.
[c] Including unskilled transport and service workers.
SOURCES: CBS, *Labour Force Survey June 1954, op. cit.,* p. 44, Table 23; and *Labour Force—Part I, op. cit.,* p. 232, Table 55 (data from Stage B of the 1961 Census).

The non-Jewish labor force constitutes a separate group, which, before the establishment of the State, was mostly employed in agriculture: in 1936, 62 per cent of employed non-Jews worked in this branch. World War II raised the demand for non-agricultural goods, so that the share of agriculture declined (as it did in the Jewish economy). The earliest reliable information is for 1955, when 48 per cent of non-Jewish men were engaged in agriculture (i.e., as "farmers, fishermen, and related workers" in the occupational classification), about the same as during the war. The labor force surveys show an uneven decline in the percentage, and by the end of the 1950's the figure was around 44 per cent.[23] The decline in the share of agriculture, and the corresponding rise in manufacturing and construction and in services, can be explained by the rise in mobility of non-Jewish workers to Jewish working areas. The amount of land per head of rural population has declined, owing to population growth and the difficulties of acquiring more land,[24] and this has affected the occupational structure in the same direction. The same factors are also responsible for a shift from self-employment: the share of employees in the male non-Jewish employed labor force has risen from 57 per cent in 1955 to 67 per cent in 1961.[25] As mentioned, the decline in the employment share of agriculture was accompanied by a rise in the share of manufacturing and construction and personal services. In these occupations the percentage of unskilled laborers was very high—over 30 per cent of manufacturing and construction workers in 1961.[26] There was no tendency to enter trade, clerical occupations, or the liberal professions.

In view of the considerable occupational mobility within each population group, one might have expected the total occupational structure to change. Table 23 shows that this did not happen and that changes have been rather small since 1955. The share of employed persons engaged in liberal and technical professions fluctuated between 10 and 13 per cent, while the share of trade declined from 11 per cent in 1955 to 8 per cent in 1965. Together, white-collar occupations and commerce came to around 37 per cent throughout the period. This is fairly high compared with other countries at a similar level of development.[27] The share of manufacturing, crafts, and construction remained fairly steady at around 29 to 33 per cent. However, the proportion of skilled workers in these occupations rose from 79 per cent in 1957 to 89 per cent in 1961. This is probably the most important change in the structure of employment to occur in the period.

The share of agriculture in employment barely declined and was around 17 per cent until 1961. Agricultural labor was recruited mainly from immigrants who arrived during the period and were settled by the government and the Jewish Agency in newly built villages.

[23] Ben-Porath, *op. cit.*, p. 30, Table 2–10, and p. 29, Table 2–8.

[24] *Ibid.*, p. 42, Table 3–4, and the discussion on pp. 43–45.

[25] CBS, *Labour Force Surveys 1955–1961* (Special Series No. 162; Jerusalem: 1964), p. 66, Table 39.

[26] *Abstract 1962*, No. 13, pp. 394–97.

[27] Gur Ofer, *The Service Industries in a Developing Economy: Israel As a Case Study* (Jerusalem and New York: Frederick A. Praeger with the Bank of Israel, 1967), Chapter 2.

TABLE 23.   Occupational Distribution of Employed Labor Force: 1955, 1957–65

(per cent)

	1955	1957	1958	1959	1960	1961	1961ᵃ	1962	1963	1964	1965
Professional, technical	10.4	11.3	10.8	11.2	11.3	11.7	11.5	10.9	12.3	12.2	13.0
Architects, engineers, etc.	..	1.0	1.1	1.0	1.0	1.2	1.7	1.9	2.2	..	..
Medical personnel	..	3.4	2.9	3.0	2.9	3.1	3.0	2.5	2.9	..	..
Teachers	..	4.7	4.2	4.1	4.6	4.6	4.5	4.2	4.7	..	..
Others	..	2.2	2.6	3.1	2.8	2.8	2.3	2.3	2.5	..	..
Administrative, managerial, and clerical	15.8	15.1	15.5	13.8	14.1	13.2	14.1	14.5	15.5	16.0	16.7
Traders, agents, salesmen	11.3	10.2	8.9	8.9	9.1	8.6	8.6	8.9	8.1	8.4	8.0
Farmers, fishermen, and related workers	17.1	16.3	17.4	16.1	17.1	16.9	16.9	16.0	14.0	12.4	12.5
Transport and communications	6.0	4.7	4.9	4.5	4.8	4.6	4.8	4.6	5.4	5.1	5.0
Skilled workers in industry and crafts	⎱ 29.0	3.6	4.0	4.1	4.2	4.4 ⎰					
Skilled workers in construction	⎰	21.2	20.8	22.8	23.0	24.5 ⎱	31.8	32.7	32.8	33.7	33.4
Unskilled industrial and construction workers	⎱ 10.4	6.4	6.3	6.1	3.9	3.7	12.3	12.4	11.9	12.2	11.4
Services	⎰	11.2	11.4	12.5	12.5	12.4					
Total	100.0	100.0	100.0	100.0	100.0	100.0	100.0	100.0	100.0	100.0	100.0

ᵃ In 1961 the occupational classification was changed slightly [see *Abstract 1963*, No. 14, note (1) on p. 509]. See also note a to Table 21.

SOURCES: CBS, *Labour Force Surveys 1955–1961, op. cit.*, p. 91, Table 47 (for 1955), and p. 95, Table 48 (for 1957–61, old series).
CBS, *Labour Force Surveys 1962* (Special Series No. 152; Jerusalem: 1964), pp. 84–87, Table 28 (for 1961, new series, and 1962).
CBS, *Labour Force Surveys 1963* (Special Series No. 176, Jerusalem: 1965), p. 42, Table 29 (for 1963).
Abstract 1966, No. 17, pp. 312–13 (for 1964 and 1965).

TABLE 24.   Jewish Employed Persons, by Industry: Selected Years, 1931–64[a]

(per cent)

	Agriculture	Industry	Construction	Transport	Commerce	Public services	Personal services[b]	Total
1931	22.1	23.8	8.7	5.5	14.1	15.2	10.6	100.0
1936	21.4	20.1	9.4	5.3	15.7	18.1	10.0	100.0
1945	13.4	31.1	4.9	5.1	14.7	20.8	10.0	100.0
1947[c]	12.6	26.5	8.7	6.3	19.4	18.6	7.9	100.0
1948	14.2	31.8	6.1	6.2	13.3	18.9	9.5	100.0
1951[c]	13.8	23.6	9.5	7.0	16.8	18.2	11.1	100.0
1954	14.7	24.5	9.2	6.7	13.1	21.8	10.0	100.0
1955	15.0	23.7	9.1	6.4	14.0	23.1	8.7	100.0
1959	14.2	25.6	9.2	6.8	12.4	24.0	7.8	100.0
1961	14.5	25.6	8.5	6.7	12.3	25.0	7.4	100.0
1962	12.4	28.2	9.0	6.4	13.1	22.8	8.1	100.0
1963	12.1	27.3	9.1	7.2	13.3	23.3	7.7	100.0
1964	10.6	28.2	9.3	7.4	13.1	23.3	8.1	100.0

[a] In the 1931–61 series, electricity and national water supply are included in "industry," and municipal waterworks and sanitary services in "public services." In the 1962–64 data, all public utilities are included in "industry."
[b] This branch roughly covers the occupational category "services."
[c] Includes income recipients other than employed persons; this affects mainly "commerce."

SOURCES: Gur Ofer, *The Service Industries in a Developing Economy: Israel As a Case Study* (Jerusalem and New York: Frederick A. Praeger with the Bank of Israel, 1967), p. 88, Table 4.6 (for 1931–61). *Abstract 1965*, No. 16, pp. 308–309, Table K/12 (for 1962–64).

Industrial structure

Data on the industrial structure of the labor force go back much further than those for occupational structure, and Table 24 presents selected years back to 1931.

The share of agriculture declined steeply during World War II, from its prewar level of 20 per cent to about 13 per cent. It then remained steady until 1961, after which it declined, reaching 11 per cent in 1964.

Industrial employment never regained its wartime peak of 31 per cent,[28] but there does appear to have been an upward trend in recent years, from 24 per cent in the early 1950's to 28 per cent in 1964.

The high employment share of housing (most of the item construction) reflects Israel's high rates of immigration and population growth; the fluctuations in this series are closely connected with changes in the rate of immigration.

Particularly interesting is the fact that the service industries have, ever since the mandatory period, accounted for over half of total employment. An analysis of this very high proportion suggests that most of the overconcentration is in public administration, health and education, other public services, and transportation.[29] There is also some overconcentration in finance, but not in trade or personal services. Several factors account for this pattern. Most important is the country's goods-intensive import surplus: for a given level of demand, the economy tends to the production of services. Other factors are the strong demand for public services and public administration, a consequence of the size and composition of immigration. The occupational structure of immigrants also helps to explain a temporary overconcentration in trade and personal services in the early 1950's, which disappeared when occupational mobility improved.

LABOR FORCE PARTICIPATION

Since 1950, the per cent of population in the labor force has been around 35 for Jews and 25 for non-Jews.[30] Both figures are low compared with developed countries: in Europe, North America, and Oceania the ratio is between 40 and 45 per cent (Table 25).

One reason for the low participation rate is the high proportion of

---

[28] The 1948 figure of 32 per cent is derived from a not very reliable estimate.
[29] Ofer, *op. cit.*, on which this paragraph is based.
[30] Table 13 and underlying worksheets.

children,[31] which is, however, to some extent offset by the low proportion of people over 40, and especially over 65. In addition, several groups—youths aged 14–17, the 55+ group, and women—have particularly low rates (Table 27).

TABLE 25.   *Labor Force Participation in Population: International Comparison*[a]

		(per cent)
	Both sexes	*Women*
Africa	35.8	14.5
Asia[b]	42.5	28.1
North America	39.7	21.3
Central and South America	35.2	13.6
Europe[b]	45.1	27.6
Oceania	40.1	18.5
Israel (1963)	35.3	18.9

[a] Averages for 1946–59.
[b] Excluding the U.S.S.R.
SOURCES: Israel—Table 13 (both sexes); *Abstract 1966*, No. 17, p. 290, Table K/1 (women in employed labor force); *Abstract 1964*, No. 15, pp. 30–31, Table B/14, and *Abstract 1965*, No. 16, pp. 40–41, Table B/15 (female population on 31.XII.1962 and 31.XII.1963).
Continent averages—U.N., Department of Economic and Social Affairs, *Demographic Aspects of Manpower, Report 1: Sex and Age Patterns of Participation in Economic Activities* (ST/SOA/Ser. A/33) (New York: 1962), p. 3.

The participation rates of the 14–17 group depend largely on school-attendance rates. Table 26 shows that Israel has a higher school-attendance rate than most of the European countries listed.[32] But a high attendance rate is not the only reason for low participation: in the late 1950's, from 6 to 13 per cent of the age group neither studied nor worked nor sought work.[33] This "residual" may explain the fact

[31] Chapter 4, pp. 61–63. See also Avner Hovne, *The Labor Force in Israel* (Jerusalem: Falk Project, 1961), p. 57, Table 29.
[32] The high participation rates in countries for which school attendance is not known indicate (except in the case of Sweden) a lower attendance rate than in Israel.
[33] School attendance from *Abstract 1964*, No. 15, p. 512, Table T/14; labor force participation from CBS, *Labour Force Surveys 1955–1961, op. cit.,*

that the participation rate did not decline when school attendance rose.

TABLE 26.   *School Attendance and Labor Force Participation at Age 14–17 in Selected Countries: Circa 1960*

(per cent of population in age group)

	School attendance[a]	Labor force participation
United States	87.5	20.4
France	68.3	..
Israel[b]	56.5	30.5
Switzerland	54.2	41.8
Venezuela	53.3	..
Chile	49.5	..
Netherlands	47.8	41.3
Ireland	43.7	..
Hungary	33.5	42.3
United Kingdom	..	65.9[c]
Sweden	..	34.7
West Germany	..	66.3
Austria	..	63.1

[a] Unweighted arithmetic mean of the rates for each of the ages 14–17.
[b] Jews only, since there are no school attendance rates for total population. Labor force participation for total in the same period is 31.5 per cent.
[c] For age 15–17. Assuming zero participation at age 14, the rate for 14–17 would be 49.4 per cent.
SOURCES: Israel—*Abstract 1966*, No. 17, p. 597, Table T/15 (school attendance); and *Abstract 1965*, No. 16, p. 298, Table K/3 (labor force participation).
 Other countries—U.N., *Demographic Yearbook 1963* (New York: 1964), Table 15 (school attendance in United States, France, Venezuela, and the Netherlands); *Demographic Yearbook 1964* (New York: 1965), Table 36 (school attendance in Switzerland, Chile, Ireland, and Hungary), and Table 8 (labor force participation).

The second low-participation group is persons over 55. The low participation here is apparently typical of immigrants from Asia-Africa. These immigrants, lacking both a trade suited to the country's conditions and the education to acquire a new one, did not even attempt to enter the labor market. In the 55–64 age group, the participation

p. 7, Table 4, and *Labour Force Surveys 1962, op. cit.*, p. xx, Table I. See also p. 71 above, on the high unemployment rate at 14–17 (the unemployed are included in labor force participants), and Table 26.

TABLE 27.   *Labor Force Participation, by Age, Sex, and Continent of Birth: 1958–65*

(per cent*)

	Total population aged 14+	aged sməf 14–17	New immigrants from Asia-Africa		
			Men aged 55–64	Women	
				Aged 18–34	Aged 35–64
	(1)	(2)	(3)	(4)	(5)
1958	53.2	31.6	61.3	24.9	15.9
1959	52.8	31.9	62.8	25.4	15.3
1960	52.9	26.2	68.7	28.4	17.5
1961	53.5	32.3	72.3	28.9	17.3
1962	54.1	31.7	74.8	29.7	19.3
1963	52.7ᵇ	30.5	77.1	30.9	21.1
1964	53.4	..	..	..	..
1965	52.8	32.1	84.0	33.6	21.2

ᵃ Per cent of total in each cell.
ᵇ New weights were introduced in 1963. The 1963 figure according to the old weights is 53.0.
SOURCES: Column (1)—*Abstract 1966*, No. 17, p. 296, Table K/4 [for 1958–61, 1963–65 (new series)]; *Abstract 1965*, No. 16, p. 298, Table K/3 [for 1962 and 1963 (old series)].
Column (2)—CBS, *Labour Force Surveys 1955–1961, op. cit.*, p. 3, Table 1 (for 1958–61); *Abstract 1963*, No. 14, p. 491, Table 3 (for 1962); *Abstract 1965*, No. 16, p. 299, Table K/4 (for 1963); *Abstract 1966*, No. 17, p. 297, Table K/5 (for 1965).
Columns (3)–(5)—*Abstracts*, as follows: *1958/59*, No. 10, p. 304, Table 11; *1959/60*, No. 11, p. 314, Table 11; *1961*, No. 12, p. 359, Table 5; *1962*, No. 13, p. 402, Table 12; *1963*, No. 14, p. 495, Table 6; *1965*, No. 16, p. 299, Table K/4; *1966*, No. 17, p. 297, Table K/5.

rate of Europe-America veterans was 92.6 per cent in 1958, compared with 61.3 per cent among new immigrants from Asia-Africa.[34] The improvement in the employment situation and specific measures to help this age group led to a considerable rise in the participation of new Asia-Africa immigrants, to 77.1 per cent in 1963.

The third low-participation group is that of women from Asia-Africa. The traditional work patterns of the countries of origin, a low educational standard, and large families all lowered the participation rate. However, in recent years it has also risen somewhat, as the effect of these factors weakens with length of residence.[35]

[34] See sources to Table 27. The figures cited here are for men.
[35] See Chapter 4, p. 59.

To sum up: Labor force participation remained constant because of two opposing trends—the rise in the proportion of children and old people during the 1950's tended to lower it, whereas the rise in the participation of old persons and women of Asia-Africa origin offset the decline. The over-all participation rate is still lower than in developed countries.

Changes in the age composition of the population and in age-specific labor force participation rates brought about shifts within the labor force. In particular, the weight of the 14–17 and the 55+ age groups rose and the weight of the 18–54 group declined. There has also been a constant rise in the share of the Asia-Africa group in the labor force.

RECENT DEVELOPMENTS

During 1964 and 1965, the labor force continued to grow and unemployment remained low (Tables 13 and 14). However, a recession began at the end of 1965 and unemployment began to rise. Measured by labor exchange registrations, the 1966 daily average unemployment was more than double the 1965 average and its duration also rose. It is estimated that unemployment (according to the Labor Force Survey concept) had risen to 7 per cent of the labor force by the end of 1966. Relief works supplied by the government almost doubled in 1966. During 1964 and 1965 the employment share of public sector services and construction and public works rose. The recession reduced employment mainly in the latter, and also in agriculture and manufacturing. Employment in services, public and private, has been fairly stable, and the weight of services in total employment has therefore grown.[36]

[36] Information on registered unemployment and relief works from *Bulletin*, XVIII (No. 3, March 1967), 29, 35. Other information in this paragraph from Ministry of Labour, *Manpower in Israel Annual Report 1966* (Jerusalem: Manpower Planning Authority, February 1967), p. 62, Table VII–1, and p. 60, Table VI–3.

6 GROWTH AND DISTRIBUTION OF PRODUCT AND RESOURCES

This chapter surveys the dimensions of Israel's economic growth. We shall focus on four aspects of this growth: the development of total resources of goods and services available to the economy and their allocation between immediate and future wants; the origin and composition of product; the sectoral structure of product; and the distribution of income.

THE GROWTH OF RESOURCES

Price changes were so large during the period reviewed that no meaningful conclusions about real economic growth can be drawn from the current price series shown in Appendix Table 1. Table 28 therefore presents indexes of total resources and their uses in constant 1955 market prices; the same data are presented in per capita terms in Table 29.[1]

The resources available to the economy are the goods and services produced that are retained for domestic use, plus that part of foreign product available for domestic use.[2] Thus, resources at the disposal of the economy ("domestic resources" for short) equal GNP *less* exports *plus* imports. For some purposes it is useful to consider total resources, i.e., GNP *plus* imports, as an aggregate allocated to exports as well as to domestic uses.[3]

---

[1] For the underlying absolute figures see Appendix Tables 2 and 3.

[2] We make no attempt to include any of the economic activities not usually included in national income estimates. The exclusion of non-marketable production (other than that conventionally included in the national accounts, such as on-the-farm consumption) probably does not entail distortions that differ significantly from those in the accounts of most developed market economies.

[3] The per cent allocation of resources is shown according to both definitions (Tables 30 and 31).

TABLE 28. Real Resources and Their Uses: 1950–65ᵃ

(index, 1955=100)

	Consumption			Domestic capital formation			Domestic use of resources	Exports	Total use of resources	Imports	GNP
	Private	Public	Total	Gross	Net	Depre- ciation					
	(1)	(2)	(3)	(4)	(5)	(6)	(7)	(8)	(9)	(10)	(11)
1950	58.9	64.3	60.1	85.7	99.4	43.7	66.8	35.7	64.1	96.4	51.4
1951	72.2	76.2	73.1	101.3	118.0	50.0	80.4	43.8	77.2	102.7	67.2
1952	77.6	72.0	76.4	87.0	93.1	68.4	79.2	59.3	77.4	90.8	72.2
1953	80.4	75.2	79.3	72.8	70.2	81.0	77.6	74.8	77.3	88.2	73.1
1954	92.4	87.9	91.4	81.2	76.9	94.3	88.8	102.7	90.0	92.1	89.1
1955	100.0	100.0	100.0	100.0	100.0	100.0	100.0	100.0	100.0	100.0	100.0
1956	109.1	143.9	116.5	94.6	89.3	110.9	110.8	114.3	111.1	117.7	108.6
1957	116.9	122.4	118.0	110.7	106.0	125.3	116.1	137.2	118.0	116.7	118.5
1958	128.7	125.7	128.1	119.0	113.3	136.2	125.7	152.7	128.0	124.0	129.6
1959	141.5	130.1	139.1	130.0	123.5	150.0	136.7	200.0	142.2	130.8	146.7
1960	151.0	138.8	148.4	138.0	128.3	167.8	145.7	251.9	154.9	145.8	158.5
1961	167.7	163.8	166.8	163.5	156.7	184.5	166.0	291.8	176.9	181.0	175.3
1962	186.0	182.5	185.2	183.7	173.0	216.7	184.9	351.9	199.3	202.9	198.0
1963	204.4	194.6	202.3	190.1	171.1	248.3	199.1	413.9	217.8	209.7	220.9
1964	226.5	204.2	221.7	231.0	217.1	273.6	224.1	444.9	243.3	241.9	243.7
1965	245.4	226.4	241.3	216.7	187.2	306.9	234.9	484.1	256.5	246.6	260.4
1965÷1950	4.2	3.5	4.0	2.5	1.9	7.0	3.5	13.6	4.0	2.6	5.1

ᵃ In this and in the other tables in this chapter giving national accounts data, the columns follow the numbering of Appendix Table 1.

SOURCE: Appendix Table 2.

TABLE 29. Real Use of Resources and GNP Per Capita: 1950–65

(index, 1955=100)

	Population	Consumption			Domestic capital formation		Domestic use of resources	Total use of resources	GNP
		Private	Public	Total	Gross	Net			
		(1)	(2)	(3)	(4)	(5)	(7)	(9)	(11)
1950	72.4	81.4	88.8	83.0	118.4	137.4	92.2	88.5	71.0
1951	85.4	84.6	89.2	85.6	118.6	138.2	94.2	90.5	78.8
1952	91.8	84.6	78.4	83.3	84.8	101.4	86.3	84.4	78.7
1953	94.3	85.2	79.8	84.1	77.3	74.4	82.3	82.0	77.5
1954	96.5	95.7	91.0	94.7	84.1	79.7	92.0	93.2	92.4
1955	100.0	100.0	100.0	100.0	100.0	100.0	100.0	100.0	100.0
1956	104.5	104.5	137.8	111.6	90.6	85.5	106.1	106.4	103.9
1957	110.3	106.0	111.0	107.1	100.4	96.1	105.3	107.0	107.4
1958	114.3	112.6	110.0	112.1	104.1	99.2	110.0	112.0	113.4
1959	117.8	120.1	110.5	118.1	110.3	104.8	116.0	120.7	124.5
1960	120.9	124.9	114.8	122.7	114.1	106.1	120.5	128.1	131.1
1961	125.1	134.0	130.9	133.4	130.7	125.2	132.7	141.4	140.1
1962	130.8	142.2	139.5	141.7	140.4	132.2	141.3	152.4	151.3
1963	136.0	150.3	143.1	148.8	139.8	125.8	146.4	160.1	162.5
1964	141.7	159.8	144.1	156.5	163.0	153.2	158.1	171.7	172.1
1965	146.6	167.3	154.4	164.6	147.7	127.7	160.2	174.9	177.6

SOURCE: Less rounded figures underlying Appendix Table 3.

Several facts emerge from the figures: (a) Throughout 1950–65, total resources available to the economy exceeded GNP, i.e., there was an import surplus which enabled Israel to use more goods and services than it could itself produce. (b) Between 1950—the first year since the end of the mandate for which detailed estimates are available— and 1965, there was a tremendous increase in domestic resources, which more than tripled, growing at an average annual rate of 8.7 per cent. Despite the rapid growth of population during the period, per capita resources rose by 74 per cent, or by 3.8 per cent annually. (c) GNP grew five times, at an average annual rate of 11.4 per cent; per capita GNP rose by 150 per cent, i.e., at an average anuual rate of 6.3 per cent. Since GNP increased faster than resources, the share of GNP in real domestic resources grew.

The data raise several questions: First, to what extent can this picture of rapid growth be the result of using faulty base-year data? After all, the 1950 estimates relate to a period of widespread price controls and unrealistic prices and exchange rates. Nevertheless, an error of 10 per cent in either direction in the 1950 GNP would not alter the general picture appreciably. Furthermore, if the data for 1950 and 1951 are discarded, the same conclusions emerge: between 1952 and 1965 the average annual rates of growth were 8.7 per cent for domestic resources and 10.4 per cent for GNP, while the per capita rates were 4.9 and 6.5 per cent, respectively.

Second, how would the conclusions be affected by including 1948 and 1949, when the economy was disrupted by war and immigration was spectacular? Here our statistical foundations are shaky. Gaathon has estimated national income in the Jewish sector of Palestine for 1947. Deflated by the cost-of-living index, his figures show that between 1947 and 1950 national income grew at an average annual rate of 31.5 per cent, enough to allow for an annual per capita growth of 5.4 per cent.[4] Better estimates might show that these rates are exaggerated, but it is unlikely that any revision would make a substantial difference.

Third, how do these rates of growth compare with those in the mandatory period? Gaathon has estimated that between 1936 and 1950 GNP per capita grew by 2 per cent annually.[5] The average rate of growth from 1950 to 1965 was more than three times as fast.[6]

[4] A. L. Gaathon, "National Income," *Encyclopaedia Hebraica*, Vol. VI (1957; Hebrew), p. 738, Table 9.

[5] *Ibid.*, p. 737.

[6] Including the data for 1948–50 in the post-mandatory period would only

Finally, how do the level and rate of growth of Israel's per capita resources or GNP compare with those of other countries? The difficulties inherent in any international comparison are considerable and well-known. However, data for per capita product in many countries (Appendix Table 5) suggest the following remarks on Israel's relative position.

Israel is well above the "underdeveloped" level; the U.N. list for 1958 includes some 75 countries with a per capita income of less than $ 200. However, Israel is still well below the most developed countries of Europe and America. Lastly, Israel's GNP has grown unusually fast, but a number of other countries, particularly those showing rapid postwar recovery, have matched its per capita rate of growth.

The allocation of resources

The resources available to the economy are allocated to consumption (public and private) and capital formation. Real per capita gross capital formation declined after 1951 and rose appreciably only after 1956, and over the whole period grew by only 25 per cent.[7] Real per capita consumption grew at an *annual* rate of 4.7 per cent. Using the alternative concept of total resources (i.e., including exports) clearly shows that the growth of resources raised exports as well as consumption.

The lumping together of private and public consumption as a measure of economic welfare rests on the assumption that in a democratic society the allocation between the two reflects consumer choice. However, it is interesting to separate the two, particularly in Israel, where special problems of defense and immigrant absorption call for relatively large public outlays. Over the whole period, per capita private consumption rose somewhat more than public consumption (by 106 per cent compared with 74 per cent); if 1952 is taken as base, the difference is much smaller, the figures being 98 and 96 per cent, respectively.

So far we have compared the rates of growth of the various components and uses of resources, measured in constant 1955 market prices, i.e., weighted by the preference system of 1955. To see how the allocation of resources changed over time, we must consider the percentage distribution of resources measured in current prices (Tables 30 and 31). These data show several trends that contrast with those shown by the constant price series.

---

enhance the differences in per capita growth rates between the two periods.

[7] The total increase for 1950–64 was 38 per cent; in 1965 there was a considerable decline.

TABLE 30.   Resources at the Disposal of the Economy and Their Uses:[a] 1950–65

(per cent)

	Consumption		Depreciation	Net domestic capital formation	Domestic use of resources	GNP	Import surplus	Domestic resources
	Private	Public						
	(1)	(2)	(6)	(5)	(7)	(11)	(12)	
1950	59.2	16.0	3.1	21.7	100.0	79.5	20.5	100.0
1951	57.1	15.5	3.3	24.1	100.0	82.7	17.3	100.0
1952	58.8	14.7	5.2	21.3	100.0	77.7	22.3	100.0
1953	61.1	14.9	6.6	17.4	100.0	78.4	21.6	100.0
1954	61.4	14.8	6.8	17.0	100.0	79.8	20.2	100.0
1955	58.2	15.8	6.4	19.6	100.0	78.7	21.3	100.0
1956	57.0	20.5	6.5	16.0	100.0	77.7	22.3	100.0
1957	58.5	16.8	6.9	17.8	100.0	80.2	19.8	100.0
1958	59.6	16.2	6.8	17.4	100.0	81.8	18.2	100.0
1959	59.8	16.1	6.8	17.3	100.0	84.6	15.4	100.0
1960	60.2	16.1	7.1	16.6	100.0	84.9	15.1	100.0
1961	58.4	16.5	7.0	18.1	100.0	84.0	16.0	100.0
1962	55.8	17.5	7.7	19.0	100.0	80.3	19.7	100.0
1963	57.4	17.2	8.2	17.2	100.0	82.4	17.6	100.0
1964	56.6	16.3	7.9	19.2	100.0	80.6	19.4	100.0
1965	58.6	17.9	8.2	15.3	100.0	83.5	16.5	100.0

[a] Computed from current price data.
SOURCE: Appendix Table 1.

TABLE 31. Total Resources and Their Uses:[a] 1950–65

(per cent)

	Consumption		Depre-ciation	Net domestic capital formation	Domestic use of resources	Exports	Total use of resources	GNP	Imports	Total resources
	Private	Public								
	(1)	(2)	(6)	(5)	(7)	(8)	(9)	(11)	(10)	
1950	57.7	15.6	3.0	21.2	97.5	2.5	100.0	77.5	22.5	100.0
1951	55.7	15.1	3.2	23.5	97.5	2.5	100.0	80.6	19.4	100.0
1952	55.8	13.9	4.9	20.2	94.8	5.2	100.0	73.7	26.3	100.0
1953	56.8	13.9	6.1	16.1	92.9	7.1	100.0	72.9	27.1	100.0
1954	55.4	13.4	6.1	15.4	90.3	9.7	100.0	72.1	27.9	100.0
1955	53.1	14.4	5.9	17.9	91.3	8.7	100.0	71.8	28.2	100.0
1956	51.8	18.7	5.9	14.6	91.0	9.0	100.0	70.7	29.3	100.0
1957	52.6	15.1	6.2	16.0	89.9	10.1	100.0	72.1	27.9	100.0
1958	53.7	14.6	6.2	15.7	90.2	9.8	100.0	73.8	26.2	100.0
1959	53.1	14.3	6.0	15.3	88.7	11.3	100.0	75.0	25.0	100.0
1960	52.6	14.1	6.2	14.5	87.4	12.6	100.0	74.1	25.9	100.0
1961	51.2	14.4	6.1	15.8	87.5	12.5	100.0	73.5	26.5	100.0
1962	47.4	14.9	6.6	16.2	85.1	14.9	100.0	68.3	31.7	100.0
1963	48.1	14.3	6.8	14.4	83.6	16.4	100.0	68.9	31.1	100.0
1964	47.9	13.8	6.7	16.3	84.7	15.3	100.0	68.3	31.7	100.0
1965	49.6	15.2	6.9	12.9	84.6	15.4	100.0	70.7	29.3	100.0

[a] Computed from current price data.
SOURCE: Appendix Table 1.

Real consumption rose faster than total real domestic resources, at the expense of real gross capital formation; but at current prices there were only slight changes in the share of the two uses after 1952.

At current prices, GNP as a per cent of domestic resources fluctuated around 78 per cent until 1957 (1951 being an exception); since then, the ratio has fluctuated around a somewhat higher level.

The trend differences between the constant and current price figures are, of course, the result of changes in relative prices. Import and export prices rose most, and GNP and consumption prices rose least; investment prices rose much more than consumption prices (Appendix Table 4). However, if we discard the statistically dubious years 1950 and 1951, the general picture is somewhat different.

Saving

Saving equals net capital formation *less* the import surplus, or, looked at another way, GNP *less* consumption and depreciation. Table 32 indicates the relative size of saving and net capital formation. Saving

TABLE 32.　　*Saving and Net Investment:*[a] *1950–65*

(per cent)

	Saving[b] as per cent of GNP	Net domestic capital formation as per cent of:		
		GNP	Domestic resources	Import surplus
1950	1.5	27.3	21.7	105.9
1951	8.2	29.1	24.1	139.0
1952	−1.2	27.5	21.3	95.7
1953	−5.3	22.1	17.4	80.6
1954	−3.9	21.3	17.0	84.4
1955	−2.2	25.0	19.6	92.1
1956	−8.1	20.6	16.0	71.7
1957	−2.4	22.2	17.8	90.1
1958	−0.9	21.3	17.4	96.0
1959	2.1	20.4	17.3	111.6
1960	1.7	19.6	16.6	109.6
1961	2.5	21.6	18.1	112.9
1962	−0.8	23.7	19.0	96.7
1963	−0.4	20.9	17.2	97.9
1964	−0.2	23.8	19.2	99.3
1965	−1.4	18.3	15.3	92.7

[a] Computed from current price data.
[b] Saving = GNP *less* (consumption *plus* depreciation).
SOURCE: Appendix Table 1.

was negative during 1952–58 and again since 1962, and was not much more than 2 per cent of GNP in 1951–61. The estimate of saving depends on the rate of exchange used to convert the import surplus to IL. Our figures use effective exchange rates.[8] Use of the official exchange rate would give higher but less meaningful estimates.

The existence of zero or even negative saving in the Israeli economy has frequently been viewed with alarm. This may be justified to the extent that the past record is used to predict difficulty in solving future problems.[9] But in considering the record on its merits, whether saving is positive or negative is important only to the extent that it determines investment and thus the rate of economic growth. Investment in Israel did not depend only, or even mainly, on saving, but on the import surplus. In fact, a comparison of annual saving with net investment, as shown in Table 32, does not suggest any clear functional relation between the two.

Investment was very high compared with GNP, but as a percentage of total resources available to the economy its relative order of magnitude was one commonly found in rapidly developing countries. This is apparent from Table 33, which presents gross investment as a per cent of total resources at the disposal of the economy in thirty-two countries. Most of the countries listed did not have a substantial import surplus and had to finance investment out of GNP; Israel's high investment, however, was made possible by the import surplus.

Thus, the simplest answer to the question why Israel failed to generate much domestic saving is that it was not necessary![10] Total resources were large enough to provide for both substantial investment and substantial increases in per capita consumption. In other words, during much of the period the import surplus permitted Israel to invest without tightening its belt. The price of maintaining a continuous import surplus will be considered in Chapter 8.

The reason for the low level of aggregate saving is better understood when the composition of saving is considered. What appears clear from all studies of saving in Israel is that private saving tended to be positive, that total saving was zero or even negative during much of the

---

[8] As defined in Joseph Baruh, "Import Taxes and Export Subsidies in Israel, 1955–61," *Bank of Israel Bulletin,* No. 18 (March 1963), 48–70.

[9] Cf. Don Patinkin, *The Israel Economy: The First Decade* (Jerusalem: Falk Project, 1960).

[10] This is not to say that saving could not have been greater had certain policies (e.g. anti-inflationary measures) been adopted, nor that it might not have been desirable to devote the import surplus to even more capital formation.

TABLE 33.   *Investment, Import Surplus, and Resources in 32 Countries: Average 1959–61*[a]

(per cent of resources at disposal of the economy)

	Gross domestic fixed capital formation	*Import surplus*
Argentina	19.8	2.3
Australia	26.0	2.5
Austria	22.5	0.2
Belgium	17.4	−2.2
Canada	22.1	3.1
Costa Rica	16.9	4.7
Cyprus	13.9	11.5
Denmark	19.4	0.6
Finland	28.1	0.5
France	17.9	−1.1
Germany (Federal Republic)	24.8	−2.9
Greece	20.9	9.9
Iceland	25.6	1.8
Ireland	13.1	2.3
Israel	22.7	15.5
Italy	22.2	−0.9
Jamaica	18.7	7.6
Japan	31.1	0.0
Luxembourg	24.0	−5.6
Mauritius	17.1	7.5
Netherlands	24.4	−3.0
New Zealand	21.9	0.9
Norway	27.5	3.3
Panama	14.1	9.4
Portugal	16.5	7.5
Puerto Rico	17.9	15.7
Sweden	21.9	0.3
Trinidad and Tobago	29.0	9.9
Union of South Africa	21.1	−2.4
United Kingdom	16.1	0.0
United States	16.4	−0.6
Venezuela	22.0	−3.3

[a] Arithmetic mean of the percentages for three years. For Belgium, Luxembourg, and Panama, average 1958–60.

SOURCES: Israel—Appendix Table 1, and *Abstract 1966,* No. 17, pp. 167–68, Table F/10.
Other countries—U.N., *Yearbook of National Accounts Statistics 1962* (New York: 1963).

period was due to the dissaving of the public and semi-public sector—a dissaving that was directly financed by the import surplus.[11] This aspect will be stressed in later chapters.

Some measures of welfare

There are several simple indicators of economic welfare, not complicated by problems of valuation and aggregation. The most common of these is average life expectancy,[12] which by 1965 was 70.5 years for men and 73.2 years for women: this is about 8 per cent above the 1949 figures and 17–18 per cent above the 1930–32 figures. Also relevant is the infant mortality rate. This dropped from 78 per thousand in 1931–35 to 52 in 1949 and 23 in 1965.[13]

Another measure is food consumption. By 1956/57, Israel's average food consumption ranked fairly high by world standards in nutritive content in terms of calories, proteins, fats, vitamins, and minerals, although in some respects, particularly in animal proteins, Israel fell short of the level found in the most prosperous countries. The 1956/57 level of nutrition was well above that of 1951, but on the whole below that of 1946.[14]

Lastly, the level of housing is a general indicator of economic welfare. Housing conditions became crowded during World War II, when civilian construction works were curtailed; the situation had not been alleviated by the time that mass immigration confronted the country with a severe housing problem. Conditions improved gradually: in 1955 average housing density of the Jewish population was, at 2.3 persons per room, higher than in 1949, but by 1961 it had declined to 2.1 persons.[15] Israel ranks high in housing amenities: by 1963, over

---

[11] There are conceptual and statistical difficulties in comparing national accounts with sample survey data. Nevertheless, the conclusion seems valid.

[12] Life expectancy figures, of course, reflect the age composition of the population.

[13] *Abstract 1966*, No. 17: life expectancy (Jews only) from p. 83, Table C/31; infant mortality (Jews only) from p. 56, Table C/2. Infant mortality rates for non-Jews are available only for more recent years (*ibid.*, p. 57, Table C/3), and also declined considerably—from 68 per thousand in 1952 to 43 per thousand in 1965.

[14] This information is from Sarah Bavly, *Food Consumption and Level of Nutrition of Urban Wage and Salary Earners' Families in Israel, 1956/57* (Special Series No. 101; Jerusalem: CBS, 1960; Hebrew).

[15] The 1955 figure is from H. Darin-Drabkin, *Housing in Israel* (Tel Aviv: 1957), p. 211; the 1961 figure is from *Statistical Abstract of Housing and Construction* (Ministry of Housing, 1964).

TABLE 34. Real Resources and Their Uses: 1951–65

(per cent increase over preceding year)

	Consumption			Gross domestic capital formation	Domestic use of resources	Exports	Total use of resources	Imports	GNP
	Private	Public	Total						
	(1)	(2)	(3)	(4)	(7)	(8)	(9)	(10)	(11)
1951	22.6	18.5	21.7	18.2	20.5	22.8	20.6	6.6	30.9
1952	7.5	-5.5	4.6	-14.1	-1.6	35.4	0.3	-11.6	7.4
1953	3.5	4.5	3.7	-16.3	-2.0	26.1	-0.1	-2.9	1.2
1954	15.0	16.8	15.3	11.5	14.4	37.3	16.3	4.5	21.9
1955	8.2	13.8	9.4	23.2	12.7	-2.6	11.1	8.6	12.2
1956	9.1	43.9	16.6	-5.4	10.8	14.3	11.1	17.7	8.6
1957	7.1	-14.9	1.3	17.0	4.8	20.0	6.1	-0.8	9.1
1958	10.1	2.7	8.5	7.4	8.2	11.3	8.5	6.2	9.4
1959	9.9	3.5	8.6	9.3	8.8	31.0	11.1	5.5	13.2
1960	6.7	6.6	6.7	6.2	6.6	26.0	8.9	11.4	8.1
1961	11.0	18.0	12.4	18.4	13.9	15.8	14.2	24.2	10.6
1962	10.9	11.4	11.0	12.4	11.4	20.6	12.7	12.1	12.9
1963	9.9	6.7	9.2	3.5	7.7	17.6	9.2	3.4	11.6
1964	10.8	4.9	9.6	21.5	12.6	7.5	11.7	15.4	10.4
1965	8.3	10.9	8.8	-6.2	4.8	8.8	5.4	1.9	6.8

SOURCE: Appendix Table 2.

93 per cent of families had electricity, and 97 per cent had running water.[16]

Developments by sub-period

Although all indicators of economic growth presented in the preceding tables show substantial increases during the period as a whole, growth was uneven. This is evident from Tables 28 and 29 and appears even more clearly from Tables 34 and 35, which show the same information as per cent increases over the preceding year instead of as cumulative indexes of growth.

TABLE 35.   *Real Use of Resources and GNP Per Capita: 1951–65*

(per cent increase over preceding year)

	Consumption			Gross domestic capital formation	Domestic use of resources	GNP
	Private	Public	Total			
	(1)	(2)	(3)	(4)	(7)	(11)
1951	3.9	0.5	3.1	0.2	2.1	11.0
1952	–0.0	–12.1	–2.7	–20.1	–8.4	–0.1
1953	0.7	1.7	0.9	–18.5	–4.6	–1.5
1954	12.3	14.0	12.7	8.8	11.7	19.2
1955	4.5	9.9	5.6	18.9	8.7	8.2
1956	4.5	37.8	11.6	–9.4	6.1	3.9
1957	1.4	–19.4	–4.1	10.8	–0.8	3.3
1958	6.3	–0.9	4.7	3.7	4.5	5.6
1959	6.6	0.4	5.3	6.0	5.5	9.8
1960	3.9	3.9	3.9	3.4	3.8	5.3
1961	7.4	14.1	8.7	14.5	10.1	6.9
1962	6.1	6.6	6.2	7.5	6.5	8.0
1963	5.7	2.6	5.0	–0.5	3.6	7.3
1964	6.3	0.7	5.2	16.6	8.0	5.9
1965	4.7	7.2	5.2	–9.3	1.3	3.2

SOURCE: Less rounded figures underlying Appendix Table 3.

The tables show considerable year-to-year fluctuations in both aggregate and per capita figures (which are strongly affected by variations in immigration). Yet there are similarities in the fluctuations of certain closely related aggregates, which suggest a possible division into sub-periods.

[16] *Abstract 1964*, No. 15, p. 180, Table G/19.

Aggregate growth was tremendous in 1951, but per capita growth was more moderate owing to large-scale immigration. Lack of data for the previous two years prevents our deciding whether this year was exceptional or the last of several years of rapid growth, although Gaathon's rough calculations for 1947–50 suggest the latter.[17] The period ending with 1951 is a distinct one in several other respects: mass immigration had virtually stopped by the end of 1951, as had the most stringent aspects of an experiment in economic policy (not since repeated), which we shall call by its most distinctive feature, austerity. Even if we cannot assume with any confidence that the two years before 1951 were also years of substantial growth, it is important to note that per capita investment was very high in both 1950 and 1951; in fact, it was not until 1961 that real gross domestic capital formation attained the per capita level of these years; real net investment per capita has exceeded the 1950–51 level in only one year (1964) since then.

In 1952 and 1953, GNP rose by less than 9 per cent (compared with 31 per cent in the single year 1951), and aggregate domestic resources fell by 3.5 per cent, because imports declined and exports rose; aggregate gross investment fell by 28 per cent. In per capita terms, GNP also declined slightly in the two years. Thus, this two-year period, when net immigration came to a temporary halt (Table 8), was the one of least growth.

The year 1954 is unusual. In no other year did per capita GNP grow so rapidly, and the other principal magnitudes also rose. All this was achieved while the import surplus declined. Furthermore, estimating methods were well developed by this time, and 1954 is so close to our base year (1955) that we can be fairly confident that these unusual developments were not merely the product of faulty statistics.[18] Although 1955 was not as spectacular as 1954, it seems closer to this year than to the later years in most developments.

The years 1956–65 were not, of course, uniform; 1956, the year of the Sinai Campaign, was one of high government consumption and large immigration; in 1957 per capita resources declined slightly, and 1959 saw an exceptional growth in per capita GNP. But compared to earlier years, annual fluctuations were moderate.

---

[17] See p. 92 above.

[18] There is some possibility that the 1954 figures were overestimates and include some elements that really belong to 1953. However, the revised 1953 and 1954 figures of the CBS (used here) still show the jump, and there are plausible grounds for believing that it actually took place.

To summarize, we can make the following division into sub-periods on the basis of the growth rates.[19]

1949–51: A period of austerity marked by large-scale immigration and relatively large capital formation. The last year, at least, was one of unusual growth in aggregate GNP and resources, but per capita growth was much more modest.

1952–53: The period of the New Economic Policy and the cessation of mass immigration; GNP growth was moderate, and resources declined owing to a decline in the import surplus. As a result, per capita GNP and resources declined.

1954–55: Resources grew rapidly, almost as fast as GNP. Per capita resources also rose faster than either before or since.

1956–64: A period of more even growth. GNP, aggregate and per capita, grew a little more slowly than in 1950–53, but per capita resources and consumption grew faster.

1965–66: A decline in economic activity which started in the latter half of 1965 reduced the rate of growth of GNP and resources, and 1966 was a year of virtual stagnation.

The Origin and Composition of Product

The GNP growth discussed in the preceding section is the outcome of economic activity in many branches, and economic policy affecting growth frequently operates primarily at the branch level. An extended discussion of each of the main industries is beyond the scope of this book. Here we comment only on the main changes in the industrial structure of product.

The GNP figures so far presented were estimated from the expenditure side. The breakdown by industrial origin is available only from income-side estimates, i.e., estimates of payments to the factors of production. The expenditure side estimates of GNP are generally higher than those from the income side, but the difference is not so large as to affect our earlier conclusions regarding the development of product.

Table 36 shows the industrial origin of net domestic product at

---

[19] An alternative division into sub-periods may be based on *changes* in the rate of growth of GNP and domestic resources:

1952: falling growth rate; 1953–54: rising growth rate, except for per capita GNP in 1953; 1955–57: falling growth rate; 1958–59: rising growth rate; 1960–62: per capita GNP and resources decelerating in 1960, per capita GNP accelerating in 1961 and 1962, per capita resources accelerating in 1961, decelerating in 1962; 1963–66: falling rate of growth, with temporary acceleration in resources in 1964.

TABLE 36.   Industrial Origin of Net Domestic Product at Factor Cost: 1952–65

(per cent)

	Agriculture, forestry, and fishing	Manufacturing, mining, and quarrying	Contract construction	Public utilities	Transport and communications	Finance, insurance, and real estate	Ownership of dwellings	General government and private nonprofit institutions	Trade and other services	Net domestic product[a]
1952	11.4	21.7	9.2	1.7	7.4	2.5	5.2	18.2	22.7	100.0
1953	11.4	22.8	7.8	2.2	7.2	2.6	5.0	19.0	22.0	100.0
1954	12.1	22.4	7.8	1.9	7.6	2.6	5.0	19.0	21.6	100.0
1955	11.3	22.5	8.4	1.7	7.4	2.7	5.4	20.0	20.6	100.0
1956	11.5	22.2	7.6	1.8	7.5	2.8	6.1	20.4	20.1	100.0
1957	12.8	21.9	8.0	1.9	7.7	2.9	5.7	19.6	19.5	100.0
1958	13.2	22.1	8.1	2.0	7.7	3.0	5.5	19.0	19.4	100.0
1959	12.1	23.0	7.6	2.2	7.9	3.3	5.6	19.3	19.0	100.0
1960	11.7	23.8	7.2	2.3	8.0	3.8	5.9	18.7	18.6	100.0
1961	11.1	24.7	7.5	2.2	8.0	4.1	6.0	18.1	18.3	100.0
1962	10.4	24.8	8.1	2.1	8.1	4.4	6.1	17.7	18.3	100.0
1963	10.4	24.5	8.2	2.0	8.1	4.7	6.8	17.2	18.1	100.0
1964	9.4	24.8	8.0	2.0	8.4	4.8	7.1	17.3	18.2	100.0
1965	8.5	24.2	7.2	2.0	8.8	5.0	7.5	18.7	18.1	100.0

[a] Not adjusted for historical depreciation or stock valuation.

SOURCES: *Abstract 1966*, No. 17, pp. 176–77, Table F/15. In this source contract construction and public utilities appear as one item; the breakdown for 1952–59 was computed according to Emanuel Levy and Others, *Israel's National Income and Expenditure, 1950–1962* (Special Series No. 153; Jerusalem: CBS, 1964); for 1960–65 from Bank of Israel, *Annual Report 1965*, p. 25, Table II–9.

factor cost, for the years 1952–65. Unfortunately, several necessary adjustments can be made only globally, so that the percentage distribution may be slightly distorted. But the general picture seems clear.

Agriculture

Agriculture has played an important dual role in the development of Palestine and Israel, as an economic activity and as the symbol of a new type of Jewish national life.[20] The ideological predilection for agriculture of the national institutions has already been mentioned; it had been held in check during the mandate, but was allowed full sway once independence was achieved. In fact, the mass influx of immigrants, the shortage of food, and the sudden availability of cultivable land combined to stimulate settlement activity: within five years the number of settlements doubled.

But settlement activity gradually abated and then came to a virtual stop as economic problems countered the ideological desire to increase the relative importance of agriculture.[21]

A major problem on the production side has been the shortage of water. As more realistic estimates were made of the annual water potential, it became clear that conventional sources (i.e., other than desalinated sea water) would not be enough for cultivating even half of the five million *dunams* (approximately 2,000 square miles) potentially cultivable under irrigation.[22] Furthermore, most water sources in Israel are in the north, whereas most cultivable land is located in the center and south of the country; topographical problems thus make the real economic cost of irrigation very high. Other problems on the production side stem from the structure of the small family farm, which, retained for ideological reasons, has difficulty in attaining the efficiency of modern farming.

A more effective curb on the growth of agriculture has been from the demand side. Supply gradually outgrew domestic demand in the tra-

---

[20] Considerable attention has been devoted to the evolution of special forms of agricultural settlement, particularly the kibbutz (collective village) and the moshav (smallholders cooperative village). See, for example, two List Institute studies: Egon Meyer, *Der Moschav* (Basel and Tübingen: Kyklos-Verlag and J.C.B. Mohr, 1967), and Martin Pallmann, *Der Kibbuz* (Basel and Tübingen: Kyklos-Verlag and J.C.B. Mohr, 1966).

[21] For a brief survey of developments in agriculture see Yair Mundlak, *Long-Term Projections of Supply and Demand for Agricultural Products in Israel— I. General View and Summary* (Jerusalem: Falk Project, 1964), Chapter 2.

[22] *Abstract 1965*, No. 16, p. 363.

ditional mixed farming products, and export markets (except for citrus) have not expanded enough to make up for this.

As a result of these developments, the share of agriculture has not grown. As Table 36 shows, its share in net domestic product, fairly constant over the period, has declined somewhat since 1960. It is in fact about what it was in 1945 and very similar to that in countries in the same per capita income class.[23] In constant prices, agricultural product grew at an average rate of 12 per cent between 1949 and 1965. This is faster than GNP, so that the fact that the share of agriculture failed to rise reflects some decline in relative agricultural prices.[24] It should be mentioned that this relative price decline was much more moderate than it would have been in the absence of the government's varied and massive program for the support of agricultural prices and farm incomes.

The composition of agricultural output is shown in Table 37. The production of animal proteins (milk, meat, and fish [25]) declined somewhat during the first part of the period, but since 1957/58 has amounted to about half of the total production. Within this group there appears to be a slight relative decline in milk and a very large relative increase in meat. The latter certainly reflects the rising standard of living.

Citrus has become relatively less important, while the share of other fruit has increased. Field crops do not show any clear trend; their share increased during the early years when cultivated area expanded most rapidly, but later declined somewhat when irrigated (though not total cultivated) area increased. A sub-branch breakdown of field crops shows a relative decline in cereals, pulses, and roughage, and an increase in industrial crops, particularly cotton and sugar beet.

Manufacturing

Manufacturing emerged as a major branch of the economy during World War II; however, the wartime share of national product could not be maintained and the branch declined to about the pre-war

[23] The U.N. *Yearbook of National Accounts Statistics 1962* (New York: 1963) gives figures on the industrial origin of domestic product. See also Simon Kuznets, "Quantitative Aspects of the Economic Growth of Nations II. Industrial Distribution of National Product and Labor Force," *Economic Development and Cultural Change,* V (supplement to No. 4, July 1957).

[24] See the sources to Table 37.

[25] Fish and changes in livestock inventory account for about half of the "others" category.

TABLE 37. Composition of Agricultural Production:[a] 1948/49–1964/65[b]

(per cent)

	Field crops	Vege-tables, potatoes	Citrus fruit	Other fruit	Milk	Eggs	Meat	Other[c]	Total
1948/49	15	12	16	7	16	15	9	10	100
1949/50	18	14	13	5	15	15	9	11	100
1950/51	13	15	14	4	16	18	8	12	100
1951/52	21	15	11	7	15	14	7	10	100
1952/53	20	16	12	7	16	12	7	10	100
1953/54	22	15	13	7	15	12	7	9	100
1954/55	21	14	11	5	15	13	12	9	100
1955/56	22	13	10	7	14	11	14	9	100
1956/57	25	12	9	6	13	13	13	9	100
1957/58	19	12	8	7	13	15	16	10	100
1958/59	20	10	9	7	13	16	17	8	100
1959/60	17	10	9	8	13	16	19	8	100
1960/61	20	9	7	9	12	17	19	7	100
1961/62	18	8	7	10	13	16	21	7	100
1962/63	17	8	9	10	14	14	22	6	100
1963/64	19	8	8	12	12	14	21	6	100
1964/65	18	8	8	11	13	14	21	7	100

[a] Calculated from constant-price data (in 1948/49 prices).
[b] Agricultural years, October–September.
[c] Honey, fish, changes in livestock inventory, and miscellaneous.
SOURCES: 1948/49–1960/61—Yair Mundlak, Long-Term Projections of Supply and Demand for Agricultural Products in Israel—I. General View and Summary (Jerusalem: Falk Project, 1964), p. 31, Table 9. (The figures in this source were calculated from various issues of Abstract.)
1961/62—Abstract 1964, No. 15, p. 340, Table L/18.
1962/63–1964/65—Abstract 1966, No. 17, p. 382, Table L/18.

TABLE 38. Composition of Industrial Output: Selected Years, 1951–63

(per cent)

	Composition, adjusted for period comparison[a]						Per cent change in weights		
	1951/52 (1)	1955 (a) (2)	1955 (b) (3)	1958 (a) (4)	1958 (b) (5)	1962/63 (6)	1951/52 to 1955 (a) (7)	1955 (b) to 1958 (a) (8)	1958 (b) to 1962/63 (9)
Mines and quarries	1.6	2.1	1.9	2.0	1.7	2.4	31.2	5.3	41.2
Food, beverages, and tobacco	30.3	22.8	23.2	23.5	23.7	23.5	−25.1	1.3	−0.8
Diamonds	2.6	3.6	3.2	3.0	2.4	5.4	38.5	−6.2	125.0
Textiles	12.7	13.8	13.4	12.7	11.9	11.2	8.7	−5.2	−5.9
Clothing	4.9	3.1	3.8	3.6	3.1	2.8	−36.7	−5.2	−9.7
Wood and furniture	6.2	5.3	6.2	6.5	5.8	5.8	−13.4	4.8	–
Paper and cardboard	0.8 }	4.4 }	2.2	2.4	2.2	2.6 }	51.7 }	9.0	18.2
Printing	2.1 }		2.2	1.8	3.3	2.8 }		−18.2	−15.2
Leather and footwear	3.2	2.3	2.9	2.5	2.3	1.7	−28.1	−13.8	−26.1
Rubber and plastics	1.5	3.4	3.2	3.3	3.0	3.6	126.7	3.1	20.0
Chemicals	7.6	8.3	7.5	10.1	9.8	6.0	9.2	34.7	−38.8
Non-metallic mineral products	7.9	8.3	7.9	7.3	8.2	7.3	5.1	−7.6	−11.0
Metals	10.2	10.0	10.2	9.8	9.1	9.0	−2.0	−3.9	−1.1
Machinery	5.1 }	6.5 }	3.2	2.9	3.7	4.6 }	27.4 }	−9.4	24.3
Electrical equipment			2.7	3.0	2.9	3.4 }		11.1	17.2
Transport equipment	1.9	3.4	3.1	4.1	5.7	6.7	78.9	32.3	17.5
Miscellaneous manufactures	1.5	2.6	3.1	1.3	1.2	1.2	73.3	−58.1	–
Total[b]	100.0	100.0	100.0	100.0	100.0	100.0			

[a] See the source for explanation.
[b] Figures may not add to 100 owing to rounding.
SOURCE: Ephraim Kleiman, The Structure of Israel Manufacturing Industries, 1952–1962 (Jerusalem: Falk Project, 1964; mimeograph), p. 28, Table B–2, and p. 352, Table H–1.

level. There was no material change until after 1958, when government economic policy became more favorable to the branch. Since then, the share of manufacturing has increased, but not very much, and is slightly less than one quarter of net domestic product.

The various CBS industrial surveys and censuses provide data for inter-temporal comparisons of the sub-branch structure of production. Changes in coverage and classification make such comparisons difficult, but a recent study of manufacturing has made numerous adjustments of the data to permit comparisons of 1951/52 with 1955, 1955 with 1958, and 1958 with 1962/63.[26] These comparisons are reproduced in Table 38.

As expected, in 1951/52 there was high concentration in the production of basic consumer goods (food, clothing, and footwear), followed by a drastic decline in their share between 1951/52 and 1955. During this period diamond production expanded and new industries were introduced, such as motor vehicles and rubber tires. After 1955, changes in the sub-branch composition of production are fairly slight, although some branches, such as chemicals and diamonds, have grown relatively fast. Kleiman has pointed out that there is a continuous process of diversification in production: many new or formerly small branches have grown so that there is less concentration in just a few branches. The Bank of Israel's input-output studies support this conclusion and indicate growing inter-relationships between different branches.[27]

Construction

The building industry appears in two items in Table 36, "contract construction" and "ownership of dwellings." The latter measures annual housing services, but the figures must be regarded as a minimum estimate because of rent control and the prevalence of owner-occupancy.[28] Contract construction measures the income originating in building

---

[26] Ephraim Kleiman, *The Structure of Israel Manufacturing Industries: 1952–1962* (Jerusalem: Falk Project, 1964; mimeograph).

[27] Michael Bruno, *Interdependence, Resource Use and Structural Change in Israel* (Special Studies No. 2; Jerusalem: Bank of Israel Research Department, 1962); and various issues of Bank of Israel, *Annual Report*.

[28] Home ownership has increased considerably in the period surveyed, and 60 per cent of dwellings were owner-occupied by 1963 (*Abstract 1964*, No. 15, p. 178). The estimates include an imputation for owner-occupancy, but this must be regarded as a lower limit.

TABLE 39. Some Indicators of Housing Activity: 1949–65

	Gross investment in housing			Employment in construction as per cent of all employment	Per cent of NDP originating in construction	Housing completions (number of units)			
	As per cent of:		Public sector share (per cent)			Public		Private	Total
	Domestic resources	Total gross fixed investment				Permanent	Temporary		
	(1)	(2)	(3)	(4)	(5)	(6)	(7)	(8)	(9)
1949	..	..	..	..	..	13,333	5,217	5,347	23,897
1950	10.9	45.1	..	..	..	16,492	13,742	7,000	37,234
1951	12.5	46.5	..	9.4	..	28,573	25,341	10,953	64,867
1952	9.5	39.0	..	..	9.2	22,366	3,305	15,142	40,813
1953	8.0	35.5	..	..	7.8	20,929	4,386	2,584	27,899
1954	8.3	37.4	..	9.0	7.8	18,274	–	7,506	25,780
1955	8.9	37.9	41.6	9.3	8.4	19,028	579	12,386	31,993
1956	7.1	33.5	40.3	8.8	7.6	18,439	2,275	11,962	32,676
1957	8.1	34.4	53.1	9.8	8.0	21,444	1,496	9,144	32,084
1958	7.2	31.9	47.5	9.8	8.1	23,200	–	10,960	34,160

1959	7.3	32.5	45.2	9.5	7.6	20,070	—	12,430	32,500
1960	6.7	30.6	40.4	9.3	7.2	17,660	—	13,330	30,990
1961	7.6	32.0	44.4	9.1	7.5	13,290	—	13,070	26,360
1962	8.5	33.6	48.4	9.6	8.1	23,850	—	14,430	38,280
1963	7.5	30.8	..	10.2	8.2	24,130	—	15,560	39,690
1964	7.3	28.8	..	10.2	8.0	19,180	—	18,800	37,980
1965	7.0	30.3	..	10.5	7.2	19,870	—	18,900	38,770

SOURCES: Columns (1), (2)—Domestic resources: Appendix Table 1. Gross fixed investment and investment in housing: *Abstract 1965*, No. 16, p. 170, Table F/10 (for 1950 and 1951); *Abstract 1966*, No. 17, pp. 168–69, Table F/10 (for 1952–65).

Column (3)—Levy and Others, *op. cit.*, pp. 100–101, Table 55. The 1950–54 figures in this source use a different definition and cannot be compared with the 1955–62 series.

Column (4)—1951, 1954: unpublished calculations underlying Gur Ofer, *The Service Industries in a Developing Economy: Israel As a Case Study* (Jerusalem and New York: Frederick A. Praeger with the Bank of Israel, 1967), Table 4.10, based on *Bulletin*, Part A (social statistics), IV (No. 2, July 1953), 193 (Hebrew)—for Jews only; and CBS, *Labour Force Survey June 1954* (Special Series No. 56; Jerusalem: 1957)—total labor force, including unemployed.
1955–61: CBS, *Labour Force Surveys 1955–1961* (Special Series No. 162; Jerusalem: 1964), p. 43, Table 30.
1962: *Abstract 1965*, No. 16, p. 306, Table K/11.
1963–65: *Abstract 1966*, No. 17, p. 302, Table K/10.

Column (5)—Table 36.

Columns (6)–(9)—1949–57: Z. Lubetzki, *Building for Residence in Israel, 1949–1963* (unpublished mimeograph), Table II–1. 1958–65: *Abstracts*, as follows: *1961*, No. 12, p. 240, Table 5 (public), and p. 239, Table 4 (private) (for 1958); *1962*, No. 13, p. 258, Table 4 (public), and p. 261, Table 6 (private) (for 1959); *1963*, No. 14, p. 310, Table 4 (public), and p. 313, Table 6 (private) (for 1960); *1964*, No. 15, p. 394, Table N/4 (for 1961); *1965*, No. 16, p. 452, Table N/4 (for 1962); *1966*, No. 17, p. 460, Table N/4 (for 1963–65).

activity, which comprises residential, non-residential, and public works, of which the first is the most important.[29]

Mass immigration necessitated large-scale building activity, much of it public. Despite great efforts, about one fifth of the population lived in temporary housing at the end of 1951, and six or seven years passed before the backlog was worked off. Additional immigration, rising incomes, and restitutions payments from Germany combined to create and maintain a large housing demand.

Table 39 provides some quantitative indicators of the importance of housing and the role of the public sector in its provision. It is clear that after 1951 housing became much less important, but its share in gross investment remains high compared with other countries.[30] The sharp decline in housing construction which began in 1965 triggered a recession.

Services

The remaining branches are frequently lumped together under the general heading of services, although it is not easy to draw the line between goods and services. Considerable attention has been devoted in Israel to the total size of these service items, and this for several unrelated reasons. First, services were identified with Jewish activity in the diaspora, which the revival of national life sought to counteract; second, the socialist concept of services as an unproductive activity; third, the fact that services are less exportable than most goods.

The total of net domestic product originating in services has generally been over 50 per cent. Whether and in what sense this can be considered an excessive concentration in services has been examined by Ofer.[31] He found that there was no correlation between per capita income level and the share of services to support the use of per capita income as a criterion for measuring a "normal" services structure.[32] Nevertheless,

---

[29] In 1965, about half of the gross investment in structures was dwellings, just under one quarter was non-residential building, and the rest was other construction works (*Abstract 1966*, No. 17, p. 171, Table F/11).

[30] For a brief survey of housing in Israel, see N. Halevi, "Housing in Israel," in *The Economic Problems of Housing*, Conference of the International Economic Association (London: Macmillan, 1967).

[31] Gur Ofer, *The Service Industries in a Developing Economy: Israel As a Case Study* (Jerusalem and New York: Frederick A. Praeger with the Bank of Israel, 1967).

[32] Ofer did use the income per capita criterion for measuring the "normal" labor force employed in services.

Israel has an unusually high concentration in services, particularly public services, compared with other countries in *any* income per capita class.

Ofer's study, covering the period 1931–61, shows that although the over-all share of services did not fluctuate much, there were important inter-branch changes. The share of commerce declined, while transportation (mainly aviation and shipping) and public services increased considerably. The last consists of "general government," which rose throughout the period, and "other public services," which expanded chiefly after the establishment of the State. We shall return to a discussion of these changes in Chapter 7.

THE SECTORAL STRUCTURE OF DOMESTIC PRODUCT

The role of the various public and semi-public institutions has already been briefly outlined in Chapter 3. It is of interest to examine the sectoral structure of national product, in a three-sector classification: (a) public—including government and national institutions; (b) Histadrut; and (c) private. Enterprises have been classified according to the extent of effective control, which is defined as at least 50 per cent ownership of voting shares. Table 40 presents estimates for selected years.

TABLE 40. *Net Domestic Product, by Sector: 1953, 1957–60*

(per cent)

	Public sector	Histadrut sector	Private sector	Total
1953	19.4	18.0	62.6	100.0
1957	20.9	20.6	58.5	100.0
1958	20.0	20.0	60.0	100.0
1959	21.6	20.3	58.1	100.0
1960	21.1	20.4	58.5	100.0

SOURCE: Haim Barkai, "The Public, Histadrut, and Private Sectors in the Israeli Economy," *Sixth Report 1961–1963* (Jerusalem: Falk Project, 1964), p. 26, Table 1.

The data show some increase in the share of both the public and the Histadrut sectors at the expense of the residual private sector between 1953 and 1957, with only slight changes thereafter. The public and Histadrut sectors each account for about one fifth of domestic product, with the private sector providing the remaining three fifths.

Barkai maintains that the share of the public sector, which is high

TABLE 41.   Net Domestic Product, by Sector and Industrial Origin: 1953 and 1959

(per cent)

	1953				1959			
	Public	Histadrut	Private	Total	Public	Histadrut	Private	Total
Agriculture	0.8	30.5	68.7	100.0	0.8	32.0	67.2	100.0
Manufacturing	1.6	19.3	79.1	100.0	4.3	22.2	73.5	100.0
Construction	9.3	18.6	72.1	100.0	10.6	31.9	57.5	100.0
Public utilities	29.2	–	70.8	100.0	100.0	–	–	100.0
Transport and communications	23.7	27.6	48.7	100.0	40.3	37.0	22.7	100.0
Finance	14.5	18.0	67.5	100.0	1.1	9.1	89.8	100.0
Trade and other services	1.2	14.6	84.2	100.0	1.7	15.8	82.5	100.0
Nonprofit institutions	73.9	11.2	14.9	100.0	–	37.6	62.4	100.0
Government services					97.0	3.0	–	100.0
Total	19.4	18.0	62.6	100.0	21.5	20.3	58.2	100.0

SOURCES: 1953—Barkai's (unpublished) revision of Creamer's estimates.
1959—Barkai, op. cit., p. 33, Table 4.

in comparison with many non-Communist countries, is actually even more significant if countries are ranked by per capita product.[33] Be that as it may, it is beyond dispute that owing to the importance of the Histadrut sector, the share of the private sector is quite low when compared with non-Communist countries. If we are interested in the extent of non-private control of production, we believe that these estimates must be regarded as the lower limits of non-private control. But if our interest is in the profit motive as opposed to other motives, it is not clear how much of the two fifths of product originating in the public and Histadrut sectors in fact deviate from the economic criteria of the private sector.

Table 41 shows the sectoral structure of domestic product by industry in 1953 and 1959. What stands out is that (government services apart) the public sector is an important producer only in public utilities and some branches of transport: roads, ports, shipping and aviation, railroads, and communications. These are primarily the fields of basic overhead investment, or what is often called infrastructure. In agriculture and manufacturing, the direct role of the public sector is quite modest.[34]

The Histadrut sector, on the other hand, is most conspicuous in agriculture, construction, bus transport, and non-profit institutions (chiefly medical care), and to a lesser extent in manufacturing.

The major changes between 1953 and 1959, in addition to the nationalization of the electric companies, were that the Histadrut share rose in construction and transport, the public sector share rose in transport and communications, and the share of both sectors in finance dropped.

THE DISTRIBUTION OF INCOME

We have seen that average welfare, as reflected by several alternative measures of per capita goods and services, has increased greatly over the years. We now turn to a consideration of how income is distributed among the population and to what extent the increased welfare has diffused throughout the population.

Several studies, based on sample survey data, have been made of the income distribution of Israel at points of time, and we compare

---

[33] Haim Barkai, "The Public, Histadrut, and Private Sectors in the Israeli Economy," *Sixth Report: 1961–1963* (Jerusalem: Falk Project, 1964), pp. 68–73.

[34] On the legal aspects of government intervention see Meir Heth, *The Legal Framework of Economic Activity in Israel* (Jerusalem and New York: Frederick A. Praeger with the Bank of Israel, 1967).

some of them in order to ascertain changes over time in the distribution of income.[35] Although these surveys have not covered the entire population, they do represent wide enough segments of it to allow important conclusions to be drawn.

Several alternative measures of income are used in considering income distribution. The first is economic income, i.e., the payment received by owners of the factors of production for their contribution to output. This measure is of paramount interest when the primary concern is with the relationship between production and distribution. However, if one is interested mainly in the welfare aspects of income, it may be preferable to consider personal income, i.e., both factor income and transfer payments. But not all personal income is at the recipient's disposal: direct taxes, for example, are deducted regardless of his personal preference. Disposable income is therefore another important measure.[36] Regardless of the income measure used, the most meaningful unit for classifying recipients is the family.

Before examining how the distribution of income has changed over time, we shall consider the general picture that emerges from the various studies.

First, there is considerable inequality in the distribution of family income in Israel. For example, it was found that in 1957/58 the bottom tenth of Jewish urban families received only 1.6 per cent of total personal income, whereas the upper tenth received 24.2 per cent: fifteen times as much. Dividing the population into richer and poorer halves shows that the average income of the richer half was three times that of the poorer half.[37]

Second, although inequality varies according to the measure of income used, it remains considerable whatever the measure. Since transfer payments and direct taxes tend to reduce the inequality of earned or economic income, personal income is distributed somewhat more equally, and there is least inequality in disposable income.

Third, there is much more inequality in per capita family income

---

[35] The major studies are: M. Zandberg, *Distribution of Income in Israel in 1954* (Jerusalem: Institute for Applied Social Research, 1956; Hebrew mimeograph); H. Ben-Shahar, *Income Distribution of Wage and Salary Earners, 1950–1957* (Jerusalem: Ministry of Finance, 1961; Hebrew mimeograph); Giora Hanoch, "Income Differentials in Israel," *Fifth Report 1959 and 1960* (Jerusalem: Falk Project, 1961).

[36] But even disposable income is not always freely disposable, for example, during a period of rationing.

[37] The figures are from Hanoch, *op. cit.*, p. 49, Table 3.

than in family income, again regardless of which measure is used; this is because the poorer groups also have the larger families.

Lastly, it would appear that despite the marked inequality described above, Israel's income distribution is "more equal than others." International comparisons of income distribution [38] made by using Lorenz curves, or simply by comparing the share of total income going to the richest tenth of the population, show that Israel's income distribution is as close to equality as that of any other nation for which data are available.[39]

Before accepting this conclusion, we must allow for the fact that the Israeli surveys, which at best cover only the Jewish urban population, exclude from 25 to 30 per cent of the population. The average income of those excluded (non-Jews and rural Jews) is lower than that of the survey population. A rough calculation suggests that their inclusion would not alter the share of the upper tenth enough to upset our conclusions.[40] But how the Lorenz curve and the derived indexes would be affected by extending the coverage depends more on the distribution of income within the excluded groups than on their average income. However, it is probably safe to assume that there would be no major change in Israel's relative position were the studies to be broadened.

Hanoch has examined the factors that explain the differences in personal income. He found that occupation, level of education, age, length of residence in the country, and continent of origin were important. Thus, comparing average incomes of different groups shows that people with professional skills receive more than unskilled workers, the better educated receive more than the less educated, new immigrants receive less than earlier immigrants, and people from Asia-Africa receive less than people from Europe-America, with the Israel-born between the two. In this analysis, Hanoch separated the influence of the several factors, so that, for example, the influence of continent of

---

[38] *Ibid.*, pp. 39–42. The comparison can be extended by reference to the data presented by Simon Kuznets in "Quantitative Aspects of the Economic Growth of Nations VIII. Distribution of Income by Size," *Economic Development and Cultural Change*, XI (No. 2, part II, January 1963).

[39] This excludes the Communist nations; however, it is not certain that inequality is particularly low in these countries.

[40] Our rough calculation assumes that the average income of the excluded 30 per cent of the population is about three quarters of the average income of the survey population (based on the ratio of agricultural to other incomes). This is not a large enough difference to affect the share of the top decile very much.

origin would not be masked by the fact that a high proportion of those coming from Asia-Africa are relatively new immigrants. When these influences are taken into account, there still remain considerable unexplained income differentials arising from random and basic factors not measured, such as variations in ability.

To understand (and perhaps to try and change) the differentials in income, the multiple-factor analysis is important. But the essential social problem of income arises from the fact that the various factors add up in a particular way: new immigrants are to a great extent from Asia and Africa and have less education and a lower level of professional skills. It is thus the unadjusted data that are of most social significance. On the average, in 1956/57 urban wage and salary earners' families from Asia-Africa received only 73 per cent as much personal income as families from Europe-America.[41] Since families from Asia-Africa are usually much larger than those from Europe-America, the difference in per capita family income is even greater.

The study of income alone may exaggerate the inequality in the distribution of welfare between continent-of-origin or length-of-residence groups. One study has tried to divide the economy into a new immigrant sector and a veteran sector and to compare the share of each such sector in production and consumption for 1954.[42] This study found that in 1954 average per capita economic income (i.e., factor payments) of the new immigrant sector was only 0.58 that of the veteran sector, while the ratio of the two sectors in per capita total (including public) consumption was 0.73.[43] Thus, direct taxes, transfer payments, and the allocation of public consumption considerably diminished the inequality in the distribution of welfare between the two sectors, compared with what it is when calculated from the dispersion of economic income alone. We shall return to the effects of public finance on income distribution in Chapter 9.

Changes in income equality

Not much is known of the distribution of income in the pre-State period. As shown in Chapter 2, there were considerable variations in product per earner in the various branches, but there are no data

---

[41] Hanoch, *op. cit.*, p. 57, Table 4.

[42] M. Rosenberg, *The Measurement of the Economic Absorption of Israel's New Immigrant Sector from a National Point of View* (Jerusalem: The Hebrew University, 1958). "New immigrants" are those who arrived in the country after May 1948.

[43] Computed from *ibid.*, p. 21.

comparable to later surveys. There is a general presumption that there was a very high degree of income equality, based on the following considerations.[44] First, the Jewish population was too new to have developed the large income differentials associated with large property and capital holdings. Second, the nationalization of land purchases reduced the possibility of a rich land owning class developing. Third, socialist equalitarian doctrine was firmly rooted among much of the population. Lastly, high labor mobility, social and economic, and particularly the shift of immigrants with professions into other pursuits reduced income inequality.

The earliest data on income distribution in the State period come from the Family Expenditure Survey of 1950/51, which shows a remarkable degree of income equality. This was in part due to the fact that the sample was restricted to Jewish families in regular employment resident in eight towns, a relatively homogeneous population, so that this survey evidently understates the degree of inequality. Clearly, had the survey included the thousands of new immigrants in transit camps and other unemployed, the findings would have been different. Other data confirm that economic welfare was distributed fairly evenly in 1951. For example, it was found that the equality of distribution of food consumption was greater in 1951 than in 1943 and 1946.[45] But here the major factor is not personal or even disposable income, but rather how income could be used: this was a period of strict rationing whose purpose was equality of food consumption.

For the years after 1951 it is possible to compare only years for which sample surveys are consistent as regards definitions and coverage.[46] The following broad conclusions seem justified by the data shown in Table 42 and the sources on which they are based.

In general, income inequality has widened considerably, although Israel is still equalitarian by international standards. Inequality rose throughout the period, though more so in the first half of the 1950's than later. This rise in inequality is shown by the increasing proportions of income going to the upper 30 per cent of the population.[47] Not only

[44] Hanoch, op. cit., pp. 42–43.

[45] Sarah Bavly, Level of Nutrition in Israel, 1951 (Special Series No. 7B; Jerusalem: CBS, 1952).

[46] For example, the income distribution of Jewish urban employed persons can be compared for 1954, 1957/58, and 1963/64 or (by tax units) for 1957/58 and 1960/61. For Jewish urban employees, the comparison can be made for, e.g., 1954, 1957/58, and 1963/64. See Table 42.

[47] Both Ben-Shahar and Hanoch come to this conclusion.

TABLE 42.   *Measures of Income Inequality: Selected Years*

	Persons receiving less than average income		Deviation from full equality[a] (1)–(2)	Lorenz index	Difference index[b]
	Per cent of population (1)	Per cent share of income (2)	(3)	(4)	(5)
Employees and self-employed					
1954 urban families	60.8	39.7	21.1	0.293	0.234
1957/58 urban survey units	59.8	35.0	24.8	0.350	0.274
1963/64 urban survey units	61.3	34.8	26.5	0.369	0.294
1957/58 tax units[c]	59.0	33.2	25.8	0.357	0.280
1960/61 tax units	59.6	33.5	26.1	0.370	0.292
Employees					
1950/51 urban families with two or more members	54.3	41.5	12.8	0.183	0.144
1954 urban families	61.2	45.3	15.9	0.260	0.201
1956/57 urban families	60.0	42.0	18.0	0.255	0.200
1959/60 urban families	60.6	40.7	19.9	0.273	0.223
1963 urban families	60.2	39.4	20.8	0.288	0.231
1954 urban survey units	60.5	42.6	17.9	0.255	0.199
1957/58 urban survey units	61.0	39.2	21.8	0.306	0.241
1963/64 urban survey units	59.9	36.6	23.3	0.324	0.259
1957/58 tax units[d]	56.4	32.1	24.3	0.345	0.270
1960/61 tax units	55.6	29.5	26.1	0.368	0.291

[a] The per cent of income that has to be shifted to those receiving less than average income in order to achieve fully equal distribution.

[b] Calculated as: the sum of the absolute differences between the per cent of income received by each decile and the per cent of income under equal distribution (i.e., 10 per cent), *divided by* the maximum value that can be taken by this sum (i.e., when all income is concentrated in the upper decile).

[c] Employees in permanent employment and self-employed with files.

[d] Employees in permanent employment.

SOURCE: *Report of the Commission of Inquiry into the Distribution of National Income* (Jerusalem: 1966; Hebrew), p. 58, Table 14 (all employed persons); p. 86, Table 27 (employees).

did some sections of the population benefit less than others from the average rise in income, but for quite long periods the lower deciles of the population did not appear to gain at all. Thus, between 1950 and 1956, the real income of the lowest fifth did not increase at all, and between 1954 and 1957/58, the real income of the lowest two fifths did not increase.[48]

However, these figures must be interpreted with caution. It is quite possible that the lower deciles of 1956 were largely composed of families who in 1950/51 were in immigrant transit camps or were otherwise unemployed and thus excluded from the 1950/51 survey. Furthermore, the problem of comparing lower deciles in two periods would be conceptually questionable in Israel even if the surveys were absolutely representative. This is because large-scale immigration has changed the population between any two points in time. Thus it is theoretically possible for every single person to be better off in period II than in period I even if average per capita income has not changed. In other words, whereas in period II many people may not have attained the average income in Israel at period I, they may be much better off than they were in period I, before they came to Israel. Considering where most immigrants came from, this point is relevant for Israel.

These qualifications lead us to reject the conclusion that between 1950 and 1956 the general rise in welfare did not reach the lower fifth of the population. But the same qualifications do not apply as strongly to the 1954–1957/58 comparison. We therefore tend to accept the conclusion that during this period the poorer classes of the population did not benefit from the average rise in welfare.

The high degree of income equality in 1950/51 seems particularly strange considering the fact that sufficient mass immigration had already taken place to bring about a marked change in the composition of the labor force as regards skills and education. Of course, the limited nature of the survey excluded many of the new immigrants. In addition, some time had to pass before mass immigration could exert its full influence on relative wages. One of the conclusions of a study on the influence of mass immigration on wages is that the influx of relatively unskilled manpower gradually widened the gap between skilled and unskilled wages.[49] We have seen that income differentials are partly

---

[48] Hanoch, *op. cit.*, pp. 46, 50. The first comparison refers to wage and salary earners only, the second refers to total urban Jewish population.

[49] Uri Bahral, *The Effect of Mass Immigration on Wages in Israel* (Jerusalem: Falk Project, 1965).

explained by occupation, level of education, continent of origin, and period of immigration. Consequently, the widening of income inequality between 1950 and 1956 is in keeping with the fact that as time went on the population included an increasing proportion of new immigrants and of people coming from Asia and Africa, and that homogeneity of occupational skills and level of education declined.

Why does the trend to greater inequality in the distribution of income continue during the later period? Most of the changes in the composition of the population had taken place by 1953. One answer is that institutional factors lengthened the period during which income distribution adjusted to changes in the composition of the population. A second possibility is that the structure of the demand for labor changed. We shall examine these suggestions in later chapters.

Throughout, disposable income was distributed more equally than personal income. Furthermore, there are indications that direct taxes became more progressive between 1950 and 1956 and between 1954 and 1957/58, so that later in the period direct taxation has had a greater dampening effect on inequality.[50]

It has often been suggested that institutional restrictions on the use of disposable income may affect inequality of economic welfare. Thus, the least inequality in economic welfare obtained during the austerity period of 1950–51. Similarly, the increasing availability of luxury goods and services (refrigerators, automobiles, telephones, foreign travel) in recent years may have affected the welfare of the rich more than that of the poor.

The distribution of welfare was not very much affected by any differential price movements in the consumption of the various income groups, at least not between 1954 and 1962. If anything, there was a slight rise in the relative prices of goods consumed by the richer deciles.[51]

International comparisons of income distribution and time series studies have shown that in recent decades there has been a tendency for inequality to lessen in developed countries. Kuznets has suggested some reasons for this trend:[52] intersectoral inequality in product per

[50] Ben-Shahar, *op. cit.* See, however, some qualifications to this conclusion raised in Chapter 9.

[51] Michael Landsberger, "Changes in the Consumer Price Indices of Different Income, Origin, and Family-Size Groups, 1954–62," *Bank of Israel Bulletin,* No. 19 (July 1963), 65, Table 1.

[52] Kuznets, "Quantitative Aspects of the Economic Growth of Nations VIII," *op. cit.,* pp. 65–67.

worker has declined; the proportion of employees in the labor force has grown; property income has declined; and equalitarian ideas have spread and gained acceptance.

As explained in other chapters, the trends in the industrial distribution of product per worker and wages have been contrary to those cited by Kuznets. The concentration of land in the hands of the public sector reduces the role of property in contributing to income inequality, and changes in property income have been towards greater inequality. Finally, the equalitarian attitude was very widely held in Palestine; in recent years public opinion has changed considerably, away from the more extreme views of the earlier period. This shift has often been rationalized on economic grounds. It is thus not surprising that income inequality has increased in Israel contrary to international trends.

CHAPTER 7 CAPITAL AND PRODUCTIVITY

This chapter is an attempt to understand the causes of the exceptionally high rate of GDP growth. We shall first discuss total GDP and then agriculture and industry.

Of the various available measures of growth, we have chosen to base the discussion on GDP per employed person. This is a close approximation to per capita GNP, which we used as an indicator of the standard of living. The transition from per capita to per employed person entails examining the changes in the number of employed persons relative to total population, which reflect the combined effect of changes in labor force participation and unemployment. As can be seen in Table 43, the percentage of employed persons in the population rose between 1949 and 1951, reflecting both increased participation and reduced unemployment. Consequently, GDP grew faster per capita than per employed person. The converse holds for 1952–53, and since 1953, per capita GDP has grown slightly faster.

We make no attempt at a comprehensive analysis of the process of economic growth; instead, we discuss a number of factors selected as likely to be important for growth. Since GDP per employed person is

TABLE 43. *Employed Persons as Per Cent of Population: 1949–65*

1949	29.3	1955	32.8	1961	34.1
1950	33.1	1956	32.6	1962	34.4
1951	34.3	1957	33.3	1963	34.0
1952	33.8	1958	32.9	1964	34.4
1953	32.2	1959	32.8	1965	34.3
1954	32.8	1960	33.2		

Source: Employed persons—see sources to Table 13.
Population—*Abstract 1966*, No. 17, p. 20, Table B/1 (mean present population).

the dependent variable, the growth of other factors of production is of major importance. We shall concentrate on tangible capital and formal education, tracing their growth in relation to the supply of labor, and assessing their effect on GDP per employed person. We know little about other variables such as the rate and efficiency of factor use and effects of scale, and we therefore touch upon them only briefly.

PRODUCTIVITY TRENDS—TOTAL GROSS DOMESTIC PRODUCT

The growth of tangible capital [1]

The stock of gross reproducible capital, including dwellings and inventories, grew more than six times between 1950 and 1966 (Table 44), i.e., at an annual rate of 13.1 per cent—compared with 5.0 per cent for the employed labor force. As a result, the amount of capital per employed person [2] grew by 7.6 per cent annually (Table 45). This may be compared with 5.1 per cent in West Germany, 2.6 per cent in Canada, 2.2 per cent in Australia, and close to zero in the United States.[3] This relatively high rate of capital growth leads one to expect that Israel also has a relatively fast rate of product growth; this has indeed been found for per capita product.[4]

An estimate of how much of total product growth is accounted for by the growth of capital stock was in Israel first made by Gaathon, who assumes a homogeneous production function linear in logarithms of the Cobb-Douglas type.[5] The elasticity of aggregate product with

---

[1] This section relies heavily on data from A. L. Gaathon, *Economic Productivity in Israel: 1950–65* (Jerusalem: 1967; mimeograph). We take this opportunity to express our deep gratitude to Dr Gaathon for his generous help, not only in this chapter but in others as well.

[2] In the rest of this section the words "per employed person" are to be understood in all references to product or capital stock, unless "aggregate" or "total" are specifically mentioned. It should also be noted that the capital stock figures include dwellings, although for some purposes non-dwelling stock might be preferable; in any case, the rates of growth are similar.

[3] Gaathon, *op. cit.*, p. 4–10, Table 4–2 (growth rate of employed labor force), and p. 2–36, Table 2–10 (country data). The country comparison is in terms of net stock, but the net figure for Israel (7.8 per cent) does not differ much from the gross figure cited above.

[4] For example, *ibid.*, p. 5–41, Appendix Table V–2.

[5] The function is: $\dfrac{V_t}{L_t} = Q_t \left(\dfrac{C_t}{L_t}\right)^{\alpha}$

where t = index of time
V = GDP

TABLE 44.   *Gross Capital Stock: 1950–66*[a]

(millions of 1955 IL)

	Fixed capital		Stocks	Total
	Dwellings	Other[b]		
1950	861.7	1,285.6	155.6	2,302.9
1951	1,104.5	1,586.9	167.9	2,859.3
1952	1,388.1	1,956.3	179.6	3,524.0
1953	1,593.2	2,276.6	226.6	4,096.4
1954	1,755.6	2,548.8	257.3	4,561.7
1955	1,964.7	2,813.0	295.7	5,073.4
1956	2,202.8	3,143.6	366.5	5,712.9
1957	2,409.3	3,546.3	401.9	6,357.5
1958	2,662.1	3,969.6	435.2	7,066.9
1959	2,910.5	4,429.7	488.4	7,828.6
1960	3,186.6	4,938.4	550.2	8,675.2
1961	3,456.2	5,479.8	617.9	9,553.9
1962	3,784.7	6,156.1	686.4	10,627.2
1963	4,196.6	6,895.9	773.5	11,866.0
1964	4,595.1	7,648.0	841.0	13,084.1
1965	5,032.3	8,542.0	957.8	14,532.1
1966	5,474.5	9,377.4	987.2	15,839.1

[a] Beginning-of-year stock.
[b] Includes livestock.
SOURCE: A. L. Gaathon, *Economic Productivity in Israel: 1950–65* (Jerusalem: 1967; pre-publication draft), pp. 2–63, Appendix Table II–3.

respect to capital, α, is measured by the actual weight of capital returns in GDP at constant prices.[6] This elasticity measures the per cent increase in aggregate product resulting from an addition of 1 per cent to the aggregate capital stock; by the nature of the function, the elasticity is also α in per employed person terms. The effect of capital on

---

L = number of employed persons
C = stock of tangible capital
α = elasticity of product with respect to capital
Q = GDP growth not "explained" by capital growth.

[6] In a Cobb-Douglas function, and under conditions of perfect competition, the share of capital returns in the national income should equal the elasticity of product with respect to capital.

the growth of GDP is accordingly found by raising the index of capital growth to the power α,[7] the result being that part of product "explained" by the growth of tangible capital. By comparing this to actual product growth, we obtain the residual growth which is not "explained" by the additional capital.

TABLE 45.   The "Explanation" of Product Growth: 1950–65

(compounded annual average rates of growth,[a] per cent)

| | Product[b] | Capital[b] | "Explained" product growth[c] | | Ratio of actual product growth to "explained" growth | |
| | | | $\alpha=\frac{1}{2}$ | Actual weights | $\alpha=\frac{1}{2}$ $(1)\div(3)$ | Actual weights $(1)\div(4)$ |
	(1)	(2)	(3)	(4)	(5)	(6)
1950–65	5.6	7.6	3.7	2.2	1.51	2.55
1953–65	6.3	6.4	3.15	2.1	2.00	3.00
1950–55	6.4	10.2	5.0	2.3	1.28	2.78
1955–60	5.4	6.9	3.4	2.1	1.59	2.57
1960–65	5.1	5.8	2.9	2.1	1.76	2.43

[a] The dates are the first and last used in the computation: e.g., 1950–55 indicates the compounded average of five annual increases.
[b] Product during year, and beginning-of-year capital stock; both magnitudes are per employed person (annual average).
[c] Computed by raising the index of capital per employed person to the power α, i.e., as [column $(2)+100]^{\alpha}-100$.
In column (4) α is the unweighted arithmetic mean of the actual weight of capital returns in GDP at constant (1955) prices for the years covered by each calculation.
SOURCE: Computed from Gaathon, op. cit., p. 4–10, Table 4–2.

Table 45 summarizes these computations. Capital grew by 7.6 per cent annually during 1950–65; assuming elasticities based on actual factor shares, GDP should as a result have grown by 2.2 per cent annually. In fact, it grew much more rapidly, by 5.6 per cent, so that capital "explained" less than half the rate of product growth [column

[7] Using the notation of note 5, we have:
$$\frac{\left(\frac{V_{t+1}}{L_{t+1}}\right)}{\left(\frac{V_t}{L_t}\right)} = \left[\frac{\left(\frac{C_{t+1}}{L_{t+1}}\right)}{\left(\frac{C_t}{L_t}\right)}\right]^{\alpha}$$

(6)]. The figures for the sub-periods show that the annual rate of capital growth declined over the years, from 10.2 per cent in 1950–55 to 6.9 per cent in 1955–60 and 5.8 per cent in 1960–65. At the same time, the annual rate of product growth also declined, from 6.4 per cent in 1950–55 to 5.1 per cent in 1960–65.

An interesting question is whether, as growth rates declined, capital accumulation became more or less important in explaining product growth. When elasticity is measured by actual factor shares, it appears that capital accumulation became increasingly important [column (6)]: actual product growth was 2.8 times "explained" growth in 1950–55,[8] the ratio declining to 2.4 in 1960–65. This result is, however, entirely due to the assumption that elasticities equal actual factor shares. The share of capital returns in GDP increased over time, and using it as the basis of computation raises the effect of capital accumulation on product. The increase in the share of capital returns might have been due to institutional forces and not to any real change in the contribution of capital to production.[9] In that case, an alternative assumption might be that the elasticity of product with respect to capital was constant throughout the period covered. In addition, it is sometimes argued (see Chapter 11) that institutional forces reduced capital returns to below the level reflected by the real productivity of capital, even in recent years. Feeling that the elasticity estimate might be too low, Gaathon (in an earlier draft) used an alternative figure of ½ and held it constant throughout. We have retained this assumption and found that capital accumulation explains a much higher part of product growth than in the first computation. Also, because elasticity is held constant, its importance as an explanation of growth declines over time, and other factors become more important [column (5)]. The fact that slightly different assumptions produce contradictory results calls for further research.[10]

---

[8] The years 1950–55 were unusual, with suppressed inflation and mass immigration at the beginning, a recession afterwards, and a boom at the end. The data are also less reliable than for later years. As a result, the degree of "explanation" jumps wildly from year to year in this period.

[9] We shall return to this point later (Chapter 11).

[10] Another attempt to estimate the contribution of capital to growth has been made by Michael Bruno in "Factor Productivity and Remuneration in Israel 1952–1961," *The Economic Quarterly*, X (No. 37–38, March 1963; Hebrew), 41–56. His work differs in both scope and method: he investigates the private sector only, and fits a production function that differs from the Cobb-Douglas. He concludes that elasticity and the "explained" part of product fall

To summarize: The growth of tangible capital only partly explains the rapid growth of product: actual product growth was 1.5 to 2.5 times as fast as could have been expected as a result of capital accumulation only, the range being given by the different assumptions used for the computation. There is no clear answer to the question of whether the role of capital became more or less important over the period.

Other factors affecting product growth

One way of trying to explain that part of product growth not accounted for by the growth of tangible capital is to measure the growth of intangible or "human" capital. Such a measurement, confined to formal education, has recently been made by Baruh.[11] Representing the economic value of education by its 1957 cost at different grades, he constructed series of aggregate and per capita education capital for 1950–61 (Table 46). He concludes that the level of formal education declined until 1953 and that since then it has not risen significantly, so that no additional explanation of GDP growth can be found here. Two opposing trends operated during the period, and this explains why the level of education remained constant: the effect of the expanding local education system is masked by the lower educational level of new immigrants compared with the veteran population (see also pp. 72–75).

While the level of formal education does not help to explain the growth of GDP, other forms of intangible capital do seem to have grown. For example, knowledge of Hebrew grew substantially: in 1950 only 52 per cent of the adult (15+) population spoke Hebrew, but by 1961 the proportion had risen to 67 per cent.[12] Levels of health and nutrition also rose.

To these one may add vocational training, both on-the-job and at special centers. There are no consistent data that enable one to gauge how much these various forms of intangible investment contributed to economic growth. However, it is plausible that their role was important.

Another explantion of the "residual" product growth may lie in rising rates of input utilization. The computations of the preceding section assumed both a constant rate of utilization of capital and a constant average number of hours worked by the employed labor force. Both assumptions are unwarranted. It is probable that capital

---

somewhere between the two assumptions used above.

[11] Joseph Baruh, "Changes in the Quality of Labor Input in Israel, 1950–61," *Bank of Israel Bulletin,* No. 25 (April 1966), 32–43.

[12] *Abstract 1963,* No. 14, p. 664, Table 43.

is used more intensively when demand is strong; and there is no information about hours worked. One indicator of effective demand conditions is the unemployment rate, which declined from 1953 until 1964 (Table 14). The rise in effective demand might have led to more intensive use of capital, partly counteracting the decline in the rate of capital accumulation per employed person.

TABLE 46.   *Per Capita Educational Stock:*
1950–61[a]

(index, 1950 = 100)

1950	100.0
1951	94.7
1952	94.3
1953	94.3
1954	94.0
1955	93.1
1956	92.1
1957	92.4
1958	92.4
1959	92.3
1960	92.9
1961	93.3

[a] Per head of population aged 25–65.
SOURCE: Joseph Baruh, "Changes in the Quality of Labor Input in Israel, 1950–61," *Bank of Israel Bulletin,* No. 25 (April 1966), p. 34, Table 1.

To sum up: The level of formal education, which in other countries has been found to provide additional explanation, has not risen since the early 1950's and does not, therefore, help to explain product growth. Other forms of human capital are apparently more important, especially those connected with the process of integrating immigrants into society, such as knowledge of Hebrew, and standards of health: once immigration had slackened, integration proceeded faster than new immigrants were added to the population. Continuous demand pressures may also have intensified the utilization of both capital and labor. The explanation of the growth of product per employed person is on the whole still unsatisfactory. Variables such as changes in the quality of tangible and intangible capital, returns to scale, and changes in the efficiency of the pricing system in allocating resources have yet to be analyzed.

THE ALLOCATION OF TANGIBLE CAPITAL

The salient feature of the industrial composition of capital stock (Table 47) is the large share of dwellings, approximately 40 per cent. In recent years the share of dwellings in annual investment has dropped to around 30 per cent,[13] but the composition of the stock has not been affected much, owing to the long life-expectancy of the (comparatively young) stock of dwellings.

TABLE 47. *Industrial Composition of Fixed Capital Stock:*[a] *Selected Years, 1950–65*

(per cent)

	1950	1953	1955	1960	1965
Agriculture	19.6	15.0	14.3	14.1	11.3
Irrigation	6.5	6.3	7.3	5.9	5.6
Manufacturing and mining	13.2	14.6	14.6	15.2	15.8
Electricity	3.5	3.1	3.3	4.4	3.7
Transport[b]	9.9	11.4	10.8	10.7	13.0
Dwellings	40.1	41.2	41.1	39.2	37.1
Public services	3.6	5.2	5.6	8.0	10.6
Other services	3.6	3.2	3.0	2.5	2.9
Total	100.0	100.0	100.0	100.0	100.0

[a] Beginning-of-year stock.
[b] Includes oil pipelines.
SOURCE: Gaathon, *op. cit.*, Appendix Table II–3.

The high level of investment in residential building is primarily a consequence of immigration. Immigrant housing was provided chiefly by the public sector, but private building activity also was indirectly affected. Another contributory factor is the rise in per capita real income. The income elasticity for residential services has been estimated at about unity, which is fairly high.[14] Another indicator of the effect of income on the demand for housing is that average area per apartment more than doubled between 1950 and 1962, although there has been no significant change in average family size. Since per capita income has risen faster in Israel than in most other countries, and since the income elasticity of dwellings is relatively high, there is more building activity

[13] *Abstract 1966*, No. 17, p. 169, Table F/10.
[14] Nissan Liviatan, *Consumption Patterns in Israel* (Jerusalem: Falk Project, 1964), p. 15, Table 1.

in this country than elsewhere. Particularly important are the personal restitutions received from Germany; a high proportion of these receipts tended to be devoted to real estate, compared with regular incomes. Lastly, the continuous inflation led savers to prefer real estate to other ways of saving. Although immigration has declined, and the share of dwellings in annual investment has since 1960 been below the level of the 1950's, there appears to be no tendency for it to drop any further, to below 30 per cent.

The public services (including government and nonprofit institutions) have an increasing share of the capital stock. Together with transportation, power generation, and water supply, public services can be considered infra-structure capital. Their combined share of the total stock grew from 23.5 per cent in 1950 to 32.9 per cent in 1965. The rest of the capital stock (36 per cent in 1950 and 30 per cent in 1965) was in manufacturing, agriculture, and other services. The share of the agricultural stock has declined steadily since 1950, while that of manufacturing has risen. This shift has been the explicit policy of the government, at least since 1955 (Table 47).

It may be asked whether the shifts in investment were profitable, i.e., whether returns to capital in manufacturing are higher than in agriculture and dwellings. Bruno found that the average return to capital in the economy was 11.5 per cent in 1958. The highest return (37.5 per cent) was to private sector services; next came agriculture and construction (14.3 per cent and 19.5 per cent, respectively). Manufacturing had a return of 12.2 per cent, and, as could be expected, infrastructure investment brought a lower-than-average or even negative rate of return.[15] There is thus no clear connection between the rates of return and trends in investment. This probably reflects the prominent role of government in directing investment by undertaking it directly, as well as by financing private enterprises at preferred terms.

Returns to Capital and Interest Rates

The increase in capital per employed person was accompanied by an increase in returns to capital between 1955 and 1960, from 8.1 per cent to 9.6 per cent, and by a decrease thereafter, to 6.8 per cent in 1961 and 6.2 per cent in 1965 (Table 48).

---

[15] Michael Bruno, *Interdependence, Resource Use and Structural Change in Israel* (Special Studies No. 2; Jerusalem: Bank of Israel Research Department, 1962), p. 53, Table III–1. These figures are not comparable to those of Table 48.

Rates of return on own capital (at current prices) have been estimated only for manufacturing, and are considerably higher, ranging between 15 and 19 per cent; but they show a similar picture of a rise in the 1950's followed by a decline.

TABLE 48. *Returns to Capital: Selected Years, 1955–65*

(per cent)

| | Total non-dwelling stock | | Own capital[a] in manufacturing, current prices |
	Current prices	1955 prices	
1955	8.1	8.1	..
1958	9.0	..	16.3
1960	9.6	9.8	19.3
1962	7.3	..	15.9[b]
1964	6.8	..	15.2[b]
1965	6.2	6.8	..

[a] Excludes owners' loans.
[b] Excludes revaluation recorded by firms after 1962 tax year.
SOURCE: *Report of the Commission of Inquiry into the Distribution of National Income* (Jerusalem: 1966; Hebrew), p. 192, Table 83 (total stock); p. 193, Table 84 (total stock at 1955 prices); p. 195, Table 85 (manufacturing).

It would be useful to compare the nominal rate of profit in manufacturing with nominal interest rates on loans received by manufacturing enterprises; such a comparison would serve as a criterion of investment profitability. We do not have sufficiently complete data for the purpose and shall therefore confine ourselves to examining trends.

In contrast to the decline in nominal profit rates since 1960, there are indications that effective nominal interest rates (i.e., nominal rates on loans linked to the Consumers Price Index) rose. Thus, effective rates on loans to manufacturing out of the government development budget averaged 8.9 per cent in 1956–59 and 13.3 per cent in 1960–61 (Table 73).

A comparison of rates of return and interest rates for the whole economy involves double-counting, since interest is already included in the rate of return. The results are, however, similar to those found in manufacturing, i.e., rates of return have declined since 1960, and

interest rates, both nominal and real, have risen.[16] Effective interest
rates on development budget loans rose from 6.9 per cent in 1956–59
to 8.6 per cent in 1960–61.[17] Average nominal rates of interest on unlinked loans in commercial banks rose from 5.6 per cent in 1951 to
8.8 per cent in 1961.[18]

The data are not reliable enough to permit us to draw conclusions.[19]
Nevertheless, they do suggest that the rapid accumulation of capital
during the 1950's resulted in diminishing marginal returns to capital
and that interest rates operated to diminish the profitability of investment still further.

CAPITAL AND PRODUCTIVITY IN AGRICULTURE

Real product per employed person in agriculture was below average
throughout 1950–62: in 1950, it was 76 per cent of average, and in
1962 it was 99 per cent. By 1965, however, the figure had reached 108
per cent.[20] Two questions therefore arise: First, why was agricultural
product per employed person initially below average? Second, why did
it rise faster than average?

The low product per employed person at the beginning of the period
can perhaps be explained in terms of settlement policy and the structure of the labor force. Remote and arid districts were often settled
because of security considerations. No other branch was affected by
this policy to the same degree, since agriculture was considered the
most suitable vocation for settlers in development areas, at least until
the mid-1950's. Manpower for these areas was largely recruited from
newcomers to the country. As a result, one finds a concentration of
new immigrants in agriculture (Table 21). Most of the new settlements
were set up as cooperative villages (moshavim) relying on mixed
farming in which settlers were entrepreneurs rather than employees, so
that a relatively high level of technical competence was required.

Another reason for the low average product around 1950 is the inclusion of non-Jewish agriculture, whose productivity was much lower

[16] The similarity is significant only if the share of own-financing in total investment remains constant.

[17] See Table 73.

[18] Meir Heth, *Banking Institutions in Israel* (Jerusalem: Falk Institute, 1966),
p. 244, Table 84.

[19] See for example Bank of Israel, *Annual Report 1964*, p. 32, Table II–10, which
contradicts the data cited here.

[20] Gaathon, *op. cit.*, Appendix Tables I–1 and III–1. The ratios cited here are
calculated at constant prices.

than that of the Jewish sector; since non-Jewish employment is concentrated in agriculture, the branch is affected more than others.

Between 1950 and 1955 agricultural product per employed person grew at an annual rate of 5.4 per cent, compared with 6.4 per cent for the whole economy. This growth occurred in spite of the fact that tangible reproducible agricultural capital per employed person grew by only 5.9 per cent annually, compared with a country average of 10.2 per cent (Table 49).

TABLE 49.   *Capital Stock and Product per Employed Person, by Industry: 1950–65*[a]

(compounded annual rates of growth,[b] *per cent)*

	Total[c]	Agriculture and irrigation	Manufacturing and mining	Transport
A. Capital stock				
1950–65	7.6	6.4	7.6	10.0
1953–65	6.4	6.7	5.4	8.0
1950–55	10.2	5.9	12.2	12.6
1955–60	6.9	5.9	6.0	7.7
1960–65	5.8	7.6	4.8	9.7
B. Product				
1950–65	5.6	8.1	4.1	9.0
1953–65	6.3	8.9	6.0	9.3
1950–55	6.4	5.4	0.1	10.4
1955–60	5.4	11.1	5.7	9.3
1960–65	5.1	8.0	6.8	7.2

[a] Beginning-of-year stock, and average product and employed labor force.
[b] The dates are the first and last used in each computation, e.g., 1950–55 indicates the compounded average of five annual increases.
[c] Includes industries for which no rates are shown here.
SOURCE: Gaathon, *op. cit.*, p. 5–39, Appendix Table V–1.

Until 1954 cultivated land per employed person remained more or less constant.[21] The relatively rapid product growth cannot thus be explained by the growth of either reproducible capital or land. The considerable investment in planning, research, and guidance (mainly by the

[21] Yair Mundlak, *Long-Term Projections of Supply and Demand for Agricultural Products in Israel—I. General View and Summary* (Jerusalem: Falk Project, 1964), p. 51, Table 21.

Settlement Department of the Jewish Agency) may provide an explanation; no equivalent research and guidance services were set up in other industries. Unfortunately, there are no data on this type of investment.[22]

The 1950–55 investment trends continued in the next sub-period. Tangible capital (including irrigation) per employed person rose somewhat more slowly than the country average (5.9 per cent compared with 6.9 per cent). But unlike in the preceding period, product per employed person grew faster than average, and this was true also of 1960–65, when there were large-scale investments in agriculture and irrigation.

The figures cited above are all at constant prices. As a result of rising productivity and since demand grew more slowly than supply, agricultural relative prices declined by 23 per cent between 1954 and 1961,[23] and the decline has continued since.[24]

In order to maintain farm incomes, production quotas and subsidies were used. These measures, together with the rise in productivity, raised relative farm incomes, and by 1965 they were at about the average level. One solution to the problem of agricultural surpluses is to gradually reduce government intervention, thereby reducing the incentive to engage in agriculture.[25] This is difficult to carry out because of the feeling, based on social and security considerations, that the existing agricultural labor force should not be reduced. Another solution is to expand the export market.

In the last resort, agricultural production is limited by two factors—land and water—the latter being the more effective limitation. Total annual water resources are estimated at 1,500 million cubic meters (about 400,000 million U.S. gallons); at present, consumption is 1,250 million cubic meters, about 80 per cent of it in agriculture.[26] Any substantial rise in agricultural output must therefore be associated with more efficient use of existing water resources. The quantity of water

[22] Another factor raising productivity is the shift from dry farming to irrigation. The effect of increased water supply is, however, not included here, since our measurement relates to value added, with water deducted as an intermediate. Only investment in irrigation installations is included.

[23] Mundlak, *op. cit.*, p. 59, Table 24. The figure cited here is an index of agricultural production prices relative to GNP prices.

[24] F. Ginor, "Structural Changes in the Israeli Economy," *The Economic Quarterly*, XIII (No. 52, February 1967; Hebrew), 362.

[25] This question is discussed in Mundlak, *op. cit.*, pp. 13–19.

[26] A. Wiener and A. Wolman, "Water Policy in Israel," *Israel Economy: Theory and Practice*, ed. Joseph Ronen (Tel Aviv: Dvir, n.d.; Hebrew), pp. 349, 351.

input per unit of land has been declining since 1960,[27] rather because of more efficient water-use than because of changes in the composition of output. Water utilization can be further improved in the future by applying new methods of irrigation and possibly by using a different pricing system for water.[28]

Existing water resources can be augmented mainly through the desalination of sea water. Water produced by this method is very expensive and, owing to the surpluses and the need to subsidize agriculture, doubts have been cast on the profitability of desalination.

Productivity in Manufacturing

Product per person engaged in manufacturing was above average throughout the period, although the annual growth rate was slower: 4.1 per cent over 1950–65, compared with 8.1 per cent in agriculture, 9.0 per cent in transport, and 5.6 per cent for the total economy (Table 49, panel B).

Capital per employed person grew roughly at the country-average rate and faster than in agriculture (Table 49, panel A). The rate of capital accumulation cannot, therefore, explain the slower-than-average growth of manufacturing product. In the sub-periods, product grew more slowly than average until 1955, and faster from then on, while capital grew faster than average until 1955, and more slowly from then on (both in per employed person terms). As a result, the share of product growth not explained by capital accumulation was very small and has risen only since 1960.

One explanation of the slow rise in product per employed person is that, as stated, there is no well-organized training and research system comparable to that in agriculture. It is more difficult to set up such a system in manufacturing, since the branch is more diversified than agriculture and much less centrally planned.

Another explanation concerns the scale of industrial plants. In agriculture the typical production unit is the smallholding, whereas in manufacturing there is a tendency for new firms to be larger than existing ones: in the initial stages of production, and sometimes for quite long, capital is under-utilized. There is no direct evidence on

[27] Bank of Israel, *Annual Report 1965*, p. 246, Table XI–9.

[28] See Mundlak, *op. cit.*, pp. 18–19, where a discussion of the shortcomings of the present pricing system can be found. The main criticism is of the attempt to equalize water prices in all districts, although the cost of water varies in different parts of the country.

this point, but we may cite a confirmatory finding. Bruno [29] found a negative correlation in 1958 between capital per man-day and the rate of return in manufacturing sub-branches. This may indicate that capital is under-utilized in capital-intensive production. While the capital intensity of new investments is increasing, manufacturing productivity may thus not grow very fast. Manufacturing may also be more sensitive to demand conditions because of the existence of excess capacity: product per employed person may rise because of better utilization of capital in boom conditions, and vice versa. This may help to explain the rise in the proportion of "unexplained" product per employed person in recent years. That manufacturing is sensitive to demand is also suggested by preliminary data for 1966, a year of recession. Although agricultural productivity rose, there was no change in manufacturing productivity.

CONCLUSIONS

In this chapter we have tried to analyze the causes of the high rate of growth of GDP per employed person.

The most important single factor was the rapid accumulation of tangible capital made possible by the import surplus. According to various assumptions, the growth of the capital stock accounts for 40 to 65 per cent of the increase in product per employed person.

The question may be asked whether such intensive investment activity can be expected to continue. Two factors may slow it down: First, the import surplus may decline, so that investment will increasingly have to rely on finance out of local savings; second, there is some evidence that returns to capital declined in the last few years, while interest rates rose. It is therefore possible that capital per employed person will grow more slowly than it has hitherto done.

The level of formal education had not risen substantially by 1961, and cannot, therefore, explain GDP growth. It may, however, rise in the future: growing income differentials between persons at various educational levels indicate that returns to education are rising;[30] so are

---

[29] *Interdependence, Resource Use and Structural Change, op. cit.,* p. 102, Table IV–5. However, the results are biased, since capital is measured gross of depreciation, while net profit is used. See E. Kleiman, "Interdependence of the Production Process," *The Economic Quarterly,* X (No. 37–38, March 1963; Hebrew), 79–89.

[30] Ruth Klinov-Malul, *The Profitability of Investment in Education in Israel* (Jerusalem: Falk Institute, 1966), Chapter 4; and a forthcoming article (in Hebrew) on "Absorption of Immigrants and Income Differentials."

school attendance rates. The effect of immigration on the level of education is diminishing as immigration becomes smaller relative to the resident population; in addition, its composition may change.

The contribution of other forms of "human capital" is difficult to evaluate; nevertheless, it cannot be ignored. Some aspects, such as the acquisition of Hebrew by adult immigrants, are bound to become less important if immigration slows down. Others, such as vocational training and rising standards of health and nutrition, may continue to be important.

A third element in the growth of product may be the continuous inflation, which has increased the rate of factor utilization; again, its importance is not known.

In agriculture, product per employed person grew faster than the all-branch average, while capital grew more slowly. This may be due to the research and guidance system, which may continue to raise productivity. However, the growth of agricultural production has lowered relative prices and made farming unprofitable. As a result, a diminishing share of factor inputs is being allocated to agriculture. The contraction of inputs may be arrested if export markets are found. An increase in agricultural output depends on more water becoming available, either through more efficient utilization of existing resources, or, if agriculture becomes more profitable, by expanding the resources.

In manufacturing, product per employed person grew more slowly than the average, while capital per employed person grew at about the average rate. There may be two reasons for this slow growth: the absence of a research and guidance system such as exists for agriculture, and the under-utilization of existing plant capacity.

Lastly, we should mention the possible role of the pricing mechanism in raising productivity. Government intervention has been extensive, making use of quantitative restrictions and price controls, taxes and subsidies. If government intervention is reduced, productivity may rise owing to an improved allocation of factors of production. This will be discussed in Chapter 11.

CHAPTER **8** INTERNATIONAL
TRANSACTIONS

Since Israel became independent, and, except for several war years, during the mandatory period as well, imports have exceeded exports; thus, a persistent deficit in the current account of the balance of payments is a distinctive feature of the economy of Israel. The extent to which this import surplus increased total resources available to the economy was discussed in Chapter 6. It was there pointed out that the import surplus made possible a high level of capital formation in the absence of net domestic saving. The role of capital formation, and thus of the import surplus, in increasing output was considered in Chapter 7. In this chapter we shall consider the volume and composition of Israel's international trade, and the financing of the import surplus and some of its implications, especially for the country's economic dependence on the rest of the world.

TRADE IN GOODS AND SERVICES

The import surplus

Table 50 summarizes the annual balance of current international transactions from 1949 to 1965. Until 1958, merchandise imports were recorded at c.i.f.; since part of the insurance and freight was carried out by Israeli firms, a corresponding receipts item appeared on the export side, thus inflating both credit and debit. Panel A of the table presents these c.i.f. data for the whole period and panel B presents the corrected f.o.b. data that are available for the years since 1958.[1]

Both imports and exports grew throughout: over 1952–65, the average annual rate of growth was about 9.5 per cent for imports and around

---

[1] The estimation procedure for the balance of payments is under constant revision; any comparison over time is thus subject to error. However, the general procedure has been fairly consistent since 1952, and we therefore frequently use this year as the base for comparison.

TABLE 50. *Balance of Payments on Current Account: 1949–65*

($ millions)

	A		B		Net
	Credit	Debit	Credit	Debit	
1949	43	263			220
1950	45.8	327.6			281.8
1951	66.6	426.1			359.5
1952	86.4	393.2			306.8
1953	102.3	365.2			262.9
1954	135.2	373.2			238.0
1955	143.9	426.6			282.7
1956	177.9	534.5			356.6
1957	222.0	557.2			335.2
1958	235.4	569.4	216.9	550.9	334.0
1959	286.3	601.7	265.7	581.1	315.4
1960	359.1	695.8	336.3	673.0	336.7
1961	425.1	856.9	397.9	829.7	431.8
1962	503.2	957.8	471.8	926.4	454.6
1963	606.7	1,011.1	576.8	981.2	404.4
1964[a]	655.7	1,225.0	619.2	1,188.5	569.3
1965[a]	749.9	1,271.0	711.4	1,232.5	521.1

A: Imports recorded c.i.f., exports f.o.b.
B: Imports and exports recorded f.o.b.
[a] Services debit includes the expenditures abroad of the national institutions. See note 21 on p. 160.
SOURCES: 1949—Michael Michaely, *Foreign Trade and Capital Imports in Israel* (Tel Aviv: Am Oved, 1963; Hebrew), p. 58, Table 25.
 1950–54—Nadav Halevi, *Estimates of Israel's International Transactions: 1952–1954* (Jerusalem: Falk Project, 1956), as quoted in slightly corrected form by Don Patinkin, *The Israel Economy: The First Decade* (Jerusalem: Falk Project, 1960), p. 52, Table 16.
 1955–65 (A)—*Bulletin*, Part B (economic statistics), XVII (March 1966), 342 (for 1955–62); Bank of Israel, *Annual Report 1964*, p. 35, Table III–1 (for 1963), and *Annual Report 1965*, p. 39, Table III–3 (for 1964–65).
 1958–65 (B)—*Abstract 1963*, No. 14, p. 407, Table 1 (for 1959); *Abstract 1965*, No. 16, p. 223, Table H/1 (for 1958, 1960–61); *Bulletin* (March 1966), *loc. cit.* (for 1962–63); *Bulletin*, XVIII (March 1967), 48 (for 1964–65). Some of the figures from the *Abstracts* have been adjusted for minor corrections in later *Bulletins*.

18 per cent for exports.[2] This is a remarkable growth rate for exports, and their ratio to imports has risen from 22 per cent in 1952 to 59 per cent in 1965. However, the absolute difference between the two is still so large that the relatively faster growth of exports has not been sufficient to reduce the import surplus. Until 1956, large fluctuations in imports made for corresponding fluctuations in the import surplus, which ranged from $ 220 to $ 360 million. In 1957–60 the import surplus was more or less stable at around $ 330 million; subsequently it grew to a peak of $ 570 million in 1964, declining to $ 520 million in 1965.[3]

TABLE 51.   *Merchandise Imports by First Destination: 1949–65*

(per cent)

	Final consumer goods	Raw materials	Fuel	Final investment goods	Total
1949	31.7	40.1	6.0	22.2	100.0
1950	25.4	40.1	7.4	27.1	100.0
1951	24.9	43.7	9.2	22.2	100.0
1952	22.1	44.7	12.4	20.8	100.0
1953	20.3	48.8	10.7	20.2	100.0
1954	16.7	56.6	10.0	16.7	100.0
1955	14.8	56.5	10.3	18.4	100.0
1956	13.4	53.8	11.0	21.8	100.0
1957	12.1	53.4	12.1	22.4	100.0
1958	12.9	54.9	9.5	22.7	100.0
1958[a]	11.5	61.0	9.5	18.0	100.0
1959	9.5	65.0	8.1	17.4	100.0
1960	8.8	63.4	6.9	20.9	100.0
1961	7.7	61.1	5.8	25.4	100.0
1962	7.0	64.2	6.3	22.5	100.0
1963	8.6	63.8	6.6	21.0	100.0
1964	9.8	60.9	5.6	23.7	100.0
1965	10.1	61.9	6.4	21.6	100.0

[a] New classification. The principal change is that spare parts were reclassified as raw materials instead of as final investment goods.

SOURCE: CBS, *Israel's Foreign Trade 1965—Part I* (Special Series No. 201; Jerusalem: 1966), p. 26, Table 15.

[2] The figures cited here are in current dollars, and the growth rates therefore differ from those cited in Chapter 6.

[3] The increase in deficit in 1964 is somewhat overstated, because from 1964 the debit includes the expenditures abroad of the national institutions.

Imports

Israel imports a wide variety of goods. Table 51 shows the CBS classification of merchandise imports into final consumer and investment goods, fuel, and other intermediates. The share of final consumer goods declined steadily, from 32 per cent in 1949 and 22 per cent in 1952 to 10 per cent in 1965. Intermediates (including fuel) rose from 46 per cent in 1949 and 57 per cent in 1952 to 68 per cent in 1965, reflecting a deepening of production: the main branches of destination were food processing, construction, and textiles. The share of investment goods, generally from one fifth to one quarter, has not changed much over the period.

The three most important service categories are government n.e.s., transport, and investment income (Table 52).

Government n.e.s. includes imports that for various reasons are not classified in a more appropriate category, so that the item is in no way an accurate measure of total government imports. First of all, it includes the Ministry of Defence imports which do not pass through the customs. Other components are the expenditures of Israeli diplomatic and economic missions abroad, and the outlays on State of Israel Bond sales.

The main transport items are the operating expenses of Israeli ships and aircraft and passenger fares to foreign carriers (panel A of Table 52). When merchandise is recorded f.o.b., freight on foreign carriers is added (panel B of the table).

A steadily growing item is investment income on foreign loans and investments in Israel. In 1952, this came to only 3.3 per cent of total imports, compared with 8.3 per cent in 1965. The composition of the item has also changed: dividends and profits have risen from 12 per cent of investment income in 1952 to 21 per cent in 1963; however, this rise may in part reflect better coverage.

The weight of services in total imports was 32 per cent in 1958 and 41 per cent in 1965.[4] However, since defense imports appear in services, these figures are an overstatement; if the item government n.e.s. is shifted to merchandise, the figures come to 22 per cent and 30 per cent, respectively. This clearly errs in the opposite direction, so that the "true" share was between 30 and 40 per cent in 1965.

---

[4] It would be misleading to make this calculation for the years before 1958, when no estimates were made for merchandise imports f.o.b., i.e., some insurance and freight were included with merchandise.

TABLE 52. Imports of Services: 1949–65

($ millions)

	Transport	Insurance	Foreign travel	Investment income	Government n.e.s.	Miscellaneous	Total
A. C.i.f. recording of merchandise imports							
1949	4	a	3	1	13	–	21
1950	4	a	3	1	13	8	29
1951	..	17	2	1	8	18	46
1952	15.0	11.5	1.3	12.8	24.0	5.4	70.0
1953	16.9	12.9	1.6	18.9	27.0	6.0	83.3
1954	16.5	12.9	1.4	19.0	26.0	4.9	80.7
1955	16.9	11.9	2.2	20.3	38.1	3.7	93.1
1956	25.2	13.8	2.1	25.6	95.4	5.4	167.5
1957	30.1	16.0	2.8	28.1	43.6	4.5	125.1
1958	33.5	18.2	3.2	33.3	55.7	7.7	151.6
1959	39.3	18.7	6.9	41.3	55.7	13.4	175.3
1960	44.2	22.4	11.4	51.2	57.5	18.3	205.0
1961	53.7	29.4	18.3	64.7	93.0	23.6	282.7
1962	68.7	27.9	26.0	69.5	113.8	38.1	344.0
1963	70.6	31.1	38.0	71.8	105.7	46.4	363.6
1964b	83.1	41.0	37.3	93.8	98.6	67.8	421.6
1965b	91.1	45.4	43.8	105.5	130.7	57.2	473.7

B. F.o.b. recording of merchandise imports

1958	57.9	20.3	3.2	33.3	55.7	7.7	178.1
1959	63.3	20.7	6.9	41.3	55.7	13.4	201.3
1960	60.7	23.6	11.4	51.2	57.5	18.3	222.7
1961	77.1	31.8	18.3	64.7	93.0	23.6	308.5
1962	88.8	30.4	26.0	69.5	113.8	38.1	366.6
1963	87.4	34.2	38.0	71.8	105.7	46.4	383.5
1964[b]	104.8	44.6	37.3	93.8	98.6	67.8	446.9
1965[b]	113.8	48.5	43.8	105.5	130.7	57.2	499.5

[a] Included in transport.
[b] Includes expenditures abroad of national institutions.

SOURCES: 1949—Michaely, *op. cit.*, fold-in Appendix.
1950—Halevi, *op. cit.*, p. 92, Table 12 (foreign travel); p. 133, Table A1 (other items).
1951—*Ibid.*, p. 92, Table 12 (foreign travel); p. 100, Table 14 (insurance); p. 133, Table A1 (other items).
1952–54—*Ibid.*, p. 26, Table 1.
1955–57—Michael Klibanski, *Balance of Payments of Israel (1957–1958)* (Special Series No. 89; Jerusalem: CBS, 1959).
1958–65 (c.i.f. recording):
1958—Bank of Israel, *Annual Report 1959*, p. 37, Table III-11.
1959–61—Bank of Israel, *Annual Report 1963*, p. 44, Table III-12 (with small correction made to 1959 figures on basis of later CBS information).
1962–63—Bank of Israel, *Annual Report 1964*, p. 42, Table III-5. This source differs from the next in that the figures have not been adjusted for national institutions expenditures abroad; see note b.
1964–65—Bank of Israel, *Annual Report 1965*, p. 47, Table III-6.
1958–65 (f.o.b. recording):
Abstracts—*1959/60*, No. 11, p. 258, Table 1 (for 1958); *1961*, No. 12, p. 302, Table 1 (for 1959); *1962*, No. 13, p. 322, Table 1 (for 1960); *1963*, No. 14, p. 408, Table 2 (for 1961); *1964*, No. 15, p. 184, Table H/2 (for 1962); *1965*, No. 16, p. 224, Table H/2 (for 1963); *1966*, No. 17, p. 218, Table H/2 (for 1964–65).

The data in this table are consistent with those of Table 50, derived in some cases from more up-to-date but less detailed published figures. In particular, minor adjustments have been made to the 1958 and 1959 data taken from the *Abstracts* listed above.

Total demand for imports depends on, *inter alia,* the import components of the various sectors of the economy, as well as the share of
each sector in total resource use. Data on import components in 1958–63
are shown in panel A of Table 53. These constant-price figures [5] suggest
that the import component of exports and public consumption rose from
1958 to 1962, while that of private consumption and investment remained constant. Owing to the method of computation, the data do
not reflect changes in the technical requirements of the branches within
each sector, but only changes in the share of each branch.[6] Thus, the
rise in the import component during 1958–62 reflects a shift of demand
to import-intensive products.

TABLE 53.   *The Import Component of Final Uses: 1958–64*

(per cent)

	Consumption		Gross investment	Exports	Total[a]
	Private	*Public*			
A. At 1963 prices					
1958	20.6	23.3	34.2	39.1	26.1
1959	20.8	24.0	29.4	39.7	25.5
1960	21.3	22.4	34.6	36.4	26.4
1961	22.1	29.2	34.8	42.8	29.0
1962	21.4	32.3	32.4	45.8	29.3
1963	21.4	28.3	31.8	41.7	28.0
B. At 1964 prices					
1962	21.1	32.6	31.2	43.9	28.6
1963	22.1	31.7	32.8	43.1	29.2
1964	22.0	29.8	33.6	44.9	29.3

[a] Excluding changes in inventories.
SOURCES: A.   Bank of Israel, *Annual Report 1963,* p. 26, Table II–8.
             B.   Bank of Israel, *Annual Report 1964,* p. 17, Table II–4.

Both the import component of exports and their weight in total uses
rose, while the weight of private consumption (whose import component

[5] It would be interesting to compare this series with current-price data; unfortunately, no comparable series is available.
[6] See Bank of Israel, *Annual Report 1962,* pp. 20–27, and *Annual Report 1963,*
pp. 22–27, where these data are discussed. Import components were calculated
on the basis of fixed technical coefficients in 80 branches. The figures in panel
A of Table 53 use fixed 1958 coefficients, while panel B uses fixed 1962
coefficients.

remained constant) declined, thus raising the average import component. The same pattern is reflected in the composition of imports during the period: the share of imports for exports rose, while that of imports for private consumption declined.

More up-to-date figures on the import component exist for 1962–64; these are shown in panel B of Table 53. It seems that during 1963 and 1964 there was no significant shift away from import-intensive products.

The year 1948 marks a major break in the regional pattern of trade. The Middle East, which had supplied about 15 per cent of the country's imports in the 1930's,[7] severed relations with Israel. The share of imports from the United Kingdom also declined in the early 1950's, and the United States emerged as a major supplier, providing (together with Canada) from 28 to 45 per cent of Israel's merchandise imports.[8] Part of this increase reflects the fact that some of the United States grants and loans, which were a major source of import financing until 1954, stipulated that the goods be purchased in the United States. After 1954, the United States share declined, while the share of Western Europe rose from about 25 per cent in 1949–50 to about 45 per cent in 1954–61, thereafter declining to 35–40 per cent. This reflects the growth and subsequent decline of German reparations in the financing of imports. The share of the United Kingdom, which in 1949–50 was below what it had been in the mandatory period, rose gradually to about 20 per cent of imports in recent years.

The general regional pattern of trade in goods and services remained more or less constant from 1958 on (Appendix Table 7). The OECD area provides about 40 per cent of imports, the dollar area about 30 per cent, and the sterling area between 15 and 20 per cent.

The regional pattern of import suppliers was also affected by changes in trade agreement policy. Clearing agreements were widespread in the early 1950's; they provided for imports to be paid for in exports rather than in foreign currency and were thus helpful at a time of hard-currency shortage, both to Israel and to the countries concerned; moreover, the agreements facilitated the transfer of goods by immigrants and investors from certain countries. Both these factors became less important after 1955, and the share of goods imported under clearing

---

[7] Michael Michaely, *Foreign Trade and Capital Imports in Israel* (Tel Aviv: Am Oved, 1963; Hebrew), p. 17, Table 8. During World War II, the Middle East supplied over half of Palestine's imports.

[8] Appendix Table 6 shows the geographic pattern of merchandise trade; Appendix Table 7 shows an alternative regional breakdown for total imports in 1958–65.

TABLE 54.   *Merchandise Exports*[a] *—Total Revenue and Value Added: 1953-65*

($ millions)

	Total revenue				Value added				Value added as per cent of total revenue			
	Agricultural products	Diamonds	Other industrial products	Total	Agricultural products	Diamonds	Other industrial products	Total	Agricultural products	Diamonds	Other industrial products	Total
1953	19.7	12.7	24.1	56.5	11.9	1.8	8.5	22.2	60	14	35	39
1954	35.6	15.6	36.6	87.8	24.9	2.2	15.7	42.8	70	14	43	49
1955	34.1	20.6	32.8	87.5	23.9	3.5	12.1	39.5	70	17	37	45
1956	44.3	24.7	36.7	105.7	32.3	4.7	16.5	53.5	73	19	45	51
1957	54.4	32.7	49.3	136.4	40.3	6.2	22.7	69.2	74	19	46	51
1958	56.8	34.3	47.1	138.2	40.9	6.9	22.1	69.9	72	20	47	51
1959	57.9	46.8	70.2	174.9	40.5	9.8	31.6	81.9	70	21	45	47
1960	63.2	56.4	89.0	208.6	43.0	12.4	43.6	99.0	68	22	49	47
1961	62.9	65.3	103.1	231.3	40.3	14.4	50.7	105.4	64	22	49	45
1962	68.4	82.6	120.4	271.4	46.5	18.2	57.8	122.5	68	22	48	45
1962[b]	68.4	82.6	120.4	271.4	54.1	15.4	66.3	135.8	79	19	55	50
1963	89.0	104.0	144.1	337.1	73.8	20.3	77.4	171.5	83	20	54	51
1964	67.0	118.2	164.2	349.4	51.5	24.7	87.1	163.3	77	21	53	47
1965	86.8	131.7	184.9	403.4	69.6	30.2	106.9	206.7	80	23	59	51

[a] F.o.b.

[b] From 1962 value added is calculated by a different method. In addition, total revenue figures include resale of ships and aircraft (no value added) of (in $ million) 0.8, 1.0, 2.9 and 3.7 in 1962 through 1965, respectively.

SOURCES: 1953–59—Michaely, *op. cit.*, p. 70, Table 33.
1960—Bank of Israel, *Annual Report 1961*, p. 36, Table III–7.
1961—Bank of Israel, *Annual Report 1962*, p. 42, Table III–7.
1962–65—Bank of Israel, *Annual Report 1965*, p. 56, Table III–11. The value added for 1962 (old series) is computed from the percentages in *Annual Report 1962*, *loc. cit.*

agreements fell from its 1955 peak of 19 per cent to 4 per cent in 1962.[9]

Exports

The composition of commodity exports can be evaluated either in terms of total receipts or in terms of foreign exchange value added. The latter represents net receipts after the deduction of the direct and indirect import component (including imported services).

In terms of total receipts the main export commodities are citrus and polished diamonds. Their combined share was over 80 per cent in 1949;[10] since then exports have become more diversified, but these two products still account for at least half of total merchandise exports. The shift has been away from citrus, with diamonds and other industrial exports both increasing their share (Table 55).

In terms of value added, these trends meant a shift away from high-value-added to low-value-added products (Table 54). This is because the weight of citrus, with a value added of over 80 per cent, is declining, while diamonds (20 per cent) and other industrial exports (about 50 per cent) have increased their shares. Altogether, there is a decline in average value added, whose counterpart—the rise in import component —was discussed above (pp. 146–47).[11]

This trend can be expected to continue, since industrial exports will go on increasing their share, and since agricultural products with a lower value added will probably rise faster than citrus. A possible decline in citrus prices may also lower value added. The value added of exports will therefore continue to grow more slowly than total receipts.

In recent years the weight of services in total exports has risen from 36 per cent in 1958 to 43 per cent in 1965 (Table 56, panel B).

The principal services item is transport, receipts from which came to $ 113 million in 1965. Two other items that have become important are tourism (foreign travel) and investment income. Tourism receipts began to increase rapidly in 1958, and jumped from $ 5.5 million in 1957 to $ 53 million in 1963; in 1964 and 1965, however, they hardly rose.[12] Investment income, which reached $ 37 million in 1965, has

---

[9] Michaely, *op. cit.*, p. 121, Table 47 (for 1955), and Bank of Israel, *Annual Report 1962*, p. 45, Table III–11 (for 1962).

[10] *Abstract 1964*, No. 15, p. 218, Table I/6.

[11] The general trend does not seem to be affected by the fact that constant-price data were used in the earlier discussion, while the data here (Table 54) are in current prices.

[12] Some of the increase in transport receipts reflect increased tourist travel on

TABLE 55. Merchandise Exports—Total Revenue and Value Added: 1953-65

(per cent)

	Total revenue				Value added			
	Agricultural products	Diamonds	Other industrial products	Total	Agricultural products	Diamonds	Other industrial products	Total
1953	34.8	22.5	42.7	100.0	53.6	8.1	38.3	100.0
1954	40.5	17.8	41.7	100.0	58.2	5.1	36.7	100.0
1955	39.0	23.5	37.5	100.0	60.5	8.9	30.6	100.0
1956	41.9	23.4	34.7	100.0	60.4	8.8	30.8	100.0
1957	39.9	24.0	36.1	100.0	58.2	9.0	32.8	100.0
1958	41.1	24.8	34.1	100.0	58.5	9.9	31.6	100.0
1959	33.1	26.8	40.1	100.0	49.4	12.0	38.6	100.0
1960	30.3	27.0	42.7	100.0	43.4	12.5	44.1	100.0
1961	27.2	28.2	44.6	100.0	38.2	13.7	48.1	100.0
1962	25.2	30.4	44.4	100.0	38.0	14.8	47.2	100.0
1962[a]	25.2	30.4	44.4	100.0	39.8	11.3	48.9	100.0
1963	26.4	30.9	42.7	100.0	44.3	11.0	44.7	100.0
1964	19.2	33.8	47.0	100.0	32.6	12.9	54.5	100.0
1965	21.5	32.6	45.9	100.0	33.7	14.6	51.7	100.0

[a] New series. See note b to Table 54.
SOURCE: Table 54.

increased mainly as a result of the considerable growth of foreign exchange reserves.

It is estimated that the value added of tourism is 75 per cent of total receipts, and in shipping it has been estimated at 15 to 18 per cent. Average value added for services was estimated at 67 per cent in 1965.[13]

During the mandatory period most exports went to the United Kingdom and the Middle East.[14] After 1948, the Middle East ceased to be a market for Israeli exports, and the United States emerged as an important customer; the United Kingdom share gradually declined, while the Western European rose (Appendix Tables 6 and 8).

The increasing importance of Western Europe as a purchaser of Israeli exports is in part connected with the development of commercial relations with West Germany, as a result of the Reparations Agreement. It also reflects the rise in industrial exports and the growing share of Western Europe in citrus exports. The United States is still the biggest market for industrial diamonds and tourism.

The mere fact that a product is exported generally indicates that the transaction is profitable for the exporter. Whether it is profitable for the economy as a whole is another matter. The divergence between input or output prices to the individual and to the economy is the central issue in any discussion of the subject. In Israel, the divergence has been most marked in the case of foreign currency—as a result of foreign exchange control (discussed in Chapter 10)—and it is therefore necessary to resort to an indirect calculation of its real social cost. An attempt to estimate the social cost per dollar of value added has been made by Bruno.[15] He found marked differences in the cost per value added dollar both within and between the major export categories. In 1958 the average cost per dollar of agricultural products (IL 1.57/$ 1) and of diamonds (IL 1.73/$ 1) were both below the

---

Israeli carriers; this does not affect the foreign travel item which consists of tourist expenditures in the country.

[13] The figure for tourism is from Y. Halperin, "Valued Added in Tourism in 1961" (unpublished seminar paper, The Hebrew University; Hebrew). The figures for shipping are based on Emil Erdreich, *The Israel Merchant Marine: An Economic Appraisal* (Jerusalem: Bank of Israel Research Department, 1962), p. 48, Table 25. For total services see Bank of Israel, *Annual Report 1965*, p. 56, Table III-1.

[14] Michaely, *op. cit.*, p. 17, Table 8.

[15] Michael Bruno, *Interdependence, Resource Use and Structural Change in Israel* (Special Studies No. 2; Jerusalem: Bank of Israel Research Department, 1962), pp. 104–14.

Table 56. Exports of Services: 1949–65

($ millions)

	Transport	Insurance	Foreign travel	Investment income	Government n.e.s.	Miscellaneous	Total
A. C.i.f. recording of merchandise imports							
1949	3	a	6	–	4	–	13
1950	4	a	4	–	3	–	11
1951	..	14.9	4.9	–	2	–	21.8
1952	24.0	10.2	4.0	0.9	2.4	0.4	41.9
1953	24.9	11.7	4.9	2.5	1.3	0.4	45.7
1954	23.8	11.7	4.9	2.3	1.3	3.4	47.4
1955	26.9	10.9	7.3	1.7	3.1	5.1	55.0
1956	32.8	11.0	6.4	4.4	5.3	8.3	68.2
1957	45.9	14.2	5.5	3.6	4.9	7.1	81.2
1958	53.1	15.8	12.2	4.9	2.3	7.3	95.6
1959	60.0	18.0	16.2	5.6	2.3	7.7	109.8
1960	70.7	22.0	26.9	7.7	6.4	15.1	148.8
1961	90.3	27.6	30.3	13.1	7.5	17.8	186.6

1962	116.4	26.9	38.4	21.3	10.4	18.4	231.8
1963	114.8	30.6	53.4	26.3	15.2	29.3	269.6
1964	126.5	42.8	54.8	28.7	21.1	32.4	306.3
1965	150.1	46.4	55.5	36.8	20.8	36.9	346.5

B. F.o.b. recording of merchandise imports

1958	35.5	14.9	12.2	4.9	2.3	7.3	77.1
1959	40.4	17.0	16.2	5.6	2.3	7.7	89.2
1960	49.3	20.6	26.9	7.7	6.4	15.1	126.0
1961	64.7	26.0	30.3	13.1	7.5	17.8	159.4
1962	86.3	25.6	38.4	21.3	10.4	18.4	200.4
1963	86.2	29.3	53.4	26.3	15.2	29.3	239.7
1964	91.5	41.3	54.8	28.7	21.1	32.4	269.8
1965	113.2	44.8	55.5	36.8	20.8	36.9	308.0

ᵃ Included in transport.

SOURCES: 1949–57—as for services imports in Table 52.
1958–65 (c.i.f. recording):
1958—Bank of Israel, *Annual Report 1959*, p. 34, Table III–7.
1950–61—Bank of Israel, *Annual Report 1963*, p. 41, Table III–9 (with small correction made to 1959 figures on basis of later CBS information).
1962–65—Bank of Israel, *Annual Report 1965*, p. 54, Table III–10.
1958–65 (f.o.b. recording)—as for services imports in Table 52.

average for total exports (IL 2.04/$ 1) and below the official IL 1.8/$ 1 exchange rate, while the cost of other industrial exports (IL 3.58/$ 1) and transport (IL 4.27/$ 1) was much higher. It thus appears that the two main export commodities, citrus and diamonds, had the greatest comparative advantage from the economy's viewpoint. However, it would be wrong to assume that exports were always encouraged to develop according to their real social cost per dollar value added. For example, textile exports, whose cost was over IL 4/$ 1 in 1958, expanded much faster than other industrial exports.[16]

It might be of interest to note also that in 1958 there was a negative correlation between the per cent of value added in total dollar receipts and the cost of the value added dollar. In other words, a high import component tended to go with a high cost per dollar value added.[17]

FINANCING THE IMPORT SURPLUS

By definition, the existence of a deficit in the current account of the balance of payments implies that there were funds to finance it. The way in which the deficit is financed is as important as its size for an analysis of a country's balance of payments.

Perhaps the most useful breakdown of the sources that finance the import surplus (often referred to as capital inflow or capital imports) is into unilateral transfers and capital transfers. Here the basic distinction is whether or not the transfer involves a transaction in financial claims (e.g., whether an inflow increases the country's indebtedness). Several subdivisions are possible: transfers may be classified by source, e.g., governments, institutions or private, or by recipient, in the same categories; various conditions are often imposed, as when funds may be used for purchases only in the donor country, and such conditions may also serve to classify the flows.

In addition to these criteria, useful for both unilateral and capital transfers, there are various distinctions that apply only to the latter. The most important are: assets or liabilities, loans or equity capital, and long-term or short-term.

---

[16] *Ibid.*, p. 110, Table IV–18. It has, however, been argued that in a rapidly expanding economy there is some danger in using current cost per dollar value added as the sole indicator of profitability; see E. Gusman and M. Mandelbaum, "On M. Bruno's Book," *The Economic Quarterly*, X (No. 37–38, March 1963; Hebrew), 142–47.

[17] Computed from Bruno, *op. cit.*, p. 111, Table IV–19. The correlation coefficient (unweighted by size of exports) for cost and value added percentage of the 18 groups shown in this source is –0.6, significant at 1 per cent.

TABLE 57. Financing the Import Surplus: 1949–65

	Import surplus	Net unilateral transfers	Net capital transfers[a]			Net unilateral transfers	Net capital transfers		
			Total	Long term	Short term		Total	Long term	Short term
	$ millions[a]					Per cent of import surplus[a]			
1949	220	118	67	43	24	53.6	30.5	19.6	10.9
1950	282	90	119	68	51	31.9	42.2	24.1	18.1
1951	359	137	165	133	32	38.2	45.9	37.0	8.9
1952	307	191	116	115	1	62.2	37.8	37.4	0.4
1953	263	173	75	69	6	65.8	28.5	26.2	2.3
1954	238	261	1	71	-70	109.7	0.4	29.8	-29.4
1955	283	210	76	76	0	74.2	26.9	26.9	0.0
1956	357	241	100	78	22	67.5	28.0	21.8	6.2
1957	335	245	79	70	9	73.1	23.6	20.9	2.7
1958	334	264	66	67	-1	79.0	19.8	20.1	-0.3
1959	315	251	55	80	-25	79.7	17.5	25.4	-7.9
1960	337	311	41	101	-60	92.3	12.2	30.0	-17.8
1961	432	346	104	176	-72	80.1	24.1	40.8	-16.7
1962	455	331	98	203	-105	72.8	21.5	44.6	-23.1
1963	404	347	73	171	-98	85.9	18.1	42.3	-24.2
1964	569	351	227	275	-48	61.7	39.9	48.3	-8.4
1965	521	341	219	248	-29	65.5	42.0	47.6	-5.6
Total 1949–65	6,011	4,208	1,681	2,044	-363	70.0	28.0	34.0	-6.0

[a] Errors and omissions are not shown so that capital imports do not equal import surplus, and the percentages do not add to 100.

SOURCE: Import surplus, Table 50; unilateral transfers, Appendix Table 9; and capital transfers, Appendix Table 10.

TABLE 58.   Institutional Sources of Net Balance-of-Payments Finance: 1949–65

(per cent)

	Unilateral transfers				Long-term capital			Unilateral transfers and long-term capital			
	Govern-ment	Institu-tional	Private	Total	Govern-ment	Private	Total	Govern-ment	Institu-tional	Private	Total
1949	—	69.5	30.5	100.0	41.9	58.1	100.0	11.2	50.9	37.9	100.0
1950	—	77.8	22.2	100.0	69.1	30.9	100.0	29.7	44.3	26.0	100.0
1951	10.2	61.3	28.5	100.0	68.4	31.6	100.0	38.9	31.1	30.0	100.0
1952	45.2	46.5[a]	8.3	100.0	67.7	32.3	100.0	53.6	29.1	17.3	100.0
1953	51.0	43.1[a]	5.9	100.0	66.4	33.6	100.0	55.4	30.7	13.9	100.0
1954	48.9	45.0[a]	6.1	100.0	71.6	28.4	100.0	53.8	35.4	10.8	100.0
1955	60.5	22.9	16.6	100.0	84.1	15.9	100.0	66.8	16.8	16.4	100.0
1956	46.6	38.6	14.8	100.0	92.0	8.0	100.0	57.7	29.1	13.2	100.0
1957	60.1	25.0	14.9	100.0	79.3	20.7	100.0	64.3	19.5	16.2	100.0
1958	57.6	28.5	13.9	100.0	63.4	36.6	100.0	58.8	22.7	18.5	100.0
1959	58.5	29.3	12.2	100.0	70.9	29.1	100.0	61.5	22.2	16.3	100.0
1960	60.3	27.9	11.8	100.0	39.8	60.2	100.0	55.3	21.0	23.7	100.0
1961	60.4	26.6	13.0	100.0	51.6	48.4	100.0	57.5	17.6	24.9	100.0
1962	57.1	22.3	20.6	100.0	62.0	38.0	100.0	59.0	13.8	27.2	100.0
1963	50.0	23.9	26.1	100.0	29.1	70.9	100.0	43.1	16.0	40.9	100.0
1964	45.4	27.3	27.3	100.0	34.2	65.8	100.0	40.5	15.3	44.2	100.0
1965	39.4	31.5	29.1	100.0	54.8	45.2	100.0	45.9	18.2	35.9	100.0

[a] Includes personal gifts, so that the item is somewhat overstated.
SOURCE: Appendix Tables 9 and 10.

A second approach is to distinguish between the various capital inflows not strictly according as they do or do not give rise to financial claims, but by their source. It may be useful to classify most of Israel's capital inflow as coming from world Jewry, the United States government, or the West German government. In some contexts, from the point of view of both recipient and donor, the form of the financial claim accompanying economic assistance may be of secondary importance.

Estimates of unilateral transfers are presented in Appendix Table 9, and of capital transfers in Appendix Table 10; both tables are in standard balance-of-payments form, and make several of the distinctions discussed above.

Table 57 shows how the current account deficit was financed. The tremendous size of unilateral transfers is immediately noticeable both in absolute numbers and relative to import surplus. This is true for the whole period as well as for almost every single year: net unilateral transfers fell below 62 per cent of the import surplus in only one year since 1952. For the whole of 1949–65, unilateral transfers financed 70 per cent of the cumulated import surplus. The remainder is financed by either long-term or short-term capital movements. Net short-term movements were small on the whole, and on balance they were negative, i.e., foreign currency reserves increased. But short-term capital played a much greater role in some years: in 1949 and 1950 they financed 11 to 18 per cent of the deficit, primarily by depleting sterling balances abroad; since 1959, other inflows have exceeded the deficit enough to make possible substantial increases in net short-term assets.

Table 58 classifies capital inflow by institutional source: government, institutions, and private. The dominant role of government and institutions is obvious, and in sharp contrast with the mandatory period. The share of private sources is much greater in capital than in unilateral transfers, but in recent years it has been growing in both.

Classifying by recipient would not change the general picture of predominantly government and institutional finance. The chief difference is that State of Israel Bonds would come under government and restitutions would be in the private category.

The long-term capital inflow by main source (world Jewry,[18] United States government economic assistance, and West Germany) is shown in Appendix Table 11. The important role of world Jewry stands out:

---

[18] Several items have been arbitrarily and in some cases inexactly allocated to "world Jewry." It is unlikely that the tenor of this discussion would be much affected by a more accurate classification.

TABLE 59. Principal Sources of Unilateral Transfers and Long-Term Capital: 1949-65ᵃ

(per cent)

	Unilateral transfersᵇ			Long-term capitalᶜ		Unilateral transfers and long-term capital as per cent of import surplus		
	World Jewry	U.S. government	German government	World Jewry	U.S. government	World Jewry	U.S. government	German government
	(1)	(2)	(3)	(4)	(5)	(6)	(7)	(8)
1949	100.0	—	—	58.1	41.9	65.0	8.2	—
1950	100.0	—	—	30.9	65.3	39.4	15.7	—
1951	89.8	10.2	—	73.0	20.8	61.2	11.6	—
1952	54.8	45.0	—	70.9	23.9	60.7	37.0	—
1953	49.0	27.1	23.7	94.0	6.3	57.0	19.5	15.6
1954	51.1	14.8	33.9	80.2	2.5	80.0	17.0	37.1
1955	39.6	9.7	50.5	62.9	30.5	46.4	15.5	37.6
1956	53.4	2.8	43.6	82.9	38.9	54.2	10.5	29.4
1957	39.9	9.8	50.1	91.8	13.0	48.2	9.9	36.7
1958	42.4	6.2	51.3	71.2	19.2	47.7	8.7	40.5
1959	41.5	3.8	54.6	75.5	24.5	52.2	9.3	43.5
1960	39.7	4.4	55.8	80.8	20.9	61.0	10.4	51.5
1961	39.6	3.0	57.4	52.4	12.3	53.1	7.4	46.1
1962	42.9	2.4	54.7	60.4	15.3	58.2	8.6	39.8
1963	50.0	1.7	48.3	103.0	18.7	86.3	9.3	41.4
1964	54.6	2.3	43.0	61.9ᵈ	15.3	63.6	8.8	26.6
1965	60.5	1.4	38.0	53.1ᵈ	20.9	64.8	10.9	24.8
Total 1949-65	51.5	7.4	41.3	68.7	20.5	59.2	12.2	28.9

ᵃ See notes to Appendix Table 11.
ᵇ Figures may not add to 100 because the detail excludes U.N. technical assistance included in the total.
ᶜ Figures may not add to 100 because the detail excludes government capital other than U.S. government, Israeli investment abroad, and "other" private capital (see Appendix Table 10), all of which are included in the total. Since some of these items are negative, the figures may add to more than 100.
ᵈ See note e to Appendix Table 11.
SOURCE: The numerators for each column are the figures in the corresponding columns of Appendix Table 11. Total unilateral transfers and long-term capital from Appendix Tables 9 and 10 respectively; import surplus from Table 50.

only once—in 1950—did world Jewry transfers come to less than half the import surplus (Table 59). For the period as a whole, world Jewry covered 59 per cent of the cumulated import surplus, the United States government 12 per cent, and West Germany 29 per cent. The share of United States aid declined considerably after 1952, and Germany has been in second place since 1954. Total long-term transfers from these three sources are almost exactly equal to the cumulated balance of payments deficit.

In addition to the items included in Table 59, one important new source of long-term loan capital should be mentioned: the loans from the International Bank for Reconstruction and Development (better known as the World Bank). Israel began official negotiations for these loans only in 1958. By the end of 1965, the World Bank had approved four loans, totaling $ 91 million.

World Jewry

Financial assistance from world Jewry, chiefly that part of it living in the United States, consists mainly of private and institutional transfers, the purchase of State of Israel Bonds, and private investment.

The private transfers are of two kinds: gifts in money and goods, and immigrant transfers. The latter vary with the size and origin of immigration, but have not been as important as they were in the 1930's. Net private transfers came to almost $ 750 million during 1949–65; in 1955–60 they averaged about $ 35 million annually, but they have risen in recent years (Appendix Table 9).

Institutional transfers may be sub-divided into those of the Jewish Agency and the Jewish National Fund (the second much the less important quantitatively), and those of other philanthrophic, educational, and welfare institutions, which range from several large organizations, such as the Joint Distribution Committee, the Hebrew University, the Israel Institute of Technology, and Hadassa, to hundreds of small institutions.

The Jewish Agency receives most of its funds from the United States; American Jews contribute generously for Jewish philanthropic causes at home and abroad, but prefer to do so through central campaign funds, which then allocate the money to various institutions. Thus, the Jewish Agency (or rather its financial instrument the Foundation Fund—Keren Hayesod) receives money allocated to the United Israel Appeal from the United Jewish Appeal; the latter may receive funds from a direct campaign or from central campaign funds. Typically, the United Jewish Appeal has allocated 60 to 65 per cent of its funds to the United Israel Appeal, with the Joint Distribution Committee receiving most of the rest.[19]

In addition to its regular campaign, the United Israel Appeal has occasionally conducted Special or Emergency Campaigns. When, at the end of 1953, Israel's short-term debt position became untenable, a new approach was attempted: Jewish communities took loans from local banks on behalf of the United Jewish Appeal. The Jewish Agency thus received a double contribution in 1954, although most of the Consolidation Loan was transferred to the Government of Israel. These loans, repayable over a five-year period, have been refunded several times; but the process leads to wide fluctuations (e.g., $ 73.7 million in 1954 and $ 26.3 million in 1955) in the annual net receipts of the United Israel Appeal.[20] The Jewish Agency spends money abroad and frequently resorts to interim financing on its own behalf; in consequence, net receipts abroad do not match annual transfers to Israel.[21]

No other single institution is a major source of funds, but taken together, other institutions account for substantial sums of between $ 20 million and $ 30 million each year.

To supplement unilateral transfers by world Jewry, the Government of Israel started issuing bonds in 1951. At that time Israel had not yet developed a reputation for credit worthiness that could facilitate large-scale financing through long-term loans or private investment. A first issue of Independence Bonds was followed by several issues of Development Loan Bonds, bearing low rates of interest (3.5 to 4 per cent) and repayable in ten to fifteen years. The sale of State of Israel Bonds was an attempt to raise loan capital that would appeal to both economic motives and sentiment. At first it was feared that sales would partly replace contributions to the United Jewish Appeal, but these fears have proved exaggerated. Annual sales have generally ranged between $ 40 million and $ 60 million, but have risen steeply in recent years, reaching $ 92 million in 1965/66.[22] The main drawback of this source is that it is a loan. The first formal redemption dates were in 1963, and in 1963/64 over $ 27 million were repaid according to

19 Michaely, *op. cit.*, p. 25, Table 11, and p. 27.
20 The composition of annual net receipts of the United Israel Appeal in 1954–65 is shown in Ministry of Finance, *Summary of Foreign Exchange Accounts for the Fiscal Year 1965/66* (Jerusalem: Foreign Exchange Department, 1966; Hebrew), p. 17.
21 The CBS now includes these transactions both in the national accounts and in the balance of payments figures.
22 Ministry of Finance, *op. cit.*, p. 13.

schedule.[23] To mitigate the burden of foreign currency repayments and to encourage investment and tourism, arrangements were made for early redemption in Israel pounds for specific purposes such as contributions to institutions, private investment, and tourist outlays in Israel.[24] Obviously, every dollar of bonds redeemed in pounds reduces future repayments by one dollar, and in this sense is income in foreign currency. But it is difficult to assess how much of this is a net addition, and how much replaces what would otherwise have been received as gifts, investments, and so forth. In so far as bond-redemption in pounds does replace other income, nothing is gained by it; in fact, it simply amounts to reducing the term of the loan and can also be viewed as deferment of foreign exchange income from the year of redemption in pounds to the year when the bond was to fall due.

The interest rate on the bonds is considered very low, particularly for the lender; but it is difficult to determine the real cost to the borrower, although it is undoubtedly much higher than the nominal interest rate. The difference is due to the high cost of issuing the bonds and to the early redemptions which raise the actual rate of fixed cost of issue.[25] Thus, whereas the bonds played an essential role during the 1951–59 period of scarce foreign exchange, the economic value of continued reliance on bond sales in recent years, considering their cost and the nature of early redemption, is open to question. Assuming bonds to be "marginal" foreign borrowing, is not the difference between the actual rate of interest on the bonds and the rate received on foreign exchange reserves too high a price to pay for holding these marginal reserves?[26]

Encouraging private investment has been an important policy aim for many years, and a law for the encouragement of investment has been in force since 1950. But until intensive efforts were made to develop

[23] There have been some early redemptions in foreign currency (e.g., to the estates of deceased bond-holders); up to April, 1966, these came to $ 40.4 million (*ibid.*).

[24] Early redemptions in pounds totaled $ 226 million from 1953/54 to 1965/66 (*ibid.*).

[25] Ben-Shahar has estimated the actual interest rate on the bonds at 6 per cent, rising to 8 per cent in 1961 with the trend to earlier redemption [*Interest Rates and the Cost of Capital in Israel, 1950–62* (Basel and Tübingen: Kyklos-Verlag and J.C.B. Mohr, 1966)].

[26] A counter argument is that the bonds cannot be turned on and off according to the current interest rate differential and are too important a long-term source to be endangered.

private long-term investment as an important third source of financing, it did not play a major role in the aid given to Israel by world Jewry.[27] There are several types of private long-term investment: commercial loans to Israeli firms by foreign firms, including banks, and investment (either equity or loan capital) in Israeli firms (including subsidiaries of foreign companies). In recent years, investment fostered by the Investment Authority has been recorded as direct investment regardless of whether it consisted of loans or of equity capital. In practice, at the time the financial transfer takes place, it is often impossible to determine how much of the money will be a loan and how much will be share capital. In some respects, there is no essential difference between the two. Both provide funds for capital formation, and both can serve the perhaps more important function of introducing foreign initiative, know-how, and commercial and industrial experience and connections. But there is a big difference between them as regards their terms: a loan must be repaid on a fixed schedule and at fixed rates of interest; whereas equity capital (requiring perhaps higher interest) may or may not be repatriated, and dividend payments are generally contingent on the successful use of the capital and may also be re-invested.

Investment by world Jewry should have included other loans either from or transferred by Jewish firms, institutions, or individuals abroad. No attempt has been made here to classify "other private" in this way. Throughout the period, organizations such as Ampal have been active in channeling loans to Israel (in addition to investment). An incomplete list of such loans shows that they came to at least 3 to 5 per cent of all foreign exchange debt outstanding in the years 1958/59 to 1962/63.[28]

United States government

Economic assistance from the United States government has taken many forms—grants, soft-currency loans, hard-currency loans, and technical assistance. This variety reflects the frequent reorganization of United States agencies dealing with economic assistance and the complexity of the process by which appropriations are approved by Congress, as well as the way in which these agencies view the changing needs of the economy of Israel and how the United States can best

---

[27] See also note b to Appendix Table 11.
[28] Dov Genachowski, "Israel's External Debt," *Bank of Israel Bulletin,* No. 20 (September 1963; Hebrew), 85.

meet these needs. Military aid, which is a substantial part of United States foreign assistance, was not included in the aid program to Israel during the period covered.

Israel's balance of payments and similar records do not include Export-Import Bank loans under United States economic assistance, though this is where they belong. The Export-Import Bank, whose main function is to encourage exports from the United States, is a major instrument for carrying out the United States government's foreign economic policy, and although the Bank is scrupulous in applying economic criteria to prospective loans, political considerations are certainly important in determining its loan policy. In 1949, when a $ 100 million loan to Israel was approved, this was a major political decision with far-reaching economic consequences: it not only formed the basis of Israel's development program but was also a declaration of confidence in the country's economic and political future.

The first loans to Israel amounted to $ 100 million, shortly followed by another $ 35 million, approved in 1949. The loans carried 3.5 per cent interest and repayment, in 24 twice-yearly payments, was to start after five years. They were used over a five-year period to pay for imports of machinery and equipment for the development of agriculture, housing, manufacturing, transport, and communications. A loan of $ 24.2 million for financing irrigation projects was approved in 1957/58. Following a $ 1.5 million loan for specific projects, $ 25 million was approved in 1961, and $ 11.2 million in 1963. In addition, Israeli firms got loans to a total of close to $ 30 million, generally guaranteed by the Government of Israel.[29]

In 1951 the United States included Israel in its Grant-in-Aid program and within three years grants of $ 185 million had been approved. The foreign exchange was to be used to purchase imports (almost all from the United States), and the equivalent in local currency was to be deposited in Israel, to be released for investment in projects approved by the United States Operations Mission in Israel (USOM). Smaller grants of various kinds continued until 1962.

Technical assistance and cultural grants also started in 1951; though not very large, they have been important in economic development.

In 1954/55, the aid program shifted from grants to loans repayable in soft currency. The local currency counterpart of the foreign exchange used for imports was lent to the Government of Israel for investment projects, at 3.5 per cent interest and to be repaid in local currency over

[29] Ministry of Finance, *op. cit.*

40 years. During 1954/55–1956/57, such loans came to about half of the United States grant program, the rest being in actual grants.

From 1954/55, the Public Law 480 Food Surplus program provided an additional source of soft-currency loans. In effect, Israel buys American surplus agricultural produce with local currency; part of the proceeds are retained for United States use in Israel, and the bulk is lent to the Israel government for development projects or (under the terms of the Cooley Amendment) to private firms. Since the local currency intended for United States use has accumulated faster than it can be spent, some of it has been lent to the Government of Israel. The first sizable loan of this kind was the IL 20 million lent in 1957/58 for investment in the Industrial Development Bank of Israel.

In 1957/58 yet another agency was set up for foreign aid loans, the Development Loan Fund (DLF). Several loans, given for purchasing equipment, were repayable in local currency.[30]

The soft-currency loans actually resemble outright grants.[31] Interest rates are low, annual repayments small, and best of all, repayments on both current and capital account accumulate locally and can therefore be reborrowed. However, the terms of these loans specify repayment in either dollars or local currency linked to the dollar. So far, only negligible amounts have been repaid in dollars or in the dollar-equivalent of exportable Israeli products, but pressure has been mounting for more hard-currency repayment.[32] Nevertheless, as the sums accumulate, they will ultimately have to be repaid in foreign exchange or the debt cancelled; the choice of either (or of a combination of the two) will probably depend on Israel's economic situation in the future.

The most important hard-currency loans are the Export-Import Bank loans, which were discussed above. With the incorporation of the DLF into the Agency for International Development (AID) in 1961/62, there was a switch to low-interest (0.75 per cent) hard-currency loans. Several such loans have already been given, and this source will probably become more important in the future.

[30] For further details of this and other forms of United States aid, see H. Ben-Shahar, *Public International Development Financing in Israel* (New York: Columbia University School of Law, 1963; mimeograph).

[31] For example, Michaely (*op. cit.*, p. 23, Table 10) includes all United States aid other than Export-Import Bank loans with unilateral transfers in his summary of the capital inflow.

[32] A sizable local currency loan recently made to an education institution is to be repaid out of future hard-currency receipts. This may be the first large hard-currency repayment.

A summary of the various forms of United States economic aid appears in Appendix Table 12.[33] Annual net receipts have fluctuated within a relatively narrow range. Except for 1949, when aid had just got started, and 1952, when the grant alone reached $ 86 million, annual receipts have usually been between $ 40 million and $ 60 million. However, there have been substantial changes in the type of aid: until 1951, it was all in the form of hard-currency loans, during 1952–54 grants predominated, and from 1955 to 1962 soft-currency loans were most important. Since 1962, hard-currency loans have once again become an important source of finance.

The United States aid program as a whole was intended to help Israel chiefly in two ways. First, by providing foreign exchange for financing imports: Export-Import Bank, DLF, and AID loans financed the import of investment goods; grants, loans, and Public Law 480 loans financed the import of food and raw materials. Second, the local currency equivalent of the dollar receipts—in effect the money used to buy the imports—was allocated to capital formation, either automatically, in the case of loans for the purchase of investment goods, or through the mechanism whereby local counterpart funds were lent to finance development projects.[34]

Almost all the United States aid funds were earmarked for the purchase of specific goods or classes of goods, almost exclusively in the United States. Either limitation is sufficient to prevent optimum use of funds, so the dual limitation which obtained in practice did so a fortiori. Equipment that could have been bought more cheaply elsewhere often came from the United States, and the volume of American farm products imported may often have been determined by the availability and terms of finance.[35]

---

[33] Since these figures are taken from the annual balance of payments estimates, they differ from the usual presentations of United States aid, which are based on appropriations rather than on actual transactions. Furthermore, our annual figures include intra-capital-account shifts, i.e., the annual net effects of the accumulation of local currency deposits and their decline when they are lent out.

[34] Ginor has attempted an interesting analysis of the effects of one type of United States aid in *Uses of Agricultural Surpluses: Analysis and Assessment of Public Law 480 Title I Program in Israel* (Jerusalem: Bank of Israel, 1963). She examines separately the foreign exchange and investment aspects of the program, and the contribution of each to the development of the economy.

[35] For example, Ginor gives ample proof of the dependence of the poultry industry on this source of economic assistance; but the question of whether this

The Federal Republic of Germany

Official transfers from West Germany have been unilateral transfers, that is, reparations and restitutions.

The Reparations Agreement, signed in September, 1952, stipulated that the Government of West Germany would pay to the Government of Israel and to Jewish institutions a sum of DM 3,450 million (equal to $821 million at the rate of exchange then prevailing) over a twelve-year period. The payment would be made in German goods,[36] and the Government of Israel would transfer $107 million in cash to Jewish institutions abroad and place the IL equivalent of 18 per cent of the remainder at the disposal of the Jewish Agency in Israel.

All the funds have already been used. The goods imported under the terms of the agreement consisted of 38 per cent ships, machinery, and equipment; 30 per cent fuel; and 24 per cent raw materials. More than 7 per cent has gone for services abroad connected with the purchases.[37]

Under a series of laws passed since 1953, the *Länder* of West Germany have been making restitution payments to victims of the Nazi regime. Residents of Israel have been receiving these as lump sum payments and pensions. Unlike the Reparations Agreement, these laws did not specify any fixed sum of payment to Israel, and the German authorities have tried to limit their total restitution obligations. Individual claims had to be presented by March, 1958, but several additional categories of people were declared eligible, so that total receipts have already surpassed predictions based on claims presented by 1958. Unlike reparations payments, which rose quickly to about $80 million and stayed at that level until 1961 when a sharp drop indicated that the final stage had been reached, restitutions payments rose from year to year, reaching $143 million in 1963. They fell somewhat in 1964 and 1965, and are expected to drop steeply once the lump sum payments are finished; but pensions will continue as long as the recipients are alive.[38]

Restitutions are paid to individuals in cash, another way in which

---

development was carried beyond what is desirable in the long run is not examined (*ibid.*).

[36] There is provision for services connected with the purchasing program and for the purchase of fuel outside Germany.

[37] Ministry of Finance, *op. cit.*, p. 17.

[38] Pension payments were about 20 per cent of total restitution transfers during the fiscal year 1963/64, but rose to 30 per cent in 1964/65 and close to 42 per cent in 1965/66 (Ministry of Finance, *op. cit.*, p. 10).

they differ from reparations, which were paid to the government in goods. One disadvantage of this has been that the government has had to make various concessions to Israeli recipients, such as premium payments and permission to use at least part of the foreign exchange as such for specific purposes, in order to make sure that all funds are transferred to Israel. In fact, not all funds were so transferred, although most probably were. Once the money does arrive, the government has control of the foreign exchange and can use it for any purpose it feels desirable. On the other hand, the government does not control the IL equivalents, and in recent years these have been a major source of inflationary pressure—made less palatable because, unlike reparations, much of the amount is directed to consumption. Government policy has therefore been to encourage holding these sums in bank deposits.

Some Implications of the Import Surplus

The figures discussed so far refer to the import surplus expressed in U.S. dollars.[39] To show the relative importance of these additional resources, the import surplus must be converted into IL and expressed as a percentage of total domestic[40] resources, as was done in Chapter 6. Table 60 shows two estimates of this ratio, one based on current and the other on constant prices. The two series both decline, but the trend is considerably more marked in constant prices. However, both measures indicate that the import surplus provided substantial additional resources.

One must be careful not to infer that the share of import surplus in total domestic resources is a measure of resources made possible by the import surplus. The *ex post* figure showing resources as composed of GNP and import surplus cannot indicate what GNP would have been had the import surplus been smaller, since GNP is affected by the import surplus of the current and previous years.

After the stress placed on the additions to welfare made possible by the import surplus, it may come as a surprise that many Israeli economists have been greatly concerned over its size and persistence and regard it as an indication of economic dependence.[41] Patinkin has gone

---

[39] More precisely, the import surplus is valued in current prices of various foreign currencies, converted to dollars at the official rates of exchange.

[40] See note a to Table 60.

[41] The problem of economic dependence has been debated at considerable length in the Israeli literature; see, for example, Daniel Creamer and Others, *Israel's National Income 1950–1954* (Jerusalem: Falk Project and CBS, 1957); Don

TABLE 60.   *Some Ratios Relating to the Concept of*
             Economic Dependence: 1950–65

(per cent)

	Per cent of domestic resources[a]			Per cent of import surplus		Exports as per cent of imports
	Import surplus		Net capital transfers[b]	Net invest- ment	Net capital transfers	
	Constant (1955) prices	Current prices	(2)×(5)			
	(1)	(2)	(3)	(4)	(5)	(6)
1950	39.5	20.5	8.7	105.9	42.2	14.0
1951	34.2	17.3	7.9	139.0	45.8	15.6
1952	28.3	22.3	8.5	95.7	37.9	22.0
1953	25.9	21.6	6.2	80.6	28.6	28.0
1954	21.0	20.2	0.1	84.4	0.4	36.2
1955	21.3	21.3	5.8	92.1	27.0	33.7
1956	22.9	22.3	6.3	71.7	28.2	33.3
1957	19.8	19.8	4.6	90.1	23.4	39.8
1958	18.9	18.2	3.6	96.0	19.7	41.3
1959	15.6	15.4	2.7	111.6	17.4	47.6
1960	14.4	15.1	1.8	109.6	12.2	51.6
1961	16.9	16.0	3.9	112.9	24.1	49.6
1962	15.8	19.7	4.3	96.7	21.6	52.5
1963	12.7	17.6	3.2	97.9	18.0	60.0
1964	14.4	19.4	7.7	99.3	39.9	53.5
1965	12.8	16.5	6.9	92.7	42.0	59.0

[a] I.e., resources for domestic use, or GNP *plus* import surplus.
[b] This is equivalent to that part of import surplus financed by capital transfers as per cent of resources.
SOURCES: Column (1)—calculated from Appendix Table 2.
         Column (2)—Table 30.
         Column (4)—Calculated from Appendix Table 1.
         Column (5)—Calculated from Appendix Table 10 and Table 50.
         Column (6)—Calculated from c.i.f. figures of Table 50.

so far as to conclude that the persistent deficit "represents the major failure of Israel economic policy... ."[42]

The term economic dependence carries a derogatory connotation going beyond the simple meaning that more resources are used than

---

Patinkin, *The Israel Economy: The First Decade* (Jerusalem: Falk Project, 1960); and Michaely, *op. cit.* Besides these, *The Economic Quarterly* (Hebrew) has carried many articles on the subject over the years, among them articles by Gaathon, Ginor, Lerner, Pines, and Ronen.

[42] Patinkin, *op. cit.,* p. 132.

are currently produced. What are the economic implications of the import surplus which cause such concern?[43] There are essentially two of them.

The first concerns the burden which the import surplus imposes on the future. A close analogy exists between an economy's living beyond its means and an individual's doing so; in both cases it appears that the excesses of the present must be paid for in the future. But is this really true? The receipt by an individual of net transfer payments, or by the economy of net unilateral transfers, imposes no future burden of repayment. The burden thus depends on how the excess is financed. As Table 57 shows, 70 per cent of Israel's import surplus was covered by unilateral transfers in 1949–65, and in no year between 1952 and 1965 has less than 60 per cent been provided free. Thus, if a single measure of economic dependence is desired which will focus attention on the future-burden aspect, it may be one showing the share in resources of that part of the import surplus *not* financed by unilateral transfers, i.e., that part which is financed either by a decrease in financial assets or an increase in liabilities [column (3) of Table 60].

The future-burden aspect of the import surplus is also reflected in attempts to focus attention on what is done with the import surplus. Thus, another measure of economic dependence is the ratio of saving to total resources.[44] In this way that part of the import surplus which finances net investment is not regarded with concern, yet that which finances consumption is considered as a sign of dependence. Here, too, instead of using the usual definition of saving [as in column (4) of Table 60] one may subtract from investment not the entire import surplus, but only that part not financed by unilateral transfers.

Michaely has suggested three supplementary ratios which focus on the future-burden aspect of the import surplus: (a) the ratio of net foreign indebtedness to Net National Product (NNP); (b) the ratio of net foreign indebtedness to total export receipts; and (c) the ratio of net foreign indebtedness to capital stock.

These and similar ratios are attempts to substitute rough macro-economic indicators for a useful but elusive measure derived from micro-economics: a measure that enables one to compare the cost of and the return to foreign investment (in the balance-of-payments sense). No such satisfactory measure has yet been devised, owing to the great

[43] We are not concerned here with non-economic interpretations of dependence, e.g., with moral or political objections to receiving aid from particular sources.
[44] Both Patinkin and Michaely stress this measure.

conceptual and statistical difficulties on both the cost and return sides of the comparison.[45]

The second major cause for concern relates to the question of whether loan funds to finance the import surplus will be available. Here, two distinct problems are involved. One is the problem of what would happen if the import surplus were to cease abruptly. Not only would total resources decrease by the amount of the decline in the import surplus, but lack of mobility in the economy and the crucial importance of imports would cause GNP to decline as well, at least temporarily. A satisfactory indicator of the magnitude of this problem, suggested by Michaely, is the ratio of the import surplus to total imports, or a similar measure, exports as a per cent of imports. This shows by how much imports would decline if the surplus disappeared suddenly; or by how much exports would have to grow in order to maintain imports. By 1963, exports had risen to 60 per cent of imports [Table 60, column (6)].

The abrupt-cessation problem may have been of great concern during 1950–53, but has not since been crucial. However, a more fundamental aspect of the question remains. Much of the capital inflow is not expected to be a permanent feature of the Israel economy; thus, the import surplus and the various suggested measures of economic dependence will decline in the future—either suddenly or gradually. But should this fact affect our appraisal of relative changes in the import surplus in the past?

Two assumptions are inherent in the attempt to appraise changes in past import surpluses on the basis of the need for eventual future decreases of the import surplus. One is that the economy should take the future decrease in the import surplus into account and prepare for it well in advance. Such preparation can range from detailed planning of investment and consumption to manipulation of relative prices in the direction they would take when the import surplus declines. Underlying the possible measures which can be taken is an important value judgement: that the economy should be protected from sudden shocks and severe dislocation.

---

[45] It is interesting to compare Ben-Shahar's estimate of the real cost of foreign loans (*Interest Rates and the Cost of Capital in Israel, 1950–62, op. cit.*) with Bruno's estimate of the marginal productivity of capital ["Factor Productivity and Remuneration in Israel, 1952–61," *The Economic Quarterly*, X (No. 37–38, March 1963; Hebrew), 41–56]. Such a comparison suggests that the real productivity of capital has been consistently much higher than the cost of loans to the economy.

A second assumption is that a gradually decreasing relative import surplus is a necessary indicator that measures, which should have been taken to prevent future shocks, have, in fact, been taken. It is not at all clear why this must be true. Let us assume for a moment that the import surplus should be reduced over a five-year period, rather than in one or two years. Then, as long as it is believed that the five-year transition period still lies in the future, present surpluses need not be reduced. Furthermore, we are actually looking for some indications that the economy is preparing for the future decrease: this may take the form of reducing present imports and using available funds to increase foreign exchange reserves or for early debt retirement, or utilizing all available funds to expand investment and production, so that potential exports or import substitutes will grow rapidly.[46] The first possibility would be reflected in a declining ratio of import surplus to total resources; the second would not. Similarly, annual changes in the import surplus could reflect shifts between the two approaches rather than movements towards or away from economic independence.

From all that has been said above, it is clear that we do not consider the attempts to measure economic dependence and how it changes to be very effective. Yet each of the indexes suggested does describe some important aspect of Israel's balance-of-payment position. Using these indexes and the earlier sections of this chapter, we can summarize some of the main developments.

Measured in constant prices, the import surplus tended to provide a declining share of total resources. In other words, using as a base the relative values of the economy in 1955, and considering changes expressed in terms of that set of values as in some sense representing physical or real changes in goods and services, we find that the net contribution of the rest of the world to Israel's total resources has declined. In current prices, there does not seem to be any strong downward trend.[47]

Net annual increases in Israel's obligations to foreigners, i.e., that part of the import surplus which represents a future burden, have fluctuated widely. But, as can be seen from Table 60 [column (3)],

---

[46] This point is emphasized by D. Pines, "Criteria of Economic Independence," *The Economic Quarterly,* VIII (No. 31, June 1961; Hebrew), 242–52.

[47] There has been a lively controversy over whether the index of economic dependence should be measured in current prices (as advocated by Patinkin) or in constant prices (as advocated by Creamer and Michaely). Pines (*op. cit.*) has shown that under certain assumptions the constant price figures are preferable.

net capital movements have never amounted to as much as 10 per cent of Israel's total resources. However, capital movements as per cent of the deficit (Table 57) were at a higher level in 1964 and 1965 than in any year since 1951. As can be seen from column (4) of Table 60, which compares net investment with import surplus, saving has been negative in many of the years; saving *plus* unilateral transfers, however, has been positive throughout.

Over the years there have been several major changes in Israel's balance-of-payments position. During 1949–51 the foreign exchange reserves were liquidated in order to obtain what was considered a necessary volume of imports.

During the next two years, when the New Economic Policy was implemented, the import surplus declined sharply, owing to lack of funds. Part of the decline in the import surplus reflects improved terms of trade following the decline of import prices from their 1951 Korean War peak.

In 1954, exports expanded and imports grew only slightly, so that the import surplus again declined. At the same time, a major campaign to increase institutional transfers improved the foreign exchange situation: short-term debts declined and some reserves were built up.

During the next three years (1955–57) the import surplus increased so rapidly as to worsen the short-term debt and reserve position, despite increasing external financial resources. The data for 1956 and 1957 in part reflect the Sinai campaign and the Suez crisis.

The year 1958 marks a turning point of sorts. Not only did the import surplus grow steadily although exports grew faster than imports, but the basic financial position changed. In 1958 it became apparent that available external sources of funds would be sufficient to permit concurrent processes of increasing imports and increasing reserves (or reducing short-term debts), and that this could continue for several years. Gradually, it became clear that the funds available would be larger and continue longer than previously believed. Thus, in allocating foreign exchange, there was a shift from closely linking monthly licensing to current estimates of cash flows, as was the practice in 1957, to a more liberal procedure based on an estimate of import needs and total sources available, which took into account inflationary pressures, debt structure, and the desired rate of reserve accumulation.

Oversimplifying somewhat, one can say that whereas in the past the foreign exchange authorities were desperately looking for funds to finance what was considered a minimum import program, in the following few years import policy was implemented in the knowledge that more than adequate sources of funds would be available.[48] The considerable rise in the deficit in 1964 once again brought the balance of payments problem to the fore. The need to curb the deficit has been used as an explanation of the recessionary policy adopted in 1965.

How long can the import surplus continue? One hesitates to make predictions because the experts have been proved wrong several times in the past. Various sources of funds have gained prominence—institutional transfers, United States aid, State of Israel Bonds, German reparations, German restitutions, and private investment—overlapping and overtaking each other in importance, so that predictions based on foreseeable declines in existing major categories were proved wrong as new sources emerged.

A re-examination of sources may nevertheless be useful, although we hesitate to call our predictions more than speculations. Among the unilateral transfers, several may be more or less permanent, or at least of fairly long duration. Private gifts need not decline, and some immigrant transfers will continue as long as immigration does. Similarly, institutional transfers will probably continue. True, the size of United Jewish Appeal funds can fluctuate greatly, but sizable amounts will be forthcoming as long as Jews abroad (particularly in America) accept the idea that the maintenance of a home in Israel open to any Jew who cares to come regardless of his means is in part an obligation of world Jewry.[49] That part of institutional transfers which consists of contributions to several hundred philanthropic, educational, and welfare institutions can certainly continue. Thus, substantial annual transfers to institutions may be expected to last for quite some time.

Other major unilateral transfers—United States grants and German reparations—have virtually ended, but restitutions may very well be appreciable for several more years, and at a lower level for perhaps another seven to ten years. Present indications are that at least some, and perhaps sizable, German economic assistance may be forthcoming as a replacement for reparations.

Among capital movements a distinction must be made between what is basically economic transactions and what lies in the no-man's-land of assistance capital. In the latter category, there are indications that

[48] This point is also made by D. Golomb, "Import Surplus—Cause or Effect," *The Economic Quarterly*, VIII (No. 29–30, February 1961; Hebrew), 150–52. However, he dates the change from 1960, whereas we date it from 1958.

[49] This source responds to emergencies and could thus increase considerably if other sources were to fail suddenly.

United States aid will continue to taper off, but certainly some agricultural surpluses can be disposed of to Israel, and even if all loan repayments shift from soft to hard currency they will be at favorable terms. State of Israel Bonds will be sold for many years, probably faster than they are redeemed, but a conservative estimate would not expect this source to provide much net capital.

Other loan capital to the government may also be no more than enough to offset the growing stream of repayments. Yet Israel's financial position is strong enough to find net annual loans of $ 20 to $ 30 million from financial institutions, if the government finds this desirable.

The last major item is private investment. This has taken the form of both loans and equity capital. Only in recent years has this source of funds been intensively developed. This item, too, reflects a mixture of economic and sentimental motives on the part of most investors; but we believe that there is room for considerable optimism concerning Israel's ability to attract normal investment capital.[50] In recent years, until the present recession, new loans and direct investment in enterprises grew tremendously. In 1963 and 1964 the effort to mobilize such investments was actually toned down, and the need for greater selectivity was stressed. An estimate of future investment, based on the average during the last few years rather than on prospects for a continuation of present trends, would arrive at a very conservative minimum estimate of $ 50 million for many years to come. Considering Israel's growth rate, we feel that an estimate of $ 80 million is conservative enough and that estimates of future investments as large as $ 150 million are not unduly optimistic. However, underlying these estimates are two assumptions: that the present recession will prove transitory, and that investment projects will be found. The problem in recent years has been what to do with the money rather than how to get it. It may be reasonable to expect that exports must expand not only to finance imports, but because new and larger industrial undertakings that can attract investments and maintain a healthy rate of growth will have to rely on export markets rather than on the small domestic market.

To summarize our discussion: It appears reasonable that Israel will be able to mobilize foreign unilateral and capital transfers for many years after the next five-year period during which some major unilateral transfers may decline drastically. A conservative estimate would place the long-term flow at between $ 200 and $ 250 million. But a less con-

---

[50] In the present context it is, of course, irrelevant whether the investment flow is purely economic or also sentimental.

servative view would raise the figure by up to $ 100 million, and this without considering any completely new major source, such as a large German loan to replace reparations, substantial new restitutions, or international assistance as part of an area peace program.

The implications of this discussion are threefold. First, substantial import surpluses may continue to be a basic feature of the economy of Israel for many years to come. Second, even if this time the pessimists are right in predicting that the country must reduce its import surplus within the next few years, the reduction need not be to the $ 150–$ 200 million level previously envisaged; a surplus of $ 250–$ 350 million, or even $ 350 million, may be maintained for several more years, if desirable. Thus, the surplus may fall to the levels which predominated up to 1960, but this may appear to be a drastic curtailment compared with more recent deficits. Lastly, the accumulation of large foreign exchange balances give the policy-makers considerable leeway in stretching out the time during which the necessary reduction in the disparity between imports and exports can be achieved; but these balances will not last long if the apparent tendency to reduce the deficit does not outlive the current recession.

PART III

ECONOMIC POLICY

We turn now to economic policy. We have already dealt with the most important policy decision: the commitment to rapid economic development, which in large measure stems from the commitment to accept and encourage immigration and to strive for the economic absorption of the immigrants.

The two most important tools of economic policy have probably been the budget and exchange control. We therefore discuss public finance in this chapter and foreign exchange policy in the next. Aspects of both combine with two other important fields of policy—money and wages— to create what has aroused more discussion than any other economic issue: Israel's inflationary experience. This is the subject of Chapter 11.

In these chapters, we attempt to distinguish between two types of policy alluded to earlier: direct activity and financial influence. In particular, our interest is to consider policies operating through the market mechanism and those circumventing it. Unfortunately, we cannot deal with a third type of policy: indirect influence. Though of great importance, it is a subject that requires separate examination and other methods of study.

In this chapter, the term "public finance" refers to all financial activities of the public sector. Funds are received by the public sector from many sources: taxes, the sale of goods and services, unilateral transfers, repayment of loans, and the creation of internal and external debt.[1] The purposes for which the funds are spent are equally varied: subsidies and other transfer payments, the purchase of goods and services on current and capital account, and loans and debt retirement.

---

[1] Of course, not all parts of the public sector rely on all these sources; central government does, local government relies primarily on taxes and transfers from central government, and the national institutions are primarily financed by unilateral transfers from abroad.

This financial activity has numerous and complex effects on the economy, some intentional and many unforeseen. None of these can here be dealt with in detail, and some will not be discussed at all. Our main concern is with the traditional effects of public finance: the allocation effect (primarily the substitution of public for private consumption), the redistributive effect, and the effect on growth.[2]

We shall start with a brief description of the major instrument of public finance—the central government's budget—and then classify fiscal policy by its effects rather than by its instruments.

THE STATE BUDGET

There is no general legal framework setting out the financial privileges, duties, and procedures of the public sector, and its principal financial activities are executed through annual budgets, the most important of which is the State budget. The annual Budget Law stipulates how much the government may spend during the coming fiscal year (April–March); it gives a detailed breakdown of the total and provides for timing of expenditures, changes in the budget, and the use of surpluses. An estimate of receipts is also included, although the legal basis for acquiring them is to be found in various other laws relating to taxation and borrowing.[3]

Ex ante *budget versus* ex post *expenditure*

The budget should enable the legislature to supervise closely the financial activities of the executive. Over the years, considerable improvements have been made in the presentation of the budget, chief among them being its organization as a performance budget and the compilation of detailed explanatory material. However, there are still many shortcomings in the budgetary process from the point of view of legislative control.[4]

One such shortcoming arises from the fact that the budget does not cover important parts of the public sector. The budgets of the national

[2] In a developing country the question of growth generally replaces the traditional problem of stability. Aspects of stability are discussed in Chapter 11.

[3] For a review of the various related laws and a discussion of the inadequacy of the legal framework, see Meir Heth, *The Legal Framework of Economic Activity in Israel* (Jerusalem and New York: Frederick A. Praeger with the Bank of Israel, 1967), Chapters 13 and 14.

[4] For a comprehensive treatment of the subject see Committee on Financial Legislation, *The Committee's Recommendations on Government Budget* (Jerusalem: Israel Political Science Association, 1961).

institutions and the local authorities, though closely related to and affecting the State budget, are separate; in fact, some of their funds may appear in the State budget. Government corporations are also excluded from the budget.[5] Not only is the line drawn between government and other public sector institutions frequently arbitrary, with economic functions shifting, but there are frequent shifts between government enterprises and government corporations, only the former being included in the budget. Thus, for some purposes it is difficult to draw meaningful conclusions from year-to-year comparisons of State budgets.[6]

Furthermore, aside from some agencies and enterprises being excluded, the *ex ante* budget is not an accurate indicator of *ex post* expenditure. Supplementary budgets have often been submitted during the fiscal year, even though the need for them is sometimes known before the original budget is approved. Many purely financial activities of the government are completely independent of the budget. Frequently, items are included for which the expenditure has already been implemented under the extrabudgetary accounts of past years.

It is extremely difficult to compare budgets with actual government expenditure. Some of the differences between the annual government balance sheets must be added to the Accountant General's reports on expenditure, but it is not always clear which balance-sheet changes represent unbudgeted expenditure and which represent purely financial transactions. Table 61 compares the *ex ante* budget with the final budget and with expenditures; because of the difficulties, columns (6) and (7) must be viewed as estimates rather than as accurate accounts. Table 62 presents the same data in percentages.

In 1948 and 1949 the budgetary process was haphazard. Insufficient data made orderly parliamentary discussion of the budget practically impossible; as a result, the most that could be done was to approve temporary three-month budgets, generally based on the preceding three months. For this reason, and because accounting methods differed considerably from those used in later years, the breakdowns of Tables 61 and 62 are not very meaningful for the early years.

It is clear that the original budget does not accurately indicate actual expenditures. Amendments and additions are made during each year, subject to legislative approval; however, these have generally been

---

[5] In the sense that their activities are not budgeted. Of course, any funds that they receive from the budget are recorded.

[6] A similar difficulty arises from shifts between gross and net recording of various operations and from the exchange rates at which foreign exchange transactions are recorded.

TABLE 61. *Budgetary and Actual Expenditure of the Government: 1948/49–1963/64*[a]

(IL millions)

	Original budget (1)	Amendments and supplementary budgets[b] (2)	Surplus carried over from previous years (3)	Total (1) through (3) (4)	Total budgetary expenditure (5)	Additional extra-budgetary expenditure[c] (6)	Total (5) + (6) (7)
1948/49[d]	..	..	..	26.7	70.1[e]	4.3	74.4
1949/50	105.0	2.2	0.1	107.3	166.8[f]	8.4	175.2
1950/51	124.5	3.9	14.0	142.4	235.7[e,g]	17.0	252.7
1951/52	198.6	—	7.2	205.8	284.7[e,g]	11.4	296.1
1952/53	283.4	4.5	12.7	300.6	358.1[e]	42.3	400.4
1953/54	361.3	45.4	27.3	434.0	396.7	86.5	483.2
1954/55	572.5	52.7	35.9	661.1	628.4	59.3	687.7
1955/56	642.3	192.4	33.1	867.8	827.4	18.5	845.9
1956/57	814.5	151.0[h]	25.7	991.2	1,099.0	123.8	1,222.8
1957/58	1,104.0	201.8	55.5	1,361.3	1,262.0	28.8	1,290.8
1958/59	1,412.1	54.6	49.6	1,516.3	1,402.8	39.8	1,442.6
1959/60	1,737.4	14.8	58.2	1,810.4	1,685.5	−31.5	1,654.0

1960/61	1,937.9	14.0	50.6	2,002.5	1,809.3	8.0	1,817.3
1961/62	2,194.1	329.7	128.2	2,652.0	2,442.0	0.9	2,442.9
1962/63	2,817.9	22.4	140.6	2,980.9	2,782.5	169.6	2,952.1
1963/64[i]	3,207.5	198.8	188.2	3,594.5	3,341.7	37.2	3,378.9

[a] Fiscal years, April 1 to March 31, except for 1948/49, which began on May 15. The double-year notation refers to fiscal years throughout this chapter.

[b] In 1955/56–1963/64 includes amendments made during the fiscal year to the estimate of earmarked income and the budget of enterprises.

[c] Includes annual changes in current asset items of the Treasury as follows:
1948/49–1952/53—bank deposits; accounts receivable; investment in securities during the year; does not include budget surplus or deficit.
1951/52–1952/53—deficit of exchange rate equalization account.
1953/54–1963/64—foreign exchange (cash and bank deposits in Israel and abroad); budget surplus or deficit (in 1954/55–1962/63); does not include current deposits and sums in transit (in Bank of Israel, banks, and Post Office Bank).
1953/54–1954/55—budget surpluses earmarked to cover deficits in exchange rate equalization account.
1955/56—wage adjustments.
1955/56–1958/59—debtors in exchange rate equalization account and surcharges.
1956/57–1963/64—reparations merchandise purchased on account of future budgets.
1959/60–1963/64—deposits of government departments with the Bank of Israel; construction of Housing Division on account of 3-year plan.

[d] Several budgets approved, each for a period of several months, by Budget Orders of the Provisional Council of State.

[e] Includes budgetary expenditure from loan funds (in IL millions): 42.6 (1948/49); 86.3 (1950/51); 75.7 (1951/52); 70.5 (1952/53).

[f] Includes IL 73.0 million participation of national institutions in the development budget.

[g] Includes part of the Ministry of Defense expenditures within the Special Budget.

[h] Includes IL 11.2 million additional defense expenditure (within Budget Law No. 2) permitted by the Finance Committee of the Knesset.

[i] Provisional figures.

SOURCES: Official Bulletin, 5708–5709; Sefer Hakhukim, 5709, 5710, 5711, 5712; Yalkut Pirsumim, 27; Reshumot, Budget Laws 38–1; Reshumot, Government of Israel Financial Reports 15–1; Ministry of Finance, Comparative Notes and Tables for the Years 1948–1953, May 27, 1954; Accountant General, Financial Reports. (All Hebrew.)

TABLE 62.   Budgetary and Actual Expenditure of the Government: 1948/49–1963/64

(per cent)

	Per cent of total budget				Per cent of total expenditure						
	Original budget	Amendments and supplementary budgets	Surplus carried over from previous years	Total	Original budget	Amendments and supplementary budgets	Surplus carried over from previous years	Total budget (5) through (7)	Total budgetary expenditure	Additional extra-budgetary expenditure	Total expenditure (9)+(10)
	(1)	(2)	(3)	(4)	(5)	(6)	(7)	(8)	(9)	(10)	(11)
1948/49	..	..	..	100.0	..	..	..	35.9	94.2	5.8	100.0
1949/50	97.9	2.0	0.1	100.0	59.9	1.2	0.1	61.2	95.2	4.8	100.0
1950/51	87.4	2.8	9.8	100.0	49.3	1.6	5.5	56.4	93.3	6.7	100.0
1951/52	96.5	—	3.5	100.0	67.1	—	2.4	69.5	96.1	3.9	100.0
1952/53	94.3	1.5	4.2	100.0	70.8	1.1	3.2	75.1	89.4	10.6	100.0
1953/54	83.2	10.5	6.3	100.0	74.8	9.4	5.6	89.8	82.1	17.9	100.0
1954/55	86.6	8.0	5.4	100.0	83.2	7.7	5.2	96.1	91.4	8.6	100.0
1955/56	74.0	22.2	3.8	100.0	75.9	22.8	3.9	102.6	97.8	2.2	100.0
1956/57	82.2	15.2	2.6	100.0	66.6	12.4	2.1	81.1	89.9	10.1	100.0
1957/58	81.1	14.8	4.1	100.0	85.5	15.7	4.3	105.5	97.8	2.2	100.0
1958/59	93.1	3.6	3.3	100.0	97.9	3.8	3.4	105.1	97.2	2.8	100.0
1959/60	96.0	0.8	3.2	100.0	105.1	0.9	3.5	109.5	101.9	–1.9	100.0
1960/61	96.8	0.7	2.5	100.0	106.6	0.8	2.8	110.2	99.6	0.4	100.0
1961/62	82.7	12.4	4.9	100.0	89.8	13.5	5.3	108.6	100.0	0.0	100.0
1962/63	94.5	0.8	4.7	100.0	95.4	0.8	4.8	101.0	94.3	5.7	100.0
1963/64	89.2	5.5	5.3	100.0	94.9	5.9	5.6	106.4	98.9	1.1	100.0

SOURCE: Table 61.

relatively small and exceeded 20 per cent of the original budget only in 1955/56; they have been over 10 per cent in four other years, and as late as 1961/62.

Perhaps more significant from the point of view of legislative control are budget-type expenditures not covered in the current budget. These have fluctuated widely, and although they have reached as much as 10 per cent of expenditures only three times, they have raised the original budget by more than 10 per cent on five occasions. However, these un-budgeted expenditures have been fairly small since 1957/58.

From the point of view of the budget as a forecast of annual expenditure, it is of interest to compare the original budget with total expenditure. Before 1958/59, the original budget proved to be a poor forecast: on only two occasions did it amount to as much as 80 per cent of final expenditure. But from 1958/59 on, the original budget did not fall very far short of total expenditures, and, in fact, overstated them in 1959/60 and 1960/61.

The structure of the budget

The budget is usually divided into an ordinary and what may be called a capital budget.[7] The ordinary expenditure items are government consumption, subsidies, transfer payments, and interest on government debt. The budget itemizes these expenditures by ministry and, in recent years, also by a detailed classification of type of service. Until 1951 defense expenditures constituted a separate (and secret) budget, but since 1951/52 they have been included with ordinary expenditures, although without a detailed breakdown. Capital expenditures include investments, grants and loans for development, and debt retirement.

Ordinary receipts include direct and indirect taxes and other obligatory payments, payments for services, and income from property and entrepreneurship. Capital receipts include unilateral transfers from abroad, foreign and internal loans (including loans from the receipts of the National Insurance Institute, which are considered as direct taxes in the national accounts), and receipts from the sale of property and loan collection.

The division between the two parts of the budget reflects the widely

---

[7] Commonly referred to as the ordinary and development budgets. In recent years the official designations have been: ordinary receipts and expenditures; receipts from counterpart funds, etc., and expenditure for development, debt retirement, etc.; a third heading, transferred receipts and expenditures, covers the central government's transfers to local authorities.

held view that regular government services should be financed from orthodox, non-inflationary sources, such as taxes and the sale of services, whereas development can be financed from loans as well, preferably long-term ones. Two separate ideas are involved here which are occasionally confused. One is that current expenditure should be financed from current receipts, i.e., that the government should not dissave. Loans, which are liabilities, can be used for asset creation. The second concerns the inflationary aspects of government finance. In this respect, the source and type of loan is much more important than whether it is used for current or capital expenditure; what counts is the total of government debt financing and whether the debt diverts existing funds or creates new money. Thus, in the early years, defense and development were both financed by the creation of money: the former, current expenditure, by selling treasury bills to the banking system, and the latter, capital expenditure, by sale of Land Bonds. Both these methods of financing were stopped in 1951, and thereafter attempts were made to limit government inflationary pressure and to create government saving through an ordinary budget surplus to be used to finance part of the capital budget.[8]

The current budget surplus (or deficit) was often spurious, since multiple exchange rates and other manipulations allowed ample room for distorting the total of current expenditures; but the idea of striving to create a current account surplus was strongly held. In recent years, attention has been diverted from the saving to the inflation aspect. Thus, the 1962/63 development budget includes sizable defense expenditures, and the 1964/65 budget reintroduced ideas long since officially kept quiet: a suggestion that local bank credit should be used to finance part of the capital budget and a sizable transfer from the capital to the ordinary budget.

The Budget Law includes two other budgets, each divided into an ordinary and a development part. One is for government enterprises—Israel Railways, the Post Office, the Development Authority, and, until 1961/62, the ports.[9] The second is a contingent budget, which includes two conceptually different types of contingent expenditures. One is actually the separation of government activities that are effectively enterprises[10] and whose expenditures are contingent upon receipts. An

---

[8] It should be noted that the division into ordinary and development budgets conforms only roughly to the standard division into current and capital transactions. Thus, a surplus (or deficit) on ordinary budget is not identical with the concept of government saving (or dissaving).

[9] Ports were excluded after a Ports Authority was set up.

[10] Ancillary agencies in the U.N. terminology for government accounts.

example of this is the Office Mechanization Centre which sells computer services, mostly to government departments. The other, mainly in the development budget, is expenditure contingent on the participation of external bodies, e.g., Jewish Agency participation in housing. For some reason, the widely publicized budget totals do not include these additional budgets, although the reports on actual expenditure (and Table 61) do. Comparisons of annual budgets that exclude the contingency budgets are highly misleading, particularly in items such as housing.

Receipts

Over the years there were significant changes in the sources of receipts. The first two columns of Table 63 show the relative importance of internal and external sources. External sources[11] reached a peak of 35 per cent of total receipts in 1954/55 and have declined since. This decline reflects changes in the composition rather than in the total of foreign aid. For example, the increased flow of restitutions from Germany (which do not appear in the government budget) more than replaced the fall in German reparations in the balance of payments.

The second section of the table shows that taxes accounted for three quarters or more of total internal receipts in 1952/53–1960/61. It is safe to assume that inflationary finance reduced the percentage considerably in the early years. Since 1961/62, the share of taxes has declined somewhat.

The last section of the table shows the share of the main types of tax. Most notable is the fact that taxes on income reached half of total tax receipts only in 1964/65. Adding taxes on property does not alter the conclusion that the reliance on indirect taxes is much greater than is customary in more developed countries, and this is strange in view of Israel's strong socialist orientation.[12] Several factors combine to explain this structure. One is the comparative difficulty of administering income tax. That the share of income taxes rose from about one quarter in 1948/49 to almost one half in 1956/57 is due chiefly to the development of more efficient collecting techniques and to the fact that the population is gradually becoming used to paying. The comparative ease of levying indirect taxes accounts for the fact that the share of direct

[11] Local currency counterparts of foreign economic assistance, primarily U.S. grants and loans, German reparations, and sale of State of Israel Bonds.

[12] The low share of property taxes, except for the forced loan in 1952/53, has long been a strong irritant to the more leftist parties.

TABLE 63.   Sources of Government Receipts: 1948/49–1964/65

(per cent)

	Total receipts			Internal receipts			Taxes[a]				
	Internal sources (1)	External sources (2)	Total (3)	Taxes[a] (4)	Other receipts (5)	Total (6)	Income (7)	Property (8)	Expenditure (9)	Transactions (10)	Total (11)
1948/49	98.1	1.9	100.0	..	..	..	25.5	4.3	62.5	7.7	100.0
1949/50	69.8	30.2	100.0	60.1	39.9	100.0	26.0	3.9	61.7	8.4	100.0
1950/51	78.5	21.5	100.0	53.1	46.9	100.0	33.3	3.0	55.9	7.8	100.0
1951/52	76.7	23.3	100.0	68.4	31.6	100.0	34.5	3.4	55.7	6.4	100.0
1952/53	70.6	29.4	100.0	83.4	16.6	100.0	35.4	16.2	43.4	5.0	100.0
1953/54	67.9	32.1	100.0	84.9	15.1	100.0	35.7	7.2	52.3	4.8	100.0
1954/55	64.6	35.4	100.0	73.0	27.0	100.0	45.7	5.8	43.6	4.9	100.0
1955/56	70.0	30.0	100.0	80.9	19.1	100.0	45.5	4.0	46.2	4.3	100.0
1956/57	76.2	23.8	100.0	79.8	20.2	100.0	47.3	2.8	45.3	4.6	100.0
1957/58	78.9	21.1	100.0	79.1	20.9	100.0	43.4	2.4	49.9	4.3	100.0
1958/59	80.8	19.2	100.0	77.5	22.5	100.0	40.9	2.4	52.3	4.4	100.0
1959/60	81.1	18.9	100.0	73.1	26.9	100.0	39.9	2.4	52.9	4.8	100.0
1960/61	85.2	14.8	100.0	75.1	24.9	100.0	39.9	3.6	51.6	4.9	100.0
1961/62	86.2	13.8	100.0	66.5	33.5	100.0	39.0	3.1	52.3	5.6	100.0
1962/63	81.2	18.8	100.0	69.6	30.4	100.0	44.6	3.7	46.3	5.4	100.0
1963/64	81.8	18.2	100.0	74.1	25.9	100.0	48.5	3.8	42.0	5.7	100.0
1964/65	83.0	17.0	100.0	76.8	23.2	100.0	50.2	4.1	40.4	5.3	100.0

[a] Here and elsewhere taxes include certain compulsory loans such as the Absorption and Immigration Loan.

SOURCES: 1948/49 [columns (1) to (3)]—State Revenue Administration. Other data from Amotz Morag, *Public Finance in Israel: Problems and Development* (Jerusalem: The Magnes Press, 1967; Hebrew), as follows: Columns (1)–(3): p. 39, Table B–3; Columns (4)–(6): p. 42, Table B–5; Columns (7)–(10): p. 51, Table B–14.

The Morag figures are compiled from Reports of the State Revenue Administration.

taxes declined from the 1956/57 peak (although it increased again after 1961/63):[13] as the tax burden increases, there is greater inducement to rely more on indirect taxation.

THE ALLOCATION OF RESOURCES

All aspects of public financial activity influence the allocation of resources: through effects on relative commodity and factor prices, through redistributive effects, and through direct purchase and production of goods and services. In this section we concentrate on one important aspect of resource allocation—the provision of public consumption, chiefly at the expense of private use of resources, either for consumption or investment. We also deal briefly with how the composition of private consumption is affected, but defer discussion of most other allocation effects to later on in this chapter and to the chapter on foreign exchange policy (Chapter 10).

Public consumption

Although the entire population shares public consumption, it does not necessarily do so equally. Health and education services are certainly not distributed equally. The usual public finance approach is to consider the allocation function as diminishing private resources through taxation and substituting public consumption. In Israel, not all of public consumption is financed by taxation, or even by the sale of services. The government budget is officially limited to the sources just mentioned for its current expenditures (subject to the qualifications discussed above), but the national institutions provide public consumption financed from foreign transfers. For this reason, it is best to consider the allocation of total resources rather than of national product alone.

Should public expenditure include private non-profit institutions? It may be argued that this is a kind of consumption which the consumer can avoid if he wishes; however, in many instances, there is little difference between it and public consumption. For example, the bulk of health insurance in Israel is provided by the Histadrut sick fund rather than by a government agency. Not only is there little theoretical ground for considering this as different from public health services, but the item is a major component of the private non-profit institutions category.

The relevant data are shown in Table 64. Within public consumption

---

[13] The situation is complicated by the fact that some indirect taxes are substitutes for devaluation, and therefore change more radically when the exchange rate is officially altered.

TABLE 64. Public Consumption Expenditure, by Type of Institution: 1950–65ᵃ

(per cent)

	Per cent of public sector agencies				Per cent of resources at disposal of economy				
	Central government[b]	Local authorities	National institutions	Total	Central government[b]	Local authorities	National institutions	Total[c]	Private non-profit institutions[d]
	(1)	(2)	(3)	(4)	(5)	(6)	(7)	(8)	(9)
1950	75.6	13.3	11.1	100.0	12.1	2.1	1.8	16.0	4.4
1951	73.8	15.4	10.8	100.0	11.4	2.4	1.7	15.5	4.4
1952	67.6	22.1	10.3	100.0	9.9	3.3	1.5	14.7	4.8
1953	65.7	24.5	9.8	100.0	9.8	3.6	1.5	14.9	5.2
1954	68.6	23.2	8.2	100.0	10.2	3.4	1.2	14.8	5.2
1955	74.3	17.7	8.0	100.0	11.7	2.8	1.3	15.8	5.3
1956	80.4	13.0	6.6	100.0	16.5	2.7	1.3	20.5	5.1
1957	76.9	14.3	8.8	100.0	12.9	2.4	1.5	16.8	5.2
1958	78.1	14.6	7.3	100.0	12.7	2.3	1.2	16.2	5.4
1959	78.3	15.4	6.3	100.0	12.6	2.5	1.0	16.1	5.8
1960	79.2	15.0	5.8	100.0	12.8	2.4	0.9	16.1	5.6
1961	79.7	14.4	5.9	100.0	13.1	2.4	1.0	16.5	5.4
1962	80.0	13.1	6.9	100.0	14.0	2.3	1.2	17.5	5.0
1963	78.8	13.9	7.3	100.0	13.5	2.4	1.3	17.2	5.1
1964	77.7	15.4	6.9	100.0	12.7	2.5	1.1	16.3	5.2
1965	78.9	16.0	5.1	100.0	14.1	2.9	0.9	17.9	5.9

ᵃ Computed from current price data.
ᵇ Includes the National Insurance Institute.
ᶜ Columns (5), (6), and (7) computed by multiplying column (8) by columns (1), (2), and (3), respectively.
ᵈ Consumption of non-profit institutions as per cent of private consumption (in specified sources) multiplied by private consumption as per cent of resources [Table 30, column (1)].
SOURCES: 1950–59—Emanuel Levy and Others, Israel's National Income and Expenditure, 1950–1962 (Special Series No. 153; Jerusalem: CBS, 1964), pp. 80–81, Table 42 (public consumption); pp. 74–75, Table 39 (private non-profit institutions); pp. 32–33, Table 15 (total private consumption).
1960–65—Abstract 1966, No. 17, p. 167, Table F/9 (public consumption); Table F/8 (non-profit institutions).

the share of national institutions has been declining, whereas the share of central government declined from 1950 to 1953 and then started to rise [columns (1) and (3)].[14] The second part of the table shows clearly that a growing share of total resources has gone to public consumption; the decline in national institutions and the increase in government since 1953 are relative not only to each other but also to total resources.

Is public consumption high compared with other countries? Barkai has compared the ratio of public consumption to total resources in Israel with the ratio of public consumption to GNP in a number of other, mostly developed, countries. He concludes that Israel devotes a fairly high proportion of resources to public consumption.[15]

Morag has examined the taxation-burden aspect of this question and concluded that the burden of taxation in Israel is on the low side compared with countries at a similar level of per capita income: in Israel in 1955/56–1962/63 the ratio of net taxes (taxes *less* subsidies) to GDP was 23 per cent, and it ranged from 20 to 30 per cent in comparable countries in 1960. The burden of taxation remained fairly low in Israel even after increasing considerably between 1952 and 1960.[16]

Ofer, examining the problem from another point of view, concludes that a disproportionately high share of product and employment is devoted to public services in Israel.[17] These findings, similar to Barkai's, do not contradict Morag's conclusions: the tax burden is relatively low despite public consumption being high because part of public consumption (that of the national institutions) is not financed from tax revenue; the inclusion of non-profit institutions (as in Ofer's data) widens the disparity between the two magnitudes. The rise of the tax burden in recent years mainly reflects the rise in the share of public services.

[14] The year of the Sinai Campaign, 1956, is exceptionally high. There seems to have been some substitution between central government and local authorities in 1952–54.

[15] Haim Barkai, "The Public, Histadrut, and Private Sectors in the Israeli Economy," *Sixth Report 1961–1963* (Jerusalem: Falk Project, 1964), pp. 70–71, Table 12.

[16] Amotz Morag, *Public Finance in Israel: Problems and Development* (Jerusalem: The Magnes Press, 1967; Hebrew), p. 40, Table B–4; for the international comparison, p. 55, Table B–18.

[17] Gur Ofer, *The Service Industries in a Developing Economy: Israel As a Case Study* (Jerusalem and New York: Frederick A. Praeger with the Bank of Israel, 1967). As stated above (p. 112), the share in employment is easier to compare, because international comparisons show a correlation between per capita income and employment in public services.

TABLE 65.   *Share of Public Services in Product and Employment: 1961*

(*per cent*[a])

	Net domestic product	Employment[b]	
		Labor Force Surveys	Census
General government			
Central government	7.6	6.0	6.8
Local authorities	1.2	1.9	2.6
National institutions	0.7	1.5	1.8
Total general government	*9.5*	*9.4*	*11.2*
Other public services			
Education	4.0	7.5	7.2
Health	3.9	4.7	4.4
Welfare	0.7	0.9	0.9
Other	2.9	2.5	2.9
Total other public services	*11.5*	*15.6*	*15.4*
Total public services	**21.0**	**25.0**	**26.6**

[a] Per cent of total NDP and total employment.
[b] Survey figures are annual averages; census figures are from Stage B of the Census, June, 1961.
SOURCE: Gur Ofer, *The Service Industries in a Developing Economy: Israel As a Case Study* (Jerusalem and New York: Frederick A. Praeger with the Bank of Israel, 1967), p. 10, Table 2.1, and p. 92, Table 4.9.

Table 65 shows the percentage share of public services in net domestic product and in employment in 1961. Using these figures for international comparisons, the most detailed of which were with the United States and the United Kingdom, Ofer found that in employment, at least, there is considerable over-concentration in general government. In other public services, there is high concentration in education, health, and welfare. The large share of education results from the combination of an unusually high proportion of population attending primary and post-primary schools and a very low pupil-teacher ratio: Ofer estimated that about three quarters of the gap between the employment-shares of education in Israel and the United States is explained by demographic factors, and the remaining quarter by the difference in the pupil-teacher ratios. The high share of health services in Israel reflects a combination of strong demand, low efficiency, and large supply of doctors.[18]

[18] *Ibid.*, p. 62, Table 3.7 (education), and pp. 65–69 (health).

There is no correlation between per capita income and the product-share of general government, so we can draw no meaningful conclusions as regards this indicator; the product-share of other public services, however, is high by any standards: almost no other country, at any income level, has such a high share.

The high concentration in public services stems, as we have seen, from a combination of several factors: there is the high demand for certain services, notably education, health, and administration, arising from mass immigration and its demographic traits; less important are supply elements, such as the number of doctors; and technical efficiency is low in some general government services because of diseconomies of scale. But the most important factor, one which operates on the demand side, is undoubtedly the import surplus. The main reason why this is particularly important in explaining over-concentration in public services has already been mentioned several times: a major share of the capital import has gone to the public sector.

A special type of public consumption is defense expenditures. Surrounded as it is by hostile neighbors, Israel must divert resources from investment or other consumption to defense. Estimates of the defense burden are usually based on the total of the items "defense" and "special budgets" in the government budget.[19] Between 1950/51 and 1955/56 resources devoted to defense (thus defined) were below 6 per cent of total resources; in 1956/57 (the year of the Sinai Campaign) the figure was 11 per cent; in the following years the percentage dropped, but hardly below 7 per cent.[20] These figures alone suggest that the financial burden of defense in Israel is similar to that of the developed NATO countries, and far heavier than in most undeveloped countries.

However, the figures must be regarded as minimum estimates. Many activities, such as border settlements, desert roads, or pipelines, are undertaken primarily for defense considerations. Expenditures on such projects would not appear under defense, but under agriculture, transport, and the like. Furthermore, there is a high cost involved in developing particular industries for defense reasons. The recording of important educational activities carried out by the army as defense

[19] For example, Don Patinkin, *The Israel Economy: The First Decade* (Jerusalem: Falk Project, 1960); and David Klein, "Aims and Targets in the State Budget," *Israel Economy: Theory and Practice*, ed. Joseph Ronen (Tel Aviv: Dvir, n.d.; Hebrew), pp. 144–63.

[20] The figures are based on Ministry of Finance current-price figures used by Klein (*op. cit.*, p. 147, Table 4) to arrive at his constant-price figures, divided by total domestic resources from Appendix Table 1.

expenditures acts in the opposite direction.[21] However, on balance, we feel sure that proper conceptual and empirical recording of the defense burden would arrive at figures much higher than those given above.

Private consumption

An obvious effect of the tax system on private consumption is that it changes relative prices of consumer goods and services. As we have seen, taxes on consumer expenditure have been used extensively. Even if a uniform *ad valorem* tax were placed on all items, consumption patterns would be affected since price elasticities differ. But taxes have been far from uniform. The most striking disparities brought about by taxation have been between imports and domestic goods. Taxes on imports have always provided a large part of total indirect tax revenue.[22] They, too, have not been uniform. It is impossible to separate discussion of import taxes and foreign exchange policy, and further consideration of this subject is therefore deferred to the next chapter.

Another striking disparity in indirect taxation is between services and goods, the latter bearing almost the entire burden. Taxes on goods are supposed to be progressive, with basic necessities being taxed least (except for tobacco and beverages) and luxury goods being taxed most heavily. Regardless of whether progressiveness was achieved or not—this is discussed in the next section—it is certainly true that the heavy taxes on such "luxury" goods as automobiles, refrigerators, and radios affected the pattern of private consumption.

Taxation also affected consumer expenditure by reducing disposable income and altering its distribution. The reduction of income, by both direct and indirect taxation, tended to reduce consumption of all normal goods, particularly those with high income elasticity, such as durables. Food expenditures are less elastic than durables, but here too, the more elastic commodities—fruit, meat, and dairy products—were more affected.

In the next section we conclude that both taxation and public transfer payments have been progressive. The total effects on consumption

[21] For a discussion of these points, see Patinkin, *op. cit.*, pp. 55–58.

[22] Customs and fuel taxes declined from almost 70 per cent of total revenue from taxes on expenditure in 1948/49 to about 40 per cent in 1951/52, and thereafter fluctuated between 38 and 48 per cent (Morag, *op. cit.*, p. 49, Table B-11). But there are other taxes on imports, not appearing under customs, which ranged from 25 to 35 per cent of customs receipts in the years 1958–61 [Joseph Baruh, "Import Taxes and Export Subsidies in Israel, 1955–61," *Bank of Israel Bulletin*, No. 18 (March 1963), 52, Table 2].

of income redistribution are difficult to compute, but two statements are obvious. Transfer of income from high to low income groups increases consumption, particularly of the more income-elastic commodities. The progressive nature of taxation has a variable effect on the consumption of goods whose income-elasticity varies with income. Liviatan has computed Engel curves for food items and has found that income elasticity for all groups other than bread and cereals declines as income class rises; particularly affected are items which are generally income elastic, such as meat and dairy products.[23] Unfortunately, estimates of Engel curves are not available for non-food items.

REDISTRIBUTION OF INCOME

In Chapter 6 it was asserted that public finance has affected the distribution of welfare: on balance, the result has been greater equality. The obvious ways in which equality is increased are by progressive taxation and expenditure.

It has been pointed out that the redistributive effects of fiscal policy should be viewed as a whole, i.e., it is immaterial (from the point of view of income redistribution) whether the desired effect is achieved by a progressive income tax, by indirect taxes, or through government expenditure.[24] While we agree that much of the debate about the redistributive effect of each tax is meaningless, there are, from the point of view of welfare economics, important differences between the various methods of redistribution. For example, an indirect tax may be avoided by changing the pattern of expenditure; this is, of course, difficult when taxes are widespread, but the consumer still has some say in determining tax incidence. He has, however, no say as regards public consumption.

Before considering the direct effect on income distribution in greater detail, it ought to be mentioned that there are many indirect effects that have not been measured at all. Taxes affect the allocation of resources and thus the income of owners of various factors of production. For example, a prohibitive protective tariff brings in no revenue, but it certainly affects the income of the factor producing the protected product. Of course, there is no point in separating fiscal measures from other government instruments of intervention. It has frequently been charged that such government intervention in the economy has made special-interest groups rich: importers, industrialists, kibbutzim, and so

[23] Nissan Liviatan, *Consumption Patterns in Israel* (Jerusalem: Falk Project, 1964), p. 39, Table 14.
[24] Morag, *op. cit.*, pp. 57–62.

forth, depending on who is making the charge. On the other hand, it is true that the income-generating effect of government expenditure also raises the incomes of poorer families. Thus, at the present state of research in these matters, it is difficult even to speculate on the net effect on income distribution of government intervention of this sort.

The most frequently discussed fiscal measures that affect income distribution are direct taxes, primarily on income. These are designed to be progressive, although some income-tax provisions, designed for incentive purposes, are clearly not progressive. Another factor limiting the equalizing effect of income taxes is that many types of personal income are not taxed, for example, transfers from abroad and employer participation in expenses, some of which accrue mainly to the higher income groups.[25] Thus, a higher tax rate may be applied to a smaller share of total personal income. An additional problem is income tax evasion and avoidance, especially at the higher income levels. This often involves exploiting loopholes in tax legislation and thus takes the form of untaxed income.

Taxes on expenditure are generally not viewed as progressive, although it is possible to design them to be so, for example, by taxing automobiles and not bread. But when indirect taxes must account for a large share of revenue, it is virtually impossible to restrict them to luxuries.

On the expenditure side, it is not easy to determine progressive or regressive effects. Some expenditures, such as transfer payments, are generally progressive, going to low-income families.[26] It is conceptually difficult to attribute government consumption to the various recipients. However, some attempts have been made to do so, and they are discussed below.

Table 66 shows the effect of taxation on the income distribution of employees' families in 1959/60. The best measure of the effect of taxation is to compare indexes of inequality before and after taxes. It is seen that income tax reduced inequality, indirect taxes increased it, and subsidies reduced it slightly. Since the effect of income tax outweighed that of indirect taxes, the net effect of taxation was to reduce inequality slightly.

Although there are no comparable data for families of the self-

---

[25] Some, such as imputed rent from owner-occupied dwellings (taxed more in theory than in practice), may be relatively more important to low-income families.

[26] Subsidies, which may be progressive (e.g., on food) or regressive (e.g., on capital), are generally included as a negative component of indirect taxes.

employed, there are several studies on the effect of income tax alone.[27] These, too, indicate that direct taxation reduces inequality.

An attempt has been made to allocate transfer payments and government services among income groups for 1960/61. This is relatively easy for transfer payments; other current outlays were allocated according to several alternative methods. All the resulting series showed that government expenditures are progressive.[28]

Table 67 summarizes the total direct effect of the budget on income distribution. Not only is the expenditure side of the budget highly progressive, but it is much more important than taxation. Taking into account the transfer payments and services of the national institutions (not covered by Table 67) would make expenditure even more progressive: their revenue plays no role in income distribution since they are financed chiefly from abroad.[29]

Considering the effects of the various aspects of fiscal policy, it is easy to accept Morag's contention that taking account of income tax alone can lead to results opposite to those desired. For example, the labor parties might achieve income tax concessions at the lower taxpaying levels (not at the lowest incomes, which are exempt). The tax would then be more progressive, but the revenue might fall and lead either to additional indirect taxes, which bear more heavily on the poorer classes, or to reduced government services, with an even more regressive effect.[30]

No firm statements can be made concerning changes over time in the total direct redistributive effect of public finance, although the effects of specific components have been studied.

Changes in income tax progressiveness have been most closely examined,[31] although here, too, conclusions are not always clear-cut. For employees, income tax was more progressive in 1954 than in 1950 (but

---

[27] For example, the *Report of the Commission of Inquiry into the Distribution of National Income* (Jerusalem: 1966; Hebrew).

[28] Robert Szereszewski, "The Incidence of State Budget Expenditure by Income Group" (unpublished M.A. thesis, The Hebrew University, 1961; Hebrew). This study is discussed by Morag, *op. cit.,* p. 61.

[29] It may be assumed that the financial activities of local authorities, who provide general services financed primarily out of property taxes, are highly progressive on both the receipts and the expenditure side.

[30] Morag, *loc. cit.*

[31] See, for example, Haim Ben-Shahar, *Income Distribution of Wage and Salary Earners, 1950–1957* (Jerusalem: Ministry of Finance, 1961; Hebrew mimeograph).

TABLE 66.   Effect of Taxation on Income Distribution of Employees' Families: 1959/60

(per cent)

Income class by monthly income (IL)	Distri-bution of families	Distribution of income					
		Total income	Income less income tax	Income less indirect taxes	Income plus sub-sidies	Income less indirect taxes plus subsidies	Income less total net taxes
	(1)	(2)	(3)	(4)	(5)	(6)	(7)
Up to 149	7.7	2.1	2.4	1.9	2.2	1.9	2.2
150–199	5.5	2.5	2.8	2.3	2.5	2.3	2.7
200–249	10.3	6.1	6.7	5.9	6.1	5.9	6.5
250–299	14.1	10.1	10.8	9.8	10.2	9.9	10.6
300–349	16.8	14.3	14.8	14.0	14.3	14.1	14.7
350–399	10.0	9.5	9.7	9.4	9.5	9.4	9.7
400–449	8.3	9.2	9.4	9.3	9.2	9.3	9.4
450–549	11.2	14.6	14.3	14.7	14.5	14.7	14.5
550 and over	16.1	31.6	29.1	32.7	31.4	32.4	29.7
Total[a]	100.0	100.0	100.0	100.0	100.0	100.0	100.0
D index[b]		0.220	0.191	0.234	0.218	0.232	0.200
Percentage change in D index[c]			−13	+6	−1	+5	−9

[a] Figures may not add to 100 owing to rounding.
[b] Computed as half the absolute sum of the differences between column (1) and each of the other columns, divided by 9.
[c] Effect of tax element deducted in the column.
SOURCE: *Report of the Commission of Inquiry into the Distribution of National Income* (Jerusalem: 1966; Hebrew), p. 222, Table 103, and p. 223.

TABLE 67.   Effect of Government Budget on the Redistribution of Income: 1960/61

Income class by monthly income (IL)	Families	Distribution					Return per IL of tax[a] (IL)
		Pre-tax income	Taxes	Post-tax income	Services	Income after taxes and services	
Per cent of total							
Total	100	100	100	100	100	100	1.0
Up to 239	30	13	10	14	34	18	3.4
240–599	54	54	42	57	50	56	1.2
600 and over	16	33	48	29	16	26	0.3
Per cent of pre-tax income							
Total		100.0	19.4	80.6	19.4	100.0	
Up to 239		100.0	14.5	85.5	50.9	136.4	
240–599		100.0	15.2	84.8	17.9	102.7	
600 and over		100.0	28.0	72.0	9.4	81.4	

[a] Return per IL of tax = services ÷ taxes.
SOURCE: M. Zandberg, "The State Budget and Redistribution of Income," *The Economic Quarterly*, VIII (No. 32, October 1961; Hebrew), 322–31. Printing errors in the *Quarterly* article corrected here.

the 1950 figures are not very reliable) and more progressive again in 1957/58; the comparison of 1956/57 with 1959/60, however, shows reduced progressiveness. For the self-employed, income tax appears to have become somewhat less progressive between 1954 and 1960. On the average for all earners, there does not seem to have been much change in progressiveness.[32]

The effects of indirect taxes can be compared only for 1956/57 and 1959/60. The figures show that the indirect tax burden increased at all income levels, but apparently more for low and middle income families, thus becoming more regressive.[33]

Subsidies on many basic commodities decreased, so that net indirect taxes were certainly more regressive in 1959/60 than in 1956/57. Over a longer period, nothing definite can be said, but it seems logical to assume that a widening of indirect taxation and reduced subsidies, combined with rising incomes, result in more regressive indirect taxation.

If we accept this assumption and the conclusion that direct taxation taxes were certainly more regressive in 1959/60 than in 1956/57. Over less progressive. The relative rise of indirect taxes after 1956/57 strengthens this conclusion. On the other hand, the relative rise in public consumption, which is progressive, may have more than compensated for changes in the effects of taxation, subject to the conceptual qualifications mentioned earlier.

THE EFFECT ON GROWTH

Public finance has been very important in fostering the rapid growth of the economy; working primarily through capital formation, it also affects employment and efficiency. In our discussion we shall concentrate on capital formation. We make no attempt to estimate the net growth effect of public finance.

Capital formation

The government has always accepted responsibility for maintaining a high rate of investment; any differences of opinion have concerned means rather than ends. Discussions of investment policy in Israel frequently suffer from confusion between the supply and demand aspects

---

[32] *Report of the Commission of Inquiry into the Distribution of National Income, op. cit.*, p. 214, Table 96 (self-employed); p. 216, Table 98 (employees); and p. 218, Table 100 (whole population).

[33] *Ibid.*, p. 220, Table 101 and p. 221, Table 102.

of the subject. Let us therefore begin by stating the obvious: when investment takes place it means that there was both a demand for and a supply of capital. Investment policy has been concerned with stimulating both demand and supply, concentrating on whichever seems to be deficient at any given time. In our discussion we shall try to distinguish between these two sides of investment policy.

TABLE 68.   *Gross Fixed Capital Formation by the Public Sector: 1952–54 and 1960–62*[a]

	As per cent of domestic resources	*As per cent of total fixed investment*				*In IL millions*
		Total	*General government*[b]	*Government enterprises*[c]	*Public corporations*[d]	
1952	6.0	24.6		13.0	11.6	81
1953	6.6	29.5		14.1	15.4	111
1954	7.1	31.8		12.4	19.4	152
1960	6.4	28.9	11.4	4.1	13.4	328
1961	6.7	28.2	9.6	3.7	14.9	416
1962	7.5	29.9	8.5	3.6	17.8	596

[a] Public housing is not included.
The calculations are at current prices. The percentage breakdown by agency is taken from the earlier source listed below, and applied to the revised capital formation data of the later source.
[b] Central government, local authorities, and national institutions.
[c] Central government enterprises such as the Post Office.
[d] Corporations in which the public sector owns or controls at least 50 per cent of the shares.
SOURCES: 1952–54—Levy and Others, *op. cit.*, pp. 94–95, Table 50.
1960–65—*Abstract 1966*, No. 17, pp. 168–69, Table F/10.

Public investment activity: No continuous series of gross fixed capital formation by purchaser is available; Table 68 presents such data for three early and three recent years. There is little difference between the two periods: except for 1952 (for which the figure is a little lower) the share of the public sector in investment was close to 30 per cent.

It is of some interest to compare Israel with other countries. Kuznets found that the government's share of gross capital formation falls as one moves from lower to higher income per capita countries:[34] the

34 Simon Kuznets, "Quantitative Aspects of the Economic Growth of Nations V. Capital Formation Proportions: International Comparisons for Recent Years,"

relatively high share of public investment in Israel is similar to what is found in countries at a much lower income level and much higher than that in countries in a similar income class. On the other hand, capital formation as a per cent of resources (or GNP) rises with the level of per capita income; here Israel's high level of investment is characteristic of the higher income countries. Thus, the ratio of public investment to total resources (in the first column of Table 68) is relatively very high.[35]

Although direct public investment may be important in itself, as it reflects part of the demand for investment, it by no means represents all direct public investment activities. The public sector, primarily the government, is a major supplier of funds for investment. As we have seen, the main instrument for this purpose has been the development budget, which at first drew its receipts from inflationary finance (mainly the sale of Land Bonds to the banking system) and foreign grants and loans, then from foreign sources, and in recent years more from internal sources. Foreign sources are for the most part an addition to the supply of capital. Internal sources (whether inflationary or not) are a mixture of new saving (compulsory or voluntary) created and existing saving channeled through the budget.

Considerable significance has been attached to changes in the size and form of public financing of capital formation. It has been asserted that the sharp decline in the public sector's share of the financing of investment between 1954 and 1958 is "one of the clearest indications of the easing of overall Government control over the economy . . . ."[36] Patinkin, too, devoted some attention to the subject. His data and discussion bring out four main points: (a) after 1954 the public sector became less important as a financer of capital formation; (b) there was a shift in the pattern of public sector investment and finance, with central government and public sector enterprises receiving a declining share of public finance, while the share of public corporations rose; (c) the share of the private sector in public investment finance rose; and (d) the emphasis in public investment financing shifted from capital grants and direct investment to loans.[37]

Economic Development and Cultural Change, VIII (No. 4, part II, July 1960), 68–69.

[35] And even this figure is an understatement, since it excludes all public housing.
[36] Harold Lubell, *The Public and Private Sectors and Investment in Israel* (RAND Corporation P–2176, 1961; mimeograph), p. 10.
[37] Patinkin, *op. cit.,* pp. 83–88.

TABLE 69. *Share of Government Development Budget Expenditures Allocated to the Public Sector:*[a] *1949/50–1962/63*

	Per cent of:				
	Total expenditure[b]		Expenditure[b] excluding housing		
	Un-adjusted	With adjust-ments[c] (i) and (ii)	Un-adjusted	With adjustments[c]	
				(iii)	(ii) and (iii)
	(1)	(2)	(3)	(4)	(5)
1949/50	82.1	39.3	78.9	..	55.0[d]
1950/51	64.7	34.3	65.9	..	52.9[d]
1951/52	77.4	49.0	77.2	74.6	62.5
1952/53	78.9	48.3	79.8	69.5	60.8
1953/54	76.1	47.9	75.3	66.7	58.9
1954/55	71.2	45.4	74.9	68.9	57.1
1955/56	67.3	50.1	72.3	71.8	64.8
1956/57	55.3	45.9	66.9	65.9	60.6
1957/58	66.7	33.3	69.7	68.2	56.3
1958/59	67.6	38.2	70.0	67.7	50.8
1959/60	76.0	38.4	76.9	73.8	59.6
1960/61	67.1	45.0	71.0	70.6	58.0
1961/62	67.8	40.7	73.8	73.1	61.2
1962/63	76.6	47.9	78.9	78.8	74.5

[a] General government (including enterprises) and public sector corporations.
[b] Does not include: advances or special expenditure for capital investments in the Bank of Israel; repayment of debts; working capital for financial activities; a fund for the redemption of the Independence and Development Loans; an exchange-rate equalization fund; and special budgets. From 1955/56 on, the expenditure from earmarked receipts does not include incomes from public sector enterprises.
[c] The variants shown are the result of the following adjustments:
  (i) Housing expenditures are considered as allocated to the private sector.
  (ii) Final destination of loans and capital transfers to the national institutions assumed to be the private sector.
  (iii) Loans given through and purchase of securities of the Israel Bank of Agriculture are considered as loans to the private sector.
[d] Only adjustment (ii).
SOURCES: 1949/50–1954/55—R. M. Barkay, *The Public Sector Accounts of Israel: 1948/49–1954/55,* 2 vols. (Jerusalem: Falk Project and CBS, 1957; mimeograph).
  1955/56–1962/63—unpublished data of CBS National Accounts Department.

All this implies a general conclusion, similar to Lubell's, that there has been some liberalization in the investment sphere, at least until 1958. Although we do not have sufficient data for a thorough examination of this contention, we do have partial figures for a longer period than Lubell and Patinkin had.[38]

As far as can be seen from Table 68 there has been no tendency for the share of public finance received by public sector corporations to rise at the expense of general government and government enterprises. But there is in any case little evidence to suggest that constant shifts between various public sector firms have any economic significance; they appear to be more the product of administrative and financial convenience. Similarly, there is as yet no evidence to suggest that a shift from shares to loans in public corporations—if it exists—has any direct connection with the exercise of control.[39]

It is interesting to look for changes in the allocation of public sector investment finance between public and private recipients. We have not been able to obtain data for investment financing by the whole public sector; Table 69 gives the percentage of development budget investment expenditures going to the public sector, according to several alternative classifications.

The first column of the table, which presents the CBS classification, shows no clear trend, with the public sector's share of government financing ranging from a peak of 82 per cent to as low as 55 per cent; in the last few years covered the range is from 66 to 76 per cent. Since public housing is conceptually difficult to classify, columns (3), (4), and (5) exclude it. This adjustment alone [column (3) compared with column (1)] makes little difference; however, public housing is affected by fluctuations in immigration, and this is reflected in 1956/57 and 1961/62, when the share of the public sector rises considerably if housing is excluded. In column (4) government investments in and loans to the Israel Bank of Agriculture are transferred from "public" to "private," since this bank is merely a channel for distributing funds to agricultural units. This adjustment makes a difference only until

---

38 The following discussion benefited greatly from consultation with David Pines, who has examined this question. We are also indebted to Mrs S. Kamir of the National Accounts Department of the CBS for much useful unpublished information.

39 It is difficult to check this statistically, because large sums are often allocated before it has been decided whether they are to be loans or shares. Similarly, several large loans were converted to shares in order to tidy up the balance sheets of public corporations.

TABLE 70. Indicators of Change in the Level of Public Investment Financing: 1950–65

	Real fixed investment:[a] index, 1950 = 100		Per cent of total fixed investment		Per cent of resources		
	Total	Financed by public sector[b]	Financed by public sector[b]	Direct government investment	Total fixed investment	Financed by public sector[b]	Direct government investment
	(1)	(2)	(3)	(4)	(5)	(6)	(7)
1950	100	100	42[c]	..	24.1	10.5	..
1951	119	110	39[c]	..	26.8	10.7	..
1952	96	119	49	24.6	24.3	13.0	6.0
1953	82	140	69	29.5	22.4	16.5	6.6
1954	90	183	81	31.8	22.2	19.3	7.1
1955	107	148	59	..	23.5	13.8	..
1956	107	130	52	..	21.3	11.1	..
1957	126	168	57	..	23.6	13.4	..
1958	133	164	53	..	22.7	12.0	..
1959	144	175	52	..	22.4	11.6	..
1960	153	189	53	28.9	22.0	11.7	6.4
1961	183	184	43	28.2	23.6	10.1	6.7
1962	204	195	41	29.9	25.2	10.3	7.5
1963	215	200	40	..	24.3	9.7	..
1964	256	233	39	..	25.4	9.9	..
1965	252	252	43	..	23.0	9.9	..

[a] Based on data at 1955 prices.   [b] For 1950–54, the computations in columns (2) and (6) use total (not fixed) capital formation, since the Lubell data for column (3) are on this basis.   [c] Direct government investment only.

SOURCES: Columns (1), (2), and (3)—Total and fixed capital formation from *Abstract 1965*, No. 16, p. 170, Table F/10 (for 1950–51); and *Abstract 1966*, No. 17, pp. 168–69, Table F/10 (for 1952–65). Per cent of publicly financed investment from Harold Lubell and Others, *Israel's National Expenditure: 1950–1954* (Jerusalem: Falk Project and CBS, 1958), p. 24, Table 2–15 (for 1950–54); Bank of Israel, *Annual Report 1955*, p. 64, Table 38 (for 1955); and Table 71 below (for 1956–65).
    Column (2) is the index of the series computed by multiplying column (1) by column (3).
    Columns (4) and (7)—Table 68.
    Columns (5) and (6)—computed from the absolute current price figures underlying columns (1) and (2), respectively, divided by domestic resources from column (7) of Appendix Table 1.

1955/56. Perhaps it is this factor, for which Patinkin's data are not adjusted, that gave the impression of a relatively larger public sector share in the early years compared with 1956–58. In column (5) there is, in addition, a similar adjustment for loans to national institutions. This further lowers the public sector share. Finally, column (2) includes public housing and classifies it as private: the public sector share drops to no more than half, ranging from 40 to 50 per cent in 1949/50–1956/57 (except in 1950/51), falling to between 33 and 38 per cent in 1957/58–1959/60, and rising again to between 40 and 48 per cent in the last three years shown. Certainly, no declining trend is evident.

Returning to the broader question of public sector financing of total fixed capital formation, Table 70 summarizes several informative statistical series. Column (3) indicates that the share of public financing of total fixed capital formation indeed dropped after 1954. But perhaps more important is the fact that 1953 and 1954 are exceptional in this respect. In fact, the share was fairly steady from 1956 to 1960, at just over 50 per cent, declining in 1960–65 to about the level of the beginning of the decade.

What happened in 1953 and 1954? Real capital formation declined in 1952 and 1953 [column (1)], as did the ratio of investment to total resources [column (5)]. The stagnation of investment—undoubtedly a result of the New Economic Policy—was primarily a stagnation of private investment; public financing as a per cent of total resources rose in both years [column (6)], and direct public investment also rose [columns (4) and (7)].[40] It thus appears that public financing of investment substituted for private investment. In 1954 total investment increased, but no more than did total resources. Much of the increase reflects a tremendous increase in public investment activity, which raised the ratio of public finance to total resources to an all-time high. In 1955, when the 1952–53 recession was clearly over, private investment reasserted itself: the share of investment in resources rose despite a drastic fall in public investment activity.

After 1955, the changes in the share of the public sector's finance of total investment are not so large, although in 1961–65 it is clearly lower than in the preceding period. Is this decline economically significant? Tables 71 and 72 present data on public finance of gross fixed capital formation as a per cent of total investment in each branch and as a per cent of total publicly financed fixed investment, for the

[40] The figures on public investment finance exclude housing; it was the housing budget which was drastically cut by the New Economic Policy.

TABLE 71.   Public Financing of Gross Fixed Capital Formation, by Industry: 1956–65

(per cent)

	Agriculture and irrigation	Manufacturing	Mining and quarrying	Transportation	Electric power	Trade and services	Dwellings	Total
1956[a]	72	39		93[b]	61	39	33	52
1957[a]	61	43		84[b]	87	34	48	57
1958	74	42	75	59	69	48	44	53
1959	72	32	71	68	54	56	44	52
1960	84	39	50	77	5	57	38	53
1961	81	36	10	56	8	42	29	43
1962	75	24	11	48	26	44	36	41
1963	83	24	21	44	23	45	32	40
1964	90	10	13	38	30	47	39	39
1965	88	6	27	54	39	50	41	43

[a] Absolute figures of public-financed fixed investment calculated from Bank of Israel source and divided by revised total fixed investment figures in the *Abstract*.

[b] Items joined because of possible classification differences between earlier and later sources.

SOURCES: Bank of Israel, *Annual Report 1957*, p. 57, Table V–2, and p. 61, Table V–4 (for 1956); *Annual Report 1958*, p. 58, Table V–4 (for 1957); *Annual Report 1965*, p. 102, Table V–17 (for 1958–65; this source is consistent with the *Abstract* figures cited). Total fixed investment for *Abstract 1966*, No. 17, p. 169, Table F/10.

TABLE 72.   Gross Fixed Domestic Capital Formation, by Industry—Total and Publicly Financed: 1956–65

(per cent)

	Agriculture and irrigation	Manufacturing	Mining and quarrying	Transportation	Electric power	Trade and services	Dwellings	Total	Total in IL millions
Total									
1956	20	13	2	11	8	13	33	100	700
1957	18	10	2	16	6	14	34	100	870
1958	20	16	1	12	5	14	32	100	941
1959	17	19	1	12	4	15	32	100	1,036
1960	16	17	1	14	3	18	31	100	1,132
1961	13	17	2	16	3	17	32	100	1,474
1962	13	16	3	14	4	16	34	100	1,995
1963	12	18	3	15	3	18	31	100	2,216
1964	9	16	3	23	2	18	29	100	2,742
1965	8	16	2	20	4	20	30	100	2,815
Public									
1956	27	10	8	16	9	9	21	100	365
1957	19	8	3	24	9	8	29	100	493
1958	27	13	1	13	7	13	26	100	503
1959	24	11	2	15	4	16	28	100	538
1960	26	12	1	20	0	19	22	100	605
1961	26	14	0	21	0	17	22	100	631
1962	24	10	1	16	2	17	30	100	816
1963	25	11	2	16	2	20	24	100	890
1964	20	4	1	22	2	22	29	100	1,072
1965	17	2	1	25	3	23	29	100	1,220

SOURCE: Computed from sources to Table 71.

years 1956–65 (that is, for the years after the sharp drop in the share of public finance).

The extent of public financing has varied greatly among branches, and, in some branches, over time. Agricultural investment was consistently and predominantly financed by the public sector. The rise in the public finance ratio in the 1960's reflects a relative increase in irrigation investments at a time when the share of agriculture in total investment was declining. Manufacturing and housing have relied least on public finance. Mining and quarrying drew considerably on public finance until 1960, and electric power (a public corporation) until 1959; thereafter, non-public sources came to the fore. The greatest fluctuations are evident in the financing of transport.

The allocation of public investment finance shows no drastic shifts between branches nor any tendency to concentration in a particular branch: no single branch has received more than 30 per cent of the total. But agriculture has received 24 to 27 per cent of total public investment finance (except in 1957 and 1960), and housing, too, has received between 20 and 30 per cent; the two together have consistently accounted for about half the total. On the other hand, manufacturing received as much as 14 per cent of total public finance only in 1961. Whereas manufacturing, electric power, and mining and quarrying together received over 20 per cent in 1956–58 and 13 to 14 per cent thereafter until 1963, their combined share was only about 7 per cent in 1964 and 1965.

Comparison of the shares of the various branches in total and in publicly financed fixed capital formation shows that trade and transport have similar shares in both; agriculture has a consistently higher share of publicly financed than of total investment, the converse being true for manufacturing and housing.

The recent decline in the share of publicly financed investment appears to reflect mainly declines in the public sector share in manufacturing, mining and quarrying, electric power, and transport. Does this mean greater liberalization? In recent years there has been a change in the pattern of finance. Several large public corporations such as the Israel Electric Company and the Dead Sea Works have been raising capital from local and foreign sources without these funds formally appearing in the development budget. Similarly, public and semi-public financial institutions, such as the Industrial Development Bank of Israel, have been carrying an increasing share of the financing of investment in manufacturing and housing; the initiative and effective control of funds are still largely in government hands, but again the development budget is circumvented. This changing pattern of finance reflects the fact that in recent years funds for development have been supplied more from internal and less from foreign sources; the government may have been able to relinquish part of its function as a supplier of funds, but it has not relinquished its role as a channeler of investment.

To sum up: This important subject has clearly not yet been adequately investigated, but on the basis of the meager knowledge presently available, it is difficult to see any clear trend indicating a reduction in public initiative or control of investment activity.

The demand for investment: The demand curve for investment may conceptually be derived from an array of potential investment projects ranked by their internal rates of return. The government affects this demand curve in many ways, and its own demand curve has already been discussed. Private demand can be increased by measures which make potential projects more profitable: government tariff, exchange rate, and pricing policy all combine to affect the profitability of investment projects. Among the relevant fiscal measures are capital grants, subsidies, and tax concessions. For example, while corporate income and profit taxes are assessed at a rate of 46 per cent, "approved" investments pay only 25 per cent, and this, after liberal depreciation allowances.

Government infra-structure investment in transport, communications, and public utilities also raises the rate of return on private investment. Although this factor is of great importance, no attempt has been made to estimate these external economies.

In addition to affecting the slope of the demand curve, the government affects its level by controlling the rate of interest. As a major source of funds, the government increases the supply of capital; if thrown into a free market, this would suffice to lower the rate of interest. But the government in fact has used several institutional arrangements for supplying its capital. Chief among them has been the low-interest loan of a proportion of the capital, with the proportion varying among projects. By manipulating the rates of interest charged as well as the proportion of the loans, the government affects the rate of interest on private capital.[41] In other words, in order to induce private firms to undertake projects which are submarginal from the

---

[41] For an analytical model of the market for capital in Israel and its application to developments in the rate of interest, see Haim Ben-Shahar, *Interest Rates and the Cost of Capital in Israel, 1950–1962* (Basel and Tübingen: Kyklos-Verlag and J.C.B. Mohr, 1965).

investor's point of view, the government lends money at rates lower than it itself pays,[42] thereby raising the rate of return on private capital.

Table 73 presents some of Ben-Shahar's estimates of interest rates and cost of capital. The distinction between effective and real rates

TABLE 73.   *Interest Rates and Cost of Capital: 1950–61*

(*per cent*)

	1950–53	1954–55	1956–59	1960–61
Effective cost of capital to the economy[a]		10–14	14–16	17–19
Real cost of capital to the economy[b]		4–8	9–11	12–14
Effective average interest rates on development budget loans				
Total	5.0	6.0	6.9	8.6
Agriculture	4.5	5.6	5.3	5.5
Manufacturing	5.5	8.1	8.9	13.3
Mining	5.5	7.0	7.5	9.5
Real average interest rates on development budget loans[b]				
Total	–6.7	0.5	2.6	4.2
Agriculture	–7.2	0.1	1.2	1.2
Manufacturing	–10.5	1.3	4.6	8.4
Mining	–6.3	1.1	3.5	5.0
Rates of participation on government loans				
Agriculture		70	60	50
Manufacturing		50	50	40
Private cost of capital[c]				
Average effective rate		25[d]		
Average real rate[b]		17[d]		

[a] Based on cost of State of Israel Bonds.
[b] Deflated by implicit price index of capital formation.
[c] Estimated return on equity capital in the share index.
[d] 1954–60.
SOURCE: Haim Ben-Shahar, *Interest Rates and the Cost of Capital in Israel, 1950–1962* (Basel and Tübingen: Kyklos-Verlag and J.C.B. Mohr, 1965), p. 83, Table 32; p. 85, Table 33; and p. 103, Table 35.

[42] After discussing several alternative measures of the cost of capital to the economy, Ben-Shahar chooses the real rate of interest on State of Israel Bonds as the most appropriate measure.

is important because of rapid price increases and occasional official devaluations.[43]

The data suggest several observations. First, effective interest rates on development budget loans averaged 5 per cent in 1950–53, rising steadily thereafter. In the early years prices rose so rapidly as to make real rates of interest on these loans negative. Real interest rates have been positive from 1954, but they have averaged as much as 4 per cent cent only from 1960.

Second, the real cost of capital to the economy has throughout been higher than the average real rates charged by the government; although both rose, the difference between them has not diminished. As the rates charged by the government rose, the rate of government participation declined, a trend that supplemented the rise in rates. The real private cost of capital has been estimated at 17 per cent for 1954–60; this is above the cost of capital to the economy and is in keeping with Ben-Shahar's model.

Third, the discriminatory nature of government loans is in keeping with other policies designed to favor agriculture: more generous rates of government participation are evident in agriculture (particularly if Jewish Agency funds are included), and interest charged is lower. In 1950–53, when effective rates discriminated only slightly, real rates favored manufacturing. But since then, as both effective and real rates rose, a large disparity has arisen in favor of agriculture, with mining between agriculture and manufacturing.

Before leaving the demand side of capital formation we should consider briefly the fundamental question of whether it was necessary to stimulate demand for investment. The assertion is often made that Israel's problem has been a shortage of supply, not demand.[44] A deficiency in demand for investment means that the supply of capital exceeds the quantity demanded at the prevailing marginal efficiency of capital. In such an event, public policy that lowers the rate of interest or shifts the demand curve will increase investment. Has this been the situation in Israel?

We do not feel that the available data are sufficient for an empirical

---

[43] Effective rates are nominal rates *plus* commissions and other hidden charges *plus* the effects of devaluation on dollar-linked loans; real rates are effective rates deflated by an implicit index of capital formation prices. For a discussion of the method and the basis of computing alternative rates, see Ben-Shahar, *op. cit.*, Chapter 5.

[44] See, for example, Michael Michaely, *Foreign Trade and Capital Imports in Israel* (Tel Aviv: Am Oved, 1963; Hebrew), pp. 126–27.

answer to this question, but they do suggest a general surmise. Bruno has estimated the marginal product of capital in manufacturing at about 22 per cent in 1961. Allowing for even very wide margins of error, the figure does not in itself suggest excess supply of and insufficient demand for capital. But that is on the assumption of competitive equilibrium, where factors of production really receive the value of their marginal product. It has been suggested that in Israel institutional arrangements have tended to give labor (on the average, not necessarily to all classes) more than the value of its marginal product. Bruno has estimated the return on capital in manufacturing at 15 per cent in 1961.[45] It is quite possible that demand, based on this rate of return, was low.[46] Government stimulation of demand by giving loans at the very low real rates shown in Table 73 raised the rate of return on private capital and thus tended to compensate for the institutional distortion in favor of labor.

It is perhaps more consistent with actual policy considerations to look not at the aggregate demand for investment, but rather at particular branches. The government's concern was not that part of the capital supply would go unused, but that it would not be used in those branches which the government considered most in need of development. The justification generally made for stimulation of demand in specific industries is that the rate of return from the point of view of the economy may be higher than the rate of return to the individual investor. The social and private rates of return may differ either because of purely economic factors such as external economies or diseconomies, or because noneconomic factors have been included in the computation of social return.

Government policy throughout has been to encourage agricultural settlement, and in later years increased attention was devoted to mining and manufacturing. It was felt that the rate of return in these fields was too low to attract investment.[47] Consequently, favorable loan terms were

[45] Michael Bruno, "Factor Productivity and Remuneration in Israel, 1952–1961," *The Economic Quarterly*, X (No. 37–38, March 1963; Hebrew), 41–56.

[46] It might seem that Ben-Shahar's rates of interest on non-government loans can be used for comparison with the return on capital. However, even the non-government loan rates reflect the predominance of public sources in the money market and cannot be used as a measure of "non-intervention" rates.

[47] Bruno's figures on capital returns in 1958 show that the return was higher in trade and services than in construction, lower in agriculture, lower still in manufacturing and transport, and zero in power and irrigation [Michael Bruno, *Interdependence, Resource Use and Structural Change in Israel*

granted to agriculture and, to a lesser degree, to industry; and agricultural settlement, irrigation, electric power, and much of transport were financed primarily from public sources. This easy finance and the low interest charged on development loans fits into the general picture of higher rates of return elsewhere. This does not imply that the government's intervention was necessarily justified or best suited to its purpose. In fact, Ben-Shahar's figures on negative or zero real interest charges for a substantial period suggest that encouragement of demand went to extremes.

Supply of capital

The influence of the government on the supply of capital to individual investors was discussed in the previous section. But there is a difference between supply of capital in this sense and the real supply of capital from the point of view of the whole economy. The amount of capital supplied in a given period is equal to domestic saving *plus* the import surplus. Consequently, the government can affect the supply of capital either by increasing domestic saving or by increasing the import surplus. We shall now consider the various components of domestic saving; the import surplus is discussed elsewhere.

Household saving: As measured by various surveys, this has been positive, and rose between 1954 and 1957/58, and between 1957/58 and 1963/64. Since rising income and greater income inequality are not credited with much of this increase in saving, the main factors must be sought in changing propensities to save. Our interest is, therefore, in fiscal policies that may have raised the propensity to save.

A large and growing proportion of household asset formation is in the form of real estate. The most common way of acquiring housing is to purchase apartments financed out of long-term mortgage loans supplemented by shorter-term loans. The increased equity through debt repayment is saving. The government has encouraged housing purchases through its own housing schemes, through tax concessions on the saving-for-housing programs, and through efforts to induce tenants of public housing to purchase their apartments.[48] In recent years, however, new

---

(Special Studies No. 2; Jerusalem: Bank of Israel Research Department, 1962), pp. 52–53, Table III–1]. This tends to support the above contention.

[48] Apparently, little was done, at least until 1957/58, to induce people who had finished paying off their mortgages to shift to other types of saving. Edmond A. Lisle, "Household Savings in Israel, 1954 to 1957/58," *Bank of Israel Bulletin,* No. 21 (April 1964), p. 100.

real estate purchases by individuals have been more in the private market than in public housing. A comparative study of saving surveys for 1954 and 1957/58 has concluded that income elasticities for housing decline as incomes rise and that housing standards are fairly constant over widely different income or social groups.[49] Since 1957/58, there have apparently been significant changes in housing standards. In any event, government fiscal policy has had only indirect effects on private housing. The lax capital gains tax on real estate, though tightened in 1964, and the lack of adequate restraints on housing credit could not prevent a large expansion in the quantity and quality of private housing; some of this expansion represents what individuals thought to be inflationproof investment. In other words, the deficiencies of fiscal and monetary policy may have led to increased saving, but if so it was in the form least desirable to the government. In fact, it might be claimed that the household saving ratios in Israel, concentrated as they are in housing, are the obverse of the conditions, government policy included, that prevented rental housing from developing.

A second important category is contractual saving.[50] Government policy can affect this kind of saving either by encouraging the formation of new types of retirement plan and stimulating the membership of existing schemes, or by restricting the proportion of fund receipts going back to members as loans. The popularity of pension and provident funds is primarily the result of the efforts of the labor movement, not of active government policy.

Tax concessions to funds were from 1957 made contingent on the acceptance of certain rules of conduct, the most important of which was the requirement to invest a high proportion of fund assets in "approved" securities, predominantly government or government-guaranteed linked bonds.[51] In addition, the funds were required to link loans granted to members.

The last major component of household saving is liquid assets, including bank deposits of all kinds and securities. The saving surveys indicate that the weight of this form of holding savings rose between 1954 and 1957/58, and balance-sheet estimates of saving indicate a much more

---

[49] *Ibid.*, p. 73.
[50] For example, fixed payments to provident and pension funds. The surveys include mortgage payments as contractual saving, while we have dealt with them in the discussion on housing.
[51] The proportion was at first 65 per cent, and was raised to 75 per cent in April, 1962, and to 80 per cent in 1964.

significant rise in recent years.[52] Although no reliable breakdowns of this item are available, certain general conclusions can be drawn. First, there has been a definite shift in personal habits as regards holding bank deposits, particularly to checking accounts.[53] This may be the result of more moderate price rises, although the real rate of return on checking accounts has been negative in recent years. Another factor is that government salaries have been paid into bank accounts since 1962.

Government policy is more evident in the rise in time deposits, particularly since 1957; special saving schemes for such purposes as housing and secondary education, were initiated and encouraged by the government. These, and time deposits in banks, have been supported by tax concessions and higher rates of return. They are also fairly liquid. High rates of return and full linkage have induced many recipients of restitution payments to retain them in special deposits,[54] but it is debatable whether this should be considered as designed to increase saving or to induce the holding of a given amount of assets in a particular, noninflationary, form. Perhaps the most important government activity has been the issue of linked securities, together with other efforts to develop a securities market. The rapid rise in holdings of securities is a recent phenomenon, and its effect on saving has not yet been adequately examined. The development of the securities market, which was quite rapid in the early 1960's, received a severe setback in the middle of the decade.[55]

Finally, the tendency of the self-employed to save by investing in their own businesses may be indirectly due to government restrictions on credit for working capital.

[52] Lisle, op. cit., p. 62, and Bank of Israel, Annual Report 1962 and Annual Report 1963 (Chapter XIX in both).

[53] The available data do not permit the separation of private from business accounts.

[54] Between 1959 and the 1962 devaluation interest on these special deposits was 6 to 7 per cent. Afterwards the rate on deposits not usable as foreign exchange remained 7 per cent, but the rate on deposits which may be so used was, for reasons difficult to understand, reduced to 4.5 per cent.

[55] On the growth of the securities market, see Marshall Sarnat, The Development of the Securities Market in Israel (Basel and Tübingen: Kyklos-Verlag and J.C.B. Mohr, 1966). The Lisle study indicates that the holding of liquid assets was, in 1957/58, mostly confined to professional and white-collar workers, and to a large extent financed by debt, not by saving (Lisle, op. cit., p. 70).

A survey of property (carried out as part of the Saving Survey, 1963/64) shows that various types of securities make up only 3 per cent of net household assets; deposits are 7 per cent and apartments are 90 per cent.

Business saving: One type of business saving—that of the self-employed —has already been mentioned under personal saving. What is generally meant by the term "business saving" is the reinvestment of earnings by firms, from depreciation funds or undistributed profits.[56] Very little information is available about this type of saving in Israel. However, several studies on the financial structure of enterprises supply enough information to suggest qualitative, if not quantitative, comments on the effects of government policy. Since business saving derives from profits, any policy which increases profits is a first step in increasing business saving. Fiscal policy has acted to increase profits by providing capital at effective real rates lower than the marginal product of capital, thus increasing the rate of return on own capital. Also, income tax concessions and generous depreciation allowances, subsidies and grants, protection, and other policy measures outside the scope of this chapter, such as cartel policy or price supports, have been of great importance in raising profits, particularly in agriculture and industry. Little is known about the use of business profits, but most studies conclude that they have been growing rapidly.[57] The decision to invest or to distribute profits is affected by many factors. Most important, perhaps, is the availability and terms of other sources of finance. It has frequently been charged that the liberal terms of the public development budget have tended to replace other sources of finance. The studies of the financial structure of industry support this charge: despite deficiencies in the data, it is clear that equity capital declined betwen 1950 and 1956, and that (until 1961) this decline was stopped as a result of stiffening development budget terms.[58] Another conclusion—subject to even greater reservations—is that business saving in industry rose steeply in 1956–61, primarily from undistributed profits. It is of interest that corporate income tax has not been refined to favor undistributed over distributed profits.

[56] Only if depreciation funds exceed real depreciation is there any net saving from this source.

[57] See, for example, the following articles in various *Bank of Israel Bulletins:* Efraim Dovrat, Nurit Wahl, and Meir Tamari, "The Financial Structure of Israel's Industrial Companies," No. 17 (January 1963), 39–93; Meir Tamari, "Changes in the Financial Structure of Israel's Industrial Companies, 1956/57 to 1961/62," No. 19 (November 1963), 14–63; *idem.,* "Financial Changes in Israel's Industrial Companies in 1962," No. 22 (December 1964), 17–31.
See also Ephraim Kleiman, *The Structure of Israel Manufacturing Industries, 1952–1962* (Jerusalem: Falk Project, 1964; mimeograph).

[58] See the articles cited in the preceding note, particularly the first two. Equity here includes loans by owners, a form popular in Israel for reasons of taxation.

Public saving: Just as business saving in the national accounts is lumped together with household saving, public saving estimates in Israel generally include the saving of non-profit institutions. Since household saving is positive while total saving is generally negative, public saving must be the culprit. As we saw in Chapter 6, some of the public dissaving stems from problems of definition and disappears when unilateral transfers from abroad are included in current receipts.

It is the accounts of the national and non-profit institutions that are most affected by the way unilateral transfers are recorded: financed to a great extent by foreign transfers, they dissave by definition.[59] The situation is in practice even more complicated, since in many of their transactions the institutions can be viewed as intermediaries between foreign transferrers and local individual recipients; in other words, the institutional allocation of transfers converts personal into institutional dissaving.[60]

Government saving is generally defined as the difference between current receipts and current expenditure. This has generally been negative. However, although this current account deficit was as much as 50 per cent of current receipts in 1950 and still over one third in 1951–53, the ratio declined steeply (except for the war year 1956) starting in 1954.[61] As mentioned earlier, since 1952 it has been declared government policy to try to finance current expenditures from tax revenues, using foreign transfers and local and foreign loans for capital transactions. There is no evidence of any serious attempt to create sizable surpluses on current account to finance capital transactions, i.e., to create government saving. Thus, despite constant exhortation on the part of the government to increase saving, little has been done in the government's own accounts.

One reservation must be made here: the questionable accounting technique of recording investment in human capital as consumption explains much of the public dissaving. Clearly, much of the burden

---

[59] The financing of the activities of the national institutions has already been mentioned (pp. 159–60). Non-profit institutions rely somewhat less on foreign transfers. In recent years they have declined relatively to total receipts, from 29 per cent in 1957 to 22 per cent in 1963. As a per cent of current receipts their share is larger—30 to 40 per cent—and has not been declining. Oded Hatzroni, "The Nonprofit Institutions in Israel, 1957–1963" (unpublished seminar paper, The Hebrew University, 1964; Hebrew).

[60] For a discussion of this point, see Patinkin, *op. cit.*, p. 97.

[61] Emanuel Levy and Others, *Israel's National Income and Expenditure, 1950–1962* (Special Series No. 153; Jerusalem: CBS, 1964), pp. 20–21, Table 9.

of financing health and education services falls on the government. Nonetheless, expanding education services need not increase government dissaving: they can be financed at the expense of other public consumption, or out of increased taxation. The latter is certainly desirable in view of the prolonged and rapid growth of private consumption.

Employment

Fiscal measures which affect the demand for or the supply of labor affect employment, both in the sense of the number of people employed and of the intensity of labor input. The main effects are through the demand side. We shall briefly consider the various effects, although our discussion will unfortunately be more qualitative than quantitative.

The Keynesian revolution of the 1930's has become standard fiscal theory as regards the role of public expenditure in maintaining stability or combating unemployment. Although, for the second aim, the importance of deficit financing has been stressed, it should be remembered that even a balanced budget acts to increase effective demand.[62] Since government consumption—the most "balanced" part of public expenditure—is an important part of total resource use and is financed by progressive taxation, it has stimulated demand for employment directly and through the multiplier effect. Furthermore, government consumption has grown steadily.

The rest of public consumption, being financed mainly from foreign transfers, is, of course, inflationary in the sense that it stimulates effective demand. Real total public consumption declined in 1952 and did not regain its 1952 level in 1953; these were years of rising unemployment. In 1957 public consumption again declined and reached the 1956 level only in 1960; but if the war year 1956 is excluded, we see that real public consumption has been growing from 1953 (Table 28). Public investment, a more flexible tool of fiscal policy, has shown greater variations.

Total public effective demand has been excessive, in the sense of being one of the principal causes of an inflation that has persisted, with only brief interludes, throughout the period surveyed. Yet to say that effective demand was excessive does not necessarily mean that public demand could have been curtailed without increasing unemployment. Labor immobility, both occupational and geographical, can explain a part of the phenomenon of concurrent inflation and

---

[62] Texts on economic principles generally discuss this as the "balanced-budget multiplier."

unemployment, and even the effective demand aspect of unemployment is affected by immobility. For example, considerable excess demand may accumulate in the Tel Aviv area, leading to inflationary pressures, before it spills over into employment generating demand in the North or South.[63] Similarly, the net effect on employment of a IL 100 million decrease (or increase) in effective demand will be quite different according as it is in private or public demand, in public health expenditure or in public housing. It is nonetheless true that during most of the inflationary years selective reductions could have been made in public expenditure without seriously worsening unemployment.

In recent years there has been much skepticism concerning the possibility of solving the unemployment problems of underdeveloped countries by means of publicly generated effective demand. Attention has been focused on factor immobility and bottlenecks. The role of investment is regarded not from its effective demand aspect but rather from its capital formation aspect. Capital formation provides a factor of production which can be complementary to labor, thus increasing employment. Furthermore, many types of capital formation are prerequisites of the development of an industrial economy: communications, roads and railways, and power.

We are unable to break down total investment, or even a particular investment, into capital which is complementary to labor and capital which is substitutable for labor. Both traditional price theory, which assumes variable factor proportions, and many specific examples compel us to believe that much of the stimulation of capital formation has led to decisions, at the margin, to replace labor with capital. But the net effect of capital formation has certainly been to provide greater opportunities. Though we cannot examine in sufficient depth the extent to which government stimulation of investment has been aimed at creating employment, or to what extent it has succeeded, we can make several rough observations concerning these important questions.

Government investment may be concerned with providing immediate or long-term employment: housing provides the former, and an irrigation scheme the latter. Since we are interested in long-term objectives rather than yearly fluctuations, we shall consider here only fixed capital formation excluding residential construction. Furthermore, our main interest is in the period 1950–60, when unemployment was one of Israel's most pressing economic problems.

---

[63] Very little attention has been devoted to the study of regional economics in Israel.

An obvious observation is that since capital per worker more than doubled between 1950 and 1960,[64] capital formation as a whole was not allocated so as to maximize employment. In the absence of detailed capital-labor ratios for the earlier period, comparable to Bruno's for 1958,[65] it is impossible to compute the extent to which the increased capital-worker ratio results from changing factor proportions within sub-branches or from changes in the sub-branch composition. A comparison of the branch structure of public investment finance (unfortunately not detailed) presented in Table 72 with Bruno's much more detailed capital-labor ratios for 1958 suggests that employment considerations were not dominant.

Bruno's estimates show that capital per worker (both direct and total input) was extremely high in electric power and much lower in all other major branches—mining, agriculture, transport, manufacturing, services, and housing (in descending order). The necessity of infrastructure investment, such as electricity, is obvious, regardless of its low direct employment aspects. But the heavy accent on agriculture and irrigation and on capital-intensive transport branches, such as shipping, is contrary to what one would have expected on the basis of employment considerations alone.

Labor input may also be stimulated on the supply side, by measures encouraging greater labor force participation or longer hours.[66] The effect of activities such as the operation of labor exchanges on labor mobility has already been discussed. More complicated are the effects of taxation.[67] It is standard practice to accuse taxation, and income tax in particular, of reducing the desire to work. There is some truth in this contention, but it seems that the magnitude of the effect is generally exaggerated. Most workers are employed according to fixed hours of work, and their decision to work is hardly affected by the rate of tax. However, there may be some influence on the willingness to work overtime or on the number of days worked per month. Married women may be deterred from participating in the labor force because "it does not pay"; however, the income tax arrangements for married couples, which allow separate returns, are not particularly ungenerous in this

[64] According to Table 44 and the source of Table 45.
[65] Michael Bruno, *Interdependence, Resource Use and Structural Change in Israel, op. cit.,* pp. 296–97, Appendix Table D–6.
[66] Immigration policy, which also appears in the budgetary activities of the Jewish Agency, is a major factor on the supply side; but we do not discuss this under fiscal policy.
[67] The following comments rely heavily on Morag, *op. cit.*

country, and the cost of household help is a much more important deterrent than income tax.

Probably most affected by tax considerations are the middle-range and upper-range employees and the self-employed, particularly professionals and highly skilled workers: their marginal rates are high, and they have considerable discretion in deciding on extra hours of work. However, premium payments and special tax rates on overtime have partly solved this problem. Another aspect, whose quantitative importance is open to conjecture, is that many people in the middle and upper income ranges fix on specific goals—a luxury apartment, a car, a trip abroad. The raising of tax rates, particularly indirect taxes on these items, of course deters potential purchasers on the margin. But for many others, it simply means that greater effort must be made to reach the goal—the net effect may thus be more work.[68]

Efficiency

For the sake of completeness we include efficiency among the factors affecting growth that are influenced by fiscal policy. There is unfortunately little that we can say about it; but two comments may not be out of place.

The connection between productivity and education has been discussed in the chapters on labor force and productivity. It was pointed out that the level of formal education fell sharply as a result of mass immigration, but that there is evidence that the decline has stopped and perhaps been reversed. This was due largely to the growth in education facilities, financed primarily by the government. Similarly, informal education helped to fill gaps in formal schooling. Nevertheless, enough has probably not been done in this respect.

A second aspect of efficiency is the allocation of resources. There is a running controversy in Israel (as well as elsewhere) between those favoring maximum reliance on free market forces and those in favor of active government intervention, direction, and control. The former assume that intervention leads to distortions in resource allocation, and hence to less than maximum output and welfare. The latter argue that although intervention might lead to misallocation of existing resources, it leads to more rapid growth, and thus to greater future

---

[68] At informal gatherings of professional people one frequently hears the complaint that "it doesn't pay to work extra"; we cannot resist commenting that there is rarely anyone present who is not used to working far beyond normal hours.

resources; even if the allocation is not ideal, the level of welfare will be enhanced. There is here a confrontation between a static and a dynamic approach. We shall not try to resolve this theoretical argument, although we shall return to it in the next chapter.[69]

We feel—and this is an opinion not supported by research on "what might have been"—that the fiscal policy measures discussed in this chapter have contributed greatly to Israel's rapid rate of growth (although this is not necessarily true for all the periods discussed). But it is not at all evident that such a wide range of preferences and discrimination was really necessary for this achievement. Furthermore, we have no doubt that much resource misallocation could have been avoided if the effects on allocation had been fully taken into account when the various government growth incentives were considered and implemented.

[69] None of the empirical studies carried out in Israel help to resolve the argument; we shall refer to some in the next chapter, but they have used their results in a framework of static welfare theory and have not examined the effects on growth.

CHAPTER **10** FOREIGN EXCHANGE
POLICY

One of the assumptions underlying the efforts to develop Jewish Palestine was that great sums had to be raised abroad, primarily from world Jewry. In consequence, the mandatory period was characterized by balance of payments deficits. This fundamental assumption was maintained afterwards too: the needs of rapid development, absorption of immigrants, and defense cannot and should not be met by domestic resources alone. The need to raise funds abroad has therefore been the prime motivating force behind balance of payments policy. Neither the government nor the national and semi-public institutions have ever relaxed their intensive efforts to mobilize foreign resources. Their success was illustrated in Chapter 8. It was, however, realized that, particularly in the early years, there would be limits to the funds raised and that efforts would also have to be made to economize in foreign exchange.

Since an excess demand for foreign exchange is defined in terms of given prices, the most obvious solution to this problem is to rely on the free market and to let demand and supply arrive at an equilibrium exchange rate. The rate could either fluctuate freely or be set officially, with changes from time to time whenever it no longer approximates an equilibrium rate.[1] The main advantage of this system is, of course, the optimum allocation of resources according to the principles of welfare economics. For several reasons virtually all policy makers and many local economists do not yet consider this system appropriate for Israel.[2] One objection rests on assumptions concerning the nature of the supply and demand curves for foreign exchange. Supply curves are

---

[1] Another alternative, the classic setting of a rate and its maintenance through fluctuations in domestic activity—the mandatory (prewar) system—conflicts with Israel's development and full-employment orientation.

[2] It might be supposed that the frequent devaluations in Israel are in effect an application of the system, but, as will be shown later, this is not so.

believed to be inelastic, since many sources, such as grants and loans, are virtually unaffected by the rate of exchange. Furthermore, the supply curves shift from year to year as external sources are found or exhausted. Demand for many types of goods also appears to be inelastic, at least in the short run, because the domestic supply of import substitutes is inelastic. Moreover, because of the domestic economic and political structure and the resulting wages, monetary, and fiscal policy, the demand curve may shift with changes in the exchange rate, so that devaluation leads to price rises which are matched by wage increases and monetary expansion. In these circumstances, not only would reliance on free market forces lead to large and frequent changes in the exchange rate, but equilibrium may, in fact, be unattainable. This possibility is strengthened when allowing for economic and political uncertainty, which could lead to a flight of capital, i.e., a move away from equilibrium.

A second objection to reliance on the free foreign exchange market mechanism, independent of the first, relates to the allocation of foreign exchange. Even granting that the free market could equate demand and supply, the resulting use of foreign exchange, based on the pattern of income distribution and individual preferences, would differ from what the government regards as socially desirable.[3]

The main instrument used to equate effective demand and supply has therefore been exchange control. Within the general framework of this control, manipulation of exchange rates and other financial inducements have been used to reduce excess demand for foreign exchange and to encourage the development of exports and import substitutes. A number of additional means have been employed to attain the latter object.

In the following sections of this chapter we consider the general framework of exchange controls, and then, briefly, import and export policy.

CAPITAL INFLOW POLICY AND EXCHANGE CONTROL

When Israel became independent, it was quite clear that import needs for defense and the absorption of immigrants would greatly exceed receipts from exports. Other traditional sources available were institutional and immigrant transfers, though the latter were slight at first.

---

[3] These views were expressed in *Report of the Committee for Foreign Exchange* (July 1953; Hebrew mimeograph), and, even more strongly, in the unpublished testimony given before the Committee.

Efforts were made to free sterling balances held in London as coverage for the Palestine pound and to encourage foreign investment and repatriation of assets held abroad, and negotiations were undertaken for large-scale international finance, the first result of which was the Export-Import Bank loan.

A system of exchange control was inherited from the mandate. Foreign exchange receipts had to be surrendered to authorized dealers, and foreign exchange expenditure required specific or general authorization. Considering the scarcity of foreign exchange and the unusual needs arising from mass immigration in the midst of active warfare, it was widely accepted at the time that controls should be maintained. To conserve foreign exchange, import licenses were issued for "necessary" imports only,[4] and virtually no foreign exchange was allocated for transactions such as foreign travel or investment abroad. Although a complicated licensing and allocation system was employed, a clearly formulated plan of annual foreign exchange use was not drawn up until 1952, when a foreign exchange budget was introduced.

The *raison d'être* of the foreign exchange budget is to relate expenditure to receipts. Several steps are involved in the process. First, the foreign exchange receipts expected during the coming year are estimated, while the various ministries concerned with issuing import licenses (or authorizing other transactions) present their estimates of the necessary allocations. The Budget Department of the Ministry of Finance then tailors the departmental requests so that total planned expenditures match total expected receipts. The expenditure estimates set out in the resulting foreign exchange budget are binding on the administrative agencies.[5]

Clearly, great importance attaches to what is included in the estimates of receipts. As we have seen, receipts cannot be confined to those from exports of goods and services but must include several non-current balance of payments items. It is thus meaningless to talk of a balanced budget; to learn something of Israel's foreign exchange position from the budgets requires one to examine which receipts are included. Most unilateral transfers[6] have been considered as legitimate sources of budgetary receipts, as well as several capital account items,

---

[4] This austere approach was somewhat relieved by the import-without-payment scheme, which will be referred to below (p. 233).

[5] The budget is formally approved by the Council of Economic Ministers, not by the Knesset. There are, of course, provisions for making changes in the budget during the year.

[6] Private gifts are not included.

generally special long-term loans (e.g., from the Export-Import Bank and State of Israel Bonds) and private investment. There has been considerable flexibility in the choice of capital items to be included as legitimate budgetary income. For example, in time of strained financial conditions, medium-term credit has been included. Furthermore, in two years (1953/54 and 1957/58) supplementary contingent budgets were included. In general, planned receipts include the main items of the long-term financial assistance which the Ministry of Finance expects to mobilize for the coming year.

The planned expenditures are set out in detail and classified by destination under such categories as consumption, investment, and exports. Whereas receipts refer to cash, goods, or the cancellation of a previous liability, budgetary expenditures refer to commitments to allocate foreign exchange. For example, the validation by the Ministry of Finance of an import license issued by an authorized Ministry is recorded as "implementation of the budget," regardless of when actual payment is to be made.[7] Thus, the budget not only limits the total amount of commitments that can be made, but also specifies in great detail how much can be spent for the various purposes. Furthermore, the licensing procedure generally relates expenditures to available sources of funds by specifying the means of payment, for example, United States grant, free currency, or even "without allocation of foreign exchange."

The annual budgets as published are not entirely comparable since there have been frequent changes in the items included, in the concept of expenditure for recording purposes, and in the accuracy of reporting. However, a survey of the budgets from 1954/55 to 1964/65 suggests several observations.[8]

The expenditure figures in the budget and those in the balance of payments current account shown in Chapter 8 do not correspond, either in size or annual changes.

Both final expenditure and receipts often exceed the *ex ante* budget, but the difference between budgetary expenditure and receipts is never very large. The discrepancies between planned expenditures and final budget utilization show that the budget was not a rigid framework.

[7] For details, see any of the Foreign Exchange Department's annual *Summary of Foreign Exchange Accounts* (Hebrew).

[8] A detailed discussion of the budget, its implementation, and the step-by-step relationship between licensing and actual imports is presented in Z. Sussman, "The Foreign Exchange Budget as a Forecast of Commodity Imports to Israel" (unpublished M.A. thesis, The Hebrew University, 1959; Hebrew).

Increases in total receipts made it possible to raise total expenditures; but the changes in specific main classes of expenditure reflect the response of the administrative system to market forces. In recent years, as more and more items came under the liberalization program, the budget has become more of a forecast than a plan. Nevertheless, it has remained the chief instrument for keeping actual expenditures more or less within a planned framework and for allocating foreign exchange to various uses.

Many aspects of exchange control are not reflected in the foreign exchange budget or even in the record of its implementation. For example, except for budgetary loans, no transactions in financial claims appear in the budget. It is the Controller of Foreign Exchange who exercises his own discretion in matters pertaining to the finance of imports: whether by means of cash, letters of credit, or suppliers credit; when, from whom, to what amount, and on what terms firms may borrow from abroad; the government's own foreign exchange debt structure; whether foreign deposits should be encouraged and what use can be made of them; what foreign investors may do with the local currency proceeds of liquidated holdings; the utilization of blocked accounts; and a host of similar economic decisions.

A detailed discussion of the various techniques of exchange control used and their development need not concern us here.[9] In brief, the main developments in the exchange control practices have been as follows.

Even when no changes were made in effective controls, there has been a tendency, particularly in the last six or seven years, to ease their bureaucratic inconveniences. For example, the banks have been empowered to deal with certain kinds of requests for foreign exchange under general directives, instead of having to apply for specific authorization for each request.

The improvement of the foreign exchange position has engendered a more liberal attitude to certain foreign exchange allocations. This first made itself felt as regards foreign companies; for example, foreign shipping companies were allowed virtually complete convertibility of earnings, and more generous provisions were made for transfers of profits by foreign investors. Allowances for Israelis traveling abroad and for other service items have been increased since 1959.

Since 1956, there has been a tendency to liberalize the import of goods. The process has two distinct aspects: more generous allocations

[9] But see, for example, A. Rubner, *The Economy of Israel* (London: Frank Cass, 1960), Chapter XVII.

(as for services) and a shift from administrative to fiscal controls. This will be considered in greater detail below.

Another function of the general financial position has been the policy of foreign aid mobilization. Although it is safe to describe the attitude towards unilateral transfers as being consistently "the more the better," there has been a change in the approach to foreign liabilities. As foreign exchange balances grew, greater selectivity was exercised in the choice of loans in 1962–65. Loans below a certain duration or above a certain rate of interest were generally not accepted; and, because of fear of inflation, loans which were considered as essentially for the purpose of evading local credit restrictions were not approved, and even private investment was mobilized with greater selectivity. However, long-term low-interest development loans have always been considered highly desirable.

The Manipulation of Relative Prices

Within the framework of exchange controls, the manipulation of relative prices was used as a major instrument of balance of payments policy. At bottom, three factors determine the relative prices of imports, exports, and production for the domestic market: the foreign-currency price of goods, determined mainly by foreign demand and supply conditions; domestic supply and demand conditions; and lastly, the effective rate at which foreign prices are converted into local prices. The first factor is outside the government's control.[10] The second is affected to some extent by all government economic policy. The last, the effective exchange rate, is set by the government, directly or indirectly, and is thus the chief means by which it can divert demand from imports to the local market, and supply from the local market to exports.

To avoid confusion, at least six conceptually different rates of exchange must be distinguished:

The official rate: Since 1957, this rate has been recognized by the International Monetary Fund as par value.

The formal rate (or rates): These are the rates at which authorized dealers are instructed to purchase and sell foreign exchange. If there is only one formal rate it is also the official rate.

The effective rates: These are the pounds per dollar actually paid by

---

[10] A possible exception is citrus; since Israel is a major supplier in the European market, its supply does affect prices, and government policy does affect citrus exports.

importers and received by exporters, regardless of whether the amounts are called exchange rates, taxes, or subsidies.

The equilibrium rate: Unlike the first three, this is a purely theoretical rate in Israel, and is the rate which would be determined by supply and demand forces in a freely competitive market.

The real rate: This is also an equilibrium rate, but not a perfectly free one. Here an attempt is made to allow for government influence, while retaining the concept of a single rate determined by the intersection of supply and demand, when these take into account the desires and actions of the government.[11]

The black market rates: These are the effective rates on illegal transactions. At no time were black market transactions of sufficient quantitative importance to warrant acceptance of the black market rate (or rates on limited free markets) as a measure of the equilibrium rate.

The process of exchange rate manipulation has been one of almost continuous devaluation, consisting of occasional formal devaluations and continuous effective devaluation through taxes and subsidies.[12] Two aspects of this process must be distinguished. The first is a general decrease in the official value of the Israel pound in terms of foreign exchange, which, at least initially, makes all imports more expensive relative to domestic goods and makes exports more profitable. The second is devaluation through multiple rates (formal or effective). Here the process of devaluation intentionally discriminates between goods.[13]

The process of formal devaluation

Until 1952, the Israel pound was officially at par with sterling, having been devalued to IL 0.357 along with sterling in September, 1949.[14] In

---

[11] An excellent theoretical analysis of the application of this concept in Israel is U. Bahral's *The Real Rate of the Dollar in the Economy of Israel* (Jerusalem: Ministry of Commerce and Industry, 1956; Hebrew).

[12] For a systematic account of the process of devaluation see Michael Michaely, *Foreign Trade and Capital Imports in Israel* (Tel Aviv: Am Oved, 1963; Hebrew), Chapter 4, and Joseph Baruh, "Import Taxes and Export Subsidies in Israel, 1955–61," *Bank of Israel Bulletin,* No. 18 (March 1963), 48–70.

[13] Of course, a uniform devaluation superimposed on a complex existing tax and subsidy system leads to new discriminatory effective rates; but this is not the main purpose of the devaluation.

[14] Before the 1949 devaluation the rate for sterling was approximately $ 4/£ 1. In practice, this rate (i.e., IL 0.25/$ 1) was applied only to the soft currencies of the period, while the direct exchange rate for hard currencies was

February, 1952, two other formal rates were added: IL 0.714/$ 1 (rate B) and IL 1/$ 1 (rate C); although the sterling rate (rate A) was still the official one at the time, transactions shifted to the higher rates over the next year until most were carried out at rate C. In April, 1953, an extra IL 0.8/$ 1 was added to rate C as a premium for industrial exports and a tax on many imports; in effect, if not yet in name, this was a new rate. In December, 1953, rates A and B were abolished, and, even though it applied to a minority of transactions, rate C was declared the official one, to be abolished only in August, 1954. By then, most transactions were at IL 1.8/$ 1; this was eventually (in July, 1955) declared the official rate and remained in force until superseded by IL 3/$ 1 at the devaluation of February, 1962.

Aside from these rates, there was also, for some of the time, a special formal rate for the transactions of public institutions: first introduced in December, 1953, at IL 1.3/$ 1, it was raised to IL 1.5/$ 1 in October, 1955, and merged into the official rate when it was raised to IL 1.8/$ 1 in April, 1958.

The techniques of effective devaluation

Effective devaluation through subsidies and taxes was continuous. Furthermore, although there were never more than three or four formal rates at any one time, effective rates were numerous and varied.

The development of effective rates for merchandise is discussed in greater detail below. Here we confine ourselves to a brief description of the changes in formal or official rates for other transactions and of the various means used to create the multiple effective rates.

Outright subsidies on receipts: Certain service exports, such as tourism and shipping and aviation, have received premiums on foreign exchange earnings. The considerations involved in granting subsidies were threefold: the extent to which the particular subsidy would increase receipts; the influence of the group demanding special treatment; avoiding legal recognition of a new rate of exchange—for example, foreign debts were frequently linked to the exchange rate prevailing for capital and interest payments.

Transfers by public institutions generally received effective rates lower than those accorded other transactions. Thus, a formal rate of IL 1.3/$ 1 (later IL 1.5/$ 1) applied to such transfers during 1954–58, when IL 1.8 was generally applicable. Thereafter, institutional

---

IL 0.333/$ 1, or $ 3/IL 1 [Michael Michaely, *Israel's Foreign Exchange Rate System* (Jerusalem: Falk Institute, 1966; preliminary draft), p. 2–2].

transfers received the official rate while most other transfers received premiums.

Most other kinds of private transfers, including private investment, while not accorded a special unfavorable rate, did not receive cash subsidies. A major exception is restitutions, which from 1957 received a premium.

Direct taxes on expenditure: Unlike merchandise imports, services imports could not easily be subjected to direct taxing and only one service item, foreign travel, has been so taxed. Fixed fees for passports and exit permits have been used (the latter were abolished a few years ago), together with a travel tax consisting of a uniform payment per person *plus* a percentage of the value of travel tickets. These have raised the effective rate on travel abroad, although currency allocations for foreign travel have been given at the official rate.

Indirect taxes and subsidies: Two types of indirect subsidy on receipts may be distinguished: those paid from government funds and those paid by non-government purchasers of the receipts. An example of the first is the subsidy given to hotels and other tourist industries which pass the subsidy on to tourists paying in foreign currency, in the form of a discount. Frequently, the subsidy consisted of allowing certain transferrers of foreign exchange to use a certain percentage of their foreign currency receipts in order to import otherwise restricted goods; the subsidy was the profit on local sales of these goods. Similarly, there were free markets for certain transactions. Foreign investors in projects not scheduled as approved investment could liquidate their assets in Israel only by depositing the proceeds in blocked accounts, which could be sold for foreign exchange to other investors; a market rate above the official rate thus served as a tax on disinvestment and as a subsidy to foreign investors. A similar subsidy to foreign investors (or tourists) was paid by holders of State of Israel Bonds who wished to sell them for dollars before redemption: by selling the bonds at a discount on the New York market, sellers gave a subsidy to the purchaser who converted them in Israel at the official rate (or in the case of tourists, at a subsidized rate).

An interesting example of a partly free market—with its own rate— is the system (in operation for several years before the 1962 devaluation) whereby recipients of restitutions could sell part of their receipts to other Israelis for travel abroad. If made through the banks such sales would have constituted a formal rate; they had, therefore, to be made in the form of foreign bonds, rather than in cash.

Import Policy

The government's double-barrelled approach is clearly evident in its import policy. On the one hand, imports have been discouraged either by quantitative restrictions or by financial measures; looked at in another way, this can be viewed as the creation of a market situation favorable to the development of import substitutes. On the other hand, there have been continuous efforts to stimulate import substitutes directly. Thus, a major criterion for both development budget loans and recognition by the Investment Center as an "approved" investment has been the effect of the proposed project on the balance of payments— import substitution or exports. Though we are concentrating here on the first aspect of policy, the second should not be overlooked. Even in surveying the first aspect of import policy alone, it is best to distinguish between general import policy and the protection of local import substitutes.

General import policy

For the ten years from 1948, control of the quantity and composition of imports was maintained primarily through the licensing system. Since it was obvious that at the official rate the available foreign exchange resources would satisfy only part of the demand, allocations for imports were made only for "necessities." However, under the import-without-payment scheme, licenses for certain types of commodities were also issued without allocation of foreign exchange. The purpose of the arrangement was twofold: to conserve officially held foreign exchange while increasing imports, on the assumption that, by giving foreign investors or Israelis holding funds abroad a higher effective exchange rate through the import of scarce goods, more funds would be transferred to Israel; and to allow some imports of luxury goods, albeit at a higher exchange rate. The import-without-payment scheme was at its peak in 1949 and 1950, accounting in 1949 for as much as one quarter of all imports,[15] but has declined over the years, although vestiges remain even today.

Import control through effective quotas means that the quantity imported is less than that demanded at the effective rate of exchange paid by importers.[16] Thus, the lucky possessor of an import license could

---

[15] See D. Kochav, "Imports Without Payment" (unpublished M.A. thesis, The Hebrew University, 1953; Hebrew).

[16] For a discussion of quotas in Israel and a diagrammatic illustration, see

sell the goods at an even higher effective exchange rate and enjoy a quota profit.

At first, licenses were issued on the basis of past trade; thus, the quota profit was enjoyed by the established importers and the recipients of import-without-payment licenses. As complaints about the system piled up, an attempt was made to shift the function of allocating licenses to business associations. This, however, was exploited for enforcing cartel arrangements.[17] In fact, no satisfactory method of allocating licenses was ever achieved.

The *Pamaz*[18] scheme of export subsidies introduced in 1953 was, in effect, a system whereby exporters were allowed to enjoy the quota profits on a wide variety of imports. Other methods of granting import licenses to exporters worked according to the same principle.

Not in all cases was the potential quota profit actually paid by the consumer. In many cases, the privileged importer was a non-profit institution (e.g., a government department, the Jewish Agency, or a medical institution). In such cases, the consumer realized the quota profit. Further, in 1949–51, the consumer enjoyed the quota profit wherever price control was effective.

Any change in the effective rate of exchange, through either devaluation or the imposition of import taxes, diverts some or all of the quota profit to the Central Bank or Treasury. Thus, as the effective rate of exchange to importers was raised as part of the New Economic Policy of 1952–54, part at least of quota profits on goods not subject to effective price control was absorbed.

It has been estimated that at the very least about one fifth of all actual imports subject to duty in 1955/56 generated quota profits which were at least partly taxed. But only when the tax exceeds the quota profits is the quota ineffective and the import limited by the tax. The estimate for 1955/56 is that about one quarter of total imports subject to duty were limited by taxes rather than by quotas.[19] Thus, although

---

Arnon Gafni, Nadav Halevi, and Giora Hanoch, *Israel's Tariff Structure and Functions* (Research Paper 3; Jerusalem: Falk Project, 1958; Hebrew). A summary of the approach and the conclusions appeared in English as "Classification of Tariffs by Function," *Kyklos*, XVI (No. 2, 1963), 303–18.

[17] This was the conclusion reached by a public committee which investigated profits in imports, and included in the unpublished report of the committee, 1958.

[18] Hebrew acronym standing for "foreign currency deposit."

[19] Gafni, Halevi, and Hanoch, *op. cit.*, p. 17, Table 3. The figure includes what was in the study defined as revenue duties and protective duties. The term

the liberalization program is generally dated as starting in 1956, a substantial amount of imports was not limited by quantitative restrictions even before the new policy.

From 1956 on, the liberalization program was continuously extended. The term as used in Israel means that import licenses are issued as required, but the licensing authorities retain the right to determine country of origin, source of finance, and terms of payment. The significant change was that quantitative controls were replaced by customs duties, purchase taxes, and special levies designed to limit the quantity imported. Investment goods and imports for the production of exports were already pretty well liberalized; the new program included other raw materials and intermediates and a wider variety of consumer goods. Both final goods and intermediate goods destined for domestic consumption were highly taxed. Of course, a good part of the taxes were substitutes for devaluation; conversely, items taxed lightly or free of duty at a time when the official exchange rate was unrealistic in effect enjoyed a subsidy. After the devaluation of 1962, many import duties were abolished and others were reduced. Thus, whereas 43 per cent of total imports in 1955/56 and 48 per cent in 1961/62 were subject to import duties, only 29 per cent were subject to duty in April–September, 1963.[20] Further, of the latter, only 9 per cent were subject to quantitative restrictions.

Table 74 shows effective exchange rates on imports.[21] In considering the figures, it should be kept in mind that the effective rate here comprises the formal rate *plus* import taxes *less* subsidies. It does not include quota profits or purchase tax on imported goods, and is therefore the rate to the importer, not to the consumer.

We shall now summarize the main developments in effective rates for imports. Changes in the effective rate for services reflect almost

---

"at least" used above means that only part of total imports were classified by function of customs duty; as a percentage of classified imports (instead of all imports subject to duty) the figures would be 43 and 57 per cent instead of 19 and 25 per cent, respectively.

[20] The first figure is from *ibid.,* p. 16, Table 2; the later figures are from B. Babayov, "Tariff Functions in Israel" (unpublished seminar paper, The Hebrew University, 1964; Hebrew).

[21] These figures (and those of Table 75) are based on the work over the years of Joseph Baruh with the Falk Project and later with the CBS and the Bank of Israel. A more comprehensive study and analysis of effective exchange rates is being conducted under the supervision of M. Michaely. Preliminary results suggest that the earlier figures are not misleading.

TABLE 74.   Formal and Effective Exchange Rates for Imports: 1952–63

(IL per $)

| | Formal rate | Effective rates[a] | | | | | Total merchandise: per cent increase over preceding year |
| | | Merchandise[b] | | | | Services | |
		Total	I	II	III		
1952	0.70[c]	0.97	0.62	0.83	1.17	0.86	..
1953	0.87[c]	1.41	1.13	1.21	1.64	1.18	45.4
1954	1.52[c]	1.83	1.39	1.64	2.09	1.80	29.8
1955	1.80	2.03	2.05	2.06	1.92	1.81	12.0
1956	1.80	2.09	2.13	2.15	1.90	1.81	3.0
1957	1.80	2.16	2.22	2.24	1.91	1.81	3.3
1958	1.80	2.28	2.45	2.36	1.94	1.82	5.6
1959	1.80	2.38	3.00	2.41	2.00	1.84	4.4
1960	1.80	2.43	3.16	2.48	2.02	1.85	2.1
1961	1.80	2.45	3.19	2.50	2.10	1.85	0.8
1962[d]	3.00	3.41	4.00	3.39	3.23	3.00	39.2
1963	3.00	3.48	4.23	3.43	3.34	3.00	2.1

[a] Price per dollar comprising the formal rate *plus* import taxes (net of drawback on imports for exports).

[b] Two different classifications were used, as follows:

1952–54: I. Food, beverages, and tobacco; II. Raw materials; III. Articles wholly or mainly manufactured. The 1955 rates reworked according to this classification are: I—1.85; II—1.91; III—2.20.

1955–63: I. Consumer goods; II. Raw materials; III. Investment goods.

[c] Average of formal rates in force at the time, weighted by the value of imports brought in under each rate.

[d] Post-devaluation rates, i.e., from February 9, 1962. For the whole of 1962 the weighted formal rate was 2.87, and the average effective rate for merchandise was 3.28.

SOURCES: 1952–54, 1962–63—Unpublished estimate of Joseph Baruh. Those for 1952–54 are a reworking (to fit definitions of later series) of data in Harold Lubell and Others, *Israel's National Expenditure: 1950–1954* (Jerusalem: Falk Project and CBS, 1958), derived from Baruh's and Kessler's work for the Economic Advisory Staff. 1955–61—Joseph Baruh, "Import Taxes and Export Subsidies in Israel, 1955–1961," *Bank of Israel Bulletin*, No.

only formal devaluations; thus, the effective rate barely changed between 1955 and the eve of the 1962 devaluation.

The rate on goods rose continuously but not steadily. From 1952 to 1955, the rise was caused mainly by the constant transfer of goods to higher formal rates. From 1956 to the 1962 devaluation, the increases were more gradual and entirely the result of increased net taxation. The large increase between 1961 and 1962[22] reflects the devaluation; it was accompanied by some reduction in taxes, but not so much as to make the effective rate approximately equal to the official rate.

No less interesting than the over-all changes is the wide diversity in rates of increase among various commodities. The aggregated classes in Table 74, being averages, show this diversity only partially. In 1952–54 the general pattern was a gradual transfer of commodities from lower to higher rates, the lower rates applying to necessities such as grains, meat, oils, sugar, and fuel. In 1955–61, the effective rates rose by 74 per cent for consumer imports (an average composed of increases of 120 per cent for food and 20–25 per cent for other items), 21 per cent for raw materials (this rise equals the average for all imports of goods), and only 9 per cent for investment goods. In the first two years after the 1962 devaluation the rate for investment goods rose much more than that for consumer goods and raw materials, i.e., much of this preferential treatment was eliminated. Perhaps more important, the differential between raw materials and investment goods was narrowed considerably.

Protection of domestic production

Two types of protective device have been used in Israel—administrative protection and tariffs, with the former predominating. In fact, it may be said that until 1962, protection was almost entirely through the administrative restriction of imports. However, even before 1962, there were changes in the approach to protection.[23]

From the first, it was accepted as axiomatic that local production should be protected. For essential commodities, however, a major consideration was to what extent local production could meet domestic

[22] But see note d to Table 74.
[23] The subject has ben surveyed by G. Gross, "The Public Committee on Customs" (unpublished seminar paper, The Hebrew University, 1962; Hebrew), and C. Gvati, "Principles of Protection of Domestic Production" (unpublished seminar paper, The Hebrew University, 1962; Hebrew). A more analytical presentation is contained in T. Goldberger (Ophir), "Principles of Protection" (unpublished M.A. thesis, The Hebrew University, 1956; Hebrew).

requirements. Thus, although agriculture in general enjoyed a high degree of protection, it was understood that it would be pointless to protect certain items, such as grain, which Israel could never produce in adequate quantities at any reasonable cost. In most other cases, an announcement of intention to produce a product was enough to stop import licenses from being granted, although licenses were occasionally granted when it was demonstrated that domestic production of intermediate goods was of such poor quality or of such uncertain delivery date as to endanger the domestic manufacture of other goods.

Protective customs duties were levied more as insurance against imports which could slip by than as a basic means of protection. A majority of the requests presented to the Public Customs Committee was for reduced rather than for protective duties. The decisions of this committee to levy a protective duty were never contingent on a reduction of administrative protection. In 1955/56, protective duties were levied on goods accounting for only 3 per cent of total imports subject to duty.[24]

Over the years, considerations of profitability were brought forward and officially accepted. From 1956, protective duties were levied to give a specific degree of protection on foreign exchange value added (i.e., on the net foreign exchange saved by substituting for imports). A public industrial council, set up in 1958, accepted the approach that shifts should be made from total administrative protection to carefully examined fiscal protection. Rules of thumb were adopted for setting protective duties, on the general principle that domestic production was entitled to the same effective rate of exchange on foreign exchange value added as exports, *plus* an additional percentage, ranging from 15 per cent on raw materials to 40 per cent on finished products.[25] In practice, however, most domestic production was still protected by absolute quota restrictions.

The change in attitude had at least one important consequence. Previously, almost blind protection was accorded to both existing and

[24] Gafni, Halevi, and Hanoch, *op. cit.*, p. 17, Table 3. Of course, this figure understates the extent of tariff protection. Weighting the protection by imports gives less weight to more effective duties, while completely effective duties get a weight of zero.

[25] It is of interest to contrast this order of preference with a reverse order applied during the 1949–53 period. At that time, when domestic production was thought "too expensive" (never defined), imports were occasionally allowed. The price differential most watched was that relating to goods in the basket of the Consumers Price Index.

newly undertaken domestic production; the new approach, though hardly applied to existing production, made itself felt in a more economic appraisal of potential production. In other words, there was greater readiness to prevent future mistakes than to correct old ones.

The New Economic Policy declared in February, 1962, heralded, among other things, a new approach to protection. A basic cause of the new policy was that administrative would be replaced by customs protection, which would gradually be reduced so that domestic production would have to compete with external production. Although this clause has not yet been applied to agricultural products, the first part, at least, has been applied to much of the country's industry during the last four years. Industrial products are examined by a public committee, which makes recommendations concerning the replacement of quantitative restrictions by duties. The way in which the new policy has been applied, the height of the tariff imposed, and the non-unitary nature of customs duties have been the subject of considerable criticism.[26]

The switch in the form of protection does not mean that there has been a significant decline in protectionism. The extent of tariff protection is also a subject of controversy, but even the lowest estimate is that the weighted average of customs duties on value added in industry (as of September, 1963) was 64 per cent, i.e., an effective exchange rate of close to IL 5/$ 1. To what extent duties will be reduced and the structure of industry altered by effective external competition still remains to be seen.

EXPORT POLICY

Israel's foreign exchange problems were so great in the first years of independence that it was believed that exports could do little to solve them. The reasoning was as follows: exports are relatively inelastic in the short run, because they must be competitive, but import substitutes can be developed by blocking imports. Consequently, although attempts were made to resuscitate exports of citrus and diamonds, most efforts were concentrated on the development of import substitutes. Gradually, greater attention was devoted to expanding exports.

It is useful to distinguish between three types of government policy to develop exports, although much overlapping between them makes

---

[26] The best example of this criticism is the last part of H. Barkai and M. Michaely, "The New Economic Policy—After One Year," appearing as "On the New Economic Policy," *The Economic Quarterly,* X (No. 39, August 1963; Hebrew), 210–32.

the distinction somewhat arbitrary: initiative in developing export industries, initiative in organization and promotion of foreign sales, and direct financial inducement.

The first type of policy is reflected in the high priority the government gave export industries in its development programs. The main instrument for implementing these programs was, of course, the development budget. Thus, both direct government investment and loans to private firms were made available to industries believed to have export potential. Similarly, government initiative in encouraging local and foreign investments through the Investment Center also accorded the same high priority to export industries.

Government efforts to promote export sales have taken many forms, from the negotiation of bilateral trade agreements to the organization of government export firms. Most of these activities combine two strands: one is indirect financial aid, such as lower shipping, insurance, sales, or interest costs; the other is acquiring export know-how.

The recognition that exports depend on a host of factors in addition to prices—packaging, quality control, delivery dates—was slow to come; but gradually more attention was devoted by the government to these factors. However, it is probably true that even in recent years not enough has been done in this direction.

Financial aid, primarily in the form of participation in costs, forms an important part of the policies discussed above. But in addition, direct financial inducements were used as a basic means of encouraging exports. The most obvious financial inducement is the rate of exchange. Changes in the formal rate were supplemented at various times by subsidies which raised the effective rate of exchange. The different types of export subsidies, which will be briefly listed below, have been studied and discussed frequently by economists in Israel.[27]

Pines has examined export subsidies according to two types of price differentials. The first is vertical discrimination, where there is a different effective price for the foreign exchange value of an export and for the value of the foreign exchange used in the production of that export, i.e., for its import component. The second type of discrimination is horizontal, where different effective rates apply to different export items. It can easily be shown that both kinds of discrimination lead to misuse of resources and even to loss of foreign exchange.[28]

[27] The most important of these studies is David Pines, *Direct Export Premiums in Israel: 1952–1958* (Jerusalem: Falk Project, 1963; Hebrew). An excellent analytical discussion of the subject is contained in Bahral, *op. cit.*

[28] Pines, *op. cit.*, Chapter 3; and Bahral, *op. cit.*

Another possible distinction is according to whether the subsidy is given directly by the government or paid by the local consumer. We shall list briefly the main subsidies used in Israel, bearing in mind both classifications.

Premiums on total export proceeds: These were used for some commodities in 1949–51. Their obvious purpose was to compensate for too low a formal rate of exchange. Their chief deficiency was that the vertical differentials involved (i.e., a higher rate for exports than for the import component) resulted in loss of foreign exchange. As an extreme example, exports could be profitable even when the foreign exchange value added was zero. The dangers in such subsidies were soon perceived, and during the 1952–55 period of gradual devaluation—formal and by means of premiums—various administrative devices were employed to limit vertical differentials to some extent.

Subsidies through import licenses: The possibility of using import quota profits as an export subsidy was quickly recognized. Some import licenses for goods destined for the local market were granted in 1952, as a reward to exporters. But the system reached its most extensive and refined form in the *Pamaz* arrangement, which was in wide use during 1953–59. This was a foreign exchange retention scheme applied to a variety of industrial and agricultural commodities, but to neither citrus nor diamonds. Exporters were allowed to retain the proceeds of their exports in foreign currency bank accounts. The value of the direct import component was to be used to import the raw materials required to maintain the output of exports; with the foreign currency value added, the producer could import raw materials in his "general line of production" and could use them either to expand exports or on the local market.

The system had several advantages. First, it relieved exporters from the cumbersome red tape of requesting foreign exchange for their import component. Some of the later attacks on the *Pamaz* system tended to forget the constricting conditions existing when the system was introduced, which frequently made the orderly planning of production and export next to impossible, and which the *Pamaz* system alleviated. But these are advantages of the retention scheme rather than of the method of subsidizing exports. Second, it eliminated a major part of the vertical differentials, since the cost to the exporter of one dollar's worth of import component for export was exactly what he could get in the local market for one dollar of *Pamaz* value added.[29] In this

[29] Not all differentials were eliminated, owing to the method of computing

respect, the *Pamaz* system was often better than more arbitrary methods of granting import licenses to exporters.

However, the *Pamaz* system led to widespread horizontal differentials, since the subsidy received by each exporter depended primarily on the local demand for his products and on his monopolistic position in the local market. The average *Pamaz* subsidy granted has been estimated as being IL 0.54 per value-added dollar in 1954 and 1955, a figure that masks a range from as low as IL 0.10 up to IL 0.80.[30] A later study has estimated *Pamaz* subsidies of as much as IL 2.4 per value-added dollar for some items in 1957. However, according to this study, the subsidy did not rise much between 1954 and 1957, at least not in the textile industry, one of the more important beneficiaries of *Pamaz*.[31]

The system was gradually weakened from 1956 on, by reducing the amounts which could be deposited in *Pamaz* accounts; by increasingly liberalizing imports, a process which undercut the monopolistic base of the system; and by extending direct premiums on value added. *Pamaz* was officially abolished in 1959, although vestiges of the system remained for some time.

Premiums on value added: These were introduced on a large scale in 1956. Export proceeds from each commodity were converted at a mixed rate: the value of the direct import component at the official rate of IL 1.8/$ 1, which is what the exporter had paid for it,[32] and the value added at the official rate *plus* a premium, which gradually rose to IL 0.85/$ 1 for most exports. This system did away with most vertical and horizontal differentials, though some persisted owing to technical difficulties.[33] The premium on value added was a fairly good, if cumbersome, substitute for devaluation and did not deserve the constant disapprobation of the International Monetary Fund, which chose to look at the multiple rates per dollar of gross exports rather than at the unitary rate per dollar of value added.[34] Of course, in so far as different exports, or exports to different countries, did not receive the same subsidy, horizontal discrimination was retained. For example, citrus and most invisibles did not receive the same treatment.

---

value added and because of other administrative complications. See Pines, *op. cit.,* Chapter 5.

[30] Falk Project, *Third Annual Report: 1956* (Jerusalem: 1957), p. 27, Table 7.

[31] Pines, *op. cit.,* p. 63, Table 10.

[32] Import duties were refunded to exporters through a drawback system.

[33] Pines, *op. cit.,* Chapter 7.

[34] This view finds expression in the annual IMF *Staff Reports* and *Recommendations on Consultations,* from 1956 to 1961.

TABLE 75. Effective Exchange Rates[a] for Exports: 1952–61

(IL per $ value added)

| | Merchandise | | | | | Services[b] | Total merchandise: per cent change over preceding year |
	Total	Citrus	Other agricultural	Diamonds	Other industrial		
1952	0.75[b]					1.00	..
1953	1.22[b]					1.35	62.7
1954	1.72[b]					1.80	41.0
1955	1.85	1.80	1.89	2.21	1.82	1.80	..
1956	2.03	1.80	2.25	2.35	2.33	1.80	9.7
1957	2.16	1.84	2.28	2.65	2.55	1.80	6.4
1958	2.33	2.08	3.95	2.65	2.35	1.80	7.9
1959	2.62	2.19	4.59	2.65	2.69	1.92	12.4
1960	2.77	2.32	5.26	2.65	2.77	1.92	5.7
1961	2.84	2.52	3.84	2.65	2.77	1.96	2.5

[a] Price per dollar value added (except as specified in note b) comprising formal rate *plus* direct subsidies from government, *plus* market subsidization through *Pamaz*. For formal rates in 1955–63 see Table 74.
[b] For services throughout and for merchandise in 1952–54, the rate is per $ of total proceeds, not value added.
SOURCES: 1952–54—Lubell, *op. cit.*, Appendix, p. 54, Table B–4.
1955–61—Baruh, *op. cit.*, pp. 56–57, Table 4 (merchandise); p. 54, Table 3 (services).

One other subsidy deserves special mention. After 1958, when the IL 0.85 premium was common, an additional premium was introduced for some commodities, either for exports to particular markets (West Africa) or for "additional" exports. Thus, marginal exports received a special rate. This practice fits the theoretical concept of a discriminating monopsonist. By 1962, many commodities were receiving a premium of IL 1.20 on at least some of their foreign exchange value added.

Changes in effective rates: Table 75 shows average effective rates of exchange on exports. The effective exchange rate is defined to include formal rates, subsidies granted directly by the government, and market subsidization through *Pamaz*.[35] The rates do not include various other indirect subsidies. In the early years, changes in the effective rates occurred primarily as the result of formal devaluation rather than of indirect subsidies. In 1955–61 there was considerable discrimination between branches; in 1955 diamonds was the only branch receiving substantial preference, but within two years a clear discriminatory pattern emerged whose order of preference was non-citrus agriculture, diamonds, other industrial (the last two changing places in 1959), citrus, and finally services.

Subsidization after the 1962 devaluation: The devaluation of February, 1962, did much to unify rates for exports, although it did not add much to most items. Not all subsidies were abolished, but since policy had become anti-export-subsidy, subsidies had to be less conspicuous. During 1962–64, therefore, greater reliance was placed on the various types of financial aid discussed above (p. 240) and on subsidies from self-administered branch equalization funds, rather than from the government budget. By taxing imports for the local market and then using the proceeds to subsidize exports, or by other cartel arrangements, the producers' organizations were, in effect, combining *Pamaz* with cash premiums on value added.

Since 1965, two approaches to export promotion can be distinguished. One is to grant additional financial inducements, either subsidies or a new devaluation. The other is to lower costs, making firms competitive at the existing exchange rate. The recession can be viewed as reflecting the latter approach. However, in 1966, some additional subsidies were introduced, although devaluation had been rejected. In effect, both approaches are being used simultaneously. At the time of writing the

---

[35] However, the estimate of *Pamaz* profits is a minimum one based on the value of direct premiums. See Baruh, *op. cit.*, p. 55.

combination does not seem to be adequate to produce a substantial rise in exports. There is also the danger that the subsidies now being given are a return to the type of discrimination at least partly eliminated in the past by the subsidy on value added.

The Discrimination Controversy

The discriminatory nature of foreign exchange policy, i.e., the use of multiple exchange rates, has been the subject of unceasing controversy among economists and policy makers.

One aspect of the controversy is Michaely's contention that policy has had a strong autarkic tendency:[36] efforts to curb the balance of payments deficit have resulted in import substitutes getting consistent preference over exports.

A comparison of Tables 74 and 75 shows that the average exchange rate for merchandise export value added was lower than for imports in 1957, higher from 1958 through 1961, and again lower after the 1962 devaluation. But this comparison does not pinpoint the real disparity in effective rates. The effective rates for imports at best show what imports actually cost importers and not what rates determined whether an item would be imported or produced locally. Protection has generally prevented the import of goods produced locally, and thus the high rates on goods not imported are not included in the computation. In other words, protection of domestic products has been at rates substantially higher than those given to exporters. The tendency to depart from automatic administrative protection in recent years, and the shift to tariff protection after the 1962 devaluation, have cerainly acted to diminish the spread between effective rates on exports and on import substitutes. Nonetheless, even now protected import substitutes receive an effective rate per dollar value added considerably higher than do exports.[37]

Has there been discrimination between exports and imports other than by setting effective exchange rates? The declared priorities policy of the government and the criteria used in granting loans and concessions would imply that over the last ten years relatively greater aid has been given to export industries. But two qualifications must be suggested.

Frequently, the means used to encourage exports are not really able

[36] Michaely, *Foreign Trade and Capital Imports in Israel, op. cit.,* p. 125.

[37] We have already noted (p. 238) that in 1958 official guidelines for customs protection called for application of the rate given to exports *plus* a substantial margin.

to distinguish between production for export and for the local market. For example, the Investment Center approves firms on the basis of a commitment to export. Many enterprises do not honor the commitment; of 111 firms approved up to 1960 which had made export commitments, only 18 fulfilled their commitments for 1962, and the total exports of the other firms amounted to only 22 per cent of the commitment (and apparently even less in 1963).[38]

The general policy of the Ministry of Commerce and Industry has been to assume that for most products the development of export potential is closely linked to the size of the domestic market. The reasoning is that as a firm grows—primarily from sales to the local market—it attains economies of scale that make exports possible. Furthermore, there is in some cases an element of attracting an enterprise by using the local market as a lure, in the expectation that eventually the local market will be unable to sustain the entire industry, and a growing proportion of sales will of necessity turn to exports. Textiles and rubber tires are examples of industries that saturated the local market and have then gone in for exports: in 1964 these branches exported 39.3 per cent and 60.4 per cent of their total output, respectively.[39] In such cases it is difficult to decide whether the aid should be called "short-term local-market preference" or "long-term export promotion." Difficulties faced by the textile industry in 1965 and, apparently much more, in 1966, call for a reassessment of the concept of local-market based export industries.

Multiple rates for imports give varying degrees of protection to import substitutes, but this aspect of discrimination has already been considered and we now turn to the discriminatory encouragement of classes of imports, i.e., we look at multiple rates as subsidies rather than taxes. Except for several necessities (favored in order to affect income distribution), the order of preference during the last ten years has been investment goods, raw materials, finished consumer goods. Michaely (op. cit.) has pointed out that lower rates on investment goods were intended to stimulate investment, whereas what they have actually done is to distort the relative prices of capital and labor. He shows that this policy is based on a fallacious identification of investment goods with investment.

[38] Based on the findings of Arela Shulroper, "Investment Encouragement Policy in Israel" (unpublished seminar paper, The Hebrew University, 1964; Hebrew), p. 21.

[39] Bank of Israel, *Annual Report 1964*, p. 266, Table XII–2.

Two diametrically opposed views have clashed in a controversy concerning discriminatory rates between commodities. One view held by many Israeli economists—at the Hebrew University, the Bank of Israel, and the Ministry of Finance—is that economic theory and experience have demonstrated the effectiveness of the price mechanism in allocating resources. Thus, static welfare economics shows that discriminatory pricing leads to misallocation at the margin. In keeping with this approach, they have advocated estimating or guessing the long-term equilibrium rate of exchange and letting the structure of production be determined by this rate.

The opposing view, as evidenced in recent years primarily by the operations of the Ministry of Commerce and Industry,[40] has been that the development of the economy can be speeded up by discriminatory practices. In more technical terminology, whereas they may be willing to accept the applicability of the marginal equations of welfare economics to static conditions, they do not believe that these can be applied to problems of development, where the major structural changes are not marginal. Relying on analogies from the infant-industry example and protectionist development theories, they present a two-step argument.

Israel is at present only in the early stages of industrialization; the existing system of comparative advantages cannot, therefore, be accepted as the correct criterion for ordering the desirability of future development.

Granting this, and the resulting desirability of using criteria other than the existing relative-price system for establishing the social desirability of particular industries, there is no reason why equal aid should be given to each case. For example, if it is believed that one industry will prove profitable to the economy even if it now needs IL 10/$ 1, whereas another will be equally profitable though it now needs IL 6/$ 1, why give both IL 10 or IL 6? In other words, they prefer to treat each item as a special case. This approach, carried to its logical conclusion, would adopt special subsidies for exports as well: there would be no excuse for forcing all exports to compete at a unitary rate. However, this part of the argument is seldom voiced.

One may support an intermediate position: to accept the need for replacing some of the existing criteria of economic advantage, and

---

[40] This has found expression in economic terms in M. Mandelbaum and M. Naveh, "Liberalization of Imports," *The Economic Quarterly,* X (No. 40, December 1963; Hebrew), 346–56.

perhaps even broaden the concept of infant industries, but to reject arbitrary measures which ignore valid, long-term economimc distinctions. For example, one might support subsidizing all industries in a development area but object to subsidizing wharfage and lading costs for exports. Actual policy has unfortunately undercut this position; the policy makers have tended to the much more extreme position described above.

To sum up, the basic argument is between those who are willing to rely on the price mechanism, with some degree of intervention, despite the inadequacies of traditional economic theory in the field of economic development, and those who prefer to rely on administrative judgement in determining the priorities and incentives to development. It might be supposed that this controversy was resolved with the New Economic Policy in 1962 when the principle of multiple exchange rates was rejected in official statements. But the implementation of the New Economic Policy and subsequent developments suggest that the fundamental controversy still remains, with little, if any, weakening of the Commerce and Industry approach.

11 INFLATION

An inflationary process is usually reflected in both the monetary and the real aspects of the economy. In the monetary sphere one expects the money supply to grow, with either a rise in the local price level or price control; effective or formal devaluation, or foreign exchange control; and a rise in nominal wages, or wage control. In the real sphere one expects the import surplus or GNP to grow and unemployment to diminish.

All these symptoms were evident during the years 1949–65, though to varying degrees. We have chosen to discuss the price index of total resources on the monetary side, and real GNP and import surplus on the real side.

Using these variables, one may ask whether an increase in total effective demand (measured by total domestic use of resources at current prices) was absorbed mainly by rising prices, by growing GNP, or by growing import surplus.[1] Table 76 summarizes the data. For the period as a whole

---

[1] Denote: U = domestic use of resources at current prices
P = price level of resources
Y = real gross national product
M = real import surplus
t = the current year.

Then $\dfrac{U_t}{U_{t-1}} = \dfrac{P_t}{P_{t-1}} \cdot \dfrac{Y_t + M_t}{Y_{t-1} + M_{t-1}}$,

and $\dfrac{Y_t + M_t}{Y_{t-1} + M_{t-1}} = \dfrac{Y_t + M_{t-1}}{Y_{t-1} + M_{t-1}} \cdot \dfrac{Y_t + M_t}{Y_t + M_{t-1}}$.

The index of U is thus broken down into the following components:

$\dfrac{P_t}{P_{t-1}}$ is the change in prices; $\dfrac{Y_t + M_{t-1}}{Y_{t-1} + M_{t-1}}$ is the effect of product growth on resources, with prices and import surplus held constant; and $\dfrac{Y_t + M_t}{Y_t + M_{t-1}}$

is the residual effect on resources of the increase in real import surplus.

the index $(1950 = 1)$ of increase in total demand was 21.2. This increase in demand was mainly absorbed by an increase in the price level of resources, the index of which was 6.03 $(1950 = 1)$. The index of increase in real resources due to GNP growth was 3.56, and that of increase due to import surplus was 0.99. One may combine price increases

TABLE 76.   *Indicators of Inflation: 1950–65*[a]

(per cent change over preceding year)

	Domestic resource use at current prices	Effect of real GNP growth on re- sources	Residual increase in uses $\frac{(1)+100}{(2)+100} - 100$	Price of do- mestic re- source use	Effect of real import surplus growth on re- sources
	(1)	*(2)*	*(3)*	*(4)*	*(5)*
1951	46.5	18.7	23.4	21.7	1.5
1952	59.2	4.9	51.8	61.8	−6.1
1953	24.6	0.9	23.5	27.2	−2.9
1954	29.0	16.2	11.0	12.7	−1.6
1955	25.5	9.6	14.5	11.5	2.8
1956	21.2	6.7	13.6	9.3	3.8
1957	12.3	7.0	5.0	7.1	−2.1
1958	12.3	7.6	4.4	3.8	0.6
1959	11.9	10.7	1.1	2.8	−1.7
1960	11.0	6.8	3.9	4.2	−0.2
1961	21.4	9.1	11.3	6.5	4.5
1962	26.8	10.7	14.5	13.9	0.6
1963	15.4	9.8	5.1	7.2	−1.9
1964	18.0	9.1	8.2	4.8	3.2
1965	13.3	5.8	7.1	8.2	−1.0
1965÷1950[b]	21.21	3.56	5.96	6.03	0.99

[a] In the notation of note 1, p. 249: column $(2) = \dfrac{Y_t + M_{t-1}}{Y_{t-1} + M_{t-1}}$;

column $(3) = \dfrac{Y_t + M_t}{Y_t + M_{t-1}} \cdot \dfrac{P_t}{P_{t-1}}$; column $(4) = \dfrac{P_t}{P_{t-1}}$; column $(5) = \dfrac{Y_t + M_t}{Y_t + M_{t-1}}$.

[b] Columns (2),(3), and (5) calculated as accumulated product of annual indexes.
SOURCE: Column (1)—Appendix Table 1.
Columns (2), (5)—Appendix Table 2.
Column (4)—Appendix Table 4.

TABLE 77. *Money Supply and Velocity of Circulation: 1948–65*

	Money supply[a] (IL million)	Per cent change over preceding year		
		Money supply	Resources velocity[b]	Velocity of demand deposits
1948	93.1	..	..	..
1949	128.9	38.5	..	..
1950	169.7	31.7	..	..
1951	224.0	32.0	11.2	25.6
1952	247.3	10.4	44.0	41.8
1953	290.1	17.3	6.3	14.4
1953	262.7[c]	..		
1954	330.5	25.8	2.5	18.9
1955	398.1	20.5	4.1	3.7
1956	469.4	17.9	2.8	–4.1
1957	560.4	19.4	–6.0	0.0
1958	645.7	15.2	–2.4	–5.3
1959	726.5	12.5	–0.6	–0.6
1960	826.1	13.7	–2.4	–7.9
1961	973.8	17.9	2.9	–0.6
1962	1,137.7	16.8	8.6	10.5
1963	1,488.9	30.9	–11.9	5.6
1964	1,682.7	13.0	4.4	1.1
1965	1,833.4	9.0	4.1	11.5
1965 ÷ 1948		21.75	..	..
1965 ÷ 1950		11.93	1.78	2.73

[a] Average.
[b] Nominal resources divided by money supply.
[c] New series excluding demand deposits in foreign currency.
SOURCES: Money supply—Don Patinkin, *The Israel Economy: The First Decade* (Jerusalem: Falk Project, 1960), p. 110, Table 39 (for 1948–53); Bank of Israel, *Annual Report 1960*, p. 228, Table XIV–3 (for 1954–57); *Annual Report 1965*, p. 318, Table XV–2 (for 1958–62); *Annual Report 1966*, p. 370, Table XV–2 (for 1963–65).
Resources—Appendix Table 1.
Velocity of demand deposits—*Abstract 1966*, No. 17, p. 518, Table Q/2.

with the growth of import surplus in order to estimate the total inflationary pressure not absorbed by product growth; this is done in column (3)
of Table 76, which shows an index of 5.96.[2]

It seems, therefore, that the additional demand was absorbed far more
by price increases than by product growth. Three questions appear relevant. First, what were the forces that initiated such a strong inflationary
pressure; second, whether there was any effective policy to curb it; and
third, what was its real price in terms of growth and allocation of resources. The rest of this chapter is an attempt to answer these questions.

We start by examining the money supply, which increased over twenty-
fold from 1948 to 1965 (Table 77). The most rapid expansion took place
until 1951, at an annual average of 34 per cent; since then, the increase
has oscillated between 10 and 20 per cent in most years.

THE CURRENCY ISSUE SYSTEM

The expulsion of Palestine from the sterling area several months before
Israel became independent made it necessary to set up a currency issue
system.

In 1948 the Anglo-Palestine Bank (later renamed Bank Leumi Le-
Israel) opened an issue department. The initial backing of the currency
was the Palestine pounds turned in by their holders in return for the new
issue; these in turn were backed by sterling accounts frozen in London.

The pressing need of the government to finance first war and then
demobilization and mass immigration and the lack of an efficient taxation
system made it necessary to increase the money supply. Consequently,
in 1949 the Issue Department was required to back no more than half
the issue in foreign currency; the remaining acceptable assets were 91-day
Treasury bills, and the way was cleared for doubling the currency issue.

During 1949, an Israeli mission to London succeeded in reaching an
agreement with the British government on the gradual thawing of the
frozen sterling reserves. But Israel was interested in these reserves for
use as foreign exchange, not as cover for the currency. Consequently,
the Currency Law was amended to include Land Bonds among the
assets (gold and foreign exchange) held against the other 50 per cent of
the currency issue.[3] Within two years foreign currency holdings ceased
to be a significant part of the backing of the currency.

[2] The computation is somewhat mechanistic, and different indexes could be
constructed that would probably show higher absorption by import surplus and
lower absorption by GNP.

[3] Whereas Treasury bills were issued to the banking system, the (long-term) Land
Bonds were issued almost exclusively to the Issue Department.

One of the aspects of the New Economic Policy was the growing re-cognition that it was necessary to separate fiscal from monetary admin-istration. After three years of preparation, the Bank of Israel was estab-lished in December, 1954, as a central bank and took over the duties of the Issue Department. The Bank of Israel Law, while calling for a "sound" backing of the currency, does not specify any fixed relationship between foreign exchange reserves and the local currency issue.

Sources of Money Supply

The currency issue system is but one component of a complex of poli-cies regarding the supply of money. Changes in money supply are, by definition, the sum of changes in credit outstanding and of foreign bal-ances, *less* changes in time and foreign exchange deposits.

Foreign exchange control requires recipients of foreign exchange to sell it to the Treasury through authorized dealers, all of which are commercial banks. Such conversions of foreign exchange directly in-crease the quantity of money unless matched by increased time deposits. In some cases, however, an authorization is given to hold foreign ex-change deposits. Thus, recipients of restitutions from Germany are allowed to hold part of their receipts in foreign exchange, and a similar arrangement exists for importers and exporters.

The amount of money created through foreign exchange conversion therefore depends on foreign exchange balances of the economy and on the willingness of the public not to convert its holdings.

Another source of money supply is credit to the government. Until the Bank of Israel was set up, the government was entitled to borrow from the banking system, a privilege used liberally until 1952, when the government stopped selling Treasury bills to the banking system. In 1954, the Bank of Israel Law made the Bank responsible for credit to the government and set a maximum of 20 per cent of the budget. However, the government still borrows small sums from the commercial banking system. In addition, the government may borrow abroad and convert its receipts. Such credit will, however, be recorded as foreign currency conversion.

Credit to the public is granted both by the Bank of Israel and by the private banking system, which is subject to various measures of credit control. The main instruments of control are definition of liquid assets, minimum liquidity requirements, and direct control of the volume of credit.

Until November, 1950, no regulations existed laying down what con-stituted liquid assets, nor were liquidity ratios specified. In practice,

Table 78.   Changes in the Quantity of Money: 1949–65

	Money supply: per cent change during year	Net foreign balances of banking system	Per cent change in money supply due to changes in			
			Bank credit		Other factors (residual)	Total
			To government	To public		
	(1)	(2)	(3)	(4)	(5)	(6)

A. First series

	(1)	(2)	(3)	(4)	(5)	(6)
1949	39.1	−13.7	78.4	47.2	−11.9	100.0
1950	35.4	−33.5	104.0	57.9	−28.4	100.0
1951	27.2	−17.0	86.8	54.0	−23.8	100.0
1952	6.5	−17.2	26.1	186.0	−94.9	100.0
1953	24.5	24.4	7.6	87.6	−19.6	100.0
1954	20.1[a]	106.8	−31.8	46.6	−21.6	100.0
1955	20.4	27.8	66.1	35.7	−29.6	100.0
1956	23.3	15.3	64.8	49.8	−29.9	100.0
1957	11.4	−29.9	91.3	104.6	−66.0	100.0
1958	14.5	91.9	46.8	89.2	−127.9	100.0
1959	10.0	140.3	8.9	196.2	−245.4	100.0

B. *Second series*[b]

1959	10.0	137.3	7.7	161.7	−206.7	100.0
1960	21.3	99.4	−2.7	91.6	−88.3	100.0
1961	10.1	151.2	−54.0	181.1	−178.3	100.0
1962	29.7	255.0	−102.7	74.7	−127.0	100.0
1963	28.1	64.5	33.6	68.1	−66.2	100.0

C. *Third series*[c]

1963	28.1	64.5	33.6	54.6	−52.7	100.0
1964	6.1	55.3	97.2	224.8	−277.3	100.0
1965	11.2	114.4	28.5	126.2	−169.1	100.0

[a] See note c to Table 77.

[b] In the later Bank of Israel *Annual Reports* the data for columns (2), (3), and (4) appear in a form different from that underlying the Patinkin source table for 1949–58. Accordingly, the change during 1959 is shown calculated both ways.

[c] The Patinkin series for bank credit to the public includes investment in domestic securities (excluding securities of subsidiaries). This item is available in later *Reports* only up to 1963, which is accordingly shown calculated both with and without the item.

SOURCES: 1949–58—Patinkin, *op. cit.*, p. 142, Appendix B (money supply, end-year figures), and p. 112, Table 40 [columns (2), (3), (4)].

1959–65—Bank of Israel, *Annual Report 1959*, p. 243, Table XIV–10, and p. 236, Table XIV–8 [columns (3) and (4) figures for 1959 consistent with Patinkin series].

Annual Report 1960, p. 246, Table XIV–10 [column (2) figures for 1959 consistent with Patinkin series].

Annual Report 1963, p. 312, Table XV–9 (banks' investment in domestic securities, 1958–63).

Annual Report 1965, p. 328, Table XV–7 [column (2), 1958–63]; p. 330, Table XV–8 [column (3), 1958–62]; p. 332, Table XV–9 [column (4), 1958–62].

Annual Report 1966, p. 379, Table XV–7 [column (2), 1963–65]; p. 381, Table XV–8 [column (3), 1963–65]; p. 385, Table XV–9 [column (4), 1963–65.]

Money supply (end-of-year figures): see source to Table 77.

banks considered cash, foreign exchange balances, and Treasury bills as liquid assets. In November, 1950, the government made a first attempt to regulate credit by requiring banks to have a liquidity ratio of 45 per cent against demand deposits. No penalties were fixed and the required ratio more or less reflected the existing one.[4]

Until 1953, the only instrument of credit control used was raising liquidity ratios; in that year they reached a marginal rate of 90 per cent, and the amount of credit was frozen altogether. Credit, however, continued to grow, partly because the banks contravened the regulations and partly because they were authorized by the government to expand credit for special purposes.

Such authorizations made freezing impractical, and since 1956 liquidity ratios and the definition of liquid assets have become important. The major variation in definition, introduced in 1957, was the exclusion of foreign exchange balances from liquid assets, so that credit could not be expanded by banks borrowing abroad. Liquidity ratios were raised continually throughout the period.

A breakdown of money supply into foreign exchange conversions, credit to the public, and credit to the government is, as the foregoing discussion implies, oversimplified. For example, the government can increase the money supply by borrowing abroad, by borrowing from the banking system, or by inducing a public enterprise to borrow on its behalf. Nevertheless, we present the data of Table 78, which shows that foreign exchange conversion was unimportant until 1958 (with the exception of 1954, when a major effort was made to raise foreign exchange reserves depleted during the preceding period). From 1958 on, its role has become a central one in affecting the supply of money, mainly owing to the flow of restitution payments from Germany, about half of which were converted annually.[5] Credit to the government was important in the austerity period 1949–51, around the time of the Sinai Campaign in 1955–57, and at the end of the period in 1963–65; credit to the public was important throughout the period.

---

[4] Forty-three per cent at the end of 1950. See D. Patinkin, "Monetary and Price Development in Israel: 1949–53," *Scripta Hierosolymitana*, Vol. III: Studies in Economic and Social Sciences, ed. Roberto Bachi (Jerusalem: The Magnes Press, 1956), Appendix Tables 2 and 3.

[5] Miriam Beham, *Monetary Aspects of the 1962 Devaluation* (Jerusalem: 1967; preliminary draft, Hebrew), pp. 58 ff.

Developments by Period

The mechanism of money creation described in the last section is but one part of the more comprehensive subject of over-all inflation policy, which can conveniently by subdivided into monetary, fiscal, and price policy. This section is devoted to a chronological discussion of these types of policy. Wage policy, which should also be examined as a source of inflation, is discussed in the next section.

1949–51: The policy of this period can be evaluated only against the background of immigration and demobilization. Large-scale investments were required, most of which had to be carried out by the public sector (for example, roads, land reclamation, and residential construction). In addition, it was necessary to reallocate consumption between the older residents and the new immigrants, in order to supply the latter with such essentials as food and clothing. Administrative tools for taxation were as yet undeveloped and the securities market was almost non-existent. The chief remaining ways were, therefore, monetary expansion and deficit budgets accompanied by price controls.[6]

As stated, the way to monetary expansion was opened by making the currency issue independent of foreign exchange balances and by expanding credit by the banking system to the government. Private credit also grew substantially. Though minimum liquidity ratios were fixed by the Ministry of Finance in 1950, they did not limit monetary expansion because the government continuously supplied the banks with liquid assets. In addition, banks were sometimes allowed to grant credit beyond their liquidity ratio, provided that it was directed at "preferred" branches (particularly agriculture).

The expansionary monetary policy was supplemented by price controls. Using the legal and administrative methods of the mandatory government, price controls, with or without rationing, were introduced in foreign exchange, in most of the goods-producing branches, and in some services. The only important price that was not interfered with by the government was wages. This large-scale intervention, usually characteristic of war periods, resulted in an increasing divergence between controlled and free-market prices. This was especially true in three areas—foreign exchange prices were too low relative to local prices; capital was too cheap relative to labor; and goods were too cheap relative to services. No serious attempts were made to correct these

---

[6] Import of capital was also used, but at this time Israel had limited access to the foreign market.

distortions by means of subsidies and taxes. But the main drawback of the system was the absence of a restrictive monetary and fiscal policy.

TABLE 79.   *Money, Prices, and Import Surplus: 1949–53*

(per cent change during year[a])

	Money supply	Consumer price index		Real balances[b]	Import surplus
		Official	Adjusted		
1949	39.1	–13.4	1.0	37.7	28.1
1950	35.3	7.1	20.4	12.4	27.6
1951	27.2	25.6	44.9	–12.2	–14.7
1952	6.5	60.2	21.6	–12.4	–14.3
1953	24.5	18.2	2.9	21.0	–9.5
1949–51 (index)	239.6	116.5	176.3	135.9	139.5
1952–53 (index)	132.6	189.4	125.1	106.0	77.6
1949–53 (index)	317.8	220.6	220.6	144.1	108.2

[a] Changes are calculated as follows: money supply from December of preceding year to December of given year; prices from January of given year to January of following year; from import surplus during given year to import surplus of following year. Hence, for the whole period 1949–53, the indexes are: money supply—December, 1953 ÷ December, 1948; prices—January, 1954 ÷ January, 1949; import surplus—1954 ÷ 1949.
[b] Money supply deflated by adjusted Consumers Price Index.
SOURCES: Money supply—Patinkin, *op. cit.*, p. 142, Appendix B.
         Official Consumers Price Index—*Abstract 1966*, No. 17, p. 273, Table J/1.
         Adjusted Consumers Price Index—Yoram Weiss, "Price Control in Israel: 1939–1963" (unpublished M. A. thesis, The Hebrew University, 1964; Hebrew), Table C23.
         Import surplus—Table 50.

As a result of monetary expansion, the public accumulated money which it could not spend. The inflationary pressures created are indicated by the data of Table 79: while money supply grew by some 140 per cent in the three years, the Consumers Price Index (which did not include black market prices) went up by only 16 per cent. As a result, black markets developed, the import surplus grew rapidly, and foreign exchange reserves approached zero. The system could no longer sustain the inflationary pressures.

An attempt to explain the lack of restrictive monetary and fiscal policy has been made by Nahum Gross.[7] On the basis of a detailed analysis of policy declarations, he maintains that the only symptom used by the government to estimate inflationary pressure was price changes; lower prices were identified with lack of inflationary pressure regardless of the rate of monetary expansion. In brief, at a time of excess demand the dominant approach was that of cost rather than demand inflation.

In spite of the errors made, it should be pointed out that some very important aims were achieved: new immigrants were provided with necessities, the share of investment in resources was high, unemployment declined, and real product increased rapidly (Tables 30, 14, and 28). Most of these achievements were, however, lost once the system broke down at the end of 1951.

1952–53: The background for this period is the collapse of the price control system as black markets developed and foreign exchange reserves dwindled. The crisis also led to the virtual cessation of immigration in 1952–53.

The new chief policy aim, often reiterated since the middle of 1951, was to reduce the import surplus and replenish foreign exchange reserves. It was also recognized that the existing price control system should be replaced by a more liberal one in order to secure more efficient production. Policy measures were based on the recognition that demand, rather than costs, should be reduced in order to achieve these aims. Accordingly, measures were concentrated in three fields: balancing the government budget, devaluation, and relaxation of price controls.

The government stopped using bank credit to finance itself; in addition, a forced loan on currency and demand deposits was levied in 1952. Income tax administration was streamlined and the tax became an increasingly important source of revenue. Also, some government land was sold to the public in order to absorb money. At the same time, expenditures were cut down.

Both the devaluation of February, 1952, and the lifting of some of the price controls raised prices. Rationing and controls remained in force for foreign exchange and some food items and were virtually abolished in other spheres. As a result, the Consumers Price Index jumped by 89 per cent in two years, although corrected for black market prices the rise was only 25 per cent (the third column of Table 79). Such price rises can be anti-inflationary, provided that money

[7] N. Gross, "Inflation and Economic Policy in Israel: The First Stage, 1949–1950" (unpublished M.A. thesis, The Hebrew University; Hebrew), p. 24.

supply is constant or growing more slowly. In fact, money supply grew by about 33 per cent in these two years. That the rate of increase slowed down was due almost entirely to fiscal policy, not monetary controls. Although liquidity ratios were raised to 90 per cent on the margin, they were not enforced very effectively.

It was the reduction in the amount of liquid assets supplied by the government rather than the higher liquidity ratios that curbed monetary expansion. Foreign balances were negligible throughout the period, so that despite the decline in import surplus they did not exert inflationary pressure; nearly all the increase in money supply stemmed from the expansion of credit to the public. As in the preceding period, attempts were made to direct credit to preferred destinations by asking the banks not to lend for consumption purposes and by granting permission to extend credit beyond the required liquidity ratio to agriculture and other preferred branches. There is no way of checking the effectiveness of credit direction, or whether there was substitution between regular and additional credit.

The results of the anti-inflationary policy were a steep rise in unemployment, stagnation of national product, and a sharp decline in the import surplus.

Unemployment rose in spite of the rather large increase in the money supply, and this may reflect the oligopolistic structure of both the product and the factor markets. Consequently, the attempt to cure demand inflation by raising prices resulted in cost inflation. The real price of reduction in imports proved to be the virtual cessation of GNP growth.

1954–60: The background of this period is the drastic change in the balance of payments situation. The Consolidation Loan received in 1954 from American Jewry (see p. 160, above) and the reparations and personal restitutions from Germany made reducing the import surplus a matter of secondary importance for the time being. The import surplus grew, making possible a large investment program. Government statements stressed economic growth and the reduction of unemployment as the main targets. The economy did in fact grow, the standard of living rose rapidly, and unemployment fell. At the same time, price level, import surplus, and money supply all rose.

Demand grew rather more slowly than in 1949–51 and was increasingly absorbed by product growth. In 1955, price increases absorbed more of the demand than did product growth; by 1959, the latter had become much more important, absorbing most of the additional demand (Table 76). Although the import surplus grew, its role in absorbing

TABLE 80. The Demand and Liquidity Surplus Created by the Government: 1956–66

(IL millions)

| | Purchases on current and capital account[a] (1) | Taxes and other net transfer payments[b] (2) | Demand surplus (1)–(2) (3) | Domestic loans granted[c] (4) | Liquidity surplus (3)+(4) = (6)+(7) (5) | Net banking credit (6) | Receipts from abroad | | |
							Total (8)+(9) (7)	Loans[d] (8)	Unilateral transfers (9)
1956[e]	537[f]	356	181	114	295	84	211	99	112
1957	491	489	2	254	256	54	202	64	138
1958	584	503	81	224	305	39	266	133	133
1959	666	624	42	207	249	5	244	135	109
1960	720	639	81	184	265	–4	269	149	120
1961	893	839	54	227	281	–48	329	190	139
1962	1,233	978	255	49	304	–61	365	292	73
1963	1,364	1,197	167	73	240	119	121	42	79
1964	1,647	1,539	108	238	346	95	251	226	25
1965	2,012	1,720	292	334	626	55	571	505	66
1966	2,446	1,929	517	103	620	210	410	392	18

[a] Net of sales.

[b] Taxes net of subsidies; other net transfers on current and capital account (including interest); the sources do not always distinguish between loans and grants to other public sector agencies; accordingly, the total amount of these loans and grants is included in this column.

[c] Loans granted less loans received (including Absorption Loan and Compulsory Saving), both net of redemptions.

[d] Net of redemptions.

[e] April–December.

[f] Apparently includes interest payments [in other years included in column (2) as a negative transfer receipt].

SOURCES: Bank of Israel Annual Reports as follows:
1956, p. 355, Table XX–1 (for 1956); 1958, pp. 236–37, Table XV–12, and p. 233, Table XV–9 (for 1957);
1960, pp. 280–81, Table XVI–4, and p. 289, Table XVI–7 (for 1958); 1961, pp. 96–97, Table VII–6 (for 1959),
and p. 108, Table VII–11 (for interest payments, 1959–61); 1962, p. 111, Table VII–9 (for Absorption Loan,
1961); 1963, p. 108, Table VII–5 (for 1960), p. 122, Table VII–10 (for interest payments, 1962), and p. 113,
Table VII–7 (for Absorption Loan, 1962); 1964, p. 141, Table VII–6 (for 1961), p. 156, Table VII–11 (for
interest payments, 1963), and p. 144, Table VII–8 (for Absorption Loan, 1963); 1965, p. 146, Table VII–6 (for
1962–63); 1966, p. 156, Table VII–5, and p. 160, Table VII–7 (for 1964–66).

the increase in demand was minor. All in all, product grew at a fairly steady annual rate of around 10 per cent in 1955–60 (Table 34), whereas the annual rate of price increase declined from around 12 per cent in 1954–55 to about 3.5 per cent in 1958–60 (Table 76).

For the first time monetary policy was formally separated from fiscal and price policy. This was done in 1954 by establishing the Bank of Israel, which was vested with authority to regulate credit and issue money, with the aim of stabilizing prices and directing credit to "productive" uses. Before turning to its monetary policy, we shall survey the government's fiscal policy.

The government creates inflationary pressure in two ways. First, when its demand for goods and services exceeds the reduction in the demand of the public; second, the public's net liquidity may be increased through the government's financial transactions as well as through its real demand. The first indicator calls for an estimate of the difference between government expenditure on goods and services (both current and capital) and the income from taxation and other payments from the public.[8] Such estimates have been made by the Bank of Israel since 1956 and are summarized in Table 80. They show that, except for 1956 (the year of the Sinai Campaign), inflationary pressure created by the government was not strong. The second indicator, liquidity, is estimated as the increase in the government's debt to the banking system and to abroad. It shows that substantial inflationary pressure was exerted by the government, mostly through financial transactions such as providing loans from the development budget. In sum, the inflationary pressure created by the government changed its form from direct demand for goods and services to monetary expansion.

As can be seen from Table 80, liquidity created by the government was fairly steady, ranging from IL 250 to IL 300 million annually. The government relied less on the banking system and more on foreign sources, the share of loans within the latter increasing. Some of these loans were not used for imports but were accumulated as foreign exchange reserves, so that their main impact was on domestic prices.

The fact that the government expanded effective demand through financial rather than fiscal operations meant that it competed with the Bank of Israel, which also dealt with monetary policy, with the explicit aim of stabilizing the value of money. This circumscribed the Bank's authority; any decisions as to the total volume of credit had to take

---

[8] The receipts side includes reductions in both liquidity and income and is, therefore, a very inexact measure of the absorption of the public's demand.

TABLE 81. Industrial Allocation of Regulated and Unregulated Credit:[a] 1955, 1958, and 1961

(per cent)

	Total	Local authorities and public services	Agri-culture	Industry	Construc-tion	Commerce and services	Other[b]
1955							
Total	100.0	7.0	30.0	28.8	6.1	16.4	11.7
Unregulated	63.2	2.5	18.1	34.7	6.3	22.7	15.7
Regulated	36.8	14.7	50.7	18.5	5.8	5.7	4.6
1958							
Total	100.0	6.4	24.8	34.4	5.6	16.0	12.8
Unregulated	49.8	2.5	16.4	29.9	6.7	22.9	21.6
Regulated	50.2	10.3	33.4	39.0	4.5	9.3	3.5
1961							
Total	100.0	11.4	19.3	30.8	5.7	16.6	16.2
Unregulated	58.2	6.3	11.9	33.0	6.6	17.7	24.5
Regulated	41.8	18.4	29.7	27.7	4.5	15.1	4.6

[a] Commercial banks only.
[b] Small artisans, finance and credit institutions, and unspecified branches.
SOURCE: Meir Heth, *Banking Institutions in Israel* (Jerusalem: Falk Institute, 1966), p. 205, Table 65 (Total), and p. 208, Table 66 (regulated and unregulated).

into account the credit offered by the government through the development budget. The Bank therefore concentrated on allocating credit rather than on setting its total volume.

The chief means used to influence the volume of credit were setting liquidity ratios and freezing credit. At the beginning of 1954 the total volume of credit was frozen, but the Bank authorized specific loans outside the quota. Between 1956 and 1960 the share of these extra loans in total credit rose from 21.9 to 31.8 per cent.[9] Since the growth of these loans was not spread evenly among banks, actual liquidity ratios varied widely. In consequence, pressure mounted to equalize them and to abandon the freezing of credit; freezing was not abolished until 1961, but liquidity ratios have been the main policy instrument since 1958.

Although, as stated, money supply grew, it is clear that its growth rate diminished. This may have been the result of the Bank's restraining policy. But the decline in the growth rate of the money supply is misleading: during the period, a large market of non-banking credit developed, in the form of consumer and black market credit. The Bank's most effective activity was the allocation of credit outside the liquidity requirements ("regulated credit"). Table 81 shows that the Bank probably did influence the credit allocation of banks, although not in all cases. The Bank's influence can be seen in the fact that a branch's share of total and regulated credit changed in the same direction. However, unregulated credit often changed in the opposite direction, partly offsetting the effect of changes in regulated credit. Again, the credit allocation statistics do not take non-banking credit into account, so that the results may be biased.

The Bank of Israel made very little use of two other instruments of monetary policy, the manipulation of interest rates and open market operations. The Bank is limited in its ability to regulate interest since maximum rates are fixed by law. Until 1957 the ceiling was 9 per cent, according to an Ottoman law. In that year, a new Interest Law raised the ceiling to 11 per cent. The Bank has not used the rediscount rate as a policy instrument to influence bank liquidity. The absence of open market operations has sometimes been explained by the underdeveloped state of the securities market.

The fact that interest rates were left at their former low level was often criticized since they were much too low to guarantee equilibrium

---

[9] Meir Heth, *Banking Institutions in Israel* (Jerusalem: Falk Institute, 1966), p. 202, Table 63.

between credit supply and demand.[10] The development of a black market in credit weakened the Bank's monetary control and created divergent rates of interest. It also helped to strengthen pressure groups that tried to gain a larger quota of legal credit. The most important contribution to raising real rates was made by private companies and the government by means of value-linked loans. Linkage, which became increasingly important after it was begun in 1955,[11] was usually to the Consumers Price Index or the foreign exchange rate.

We shall comment briefly on price policy. The tendency to replace direct controls by subsidies and indirect taxes continued. Many of the subsidies were designed to lower those prices that affected the Consumers Price Index, and through it wages. However, another type of subsidy, aimed at increasing output or maintaining incomes, became more important. In the foreign exchange market, where quantitative restrictions were still used, taxes and subsidies also increasingly replaced quota controls (see Chapter 10), and import duties and export subsidies accounted for an increasing share of net indirect taxation. In agriculture, subsidies were used to maintain incomes rather than to keep consumer prices down, and were combined with quantitative restrictions on output. It is interesting to ask whether the complicated system of net indirect taxes resulted in a growing divergence of actual from free market prices. One way of gauging this is to compute subsidies and taxes as a percentage of GNP, and for our purpose their sum rather than the difference between them seems appropriate since both add to the divergence from free market prices. Table 82 shows that the weight of taxes and subsidies on local product did not rise during the period; however, those on foreign trade did, and this reflects, to some extent at least, convergence towards rather than divergence from a free foreign exchange (see Chapter 10). On the whole, it was the composition rather than the size of taxes and subsidies that changed.

To sum up: By 1960 there was full employment, accompanied by a high rate of product growth (Tables 14 and 34). Though the import surplus was large, foreign exchange reserves rose steadily, mainly because of personal restitutions payments. At the same time, inflationary pressures continued to mount and found several outlets. First, increasing

[10] See, for example, Heth, *op. cit.*, pp. 100–103, and H. Barkai and M. Michaely, "The New Economic Policy—After One Year," *The Economic Quarterly*, X (No. 37–38, March 1963; Hebrew), 23–39.

[11] There were, in fact, a few isolated examples of value linkage even earlier. See Marshall Sarnat, *Saving and Investment Through Retirement Funds in Israel* (Jerusalem: Falk Institute, 1966), pp. 72–73.

pressure on the price of foreign exchange entailed a cumbersome system of taxing imports and subsidizing exports. Second, there was increasing pressure on the credit market and a black market for credit developed. The government continued to exert inflationary pressure, although conversions of foreign exchange balances accumulated by the public gradually became more important.

TABLE 82. Indirect Taxes and Subsidies: 1950–65

(per cent of GNP at market prices)

| | On domestic production | | Foreign trade | |
	Taxes	Subsidies	Import taxes	Export subsidies
1950	9.2	–	2.4	–
1951	9.7	1.0	1.7	–
1952	7.4	–	1.7	..
1953	9.1	2.0	2.1	..
1954	9.8	0.6	2.3	..
1955	8.1	1.4	4.1	0.1
1956	7.8	1.3	4.8	0.3
1957	9.3	2.3	6.0	0.9
1958	9.1	2.2	6.6	1.2
1959	9.4	2.0	7.7	1.7
1960	9.7	2.0	7.7	2.4
1961	10.5	1.4	8.2	2.8
1962	10.4	1.6	6.5	0.7
1963	10.2	1.8	5.8	0.4
1964	10.1	1.8	6.1	0.4
1965	9.7	1.6	5.9	0.4

SOURCE: Abstract 1966, No. 17, pp. 156–57, Table F/1.

1961–64: In some respects this period is similar to the preceding one. GNP continued to increase at an annual rate of about 11 per cent and full employment prevailed. However, inflationary pressure increased considerably and took a new form. By 1958 personal restitutions payments had already become the principal source of the increase in foreign exchange balances and, pari passu, in money supply. This contrasted with the previous years when most transfers from abroad accrued directly to the government.

During 1961 it became clear that devaluation was unavoidable. The import surplus rose from $ 315 million in 1959 to $ 432 million in 1961 (Table 50) and although the import surplus was still exceeded by capital imports (Table 57), it was felt that its growth must be curbed. In addition, the system of effective devaluation through taxes and subsidies had become too cumbersome. Expectations of devaluation during 1961 led the public to reduce its foreign currency conversions; this reduced inflationary pressure, but several other factors worked in the opposite direction. First, the banks continued to convert their foreign balances and expand credit.[12] Second, the government increased its reliance on foreign loans for financing its activities. Private loans and investments from abroad also rose steadily (Table 58).

The devaluation of February, 1962, was therefore carried out at a time of inflationary pressure and a large stock of private foreign currency balances whose owners converted them after devaluation.

As a result, the money supply grew by 30 per cent during 1962 (Table 78), continuing to grow, but more slowly, in 1963 and 1964. In addition, a bill-brokerage market developed rapidly and became the main form of non-banking credit. Bill brokerage is an arrangement whereby owners of deposits lend them out through the mediation of banks, with or without a bank guarantee. The effective rate of interest on such loans is about 12 to 17 per cent,[13] compared with the legal maximum of 11 per cent. The weight of bill brokerage in the total growth of credit rose rapidly, from 24 per cent in 1961 to 42 per cent in 1964.[14] The growth of this type of credit is reflected in the velocity of demand deposits, which rose from 16.2 in 1961 to 19.1 in 1964.[15] The recorded increase in money supply is therefore an understatement.

The increase in money supply and in its velocity caused prices to rise far beyond what was to be expected from the rise in import costs due to devaluation.[16] Although real product grew fast, prices also rose, and the import surplus grew from $ 432 million in 1961 to $ 569 million in 1964 (Table 50). Although foreign exchange balances were higher in 1964 than in 1961, the basic problem of balance of payments deficit was not solved and inflationary pressure, which caused the failure of the devaluation, was much more severe.

During the period, the net effect of government policy was inflationary. Between 1957 and 1961 the direct demand surplus had been negligible, but it rose considerably in 1962. The liquidity surplus declined in 1962 and 1963, but not sufficiently to offset the increase in direct

12 Beham, *op. cit.,* pp. 74–75.
13 Heth, *op. cit.,* p. 325, note 12.
14 *Ibid.,* p. 338, Table 117. Most of the rise occurred from 1961 to 1962.
15 *Abstract 1966,* No. 17, p. 518, Table Q/2.
16 Bank of Israel, *Annual Report 1962,* p. 76, Table VI–2.

demand (Table 80). This decline in loans reflects the government's efforts to curb inflation, all of them directed at the credit market; they included the flotation of a short-term loan, provisions for early redemption of mortgages, and the redemption of some of the government's debt to the Bank of Israel. These measures are reflected in the 1962–63 figures; in 1964 the government resumed lending to the public. Since its direct expenditures, both on current and capital account, rose steeply, the anti-inflationary steps taken proved ineffective. In 1961–62 the government relied exclusively on foreign receipts to finance the demand surplus; from 1963, it returned to borrowing from the banking system.

While it contributed to the inflationary pressure—creating a demand surplus and raising liquidity—the government attempted to freeze costs and prices by direct, though informal, intervention. In 1962 a Price Headquarters was set up whose function was to exert pressure on producers not to raise prices. However, government pressure was not equally effective in all branches: as in the early 1950's, agriculture and manufacturing were most susceptible, while the price of services rose faster than it would have done in the absence of intervention. The average price level continued to rise in spite of the intervention, because of monetary expansion.

As early as 1961, the Bank of Israel tried to curb the growth of credit. Time deposits up to 18 months were included with demand deposits for the purpose of the liquidity regulations; the Bank also reduced loans in excess of the liquidity quota. These measures proved inadequate, because of the current supply of liquid assets through foreign exchange conversions and because the banks were willing to pay the fine for excess liquidity.

The total failure of the government and the Bank of Israel to carry out an anti-inflationary policy and a successful devaluation has often been debated.[17] It seems to us that several factors contributed. The government itself expanded demand continuously. This may have been due to some ministries expanding their activities in spite of a general anti-inflationary policy. It may also have been that the government attempted to combat cost rather than demand inflation, as suggested by the efforts invested in the Price Headquarters and the (unsuccessful) attempt to freeze wages for a year. The Bank was unable to cope with

---

[17] Beham, *op. cit.*; Barkai and Michaely, *op. cit.*; D. Horowitz, "Comments on Criticism," *The Economic Quarterly*, X (No. 37–38, March 1963; Hebrew), 40; M. Zandberg, "The New Economic Policy," *The Economic Quarterly*, X (No. 40, December 1963; Hebrew), 339–45.

the large-scale conversions of foreign exchange, and later with the increasing scale of loans by the government.

Recent trends: The recognition of failure has had a very far-reaching influence on the government's recent policy: although by 1965 the internal price level had risen by more than 20 per cent over 1962 (Appendix Table 4), there has been reluctance to adjust the foreign exchange price by means of devaluation for fear of accelerated inflation. As an alternative, the government has tried to improve the balance of payments situation through a deflationary policy. In 1966 government and private investment both declined sharply, unemployment increased, and product hardly grew at all. As a result, the import surplus declined. This was wholly due to the income effect, internal prices continuing to rise; it therefore depends on there being a recession—the long-run problem of reducing the import surplus and maintaining full employment has yet to be solved.

WAGE POLICY

A frequently voiced explanation of the government's inflationary policy and the inability of the Bank of Israel to exert a restraining influence is that there were excessive wage increases, and that any anti-inflationary policy consistent with full employment must start by changing the institutional set-up of the labor market rather than from monetary and fiscal policies. We shall now examine wage policy in the light of this argument.

Individual negotiations for wages and working conditions are rare in Israel; collective bargaining is the common practice. The Histadrut, in which about 90 per cent of all employees are organized, is the chief representative of labor. Employers are represented by the Manufacturers Association, whose influence, however, is not comparable to that of the Histadrut. Formally, the government appears only as an employer (represented by the Civil Service Commission), but government wage policy as regards other sectors is reflected in party discussions. Since the Histadrut is dominated by Mapai, which is also the largest party in the government coalition, it can get government backing in wage negotiations but must also take macro-economic factors into consideration.

Wages consist mostly of the basic wage, the cost-of-living (COL) allowance, and fringe benefits. Basic wage rates are fixed separately for each industry or occupation, negotiations being conducted between the appropriate trade union and employers association. Trade unions are affiliated with the Histadrut, and any agreement reached requires the approval of the Histadrut Trade Union Department. The COL allowance, on the other hand, is negotiated directly by the Trade Union Department and the Manufacturers Association. Since 1952, the results of these negotiations have been extended to virtually all employees, an extension formalized by a 1959 Ministry of Labor regulation.

The cost-of-living allowance

The COL allowance system was introduced under the mandatory government. In 1942, after wartime price rises, a commission was appointed to inquire into wage problems. Its recommendations, which remained in force until September, 1948, were that (a) allowances were to be paid according to changes in the Consumers Price Index prepared by the government; (b) changes in the allowance were to be made every three months; (c) no allowance was paid on that part of the monthly basic wage which exceeded a given maximum.

Ever since, the COL allowance has followed broadly the pattern set in 1942. The details have often been changed: first, the interval between payments was in 1957 formally lengthened from three to six months, and in practice it has nearly always been a full year since then;[18] second, the ceiling on the basic wage receiving the allowance has been raised continually; third, the basket for calculating the COL allowance has been changed from time to time.[19]

The economic effects of the COL allowance have been the subject of constant debate. It may be worth while to begin with the most important bone of contention, namely, whether or not the allowance is the cause of a persistent cost inflation. There are two sets of factors which lead to price rises and consequently to a payment of the allowance. The first is a rise in the money supply or changes in liquidity preferences, or other factors causing demand inflation; the second is a rise in import prices or taxes or in basic-wage claims, which may induce a cost inflation. When the first type of factor is at work, it is plausible that even without the COL allowance mechanism, producers would increase their demand for labor, and under full employment the price of labor would rise. Under such conditions, therefore, the COL allowance merely accelerates and lubricates economic processes that would occur in any case. In itself, the allowance cannot be regarded as causing a further price rise, but only as an agent of income redistribution. Its

---

[18] *Abstract 1966,* No. 17, p. 348, Table K/40.
[19] A detailed survey of the COL allowance agreements may be found in Uri Bahral, *The Effect of Mass Immigration on Wages in Israel* (Jerusalem: Falk Project, 1965), Appendix A, pp. 59–66.

major shortcoming is that the rise is uniform among various branches, which do not profit equally from inflation. Eventually, wage rises would tend to be equalized throughout the economy, but equalizing in advance may produce pressure from the less well-to-do branches for the government to expand the money supply.

A change in the exchange rate usually aims at reducing the import surplus both by changing the price of imports relative to local product and by reducing aggregate demand. In this case, paying a COL allowance means keeping real wages constant, and, if total demand is to be reduced, curtailing profits and possibly increasing unemployment. An increase in taxation poses a similar problem, especially if it is applied as an anti-inflationary device aimed at reducing nominal incomes. The rise in prices automatically raises wages, so that as far as employees are concerned the tax cannot achieve its objective. Since profits are reduced, unemployment and cost inflation may ensue. An increase in basic wage claims followed by a rise in prices and a COL allowance may also initiate a cost-inflation chain reaction. While the COL allowance may be appropriate in conditions of demand inflation, it is an obstacle to anti-inflationary fiscal policy and successful devaluation.

Throughout most of the period the increase in money supply stemmed from government deficit financing and from foreign-exchange conversion, i.e., from demand factors independent of the labor market. The COL allowance system was therefore useful, the more so because prices rose very rapidly, and, in the absence of an automatic mechanism, would probably have resulted in numerous labor disputes. In recent years, however, the need for an anti-inflationary fiscal policy and devaluation has made the system less workable.

A special committee set up by the Histadrut and the Manufacturers Association in 1965 in effect recommended continuing with the system but excluding import prices from the Consumers Price Index.[20] Another suggestion was to exclude indirect taxes from the Index, although the committee made no firm recommendation on this point. None of these changes has yet been introduced.

Also of importance is the maximum wage for payment of the allowance, since this sets a limit on the total amount paid as well as influencing wage differentials. In periods of rapidly rising prices, the ceiling causes differentials to contract. This happened in 1952–53; thereafter, the ceiling was raised from time to time, and, on the whole,

[20] *Report of the Committee of Experts Inquiring into the Cost-of-Living Allowance* (Tel Aviv: November 1966; Hebrew mimeograph), pp. 1–2.

differentials widened.[21] The 1965 committee recommended abolishing the ceiling altogether.

Over the years, the COL allowance has become a less important element of the rise in nominal wages. In 1955–58 it accounted for about one half to two thirds of the rise, and from then on for about one third (except in the two years following devaluation, when it again accounted for one half to two thirds).[22]

The over-all level of wages

Unlike the COL allowance, which is centrally determined and covers all employees, basic wages are negotiated separately for various trades and occupations, subject to the approval of the Histadrut's Trade Union Department. Here the Histadrut's policy is less clear-cut than in the case of the COL allowance, and it has changed radically over the years.

During the period of austerity the price of labor was the only uncontrolled price. The Histadrut was against freezing wages, and there were several strikes, of which the most serious one occurred in 1951 in the metal industry and resulted in a 19 per cent wage increase. It was the Histadrut's attitude that wages could go up without causing unemployment since profits were "excessive." Even when unemployment rose sharply between 1952 and 1954 no attempt was made to freeze real wages,[23] let alone reduce them. Instead, two solutions to unemployment were proposed: to reduce the supply of labor by a ban on overtime, and to raise aggregate demand for local products. Thus, it was proposed to carry out public works and to expand credit to enterprises in order to absorb the unemployed, i.e., to increase the money supply in order to create effective demand. It was also proposed to ban the import of finished goods "which could be produced locally at reasonable prices and quality"—the traditional demand for protection against foreign competition in order to create employment.[24]

As mentioned, there was no suggestion of lowering or even freezing wages in order to raise the demand for labor. On the contrary, real daily wages in manufacturing rose by 3 per cent in 1952.[25] Whether a reduction in wages would have been of greater help in reducing

[21] Bahral, *op. cit.*, p. 6 and p. 55, Figure 8.
[22] Bank of Israel, *Annual Reports,* the chapter on wages.
[23] That is, to pay the COL allowance without raising basic wages.
[24] Histadrut Council, June, 1953.
[25] Don Patinkin, *The Israel Economy: The First Decade* (Jerusalem: Falk Project, 1960), p. 143, Appendix B.

unemployment than the means listed above has been the subject of a lively debate.

The Histadrut has been accused of looking after those with jobs, who were mostly well established in the country, while ignoring the new immigrants who formed the bulk of the unemployed.[26] The counter argument was that the employed and the unemployed were non-competing groups because the latter were unskilled and knew no Hebrew. Lowering wages would, therefore, not have helped the unemployed but would have led to a further decline in effective demand, making the situation even worse. However, the question is not just one of substitutability among workers, but of substitutability between labor and capital. The high relative cost of unskilled labor led producers to substitute capital for labor. That more labor would in fact have been employed at lower wages is indicated by the black market for labor in agriculture, where new immigrants were at the time employed at less than the official wage.

On the whole, the Histadrut's policy until 1954 tended to produce cost inflation, since it recommended wage increases regardless of the unemployment situation. This policy had to be reconsidered because of widening wage differentials, the growing power of the professional and civil service unions, and the weakening of central control in general (see pp. 277–78 below), as well as because of unemployment. It was felt that if the unions were left to themselves, cost inflation might become even more acute.

The Histadrut eventually took the stand that the total basic-wage bill should rise in proportion to real national product, so that the share of labor would remain fixed. The average wage per employee, however, would not be fixed but would depend on the number of employees as well as on product growth. The rise in the various branches would, under these limitations, depend on profitability in the branch.[27]

This policy was temporarily abandoned at the time of the 1962 devaluation. For the first time the Histadrut agreed to a two-year basic-wage freeze (with the COL allowance remaining in force, however), for fear of cost inflation and of rendering the devaluation ineffective. It might also have been an attempt to gain a breathing space during which the Histadrut could restore its central authority over the separate wage negotiations of affiliated unions.

[26] S. Riemer, "Wages in Israel," *Encyclopaedia Hebraica,* Vol. VI (1957; Hebrew), 802–807.

[27] Ninth Histadrut Conference, 1960.

The result was a complete failure. Between 1962 and 1964 the inflationary process caused the demand for labor to increase, wages broke all institutional bounds, and wage increases were effected mainly by mass promotions on existing scales: wage drift accounted for about two thirds of total wage increases at this time, being particularly pronounced in the civil service.[28]

The wage drift in the civil service resulted in an anomalous internal wage structure, and at the beginning of 1962 a government commission was appointed to recommend a new salary scale for the civil service and public corporations. Subsequent developments will be described below (pp. 278–79). Briefly, civil service salaries rose by 30 per cent, the full impact of the rise coming in 1965 and coinciding with lower-than-usual rates of product growth and monetary expansion (Tables 34 and 77). For the first time since the early 1950's, the country faced rising unemployment.

The share of wages in national income

In the light of the foregoing discussion, it is of interest to investigate whether wage claims, in all their forms, contributed to cost inflation. A possible approach to the problem is to examine the share of labor returns in national income.

Let us suppose, as a starting point, that the wage bill rises in proportion to product in the absence of inflation, so that its share remains fixed.[29] If the share of wages in fact declines, one explanation is that there is a lag due to demand inflation; conversely, if the share rises, a possible explanation is that there is cost inflation.

The share of wages in national income in 1955–65 is shown in Table 83 [column (2)]. The effect of variations in the percentage of employees in the employed labor force can be eliminated by holding it constant at the 1955 level, and this has been done in column (3).[30] Both series show that the share of wages declined between 1955 and 1961, and there is some evidence that it also declined in 1952–55.[31]

28 Bank of Israel, *Annual Reports,* the chapter on wages.
29 This corresponds to assuming a Cobb-Douglas type production function for the economy.
30 An alternative method of making the adjustment is to impute the average wage of employees to the self-employed. The index of labor share according to a fixed employee percentage will be in the ratio e_0/E_0 to the alternative index, when e_0 is the number of employees and E_0 the total number of employed persons, in the base year o.
31 M. Bruno, "Factor Productivity and Remuneration in Israel, 1952–1961,"

According to this—very weak—test, there is no indication of cost inflation. Since 1962 the picture is less clear-cut. In 1962 wages rose
slightly faster than product, reflecting the COL allowance paid as a
result of the devaluation. Again, in 1964 and 1965, the share of labor
rose as a result of increased basic wages. The last years of the series may
therefore indicate cost inflation.

TABLE 83.   *The Share of Wages in National Income:*
             1955–65

(per cent)

	Employees as per cent of employed persons	Share of wages in national income	
		Unadjusted	Adjusted for weight of employees[a]
	(1)	(2)	(3)
1955	64.5	53.7	53.7
1956	65.1	52.7	52.2
1957	65.2	52.2	51.6
1958	65.3	51.8	51.2
1959	66.2	51.4	50.1
1960	66.2	51.0	49.7
1961	67.4	51.2	49.0
1962	68.7	52.8	49.6
1963	69.5	50.3	46.7
1964	70.1	51.0	46.9
1965	70.6	52.1	47.6

[a] Assuming 1955 percentage of employees in employed labor force;
    i.e., calculated as [column (2) ÷ column (1)]×64.5 per cent.
SOURCES: See sources to Table 84.

The decline in the share of the total wage bill during 1955–65
reflects the fact that the unit price of labor rose more slowly than
product per worker. Table 84 shows that nominal wages per employee
rose 2.8 times from 1955 to 1965, whereas nominal product per employed person more than tripled.

We can therefore conclude that there has been some redistribution
of income between 1952 and 1963; returns to labor have declined as
a proportion of national income; and income per employee rose more
slowly than income per employed person. However, the worsening of

The Economic Quarterly, X (No. 37–38, March 1963; Hebrew), 41–56.

TABLE 84.   *National Income per Employed Person*
and Wages per Employee: 1955–65

(per cent change over preceding year)

	Nominal national income per employed person	Wages per employee		Consumers Price Index
		Nominal	Real	
1956	14.2	11.0	4.2	6.5
1957	9.8	8.5	2.0	6.4
1958	12.6	11.4	7.7	3.4
1959	9.4	7.2	5.7	1.4
1960	7.3	6.3	3.9	2.3
1961	12.5	11.0	4.0	6.7
1962	11.6	13.0	3.2	9.5
1963	19.1	12.0	5.1	6.6
1964	11.3	12.0	6.5	5.2
1965	15.1	16.6	8.3	7.7
1965÷1955	3.172	2.806	1.636	1.715

SOURCES: National income—*Abstract 1966*, No. 17, pp. 156–57, Table F/1.
Wage-bill—Bank of Israel, *Annual Report 1961*, p. 24, Table II–13 (for 1955–60; the figure was derived by applying to national income from the *Abstract* the per cent of wage-bill out of product derived from this source and linked on 1961 to the slightly different series in *Annual Report 1965*).
Annual Report 1965, p. 217, Table X–7 (for 1961–65; the figures in this source are consistent with the national income data in the *Abstract*).
Employment data—Bank of Israel, *Annual Report 1961*, loc. cit. (for 1955–60).
Annual Report 1965, p. 214, Table X–4 (for 1961–65; total employed persons calculated for 1962–64 from per cent of employees out of total given in other issues of the *Annual Report*).
Consumers Price Index—*Abstract 1966*, No. 17, p. 273, Table J/1.

the wage-earner's position is relative rather than absolute, since real wages per employee have risen steadily. Bruno has tried to explain why wages have lagged behind product.[32] His contention is that in the early 1950's the marginal product of labor and its price were not in equilibrium and that during the period market forces drove wages towards equilibrium.

Another criterion for the existence of cost inflation is the connection between unemployment and the rise in average wages. We have partial

[32] *Ibid.*

evidence for 1952–53[33] indicating that wages rose as well as unemployment, and this points to cost inflation. From 1954 to 1964, wages rose while unemployment declined, so that demand inflation is indicated, but in 1965 unemployment again rose together with wages.

Our conclusion is, therefore, that there is no evidence that the COL allowance or basic-wage increases were, during most of the period, causes of inflation. But recently, inflation may have been generated through wage claims, especially by public sector employees in the professional and administrative categories.

Wage differentials

Average-wage policy depends on policy regarding differentials, since it is the changes in the separately negotiated basic wages that ultimately determine the rise in average wages. Here the extent of central Histadrut control is important. Another important issue is whether the two policies are consistent.

When the State was established, there was no explicit policy on wage differentials. The equalitarian approach was illustrated in the Histadrut itself, where the family wage was customary; this means that employees of all grades got the same salary, supplemented by allowances based on family size. Family allowances were also introduced in firms which did not have a standard basic wage but which operated under collective agreements. Apart from this system, which did not apply to many workers, there was no comprehensive policy regarding the structure of the basic wage.

During 1952–54 it became clear that changes in the composition of the labor force and the rapid accumulation of capital generated pressures on the market that tended to widen differentials and that the Histadrut could no longer ignore them. By 1955 this had become the central issue of Histadrut wage policy. The turning point was a series of strikes in 1955; these led to the establishment of a commission of inquiry in 1956, which regraded professional manpower in the civil service. At the same time, the Histadrut set up a special department for professional employees. Although the Histadrut recognized the necessity for widening wage differentials, it participated in the process reluctantly. As the central organization of employees in the country, it regarded the trend as a danger to its unity. Moreover, the prevailing social outlook within the Histadrut was opposed to the widening of differentials. When some affiliated unions began to negotiate independent

[33] See note 25, p. 272.

salary agreements, the Histadrut for the first time faced a serious challenge to its monopoly of wage bargaining. In 1958 there was a successful strike of secondary school teachers, and they demanded to be recognized as an independent union. At the same time, the doctors and engineers unions became stronger, as did other smaller professional associations, and by the beginning of the 1960's they, too, negotiated their salaries independently of the Histadrut.

In 1958 the Histadrut formulated its first wage differentials policy: to freeze differentials between different occupations so that a change in one group would entail corresponding changes in all groups linked to it.[34] This decision was often attacked, because rapid shifts in the structure of the labor force do not permit relative wages to remain fixed for any length of time. In fact, it was not effective. Differentials between skill levels widened, as did inter-industry differentials. The trend was partly a reflection of inter-industry differences in skill-mix and partly of the unequal bargaining power of the various unions. Broadly speaking, the Histadrut supported larger wage claims for manufacturing, agriculture, and construction than it did for services. This attitude undoubtedly stemmed from its socialist tradition, which classified economic activity as "productive" or "unproductive." Another consideration was the fact that goods are generally more exportable than services, and the Histadrut wanted to draw labor into agriculture and industry for balance of payments purposes. It failed to implement this policy, and wage differentials between manufacturing and public services widened during 1958–62 in favor of the latter.[35] In this process the professional and administrative trade unions became the strongest in the Histadrut; its inability to control them has been especially evident since 1962.

At the beginning of 1962 a commission was appointed in order to streamline the multiple salary scales in the civil service and government corporations. The commission recommended a single uniform scale for all employees in these institutions. Members of the professions successfully objected to a system which would do away with the flexibility and independence that they had enjoyed in wage negotiations since the mid-1950's and refused to be included in the uniform scale. In 1964, when the wage freeze came to an end, they submitted wage claims through their own unions, a practice which was followed by several

---

[34] Sometimes the linkage of various wage-scales was part of collective agreements; sometimes it formed the basis of collective bargaining without any formal ground.

[35] Bank of Israel, *Annual Report 1962*, p. 159, Table IX–3.

other unions that were becoming more independent of the Histadrut's authority in wage matters. The result was a 30 per cent rise in civil service salaries during the single year 1965, followed by smaller rises in other branches. In effect, civil servants became the price leaders of the labor market.

The crumbling of Histadrut authority was also reflected in the big increase since 1960 in the number of days lost through strikes; unlike those of the 1950's, these were for the most part not sanctioned by the Histadrut. In practice, the Histadrut's chief remaining way of controlling wages was the COL allowance.

THE EFFECTS OF INFLATION

It is generally acknowleged that inflationary pressure has been too strong. It is not clear whether no inflationary pressure at all would have been preferable or what the optimum inflationary pressure should have been. The benefits of inflation may be that it helps reduce unemployment, enhances growth, and is an administratively cheap way of taxation. Its adverse effects are mainly apt to occur in the fields of saving and investment, balance of payments position, and income distribution.

Saving:[36] Inflation is usually said to reduce private as well as business saving in two ways, by increasing real balances and by reducing real interest rates. As can be seen, real balances grew during most of the period (Tables 76, 77, and 79), presumably reducing private saving. Until 1954 no attempt was made to link the rate of interest to the price level, so that the real rate was very low and sometimes negative.[37] As a result, the securities market was paralyzed, and firms lacked the incentive to accumulate undistributed profits, since unlinked loans were cheaper. The other form of private saving prevalent was contractual saving through provident and pension funds and through mortgages. Provident funds were among the first to try to link loans to the Consumers Price Index (or related indexes) in order to preserve the value of members' savings. Eventually mortgage banks, private firms, and the government (for its development budget loans) all used linkage. As a result, the securities market revived, time deposits grew, and firms

---

[36] Much of the following paragraphs rests on discussions with Marshall Sarnat in connection with his book, *The Development of the Securities Market in Israel* (Basel and Tübingen: Kyklos-Verlag and J.C.B. Mohr, 1966).

[37] The interest rate on development budget loans was between 4 and 6 per cent, prices rising by much more during this period.

had somewhat more inducement to finance investment out of earnings. The main forms of private saving remained, however, with provident funds and mortgage banks. In 1957, contractual saving accounted for 97 per cent of the saving of wage-earners' families, and a similar percentage was found for 1959.[38]

It was argued in Chapter 6 (p. 97) that since it was possible to maintain a high rate of investment independently of the rate of saving, no serious harm was done by saving being low. This may change in the future, to the extent that the share of unilateral transfers in total capital import declines or to the extent that total capital import declines. In either case, private savings are bound to play a more important role in total investment. In the past, however, inflation has affected not so much the total size of investment as its allocation. Provident funds are obliged, by government regulations, to invest in government and government-approved securities. Actually, it often happens that such securities are sold to the provident funds as a substitute for a development budget loan directly granted by the government. The allocation of private saving to investment projects is therefore largely controlled by the government. Saving through mortgage banks is channeled by and large to housing projects, the majority of which are also under government control. Consequently, contractual saving gives the government far-reaching control over investment.

The allocation of investment was also affected by the structure of interest rates on loans. The too-low rates on bank loans led to capital being wasted and to the development of a non-banking loan market in which interest rates were much higher. As a result, pressure groups were formed in order to gain cheap credit, and it became difficult to apply economic criteria to credit allocation.

Balance of payments: Inflation raises the import surplus by raising effective demand and by reducing the price of imports as compared with local products. However, as with saving, the absolute size of the import surplus in the past is not the only issue; built-in inflation may make adjustment to a smaller import surplus much more difficult in the future. Furthermore, there is the effect on the allocation of resources, which operates through relative prices. While GNP prices rose by 84 per cent in 1954–64, the official exchange rate rose by only 67 per cent. The reasons for avoiding outright devaluation are discussed elsewhere (Chapter 10), but the result was that import quotas and taxes and

[38] *Survey of Family Savings: 1957/58 and 1958/59—Preliminary Report* (Research Paper 8; Jerusalem: Falk Project, 1960), p. 7.

export subsidies were used in order to raise the effective exchange rate, so that the price of foreign exchange varied for different uses. The adverse effects of the multiple-rate system are also discussed in Chapter 10; here we stress only that the government acquired administrative powers to decide on foreign exchange prices and import quotas, not only because of a conscious preference for administrative control as opposed to market forces, but because of the inflationary process coupled with the reluctance to carry out open devaluation.

Income distribution: Because of the COL allowance, wage and salary earners did not lose from inflation. The decline in the share of labor returns in national income seems to be an adjustment from an initial state of disequilibrium rather than the result of inflation. The inflationary process, however, made the adjustment easier.

By itself, inflation should have narrowed wage differentials through the ceiling on the COL allowance, but, in fact, differentials widened, reflecting the changes in the structure of manpower. On the whole, therefore, no substantial changes in income distribution can be attributed to inflation.

Summary

We have in this chapter tried to survey the conditions which have made inflation a characteristic of the economy since the State was established. Several factors contributed to the inflationary process. The government's policy was inflationary throughout most of the period. In the austerity years it used deficit financing; for two years it tried to combat inflation, but then reverted to indirect inflationary policies, financing the development budget by converting foreign exchange and borrowing from the banking system. Although the government's excess liquidity declined for a few years, it rose again in the 1960's. Our discussion indicates that, except for short periods, demand rather than cost inflation prevailed. The government's price policy, which aimed at curbing price rises, therefore proved ineffective, regardless of whether it was implemented by direct controls or by subsidies.

The Bank of Israel did have an anti-inflationary policy, but was unable to counteract the government's policy. It is, however, often argued that even within its limitations the Bank would have been more effective had it raised interest rates and dealt in the open market.

Another major source of inflation has, since 1958, been the flow of foreign unilateral transfers directly to the public; its influence was accentuated after the 1962 devaluation. No effective measures were taken to counteract it.

There is little evidence that wage claims (either for COL allowance or basic rates) were, during most of the period, important as a source of inflation. However, in 1952–53, and again in 1965, wages rose in spite of increasing unemployment; also, in conditions of devaluation or an anti-inflationary fiscal policy, the existing COL allowance system may prove inflationary.

The main question, to which we do not attempt to give a quantitative answer, is whether the inflationary policy was on the whole justified. On the credit side, one may put the reduction of unemployment and some of the growth in GNP. On the debit side there are two issues. First, the difficulties that will confront the economy when it has to adjust to a smaller import surplus and greater saving; second, the loss in output due to misallocation of resources. The distortion in allocation has been mainly in investment and foreign trade, the result of unrealistic and widely diverging prices for credit and foreign exchange.

STATISTICAL APPENDIX

APPENDIX TABLE 1.   *Nominal Resources and Their Uses: 1950–65*

	Consumption			Domestic capital formation		
	Private	*Public*	*Total* (1)+(2)	*Gross*	*Net* (4)–(6)	*Depre- ciation*
	(1)	(2)	(3)	(4)	(5)	(6)
1950	341	92	433	143	125	18
1951	482	131	613	231	203	28
1952	791	197	988	356	287	69
1953	1,024	250	1,274	401	291	110
1954	1,326	320	1,646	515	368	147
1955	1,578	428	2,006	707	533	174
1956	1,872	675	2,547	740	526	214
1957	2,160	620	2,780	910	657	253
1958	2,466	672	3,138	1,005	722	283
1959	2,772	748	3,520	1,114	798	316
1960	3,096	829	3,925	1,218	854	364
1961	3,648	1,030	4,678	1,565	1,130	435
1962	4,410	1,384	5,794	2,120	1,504	616
1963	5,247	1,568	6,815	2,319	1,574	745
1964	6,098	1,755	7,853	2,924	2,071	853
1965	7,164	2,188	9,352	2,863	1,866	997

[a] Exports are recorded f.o.b., imports, c.i.f.; factor payments from and to the rest of the world (shown as a single net item in source a.) are included in exports and imports, respectively.

The dollar figures underlying the IL data in source a. are not precisely the same as those appearing in Chapter 8, Table 50, but have been adjusted by the National Accounts Division of the CBS to conform to national accounting definitions. They have here been converted to IL at effective exchange rates from the other sources listed. The calculation was done separately for merchandise, factor services, and non-factor services.

1950–51—at sterling rate ($2.8/IL 1).

1952–54—rates used in source b. adjusted to definitions of source c.

1955–61—source c. (factor services assumed to be at official rate of IL 1.8/$1).

1962—imports: 1961 rates (source c.) given weight of 5½ weeks; arithmetic mean of effective rates for March and December, 1962 (source d.) given weight of 46½ weeks, to take account of devaluation which occurred on February, 9. The 1962 rate for services imports was assumed to be the new official rate of IL 3.0/$ 1.

(IL millions)

Domestic use of resources (3)+(4) (7)	Exports[a] (8)	Total use of resources (7)+(8) (9)	Imports[a] (10)	GNP (9)-(10) (11)	Import surplus (10)-(8) (12)
576	15	591	133	458	118
844	22	866	168	698	146
1,344	73	1,417	373	1,044	300
1,675	128	1,803	489	1,314	361
2,161	231	2,392	667	1,725	436
2,713	258	2,971	837	2,134	579
3,287	325	3,612	1,059	2,553	734
3,690	416	4,106	1,145	2,961	729
4,143	452	4,595	1,204	3,391	752
4,634	588	5,222	1,303	3,919	715
5,143	743	5,886	1,522	4,364	779
6,243	886	7,129	1,887	5,242	1,001
7,914	1,390	9,304	2,946	6,358	1,556
9,134	1,793	10,927	3,400	7,527	1,607
10,777	1,951	12,728	4,037	8,691	2,086
12,215	2,222	14,437	4,235	10,202	2,013

Merchandise exports: the calculation was done from monthly data for four main commodity groups (citrus, other agricultural, diamonds, other industrial). 1961 rates (source c.) were applied to January *plus* 31 per cent of February, and the new official rate was applied to the rest of the year (69 per cent of February *plus* March through December).

Services exports: as for services imports.

1963–65—dollars converted at official rate *plus* import tax or export subsidy, from source a.

SOURCES: a. *Abstract 1966,* No. 17, pp. 156–57, Table F/1.
   b. Harold Lubell and Others, *Israel's National Expenditure: 1950–1954* (Jerusalem: Falk Project and CBS, 1958).
   c. Joseph Baruh, "Import Taxes and Export Subsidies in Israel, 1955–61," *Bank of Israel Bulletin,* No. 18 (March 1963), p. 52, Table 2, and p. 57, Table 4.
   d. Bank of Israel, *Annual Report 1962,* p. 33, Table III–1.

APPENDIX TABLE 2. Real Resources and Their Uses: 1950–65

(Millions of 1955 IL)

	Consumption			Domestic capital formation			Domestic use of resources (3)+(4)	Exports	Total use of resources (7)+(8)	Imports	GNP (9)-(10)	Import surplus (10)-(8)
	Private (1)	Public (2)	Total (1)+(2) (3)	Gross (4)	Net (4)-(6) (5)	Depreciation (6)	(7)	(8)	(9)	(10)	(11)	(12)
1950	930	275	1,205	606	530	76	1,811	92	1,903	807	1,096	715
1951	1,140	326	1,466	716	629	87	2,182	113	2,295	860	1,435	747
1952	1,225	308	1,533	615	496	119	2,148	153	2,301	760	1,541	607
1953	1,268	322	1,590	515	374	141	2,105	193	2,298	738	1,560	545
1954	1,458	376	1,834	574	410	164	2,408	265	2,673	771	1,902	506
1955	1,578	428	2,006	707	533	174	2,713	258	2,971	837	2,134	579
1956	1,722	616	2,338	669	476	193	3,007	295	3,302	985	2,317	690
1957	1,844	524	2,368	783	565	218	3,151	354	3,505	977	2,528	623
1958	2,031	538	2,569	841	604	237	3,410	394	3,804	1,038	2,766	644
1959	2,233	557	2,790	919	658	261	3,709	516	4,225	1,095	3,130	579
1960	2,383	594	2,977	976	684	292	3,953	650	4,603	1,220	3,383	570
1961	2,646	701	3,347	1,156	835	321	4,503	753	5,256	1,515	3,741	762
1962	2,935	781	3,716	1,299	922	377	5,015	908	5,923	1,698	4,225	790
1963	3,225	833	4,058	1,344	912	432	5,402	1,068	6,470	1,755	4,715	687
1964	3,574	874	4,448	1,633	1,157	476	6,081	1,148	7,229	2,025	5,204	877
1965	3,872	969	4,841	1,532	998	534	6,373	1,249	7,622	2,064	5,558	815

SOURCES: Imports and exports—figures in current dollars underlying Appendix Table 1 deflated by price indexes (1955=100) based on computations of M. Evans ["An Econometric Model of the Israeli Economy" (forthcoming)], and then converted to 1955 IL by applying the effective exchange rate for 1955. Other data—*Abstract 1966*, No. 17, pp. 158–59, Table F/2.

APPENDIX TABLE 3.   Real Resources and Their Uses Per Capita: 1950–65

(1955 IL)

| Mean present population (thousands) | Consumption | | | Domestic capital formation | | Domestic use of resources (3)+(4) (7) | Total use of resources (9) | GNP (11) |
	Private (1)	Public (2)	Total (1)+(2) (3)	Gross (4)	Net (5)			
1,266.8	734	217	951	478	418	1,429	1,502	865
1,494.3	763	218	981	479	421	1,460	1,536	960
1,606.2	762	192	954	383	309	1,337	1,432	959
1,650.3	768	195	963	312	227	1,275	1,392	945
1,689.5	863	222	1,085	340	243	1,425	1,582	1,126
1,750.4	902	244	1,146	404	305	1,550	1,697	1,219
1,828.4	942	337	1,279	366	260	1,645	1,806	1,267
1,930.5	955	271	1,226	406	293	1,632	1,816	1,310
2,000.1	1,015	269	1,284	421	302	1,705	1,902	1,383
2,062.1	1,083	270	1,353	446	319	1,799	2,049	1,518
2,117.0	1,126	280	1,406	461	323	1,867	2,174	1,598
2,189.6	1,208	320	1,528	528	381	2,056	2,400	1,708
2,289.7	1,282	341	1,623	567	403	2,190	2,587	1,845
2,380.3	1,355	350	1,705	564	383	2,269	2,718	1,981
2,480.7	1,441	352	1,793	658	466	2,451	2,914	2,098
2,566.8	1,509	377	1,886	597	389	2,483	2,969	2,165

(Rows correspond to years 1950, 1951, 1952, 1953, 1954, 1955, 1956, 1957, 1958, 1959, 1960, 1961, 1962, 1963, 1964, 1965.)

SOURCES: Population from CBS, Abstract 1966, No. 17, p. 20, Table B/1; Aggregate data in 1955 IL from Appendix Table 2.

APPENDIX TABLE 4. Resources and Resource Use—Implicit Price Indexes: 1950–65

(1955=100)

| | Consumption | | Gross domestic capital formation | Domestic resources | Exports | Imports | GNP |
| | Private | Public | | | | | |
	(1)	(2)	(4)	(7)	(8)	(10)	(11)
1950	36.7	33.5	23.6	31.8	16.3	16.5	41.8
1951	42.3	40.2	32.3	38.7	19.5	19.5	48.6
1952	64.6	64.0	57.9	62.6	47.7	49.1	67.7
1953	80.8	77.6	77.9	79.6	66.3	66.3	84.2
1954	90.9	85.1	89.7	89.7	87.2	86.5	90.7
1955	100.0	100.0	100.0	100.0	100.0	100.0	100.0
1956	108.7	109.6	110.6	109.3	110.2	107.5	110.2
1957	117.1	118.3	116.2	117.1	117.5	117.2	117.1
1958	121.4	124.9	119.5	121.5	114.7	116.0	122.6
1959	124.1	134.3	121.2	124.9	114.0	119.0	125.2
1960	129.9	139.6	124.8	130.1	114.3	124.8	129.0
1961	137.9	146.9	135.4	138.6	117.7	124.6	140.1
1962	150.3	177.2	163.2	157.8	153.1	173.5	150.5
1963	162.7	188.2	172.5	169.1	167.9	193.7	159.6
1964	170.6	200.8	179.1	177.2	169.9	199.4	167.0
1965	185.0	225.8	186.9	191.7	177.9	205.2	183.6

SOURCE: Current price data (Appendix Table 1) divided by constant price data (Appendix Table 2).

APPENDIX TABLE 5.   *Per Capita Product in Thirty Countries:*[a]
1953, 1958, and 1961

(dollars)

	1953	1958	1961
United States	2,080	2,324	2,572
Canada	1,521	1,767	1,774
Luxembourg	1,037	1,332	1,438
Sweden	981	1,309	1,592
New Zealand	1,053	1,291	1,439
Australia	1,004	1,215	1,380
Belgium	903	1,093	1,198
France	853	1,089	1,149
United Kingdom	814	1,084	1,244
Norway	785	1,012	1,208
Denmark	791	975	1,256
Germany (Federal Republic)	611	920	1,232
Netherlands	531	767	939
Finland	687	751	982
Austria	407	656	831
Israel	(400)	(600)	(750)
Puerto Rico	405	581	761
Trinidad and Tobago	330	529	643
Italy	353	493	618
Ireland	409	472	583
Cyprus	332	410	404
Union of South Africa	316	385	414
Jamaica	201	357	419
Panama	320	352	365
Costa Rica	308	348	336
Greece	190	307	373
Japan	196	285	464
Mexico	212	255	275
Mauritius	228	221	226
Portugal	175	212	260

[a] Gross domestic product at factor cost, except for Israel, where net national product at factor cost (national income) was used. Countries are ranked according to the 1958 figures.

SOURCES: Israel—National income from *Abstract 1964*, No. 15, pp. 136–37. For conversion into dollars, a rate of IL 2.50/$ 1 was taken for 1961, and moved back to the other years over the local Consumers Price Index.

Other countries—U.N. *Yearbook of National Accounts Statistics 1962* (New York: 1963), pp. 314–17, International Table 3. For the exchange rates used see notes in the source.

APPENDIX TABLE 6.   The Geographic Pattern of Merchandise Trade: 1949–65

(per cent)

	Total[a]	United States and Canada	Latin America[b]	United Kingdom	Western Europe[c]	Eastern Europe[d]	Asia Africa and Oceania[e]
A. Imports							
1949	100.0	35.7	8.3	9.5	25.5	9.5	11.5
1950	100.0	42.4	7.3	9.1	24.6	5.8	10.8
1951	100.0	38.0	4.0	10.9	32.0	3.1	12.0
1952	100.0	45.3	2.8	8.7	31.1	1.7	10.4
1953	100.0	39.7	3.2	12.2	37.6	0.9	6.4
1954	100.0	34.0	2.2	10.9	45.8	2.8	4.3
1955	100.0	33.8	1.9	11.6	45.0	2.0	5.7
1956	100.0	37.1	2.7	11.2	43.0	1.2	4.8
1957	100.0	30.8	2.3	13.4	46.0	2.3	5.2
1958	100.0	33.9	3.2	13.2	42.7	2.1	4.9
1959	100.0	33.5	1.8	12.6	44.1	1.6	6.4
1960	100.0	33.2	0.7	12.9	46.0	0.8	6.4
1961	100.0	33.0	0.6	14.5	45.8	1.1	5.0
1962	100.0	37.2	1.4	17.2	37.7	1.4	5.1
1963	100.0	31.4	1.2	21.7	38.1	1.6	6.0
1964	100.0	28.1	1.4	20.4	42.6	2.2	5.3
1965	100.0	28.3	2.0	21.4	39.2	2.1	7.0
B. Exports							
1949	100.0	17.0	0.4	53.7	21.5	6.0	1.4
1950	100.0	25.1	0.3	31.3	30.5	10.7	2.1

1951	100.0	24.9	32.8	0.9	34.5	4.6	2.3
1952	100.0	28.1	29.2	0.7	33.9	6.1	2.0
1953	100.0	23.6	26.1	0.5	44.3	3.5	2.0
1954	100.0	18.2	23.0	1.3	49.0	5.2	3.3
1955	100.0	20.0	20.9	1.3	49.1	3.9	4.8
1956	100.0	19.6	22.3	0.5	45.4	4.6	7.6
1957	100.0	15.9	20.6	0.6	51.7	3.6	7.6
1958	100.0	15.7	21.8	0.8	47.6	5.1	9.0
1959	100.0	17.3	19.6	1.6	46.3	4.8	10.4
1960	100.0	15.3	17.2	1.7	51.1	1.9	12.8
1961	100.0	17.7	14.9	1.1	48.7	2.7	14.9
1962	100.0	17.9	14.2	1.0	50.3	3.0	13.6
1963	100.0	15.4	14.1	1.0	53.0	2.8	13.7
1964	100.0	16.7	12.7	1.7	49.0	4.0	15.9
1965	100.0	16.4	12.1	1.4	48.9	3.9	17.3

[a] Excludes merchandise not classified by origin or destination: about 7 to 14 per cent of total imports, and 1 to 4 per cent of total exports.

[b] Central America, South America and Mexico.

[c] European countries (including Yugoslavia) not in the Soviet bloc, and Turkey.

[d] Includes U.S.S.R., excludes Yugoslavia.

[e] Excludes Turkey.

SOURCES: 1949-53—Michael Michaely, *Foreign Trade and Capital Imports in Israel* (Tel Aviv: Am Oved, 1963; Hebrew), p. 84, Table 40.
1954-57—CBS, *Abstract 1958/59*, No. 10, pp. 272-73, Table 11 (imports) and pp. 274-75, Table 12 (exports).
1958—*Abstract 1959/60*, No. 11, pp. 281-82, Table 10.
1959—*Abstract 1961*, No. 12, pp. 330-31, Table 9.
1960—*Abstract 1964*, No. 15, pp. 214-17, Table I/5.
1961—*Abstract 1963*, No. 14, pp. 446-49, Table 9.
1962—*Abstract 1965*, No. 16, pp. 258-60, Table I/7.
1963-65—*Abstract 1966*, No. 17, pp. 252-54, Table I/7.

APPENDIX TABLE 7. *The Regional Pattern of Imports: 1958–65*[a]

(per cent)

	Total	Dollar area	Sterling area	OECD area	Soviet area	Other
1958						
Merchandise	100.0	30.1	15.2	39.3	1.9	13.5
Services	100.0	36.8	15.9	43.3	0.7	3.3
Total	100.0	32.3	15.4	40.6	1.5	10.2
1959						
Merchandise	100.0	30.1	14.4	38.5	1.4	15.6
Services	100.0	35.1	16.4	38.7	0.4	9.4
Total	100.0	31.8	15.1	38.6	1.1	13.8
1960						
Merchandise	100.0	32.7	14.6	42.6	0.8	9.3
Services	100.0	30.3	19.0	36.4	0.3	14.0
Total	100.0	31.8	16.1	40.5	0.7	10.9
1961						
Merchandise	100.0	32.7	14.6	42.7	0.8	9.2
Services	100.0	26.6	16.3	44.4	0.3	12.4
Total	100.0	30.3	15.3	43.3	0.6	10.5
1962						
Merchandise	100.0	36.0	19.4	34.6	1.5	8.5
Services	100.0	27.0	15.4	45.8	0.7	11.1
Total	100.0	32.2	17.7	39.2	1.2	9.7
1963						
Merchandise	100.0	28.5	21.6	34.9	2.1	12.9
Services	100.0	34.3	15.3	39.8	0.5	10.1
Total	100.0	30.8	19.0	36.9	1.5	11.8
1964						
Merchandise	100.0	26.3	21.7	40.7	2.4	8.9
Services	100.0	32.2	15.7	41.6	0.7	9.8
Total	100.0	28.5	19.5	41.0	1.8	9.2
1965						
Merchandise	100.0	26.4	21.2	36.6	2.0	13.8
Services	100.0	34.0	14.2	41.2	0.9	9.7
Total	100.0	29.5	18.4	38.5	1.5	12.1

[a] F.o.b.
SOURCES: 1958—*Abstract 1962*, No. 13, pp. 328–29, Table 3.
     1960—*Abstract 1964*, No. 15, pp. 186–87, Table H/3.
     1959, 1961–65—*Abstract 1966*, No. 17, pp. 220–21, Table H/4.

APPENDIX TABLE 8.   *The Regional Pattern of Exports: 1958–65*[a]

(per cent)

	Total	Dollar area	Sterling area	OECD area	Soviet area	Other
1958						
Merchandise	100.0	14.9	28.3	40.4	4.9	11.5
Services	100.0	30.1	26.5	37.1	1.0	5.3
Total	100.0	20.3	27.6	39.2	3.6	9.3
1959						
Merchandise	100.0	17.6	27.2	41.7	3.0	10.5
Services	100.0	35.0	25.5	38.5	0.9	0.1
Total	100.0	23.5	26.6	40.6	2.3	7.0
1960						
Merchandise	100.0	15.0	25.8	45.2	1.8	12.2
Services	100.0	35.7	26.0	25.6	0.6	12.1
Total	100.0	22.8	25.9	37.8	1.4	12.1
1961						
Merchandise	100.0	15.0	25.8	45.2	1.8	12.2
Services	100.0	35.7	26.0	25.7	0.6	12.0
Total	100.0	23.3	25.9	37.4	1.3	12.1
1962						
Merchandise	100.0	17.4	21.8	43.4	3.2	14.2
Services	100.0	34.6	21.6	31.5	0.8	11.5
Total	100.0	24.7	21.7	38.3	2.2	13.1
1963						
Merchandise	100.0	15.2	21.5	48.1	2.8	12.4
Services	100.0	41.6	21.7	26.0	0.4	10.3
Total	100.0	26.1	21.6	38.9	1.8	11.6
1964						
Merchandise	100.0	16.6	21.3	43.7	4.2	14.2
Services	100.0	35.8	20.0	33.0	0.3	10.9
Total	100.0	25.0	20.8	39.0	2.5	12.7
1965						
Merchandise	100.0	16.6	22.2	44.0	4.2	13.0
Services	100.0	37.2	19.7	32.9	0.7	9.5
Total	100.0	25.5	21.1	39.2	2.7	11.5

[a] F.o.b.

SOURCES: See sources to Appendix Table 7.

APPENDIX TABLE 9.   *Unilateral Transfers: 1949–65*

	Personal			Institutional	
	Total	In cash	In kind	Total	In cash
1949[a]	36	..	..	82	..
1950[a]	20	..	..	70	..
1951[a]	39	..	..	84	..
1952: Credit	16.3	2.4	13.9	89.0	46.2
Debit	0.5	0.1	0.4	–	–
Net credit	15.8	2.3	13.5	89.0	46.2
1953: Credit	11.0	3.4	7.6	75.2	47.5
Debit	0.8	0.2	0.6	0.8	0.2
Net credit	10.2	3.2	7.0	74.4	47.3
1954: Credit	16.7	8.4	8.3	120.6	90.1
Debit	0.9	0.1	0.8	3.2	2.9
Net credit	15.8	8.3	7.5	117.4	87.2
1955: Credit	35.6	24.5	11.1	52.7	47.6
Debit	0.6	0.2	0.4	4.5	4.5
Net credit	35.0	24.3	10.7	48.2	43.1
1956: Credit	36.1	25.8	10.3	92.7	87.6
Debit	0.4	0.3	0.1	..	..
Net credit	35.7	25.5	10.2	92.7	87.6
1957: Credit	37.2	21.5	15.7	61.3	55.7
Debit	0.5	0.3	0.2	..	..
Net credit	36.7	21.2	15.5	61.3	55.7
1958: Credit	37.4	28.8	8.6	75.1	65.9
Debit	0.7	0.3	0.4	..	..
Net credit	36.7	28.5	8.2	75.1	65.9
1959: Credit	31.4	22.4	9.0	73.6	65.5
Debit	0.9	0.6	0.3	–	–
Net credit	30.5	21.8	8.7	73.6	65.5
1960: Credit	37.8	29.1	8.7	86.7	81.3
Debit	1.0	0.8	0.2	–	–
Net credit	36.8	28.3	8.5	86.7	81.3
1961: Credit	46.3	37.8	8.5	92.0	86.4
Debit	1.3	1.2	0.1	–	–
Net credit	45.0	36.6	8.4	92.0	86.4
1962: Credit	69.1	58.5	10.6	73.8	71.8
Debit	1.1	0.7	0.4	–	–
Net credit	68.0	57.8	10.2	73.8	71.8
1963: Credit	93.5	83.0	10.5	82.7	82.7
Debit	3.0	0.8	2.2	–	–
Net credit	90.5	82.2	8.3	82.7	82.7
1964: Credit	100.2	90.4	9.8	97.1	94.4
Debit	4.3	1.2	3.1	1.2	1.2
Net Credit	95.9	89.2	6.7	95.9	93.2
1965: Credit	103.3	94.6	8.7	108.5	106.0
Debit	4.1	1.3	2.8	1.4	1.4
Net credit	99.2	93.3	5.9	107.1	104.6

[a] Net credit.
[b] Includes personal gifts.
[c] Arbitrary separation of U.N. from U.S. technical assistance, based on later data.

SOURCES: 1949—Michaely, *op. cit.*, Appendix (fold-in).
        1950–54—Nadav Halevi, *Estimates of Israel's International Trans-actions: 1952–54* (Jerusalem: Falk Project, 1956), p. 108, Table 18.
        1955–65—*Abstracts* as follows: *1958/59*, No. 10, p. 248, Table 1 (for

($ millions)

In kind	Total	U.S.	Government Repara-tions	Resti-tutions	U.N. technical assistance	Total unilateral transfers
..	–	–	–	–	–	118
..	–	–	–	–	–	90
..	14	14	–	–	–	137
42.8 [b]	86.4	86.0	–	–	0.4 [c]	191.7
–	–	–	–	–	–	0.5
42.8	86.4	86.0	–	–	0.4	191.2
27.7 [b]	88.2	46.9	40.9	–	0.4 [c]	174.4
0.6	–	–	–	–	–	1.6
27.1	88.2	46.9	40.9	–	0.4	172.8
30.5 [b]	127.4	38.6	82.3	6.1	0.4 [c]	264.7
0.3	–	–	–	–	–	4.1
30.2	127.4	38.6	82.3	6.1	0.4	260.6
5.1	127.2	20.5	87.5	18.8	0.4	215.5
–	–	..	..	..	..	5.1
5.1	127.2	20.5	87.5	18.8	0.4	210.4
5.1	115.5	6.8	82.5	25.7	0.5	244.3
–	3.4	..	3.3	..	0.1	3.8
5.1	112.1	6.8	79.2	25.7	0.4	240.5
5.6	152.6	24.1	82.1	45.9	0.5	251.1
–	5.2	..	4.2	0.9	0.1	5.7
5.6	147.4	24.1	77.9	45.0	0.4	245.4
9.2	156.0	16.4	72.9	66.3	0.4	268.5
–	4.2	–	3.2	0.9	0.1	4.9
9.2	151.8	16.4	69.7	65.4	0.3	263.6
8.1	150.7	9.5	70.0 '	70.8	0.4	255.7
–	3.8	–	3.6	0.1	0.1	4.7
8.1	146.9	9.5	66.4	70.7	0.3	251.0
5.4	193.6	13.9	78.8	100.6	0.3	318.1
–	6.0	–	3.1	2.8	0.1	7.0
5.4	187.6	13.9	75.7	97.8	0.2	311.1
5.6	213.2	10.4	90.9	111.5	0.4	351.5
–	3.9	–	2.6	1.0	0.3	5.2
5.6	209.3	10.4	88.3	110.5	0.1	346.3
2.0	197.5	8.0	51.3	137.9	0.3	340.4
–	8.6	–	4.3	4.0	0.3	9.7
2.0	188.9	8.0	47.0	133.9	–	330.7
–	183.1	5.9	34.0	142.8	0.4	359.3
–	9.7	–	5.5	3.9	0.3	12.7
–	173.4	5.9	28.5	138.9	0.1	346.6
2.7	165.6	8.2	22.8	134.2	0.4	362.9
–	6.1	–	5.9	–	0.2	11.6
2.7	159.5	8.2	16.9	134.2	0.2	351.3
2.5	137.6	4.7	19.8	112.7	0.4	349.4
–	3.3	–	3.1	–	0.2	8.8
2.5	134.3	4.7	16.7	112.7	0.2	340.6

1955–57); *1959/60,* No. 11, p. 258, Table 1 (for 1958); *1961,* No. 12, p. 303, Table 1 (for 1959); *1962,* No. 13, p. 322, Table 1 (for 1960); *1963,* No. 14, p. 408, Table 2 (for 1961); *1964,* No. 15, p. 184, Table H/2 (for 1962); *1965,* No. 16, p. 224, Table H/2 (for 1963); *1966,* No. 17, p. 218, Table H/2 (for 1964–65). The data from the *Abstracts* are supplemented by additional details from the Balance of Payments Section of the CBS.

APPENDIX TABLE 10.   *Balance-of-Payments Capital Account: 1949–65*

				Long-term capital		
	Total long-term			*Government capital*[a]		
		Total	*State of Israel Bonds*	*Foreign currency loans*	*Local currency loans*	*Other government*	*Total*
1949[b]	43	18	–	18	–	–	25
1950[b]	68	47	–	47	–	–	21
1951[b]	133	91	55	36	–	–	42
1952 : Credit		86.8	47.2	39.4	–	0.2	58.3
Debit		9.0	0.9	8.1	–	–	21.2
Net credit	114.9	77.8	46.3	31.3	–	0.2	37.1
1953 : Credit		61.6	38.5	22.7	–	0.4	31.9
Debit		15.4	2.4	13.0	–	–	8.5
Net credit	69.6	46.2	36.1	9.7	–	0.4	23.4
1954 : Credit		87.7	41.0	47.8	–	–1.1	47.4
Debit		36.7	11.8[d]	19.0	–	5.9	27.2
Net credit	71.2	51.0	29.2	28.8	–	–7.0	20.2
1955 : Credit		67.6	32.2	10.0	25.4	..	15.9
Debit		3.4	..	2.1	..	1.3	3.8
Net credit	76.3	64.2	32.2	7.9	25.4	–1.3	12.1
1956 : Credit		114.9	53.3	29.0	32.6	..	34.7
Debit		42.8	5.9	36.7	..	0.2	28.4
Net credit	78.4	72.1	47.4	–7.7	32.6	–0.2	6.3
1957 : Credit		126.5	53.7	52.4	20.4	..	37.0
Debit		71.5	9.0	62.0	..	0.5	22.6
Net credit	69.4	55.0	44.7	–9.6	20.4	–0.5	14.4
1958 : Credit		126.8	50.8	56.7	19.3	–	60.8
Debit		84.5	17.1	63.3	–	4.1	36.4
Net credit	66.7	42.3	33.7	–6.6	19.3	–4.1	24.4
1959 : Credit		133.8	57.6	55.4	18.4	2.4	50.8
Debit		76.8	22.3	49.4	0.1	5.0	27.4
Net credit	80.4	57.0	35.3	6.0	18.3	–2.6	23.4
1960 : Credit		119.2	58.7	27.7	29.0	3.8	96.0
Debit		79.0	30.4	43.7	0.5	4.4	35.1
Net credit	101.1	40.2	28.3	–16.0	28.5	–0.6	60.9
1961 : Credit		168.8	63.3	71.6	32.3	1.6	123.0
Debit		78.0	31.2	40.6	2.5	3.7	37.7
Net credit	176.1	90.8	32.1	31.0	29.8	–2.1	85.3
1962 : Credit		213.7	66.5	127.1	20.1	–	134.9
Debit		87.7	33.1	48.5	2.6	3.5	57.8
Net credit	203.1	126.0	33.4	78.6	17.5	–3.5	77.1
1963 : Credit		214.2	79.4	111.0	21.0	2.8	189.9
Debit		164.6	56.2	97.3	5.9	5.2	69.1
Net credit	170.4	49.6	23.2	13.7	15.1	–2.4	120.8
1964[f]: Credit		224.1	98.7	84.6	36.1	4.7	228.1
Debit		130.1	74.2	25.2	5.4	25.3	47.0
Net credit	275.1	94.0	24.5	59.4	30.7	–20.6	181.1
1965[f]: Credit		243.7	100.4	116.6	26.1	0.6	162.9
Debit		108.0	67.1	26.8	6.2	7.9	51.1
Net credit	247.5	135.7	33.3	89.8	19.9	–7.3	111.8

[a] Includes both loans from and to governmental agencies. Thus, e.g., loans from U.S. agencies to private firms are included here.
[b] Net credit.
[c] Includes sale of securities vested by the government.
[d] Mainly exchange of Independence Bonds for Development Bonds.
[e] Net figure.
[f] The inclusion in services imports of national institutions transactions abroad (see note

($ millions)

Private capital			Short-term capital					Total capital
Investment in Israel	Investment abroad	Other private	Total Short-term	Loans and credit	U.S. local currency deposits	Other deposits	Foreign exchange balances and gold	
..	..	..	24	–	–	–	24	67
..	..	..	51	–	–	–	51	119
..	..	..	32	–	–	–	32	165
35.2	7.2[e]	15.9						
0.1	1.1	20.0						
35.1	6.1	-4.1	1.5	-4.6	1.9	0.3	3.9	116.4
30.4	1.5[e]	–						
1.1	1.8	5.6						
29.3	-0.3	-5.6	5.7	9.3	2.7	1.3	-7.6	75.3
28.0	1.9[e]	17.5						
0.1	2.6	24.5						
27.9	-0.7	-7.0	-70.2	-39.8	4.7	1.2	-36.3	1.0
15.8	0.1	..						
–	0.9	2.9[e]						
15.8	-8.0	-2.9	0.0	4.6	6.2	-1.5	-9.3	76.3
22.1	0.1	12.5						
4.5	4.5	19.4						
17.6	-4.4	-6.9	22.0	15.1	8.1	-4.5	3.3	100.4
25.2	0.2	11.6						
6.2	0.9	15.5						
19.0	0.7	-3.9	9.2	0.5	4.9	-2.1	5.9	78.6
16.4	0.1	44.3						
2.6	2.2	31.6						
13.8	-2.1	12.7	-1.0	17.8	26.6	-0.7	-44.7	65.7
25.5	0.4	24.9						
0.1	11.0	16.3						
25.4	-10.6	8.6	-25.6	-20.6	27.1	6.5	-38.6	54.8
55.6	0.1	40.3						
2.2	10.0	22.9						
53.4	-9.9	17.4	-60.1	-5.6	19.0	28.3	-101.8	41.0
62.8	0.8	59.4						
2.6	8.8	26.3						
60.2	-8.0	33.1	-71.9	-0.3	12.3	11.0	-94.9	104.2
96.3	–	38.6						
7.1	6.9	43.8						
89.2	-6.9	-5.2	-104.7	6.0	9.8	20.1	-140.6	98.4
162.6	–	27.3						
10.2	17.0	41.9						
152.4	-17.0	-14.6	-97.7	-16.1	7.3	20.2	-109.1	72.7
156.7		71.4						
10.8		36.2						
145.9		35.2	-47.7	25.8	-21.9	-24.1	-27.5	227.4
98.2		64.7						
0.2		50.9						
98.0		13.8	-28.8	80.3	7.4	-10.5	-106.0	218.7

b, Table 50), affects several items. These transactions are classified as "private" by the CBS.

SOURCES: 1949–51—Michaely, *loc. cit.*
  1952–54—Halevi, *op. cit.*, p. 54, Table 3; p. 58, Table 6; p. 126, Table 21; p. 129, Table 22.
  1955–65—as for unilateral transfers (see sources to Appendix Table 9), with additional detail from the Balance of Payments Section of the CBS.

APPENDIX TABLE 11.   Principal Sources of Unilateral Transfers and Long-Term Capital: 1949–65

($ millions)

	Unilateral transfers			Long-term capital		Transfers and capital		
	World Jewry (1)	U.S. government^a (2)	German government (3)	World Jewry^b (4)	U.S. government^c (5)	World Jewry (1)+(4) (6)	U.S. government (2)+(5) (7)	German government^d (8)
1949	118	–	–	25	18	143	18	–
1950	90	–	–	21	44.4	111	44.4	–
1951	123	14	–	97	27.7	220	41.7	–
1952	104.8	86.0	–	81.4	27.5	186.2	113.5	40.9
1953	84.6	46.9	40.9	65.4	4.4	150.0	51.3	40.9
1954	133.2	38.6	88.4	57.1	1.8	190.3	40.4	88.4
1955	83.2	20.5	106.3	48.0	23.3	131.2	43.8	106.3
1956	128.4	6.8	104.9	65.0	30.5	193.4	37.3	104.9
1957	98.0	24.1	122.9	63.7	9.0	161.7	33.1	122.9
1958	111.8	16.4	135.1	47.5	12.8	159.3	29.2	135.1
1959	104.1	9.5	137.1	60.7	19.7	164.8	29.2	137.1
1960	123.5	13.9	173.5	81.7	21.1	205.2	35.0	173.5
1961	137.0	10.4	198.8	92.3	21.6	229.3	32.0	198.8
1962	141.8	8.0	180.9	122.6	31.1	264.4	39.1	180.9
1963	173.2	5.9	167.4	175.6	31.8	348.8	37.7	167.4
1964	191.8	8.2	151.1	170.4^e	42.1	362.2	50.3	151.1
1965	206.3	4.7	129.4	131.3^e	51.8	337.6	56.5	129.4
Total 1949–65	2,152.7	313.9	1,736.7	1,405.7	418.6	3,558.4	732.5	1,736.7

a Grants and technical assistance.
b Some of the net private foreign investment included here is undoubtedly from non-Jews.
c All loans from U.S. government agencies, including Export–Import Bank.
d Unilateral transfers only, since there are no separate figures for loans.
e Net of investment abroad by Israel.

SOURCES: World Jewry—Appendix Table 9, columns (1)+(4) (private and institutional transfers); and Appendix Table 10, columns (3)+(8) (State of Israel Bonds and private investment in Israel).
U.S. government—Appendix Table 12, column (1) (unilateral transfers); column (4)+(9) (long-term capital).
German government—Appendix Table 9, columns (9)+(10) (reparations and restitutions).

APPENDIX TABLE 12. United States Economic Assistance: 1949-65

($ millions)

Year	Grants and technical assistance (1)	Soft currency capital transactions					Hard currency loans			Total aid, (1)+(6)+(9) (10)
		Loans			U.S. deposits, net credit (5)	Total net credit (4)+(5) (6)	Credit (7)	Debit (8)	Net credit (7)-(8) (9)	
		Credit (2)	Debit (3)	Net credit (2)-(3) (4)						
1949	–	–	–	–	–	–	18	–	18	18
1950	–	–	–	–	–	–	44.4	–	44.4	44.4
1951	14	–	–	–	–	–	27.7	–	27.7	41.7
1952	86.0	–	–	–	1.9	1.9	31.0	3.5	27.5	115.4
1953	46.9	–	–	–	2.7	2.7	12.0	7.6	4.4	54.0
1954	38.6	–	–	–	4.7	4.7	2.8	1.0	1.8	45.1
1955	20.5	25.4	..	25.4	6.2	31.6	..	2.1	-2.1	50.0
1956	6.8	32.6	..	32.6	8.1	40.7	..	2.1	-2.1	45.4
1957	24.1	20.4	..	20.4	4.9	25.3	..	11.4	-11.4	38.0
1958	16.4	19.3	–	19.3	26.6	45.9	5.3	11.8	-6.5	55.8
1959	9.5	18.4	0.1	18.3	27.1	45.4	14.0	12.6	1.4	56.3
1960	13.9	29.0	0.5	28.5	19.0	47.5	5.3	12.7	-7.4	54.0
1961	10.4	32.3	2.5	29.8	12.3	42.1	6.0	14.2	-8.2	44.3
1962	8.0	20.1	2.6	17.5	9.8	27.3	31.6	18.0	13.6	48.9
1963	5.9	21.0	5.9	15.1	7.3	22.4	35.6	18.9	16.7	45.0
1964	8.2	36.1	5.4	30.7	-21.9	8.8	32.5	21.1	11.4	28.4
1965	4.7	26.1	6.2	19.9	7.4	27.3	55.4	23.5	31.9	63.9
Total 1949-65	313.9	280.7	23.2	257.5	116.1	373.6	321.6	160.5	161.1	848.6

SOURCES: 1950-54—Halevi, *op. cit.*, p. 126, Table 21.
1949, 1955-65—see sources for these years in Appendix Table 9. Data from *Abstracts* are supplemented by details from the Balance of Payments Section of the CBS.

BIBLIOGRAPHY AND INDEXES

BIBLIOGRAPHY

Abcarius, M. F. *Palestine Through the Fog of Propaganda.* London: Hutchinson, n.d.

Abramovitz, Z., and Guelfat, I. *The Arab Economy.* Tel Aviv: Hakibbutz Hameuchad, 1944; Hebrew.

American Jewish Year Book 1961. Vol. LXII. Philadelphia: Jewish Publication Society of America.

Babayov, B. "Tariff Functions in Israel." Unpublished seminar paper, The Hebrew University, 1964; Hebrew.

Bahral, Uri. *The Real Rate of the Dollar in the Economy of Israel.* Jerusalem: Ministry of Commerce and Industry, 1956; Hebrew.

———. *The Effect of Mass Immigration on Wages in Israel.* Jerusalem: Falk Project, 1965.

Bank of Israel. *Annual Reports.* Jerusalem.

Barkai, Haim. "The Public, Histadrut, and Private Sectors in the Israeli Economy," *Sixth Report 1961–1963.* Jerusalem: Falk Project, 1964.

———, and Michaely, M. "The New Economic Policy—After One Year," *The Economic Quarterly,* X (No. 37–38, March 1963), 23–39; Hebrew.

———, and ———. "On the New Economic Policy," *The Economic Quarterly,* X (No. 39, August 1963), 210–32; Hebrew.

Barkay, R. M. *The Public Sector Accounts of Israel: 1948/49–1954/55.* 2 vols. Jerusalem: Falk Project and CBS, 1957 (mimeograph).

Baruh, Joseph. "Import Taxes and Export Subsidies in Israel, 1955–61," *Bank of Israel Bulletin,* No. 18 (March 1963), 48–70.

———. "Changes in the Quality of Labor Input in Israel, 1950–61," *Bank of Israel Bulletin,* No. 25 (April 1966), 32–43.

Bavly, Sarah. *Level of Nutrition in Israel 1951.* (CBS Special Series No. 7B.) Jerusalem: 1952.

BAVLY, SARAH. *Food Consumption and Level of Nutrition of Urban Wage and Salary Earners' Families in Israel, 1956/57.* (CBS Special Series No. 101.) Jerusalem: 1960; Hebrew.

BEHAM, MIRIAM. *Monetary Aspects of the 1962 Devaluation.* Preliminary draft, Jerusalem: 1967; Hebrew.

BEN-PORATH, YORAM. *The Arab Labor Force in Israel.* Jerusalem: Falk Institute, 1966.

BEN-SHAHAR, HAIM. *Income Distribution of Wage and Salary Earners, 1950–1957.* Jerusalem: Ministry of Finance, 1961; Hebrew.

———. *Public International Development Financing in Israel.* New York: Columbia University School of Law, 1963 (mimeograph).

———. *Interest Rates and the Cost of Capital in Israel, 1950–1962.* Basel and Tübingen: Kyklos-Verlag and J.C.B. Mohr, 1965.

BONNE, A. *Palestine, The Country and the Economy.* Tel Aviv: Dvir, 1936; Hebrew.

British Policy in Palestine. Cmd. 1700. Reprinted in Jewish Agency. *Book of Documents Submitted to the General Assembly of the United Nations. 1917–1947.* New York: 1947.

BRUNO, MICHAEL. *Interdependence, Resource Use and Structural Change in Israel.* (Bank of Israel Research Department Special Studies No. 2.) Jerusalem: 1962.

———. "Factor Productivity and Remuneration in Israel, 1952–1961," *The Economic Quarterly,* X (No. 37–38, March 1963), 41–56; Hebrew.

CENTRAL BUREAU OF STATISTICS. *Statistical Abstract of Israel.* Jerusalem: annual issue (referred to as *Abstract*).

———. *Statistical Bulletin of Israel.* Jerusalem: monthly issue (referred to as *Bulletin*).

———. *Family Expenditure Surveys: 1950/51—1956/57—1959/60.* (Special Series No. 148.) Jerusalem: 1963.

———. *Israel's Foreign Trade 1965—Part I.* (Special Series No. 201.) Jerusalem: 1966.

———. *Labour Force—Part I.* (Census Publication No. 9.) Jerusalem: 1963.

———. *Labour Force Survey June 1954.* (Special Series No. 56.) Jerusalem: 1957.

———. *Labour Force Surveys 1955–1961.* (Special Series No. 162.) Jerusalem: 1964.

———. *Labour Force Surveys 1962.* (Special Series No. 152.) Jerusalem: 1964.

————. *Labour Force Surveys 1963.* (Special Series No. 176.) Jerusalem: 1965.

————. *Languages, Literacy and Educational Attainment—Part I.* (Census Publication No. 15.) Jerusalem: 1963.

————. *Projections of the Population of Israel up to 1969.* (Special Series No. 179.) Jerusalem: 1965.

COMMITTEE ON FINANCIAL LEGISLATION. *The Committee's Recommendations on Government Budget.* Jerusalem: Israel Political Science Association, 1961.

CREAMER, DANIEL, and OTHERS. *Israel's National Income 1950–1954.* Jerusalem: Falk Project and CBS, 1957.

DARIN-DRABKIN, H. *Housing in Israel.* Tel Aviv: 1957.

DEPARTMENT OF STATISTICS. *Special Bulletin 20.* Government of Palestine, n.d.

————. *Statistical Abstract of Palestine 1944–45.* Jerusalem: Government of Palestine, 1946.

DOVRAT, E., WAHL, N., and TAMARI, M. "The Financial Structure of Israel's Industrial Companies," *Bank of Israel Bulletin,* No. 17 (January 1963), 39–93.

EASTERLIN, RICHARD A. "Israel's Development: Past Accomplishments and Future Problems," *Quarterly Journal of Economics,* LXXV (February 1961), 63–86.

ERDREICH, EMIL. *The Israel Merchant Marine: An Economic Appraisal.* Jerusalem: Bank of Israel Research Department, 1962.

GAATHON, A. L. "Economic Planning in Israel," *Israel Economy: Theory and Practice,* ed. Joseph Ronen. Tel Aviv: Dvir, n.d., pp. 179–202; Hebrew.

————. "National Income," *Encyclopaedia Hebraica,* Vol. VI (1957), 729–39; Hebrew.

————. *Economic Productivity in Israel: 1950–65.* Pre-publication draft, Jerusalem, 1967.

GABRIEL, R. K. *Marriage and Births in Israel.* Jerusalem: The Hebrew University, 1960; Hebrew (mimeograph).

GAFNI, A., HALEVI, N., and HANOCH, G. *Israel's Tariff Structure and Functions.* (Research Paper 3.) Jerusalem: Falk Project, 1958; Hebrew.

————. "Classification of Tariffs by Function," *Kyklos,* XVI (No. 2, 1963), 303–18.

GENACHOWSKI, DOV. "Israel's External Debt," *Bank of Israel Bulletin,* No. 20 (September 1963), 62–117; Hebrew.

GINOR, FANNY. *Uses of Agricultural Surpluses: Analysis and Assessment of Public Law 480 Title I Program in Israel.* Jerusalem: Bank of Israel, 1963.

————. "Structural Changes in the Israeli Economy," *The Economic Quarterly,* XIII (No. 52, February 1967), 353–63; Hebrew.

GOLDBERGER (OPHIR), T. "Principles of Protection." Unpublished M.A. thesis, The Hebrew University, 1956; Hebrew.

GOLOMB, D. "Import Surplus—Cause or Effect," *The Economic Quarterly,* VIII (No. 29–30, February 1961), 150–52; Hebrew.

GOVERNMENT OF PALESTINE, *Report of the Wages Committee.* 1943.

————. *A Survey of Palestine.* 3 vols. and Supplement. Government Printer, 1946, 1947.

GROSS, G. "The Public Committee on Customs." Unpublished seminar paper, The Hebrew University, 1962; Hebrew.

GROSS, N. "Inflation and Economic Policy in Israel: The First Stage, 1949–1950." Unpublished M.A. thesis, The Hebrew University; Hebrew.

GRUENBAUM (GAATHON), L. *National Income and Outlay in Palestine 1936.* Jerusalem: Jewish Agency, 1941.

————. *Outlines of a Development Plan for Jewish Palestine.* Jerusalem: Jewish Agency, 1946.

————. *Four Year Development Plan of Israel, 1950–1953.* Tel Aviv: Prime Minister's Office, Department of Economic Research, 1950.

GUREVICH, D., GERTZ, A., and BACHI, R. *The Jewish Population in Palestine.* Jerusalem: Jewish Agency, 1944; Hebrew.

GUSMAN, E., and MANDELBAUM, M. "On M. Bruno's Book," *The Economic Quarterly,* X (No. 37–38, March 1963), 142–47; Hebrew.

GVATI, C. "Principles of Protection of Domestic Production." Unpublished seminar paper, The Hebrew University, 1962; Hebrew.

HALEVI, NADAV. *Estimates of Israel's International Transactions: 1952–1954.* Jerusalem: Falk Project, 1956.

————. "The Israeli Labor Movement," *The Annals of the American Academy of Political and Social Science,* CCCX (March 1957), 172–81.

————. "Housing in Israel," *The Economic Problems of Housing.* Conference of the International Economic Association. London: Macmillan, 1967.

HALPERIN, ASHER. "Palestine's Balance of Payments 1932–1946." Unpublished doctoral thesis, Princeton University, 1954.

HALPERIN, Y. "Value Added in Tourism in 1961." Unpublished seminar paper, The Hebrew University; Hebrew.

HANOCH, GIORA. "Income Differentials in Israel," *Fifth Report 1959 and 1960*. Jerusalem: Falk Project, 1961.

HATZRONI, ODED. "The Nonprofit Institutions in Israel, 1957–1963." Unpublished seminar paper, The Hebrew University, 1964; Hebrew.

HETH, MEIR. *Banking Institutions in Israel*. Jerusalem: Falk Institute, 1966.

————. *The Legal Framework of Economic Activity in Israel*. (Praeger Special Studies in International Economics and Development.) Jerusalem and New York: Frederick A. Praeger in cooperation with the Bank of Israel, 1967.

HIMADEH, S. B. (ed.) *Economic Organization of Palestine*. (Social Science Series No. 11.) Beirut: American University, 1938.

HOROWITZ, DAVID. *The Economy of Palestine and its Development*. Rev. ed. Tel Aviv: Mosad Bialik, 1948; Hebrew.

————. *The Economy of Israel*. Tel Aviv: Massada, 1954; Hebrew.

————. "Comments on Criticism," *The Economic Quarterly*, X (No. 37–38, March 1963), 40; Hebrew.

————, and HINDEN, RITA. *Economic Survey of Palestine*. Tel Aviv: Jewish Agency, 1938.

HOVNE, AVNER. *The Labor Force in Israel*. Jerusalem: Falk Project, 1961.

HUREWITZ, J. *The Struggle for Palestine*. New York: Norton, 1950.

JEWISH AGENCY, *Memorandum Submitted to the Palestine Royal Commission*. London: 1935.

————. *The Jewish Case before the Anglo-American Committee of Inquiry on Palestine*. Jerusalem: 1947.

————. *The Jewish Plan for Palestine*. Jerusalem: 1947.

————. *Statistical Handbook of Jewish Palestine 1947*. Jerusalem: 1947.

————. *Immigration Papers*, No. 20 (November 1952); Hebrew.

KLEIMAN, EPHRAIM. *The Structure of Israel Manufacturing Industries, 1952–1962*. Jerusalem: Falk Project, 1964 (mimeograph).

————. "Interdependence of the Production Process," *The Economic Quarterly*, X (No. 37–38, March 1963), 79–89; Hebrew.

KLEIN, DAVID. "Aims and Targets in the State Budget," *Israel Economy: Theory and Practice*, ed. J. Ronen. Tel Aviv: Dvir, n.d., pp. 144–63; Hebrew.

KLIBANSKI, MICHAEL. *Balance of Payments of Israel, 1957–1958*. (CBS Special Series No. 89.) Jerusalem: 1959.

KLINOV-MALUL, RUTH. *The Profitability of Investment in Education in Israel*. Jerusalem: Falk Institute, 1966.

———. "Absorption of Immigrants and Income Differentials." Forthcoming; Hebrew.

KOCHAV, D. "Imports without Payment." Unpublished M.A. thesis, The Hebrew University, 1953; Hebrew.

KUZNETS, SIMON. "International Income Levels," *Economic Change*. New York: Norton, 1953.

———. "Quantitative Aspects of the Economic Growth of Nations II. Industrial Distribution of National Product and Labor Force," *Economic Development and Cultural Change*, V (Supplement to No. 4, July 1957).

———. "The Economic Structure and Life of the Jews," *The Jews*, Vol. II, ed. Louis Finkelstein. 3rd ed. New York: Harper and Brothers, 1960.

———. "Quantitative Aspects of the Economic Growth of Nations V. Capital Formation Proportions: International Comparisons for Recent Years," *Economic Development and Cultural Change*, VIII (No. 4, part II, July 1960).

———. "Quantitative Aspects of the Economic Growth of Nations VIII. Distribution of Income by Size," *Economic Development and Cultural Change*, XI (No. 2, part II, January 1963).

LANDSBERGER, MICHAEL. "Changes in the Consumer Price Indices of Different Income, Origin, and Family-Size Groups, 1954–62," *Bank of Israel Bulletin*, No. 19 (November 1963), 64–74.

LEVY, EMANUEL, and OTHERS. *Israel's National Income and Expenditure, 1950–1962*. (CBS Special Series No. 153.) Jerusalem: 1964.

LISLE, EDMOND A. "Household Savings in Israel, 1954 to 1957/58," *Bank of Israel Bulletin*, No. 21 (April 1964), 46–113.

LIVIATAN, NISSAN. *Consumption Patterns in Israel*. Jerusalem: Falk Project, 1964.

LOFTUS, P. J. *National Income of Palestine 1944*. Jerusalem: Government Printer, 1946.

———. *National Income of Palestine 1945*. Jerusalem: Government Printer, 1948.

LUBELL, HAROLD. *The Public and Private Sectors and Investment in Israel.* RAND Corporation P-2176, 1961 (mimeograph).
———, and OTHERS. *Israel's National Expenditure: 1950-1954.* Jerusalem: Falk Project and CBS, 1958.
LUBETZKI, Z. *Building for Residence in Israel, 1949-1963.* Unpublished mimeograph, 1965.

MANDELBAUM, M., and NAVEH, M. "Liberalization of Imports," *The Economic Quarterly*, X (No. 40, December 1963), 346-56; Hebrew.
MEYER, EGON. *Der Moschav.* Basel and Tübingen: Kyklos-Verlag and J.C.B. Mohr, 1967.
MICHAELY, MICHAEL. *Foreign Trade and Capital Imports in Israel.* Tel Aviv: Am Oved, 1963; Hebrew.
———. *Israel's Foreign Exchange Rate System.* Jerusalem: Falk Institute, forthcoming.
MILLS, E. *Census of Palestine.* 2 vols. Government of Palestine, 1933.
MINISTRY OF FINANCE, *Summary of Foreign Exchange Accounts.* Jerusalem: Foreign Exchange Department, annual issue; Hebrew.
MINISTRY OF LABOUR. *Manpower in Israel Annual Report 1966.* Jerusalem: Manpower Planning Authority, February 1967.
MORAG, AMOTZ. *Public Finance in Israel: Problems and Development.* Jerusalem: The Magnes Press, 1967; Hebrew.
MUNDLAK, YAIR. *Long-Term Projections of Supply and Demand for Agricultural Products in Israel—I. General View and Summary.* Jerusalem: Falk Project, 1964.

NATHAN, R. R., GASS, O., and CREAMER D. *Palestine: Problem and Promise.* Washington: Public Affairs Press, 1946.
NIZAN, A. *The Standard of Living in Palestine (Israel) During the Last 20 Years.* (CBS Special Series No. 7A.) Jerusalem: 1952; Hebrew.
NOVOMEYSKY, M. "The Industries of Palestine," *Bulletin 4/5 of the Palestine Economic Society* (May 1925).

OFER, GUR. *The Service Industries in a Developing Economy: Israel As a Case Study.* (Praeger Special Studies in International Economics and Development.) Jerusalem and New York: Frederick A. Praeger in cooperation with the Bank of Israel, 1967.
OTTENSOOSER, ROBERT DAVID. *The Palestine Pound and the Israel Pound.* Geneva: Librarie E. Droz, 1955.

PALLMANN, MARTIN. *Der Kibbuz*. Basel and Tübingen: Kyklos-Verlag and J.C.B. Mohr, 1966.

PATINKIN, DON. "Monetary and Price Developments in Israel: 1949–53," *Scripta Hierosolymitana*. Vol. III: *Studies in Economic and Social Sciences*. Ed. Roberto Bachi. Jerusalem: The Magnes Press, 1956, pp. 20–52.

———. *The Israel Economy: The First Decade*. Jerusalem: Falk Project, 1960.

PINES, DAVID. "Criteria of Economic Independence," *The Economic Quarterly*, VIII (No. 31, June 1961), 245–52; Hebrew.

———. *Direct Export Premiums in Israel: 1952–1958*. Jerusalem: Falk Project, 1963; Hebrew.

PIRKER, THEO. *Die Histadrut*. Basel and Tübingen: Kyklos-Verlag and J.C.B. Mohr, 1965.

Report of the Commission of Inquiry into the Distribution of National Income. Jerusalem: 1966; Hebrew.

Report of the Committee of Experts Inquiring into the Cost-of-Living Allowance. Tel Aviv: November 1966; Hebrew (mimeograph).

Report of the Committee for Foreign Exchange. July 1963; Hebrew (mimeograph).

Report of the Palestine Royal Commission. Cmd. 5479. London: 1937 (Peel Report).

RIEMER, S. "Wages in Israel," *Encyclopaedia Hebraica*, Vol. VI (1957), 802–807; Hebrew.

RONEN, JOSEPH (ed.). *Israel Economy: Theory and Practice*. Tel Aviv: Dvir, n.d.; Hebrew.

ROSENBERG, M. *The Measurement of the Economic Absorption of Israel's New Immigrant Sector from a National Point of View*. Jerusalem: The Hebrew University, 1958.

RUBNER, A. *The Economy of Israel*. London: Frank Cass, 1961.

RUPPIN, ARTHUR. *Three Decades of Palestine*. Jerusalem: Schocken, 1936.

SARNAT, MARSHALL. *Saving and Investment Through Retirement Funds in Israel*. Jerusalem: Falk Institute, 1966.

———. *The Development of the Securities Market in Israel*. Basel and Tübingen: Kyklos-Verlag and J.C.B. Mohr, 1966.

SCHMELZ, O. *Standard of Education of the Population, June 1954*. (CBS Special Series No. 66.) Jerusalem: 1958.

Shaw Report. Cmd. 3530. London: 1930.

SHULROPER, ARELA. "Investment Encouragement Policy in Israel." Unpublished seminar paper, The Hebrew University, 1964; Hebrew.

SICRON, MOSHE. *Immigration to Israel: 1948–1953.* Separate Statistical Supplement. Jerusalem: Falk Project and CBS, 1957.

———, and GIL, B. *Jewish Population by Sex, Age and Country of Birth, 1931–1954.* (CBS Special Series No. 37.) Jerusalem: 1955.

SIMPSON, SIR JOHN HOPE. *Palestine: Report on Immigration, Land Settlement and Development.* Cmd. 3686. London: 1930.

Survey of Family Savings: 1957/58 and 1958/59—Preliminary Report. (Research Paper 8.) Jerusalem: Falk Project, 1960.

SUSSMAN, Z. "The Foreign Exchange Budget as a Forecast of Commodity Imports to Israel." Unpublished M.A. thesis, The Hebrew University, 1959; Hebrew.

SZERESZEWSKI, ROBERT. "The Incidence of State Budget Expenditure by Income Group." Unpublished M.A. thesis, The Hebrew University, 1961; Hebrew.

TAMARI, MEIR. "Changes in the Financial Structure of Israel's Industrial Companies, 1956/57 to 1961/62," *Bank of Israel Bulletin,* No. 19 (November 1963), 14–63.

———. "Financial Changes in Israel's Industrial Companies in 1962," *Bank of Israel Bulletin,* No. 22 (December 1964), 17–31.

ULITZUR, A. *National Capital and the Building of Palestine.* Jerusalem: Palestine Foundation Fund, 1939; Hebrew.

UNITED NATIONS. *Demographic Yearbook.* New York: various issues.

———. Department of Economic and Social Affairs, *Demographic Aspects of Manpower, Report 1: Sex and Age Patterns of Participation in Economic Activities.* (ST/SOA/Ser. A/33.) New York: 1962.

———. *Yearbook of National Accounts Statistics 1962.* New York: 1963.

WEISS, YORAM. "Price Control in Israel: 1939–1963." Unpublished M.A. thesis, The Hebrew University, 1964; Hebrew.

WIENER, A., and WOLMAN, A. "Water Policy in Israel," *Israel Economy: Theory and Practice,* ed. Joseph Ronen. Tel Aviv: Dvir, n.d.; pp. 349–56; Hebrew.

WOOD, G. E. *Survey of National Income of Palestine.* Jerusalem: Government Printer, 1943.

WOYTINSKY, W. S. and E. S. *World Population and Production.* New York: Twentieth Century Fund, 1953.

ZANDBERG, M. *Distribution of Income in Israel in 1954.* Jerusalem: Institute of Applied Social Research, 1956; Hebrew (mimeograph).
———. "The State Budget and Redistribution of Income," *The Economic Quarterly,* VIII (No. 32, October 1961), 322–31; Hebrew.
———. "The New Economic Policy," *The Economic Quarterly,* X (No. 40, December 1963), 339–45; Hebrew.

SUBJECT INDEX

Numbers in bold type refer to sections

NAME INDEX

Numbers in italics refer to tables

Abcarius, M. F., 37n
Abramovitz, Z., 16n

Babayov, B., 235n
Bachi, Roberto, 32n, 33n
Bahral, Uri, 121n, 230n, 240n, 270n, 272n
Barkai, Haim, 42n, 43n, 46n, 113, *114*, 115n, 191, 239n, 265n, 268n
Barkay, R. M., *203*
Baruh, Joseph, 73n, 97n, 129, *130*, 194n, 230n, 235n, *236*, *243*, 244n, *285*
Bavly, Sarah, 99n, 119n
Beham, Miriam, 256n, 267n, 268n
Ben-Porath, Yoram, 38n, 60n, 71n, 81n
Ben-Shahar, Haim, 116n, 119n, 122n, 161n, 164n, 170n, 197n, 210n, 211, 212, 213n, 214
Bonné, Alfred, 13n
Bruno, Michael, 109n, 128n, 132, 138, 151, 154n, 170n, 213, 221, 274n, 276

Creamer, Daniel, 14n, *25*, 28n, 31n, 36n, 37n, 38n, 167n, 171n

Darin-Drabkin, H., 99n
Dovrat, Efraim, 217n

Easterlin, Richard A., 18n, 72n
Erdreich, Emil, 151n

Evans, Michael, *286*

Gaathon, A. L., 6n, 21, 22n, 23n, 24n, 26, 28n, 36n, 38n, 43n, 92, 102, 125, *126*, *127*, 128, *131*, 134n, *135*, 168n
Gabriel, R. K., 59n
Gafni, Arnon, 234n, 238n
Gass, O., 14n, *25*, 28n, 31n, 36n, 37n, 38n
Genachowski, Dov, 162n
Gertz, A., 32n, 33n
Gil, B., *15*, *18*
Ginor, Fanny, 136n, 165n, 168n
Goldberger (Ophir), T., 237n
Golomb, David, 173n
Gross, G., 237n
Gross, Nahum, 259
Gruenbaum, L., see Gaathon, A.L.
Guelfat, I., 16n
Gurevich, D., 32n, 33n
Gusman, E., 154n
Gvati, C., 237n

Halevi, Nadav, 47n, 112n, *141*, *145*, 234n, 238n, *294*, *297*, *299*
Halperin, Asher, 21n
Halperin, Y., 151n
Hanoch, Giora, 73n, 116n, 117, 118n, 119n, 121n, 234n, 238n
Hatzroni, Oded, 218n
Heth, Meir, 42n, 115n, 134n, 180n, *263*, 264n, 265n, 267n
Himadeh, S. B., 13n

319

ABOUT THE AUTHORS

Nadav Halevi was born and educated in the United States and received his Ph.D. degree in economics from Columbia University. Since 1953, he has made his home in Israel. After conducting several studies at the Falk Institute for Economic Research in Israel, he served for three years as Economic Adviser to the Foreign Exchange Division of the Ministry of Finance. He has been on the faculty of the Department of Economics of the Hebrew University, Jerusalem, since 1960.

Dr Halevi's publications include *Estimates of Israel's International Transactions: 1952–1954* and various articles on the economy of Israel, dealing primarily with its international trade and finance.

Ruth Klinov-Malul received her doctorate from the Hebrew University in 1964, and has been on the faculty of the Department of Economics of the University since 1965. Much of her previous work has been concerned with problems of labor economics.

Her publications include an article on productivity in Israeli cotton spinning mills, *The Supply of Professional Manpower from Israel's Educational System* (in collaboration with Professor H. Muhsam and Dr G. Hanoch), and *The Profitability of Investment in Education in Israel*—all based on research conducted at the Falk Institute.